Child Care and Education

SECOND EDITION

WITHDRAWN FROM
ST HELENS COLLEGE LIBRARY

Carolyn Meggitt

HODDER
EDUCATION
AN HACHETTE UK COMPANY

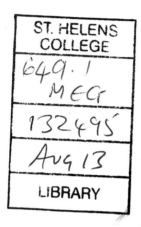
Orders: please contact Bookpoint Ltd, 130 Milton Park, Abingdon, Oxon OX14 4SB. Telephone: +44 (0)1235 827720. Fax: +44 (0)1235 400454. Lines are open from 9.00a.m. to 5.00p.m., Monday to Saturday, with a 24-hour message-answering service. You can also order through our website **www.hoddereducation.co.uk**

If you have any comments to make about this, or any of our other titles, please send them to educationenquiries@hodder.co.uk

British Library Cataloguing in Publication Data
A catalogue record for this title is available from the British Library

ISBN: 978 1 4441 8781 6

Published 2013
Impression number   10 9 8 7 6 5 4 3 2 1
Year   2016 2015 2014 2013

Hachette UK's policy is to use papers that are natural, renewable and recyclable products and made from wood grown in sustainable forests. The logging and manufacturing processes are expected to conform to the environmental regulations of the country of origin.

Cover photo © Hodder Education
Typeset by Datapage (India) Pvt. Ltd.
Printed in Italy for Hodder Education, an Hachette UK Company, 338 Euston Road, London NW1 3BH.

Contents

Acknowledgements

I would like to thank the following people for their contributions: Laura Meggitt (Community Play Specialist) for her valuable insights and for providing many of the early years case studies; Kirsty Meggitt (Recruitment Consultant) for help with the section on SMART targets in Unit 5.

I would also like to thank the editorial team at Hodder Education: Stephen Halder, Publisher; Chloé Harmsworth, Senior Desk Editor; Gemma Parsons, Development Editor; Llinos Edwards, Freelance Copy Editor; and Kevin Doherty, Freelance Proofreader, for all their hard work and support.

This book uses intellectual property/material from books previously co-authored with Tina Bruce and Julian Grenier, who willingly agreed to its inclusion in this book in order to share what is important for high-quality early childhood practice.

Carolyn Meggitt

Photo credits

1 An introduction to working with children: Unit 1

This is an introductory Unit designed to give you an overview of some of the different types of settings and local provision for children in your area. You will learn how to prepare for working in settings and the responsibilities of your role. The content also includes understanding children's individual needs and how to treat children fairly. You will gain an insight into your preferred learning style and develop your ability to study.

Learning outcomes

During this unit you will learn about:

1. *Some of the different types of settings and local provision for children.*

2. *How to prepare for your placement including: dress code, behaviour, time-keeping, and positive attitudes.*

3. *The responsibilities and limits of your role in placements.*

4. *Children's individual needs and necessity for fairness and inclusive practice.*

5. *Your own preferred learning style and how to develop relevant study skills.*

The different types of setting and local provision for children

A wide range of organisations exists to provide services for young children and their families. These include statutory (public) services, voluntary services and private services. Many of the settings provide both care and education for children. Parents can choose child care from the settings shown in Figure 1.1.

Statutory (public) services

Statutory services are those that are funded by government and that have to be provided by law (or statute). Some services are provided by *central* government departments – for example:

- the National Health Service (NHS)
- the Department for Education.

These large departments are funded directly from **taxation** – income tax, VAT and National Insurance. Other **statutory services** are provided by *local* government – for example:

- the housing department
- the local education authority
- the social services department.

These are largely funded through **local taxation** (Council Tax) and from grants made by central government.

Voluntary services

These are health, education and social care services that are set up by **charities** to provide services that local authorities can buy in and so benefit from their expertise. Voluntary organisations are:

- non-profit-making
- non-statutory
- dependent on donations, fundraising and government grants.

Example: The **National Council of Voluntary Child Care Organisations (NCVCCO)** is an organisation whose members are all registered charities that work with children, young people and their families. They range from very large national organisations (such as Barnardo's) to small, locally based charities.

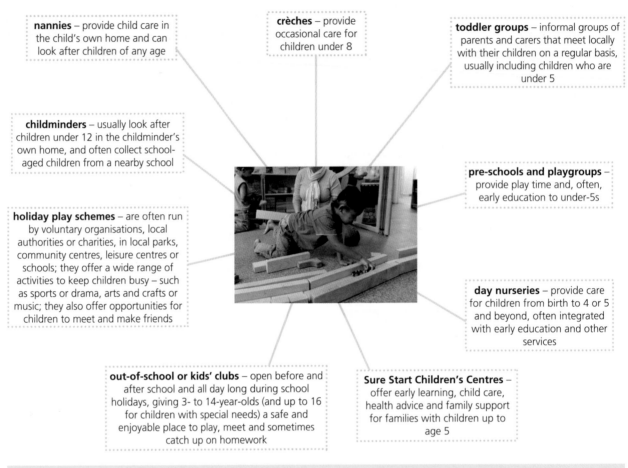

nannies – provide child care in the child's own home and can look after children of any age

crèches – provide occasional care for children under 8

toddler groups – informal groups of parents and carers that meet locally with their children on a regular basis, usually including children who are under 5

childminders – usually look after children under 12 in the childminder's own home, and often collect school-aged children from a nearby school

pre-schools and playgroups – provide play time and, often, early education to under-5s

holiday play schemes – are often run by voluntary organisations, local authorities or charities, in local parks, community centres, leisure centres or schools; they offer a wide range of activities to keep children busy – such as sports or drama, arts and crafts or music; they also offer opportunities for children to meet and make friends

day nurseries – provide care for children from birth to 4 or 5 and beyond, often integrated with early education and other services

out-of-school or kids' clubs – open before and after school and all day long during school holidays, giving 3- to 14-year-olds (and up to 16 for children with special needs) a safe and enjoyable place to play, meet and sometimes catch up on homework

Sure Start Children's Centres – offer early learning, child care, health advice and family support for families with children up to age 5

Figure 1.1 Different child care settings

Private sector

The private sector consists of organisations set up to provide health, education and social care services 'at a price'. They are income-generating and profit-making services, which include:

- 'public' and independent or private schools
- private care homes and hostels
- complementary and alternative medicine and therapies, some hospitals and private health screening services
- child care providers (e.g. private nurseries and crèches; workplace nurseries).

Multi-agency work

A range of different professionals and agencies from across health, social and educational services works together to support children.

Social services for children

Social Services departments are a statutory service, organised at a local level; they provide a range of care and support for children and families, including:

- families where children are assessed as being **in need** (including disabled children)
- children who may be suffering '**significant harm**'
- children who require looking after by the local authority (through **fostering** or **residential care**), and
- children who are placed for **adoption**.

Looked-after children

Children who are in the care of local authorities are described as 'looked-after children'. They are one of the most vulnerable groups in society. The majority of children who remain in care are there because they have suffered abuse or neglect.

There are two main reasons for children being in local authority care.

1 Children who are subject to a **care order** made by the courts under Section 31 of the Children Act 1989 (about 65 per cent of all looked-after children); for the courts to grant a care order, they have to be satisfied that a child is suffering or would suffer 'significant harm' without such intervention.

2 Children who are accommodated by the local authority on a voluntary basis under Section 20 of the Children Act 1989 (about a third of all looked-after children).

At any one time, around 60,000 children are looked after in England, although some 90,000 pass through the care system in any year. A total of 42 per cent of looked-after children return home within six months. The system aims to support rehabilitation back into families where possible.

Foster care

Children are generally looked after in foster care. A minority will be cared for in **children's homes** and some by prospective adoptive parents. Irrespective of the setting in which children are accommodated, all looked-after children will have a social worker and carers (e.g. foster carers, residential care staff) responsible for their day-to-day care, who should be involved in making plans or decisions about the child.

Education services for children

Since 1972, schooling has been compulsory for all children between the ages of five and 16. A very small number of children are home-schooled. There are strict regulations to ensure that they receive appropriate education.

The Early Years Foundation Stage: from birth to five

The Early Years Foundation Stage (EYFS) sets standards for the development, learning and care of children from birth to five years. All registered providers of early years care are required to use the EYFS **statutory** framework, so it applies to

childminders as well as to nursery schools, after-school clubs and nurseries or schools. See Unit 10 for further information about the EYFS.

All three- and four-year-olds are now entitled to free early education for 12.5 hours per week for 38 weeks of the year. Many children under five attend:

- maintained (or state) nursery schools
- nursery classes attached to primary schools
- playgroups or pre-schools in the voluntary sector
- privately run nurseries
- children's centres
- home learning environment (HLE) – many young children are cared for by childminders (in the childminder's home) or by nannies or grandparents.

From the age of five, children attend:

- **infant schools** (for children aged five to seven years)
- **primary schools** (for children aged five to 11 years)
- preparatory and independent schools (private sector)
- after-school clubs.

Integrated provision for children

Children's centres serve children and their families from the antenatal period until children start in reception or Year 1 at primary school. Each centre strives to provide to families with babies and/or pre-school children the services listed in Table 1.1.

Children's centres act as a 'service hub' within the community, offering not only a base for childminder networks, but also a link to other day care provision, out-of-school clubs and extended schools, for example. Centres may also offer other services, such as training for parents (e.g. parenting classes, basic skills, English as an additional language), benefits advice, child care services for older children, and toy libraries.

Within any local authority in the UK there are child care and education settings that come into the

Good-quality early learning integrated with full-day care provision (a maximum of ten hours a day, five days a week, 48 weeks a year)	Good-quality teacher input to lead the development of learning within the centre
Parental outreach	Family support services
A base for a childminder network	Child and family health services, including antenatal services
Support for children and parents with special needs	Effective links with Jobcentre Plus, local training providers, and further and higher education institutions

Table 1.1 Services offered by Children's Centres

category of voluntary provision. Two examples are described below.

1 **Community nurseries:** community nurseries exist to provide a service to local children and their families. They are run by local community organisations – often with financial assistance from the local authority – or by charities such as Barnardo's and Save the Children. Most of these nurseries are open long enough to suit working parents or those at college. Many centres also provide, or act as a venue for, other services, including parent and toddler groups, drop-in crèches, toy libraries and after-school clubs.

2 **Pre-School Learning Alliance Community Pre-Schools:** Pre-School Learning Alliance Community Pre-Schools (playgroups) offer children aged between three and five years an opportunity to learn through play.
   - *They usually operate on a part-time sessional basis.*
   - *Sessions normally last two-and-a-half hours each morning or afternoon.*
   - *Staff plan a varied range of experiences that takes into account children's previous experiences and developing needs.*

The nationally set Foundation Stage Early Years framework, approved by the Department for Education (DfE), is adapted by each group to meet the needs of the children and to allow them to make the most of a variety of learning opportunities that arise spontaneously through play.

At many pre-school playgroups, parents and carers are encouraged to be involved, and there are often parent and toddler groups which meet at the same site.

Leisure activities and recreation services

These services provide children and their families with activities and opportunities for recreation and sport. Some of these are provided by the local authority and are either provided free or at a subsidised cost; others are privately owned and run. See Figure 1.2 for examples.

Local provision for children

Most local authorities have a department to coordinate all the services to children within their locality. These departments are often called Early Years Services, and deal exclusively with the needs of young children and their families. The range of services provided varies greatly from one local authority to another, but typically will include the following services (those marked * must be provided by law).

- **Housing:** children and their families in need, e.g. homeless families and those seeking refuge, are a priority. Services include providing bed and breakfast accommodation or council housing.*
- **After-school clubs:** these offer supervised play opportunities in a safe, supportive and friendly environment. They usually cater for children from five to 11 years, but some centres have facilities for under-fives.*
- **Nursery education:** most authorities are not able to offer full nursery education to all children within their locality. Nursery classes are usually attached to statutory primary schools. Nursery schools are separate.

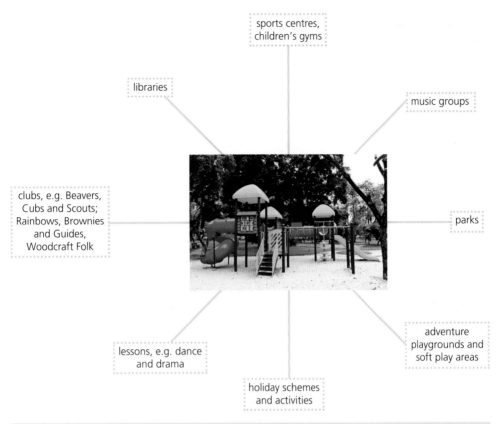

sports centres, children's gyms

libraries

music groups

clubs, e.g. Beavers, Cubs and Scouts; Rainbows, Brownies and Guides, Woodcraft Folk

parks

adventure playgrounds and soft play areas

lessons, e.g. dance and drama

holiday schemes and activities

Figure 1.2 Examples of leisure activities and recreation services

- **Community places for families with low incomes:** most local authorities keep a number of full-day nursery places at Children's Centres, specifically for children in families with low incomes.
- **Regulation and registration of services:** such as childminders, private fostering and private or voluntarily run day care and family centres.*
- **Social workers:** work with families where children are assessed as being 'in need'; they give practical support and advice on a wide range of issues including adoption and foster care.*
- **Infant or primary education:** children must attend full-time school from the age of five, and must follow the National Curriculum.*
- **Residential holidays:** provide opportunities for children to develop self-reliance, as well as providing a break for many children who otherwise would not have the chance of a holiday.

- **Holiday play schemes:** full-day programmes of activities during the school holidays.
- **Advice, information and counselling:** local authorities have a duty to provide information and counselling to families where there is a child in need.*
- **Children's centres:** these include early learning, parent information services, and support for children and parents with special needs.*
- **Respite care:** families caring for a child with additional needs may be offered a residential holiday for their child so that they can have a break – or respite – from caring for them full-time.*

These services are usually listed and coordinated by a local **Council for Voluntary Service**. Voluntary organisations sometimes also provide some of the statutory services and will receive payment from the local authority or government for these services – for example, after-school clubs.

Finding out about your area

1. **Design a booklet** that you could give to a family who are new to your area to inform them about the following sources of information.
   a) Where to find information on:
      - support groups for parents
      - mother and toddler groups
      - pre-school groups (playgroups)
      - nursery schools and infant schools.
   b) How to access information on:
      - health care for their family – hospitals, accident and emergency departments
      - location of health clinics, GP centres
      - Community Health Councils – these are independent bodies that represent the views of patients and users of the Health Service.
   c) Where to find out what benefits and allowances families may be entitled to receive – for example:
      - child benefit
      - lone-parent benefit
      - housing benefit.
2. **List some useful general voluntary organisations** that exist to support families with young children, with addresses, telephone numbers and, where possible, their website addresses.

Sources of information and guidance

Some useful sources of information about Early Years Services are listed below.

- *Charities Digest*: available in the reference section of public libraries and most college libraries.
- www.charitynet.org.uk.
- Citizens Advice Bureau: trained staff provide free, impartial advice and help on legal, social and financial matters to anyone who contacts them.
- Public library: for information on all local voluntary groups, often on computer link.
- *Yellow Pages*/phone book: usually listed under 'Charitable and Voluntary Organisations'.
- Local Authority (Council) Information Service: useful addresses of voluntary organisations.
- Post offices and Benefit Agency Offices (DSS): for leaflets explaining the benefits and allowances available for families with young children.

Preparing for your placement

How to prepare for placement

During the course, you will be allocated a range of placements, which may include nurseries and schools working with children across a diverse age range. These are arranged by your study centre and should enable you to carry out all the requirements set out in your Course Handbook. The variety of placements available will depend on where you are studying and the local structure of early years care and education provision.

Every work setting will be different depending on staff, premises, function, attitude, outlook and, of course, the children! There is plenty to learn from those who have experience and are willing to share their expertise with you and offer advice. You will have the opportunity to decide if you have a preferred age range, which may be useful when you seek employment. Similarly, you may feel more comfortable and confident in some staff teams than others. This may be because of organisational factors or attitudes – try to analyse what makes the difference.

If you are following the career path that is right for you, then it is probable (and preferable) that you enjoy your training placement time more than your study centre time! If this is not the case, think carefully about your choices for now and the future. Child care and education are one field in which you cannot achieve through written work alone. Students who show little initiative, have poor communication and display little interest in placement are unlikely to receive satisfactory PDPs (Professional Development Profiles) and so will not succeed, whereas those who are very good in their placements can usually be given the necessary support to complete written tasks successfully to achieve the award.

Before starting your placement

Many students are nervous when starting in a new placement, and staff will be aware of their concerns. The information that follows will help you to feel more confident and to feel settled more quickly.

Making contact

Find out exactly where the placement is – practise the route beforehand so that you allow enough time; make sure you have the telephone number and that you know who to report to. (Many placements will be happy to show you around prior to starting work.) At this first visit you could ask the following questions.

- What hours will I be working?
- What should I wear?
- What sort of things will I have to do?
- What shall I do if I am ill or cannot attend?
- What shall I do at lunchtime?

What are the placement responsibilities?

Many training placements have a wealth of experience in helping students on a number of courses and may have a designated person (e.g. a placement supervisor) to liaise with the study centre.

- They welcome well-motivated students and will afford time and advice for those willing and keen to accept it.
- They understand that there are course requirements that you need to be able to implement, but they will also expect you to carry out tasks they have planned and arranged, and to follow the policies and procedures laid down in their setting.

Take advantage of any extra opportunities you may have to attend special events or outings as these provide valuable experience in seeing children in a range of situations and environments.

What are your responsibilities as a student in the placement?

Your responsibilities are as follows:

- attendance
- appearance
- paperwork
- cooperation and teamwork
- positive attitude.

Attendance and time-keeping

Check attendance times

Make sure you have checked the following with your supervisor: your starting time, break and lunch times, and finishing time. There is sometimes some flexibility if you have limited transport choices or have unavoidable appointments.

Be flexible

Always offer to make up missed time, and be prepared to stay longer on some occasions, if possible, to help complete a job and prepare for the following day (for example, when displays are being changed – much easier to do without children around!).

Reliability and punctuality

These are very important, and poor performance in these aspects can lead to tensions between you and staff. Their main concern must be the children in their care, and they will be less likely to cooperate with you and to give responsibility for tasks if you cannot be relied upon to arrive on time and be prepared.

Absence from placement

If, for some good reason, you cannot attend, you must contact your placement and inform them as soon as possible (preferably before the children arrive) so that alternative arrangements can be made, indicating whether you are likely to be able to attend on the next scheduled date. You should also inform your study centre to avoid a visiting tutor making an unnecessary journey. Whenever possible, missed days should be 'made up'.

Dress code and appearance

Your study centre will give guidance on your appearance, particularly if there is a dress code or uniform (often a sweatshirt over dark trousers).

- Choose clothing carefully, bearing in mind the types of activity you are likely to be involved in.
- Footwear should be comfortable and not too heavy.
- Hair should be tied back if long; head lice are easily passed on by young children in group settings – you

can help to avoid getting them yourself by ensuring that you keep your hair well brushed and tying it back.

- Avoid long fingernails and do not wear nail varnish – flakes chipping off into the snack you are preparing are neither appetising nor hygienic!
- Similarly, avoid all jewellery other than a watch – small children pull on chains and dangly earrings, and heavy rings and bracelets are inappropriate for dealing with play dough or paint, or for changing nappies.

Paperwork

Although time is always precious, try to identify a time each week or fortnight when you can sit down with your supervisor and discuss your progress. You should talk about:

- what competencies you feel you have achieved
- how you might achieve those that do not occur during the normal daily routine
- what activities you have planned and need to carry out
- forthcoming plans and events that involve you.

Practice Evidence Records (PERs) and the Practice Evidence Record Tasks

This is a mandatory part of the evidence you need to submit to gain the CACHE Level 2 qualification (See also Unit 6 pages 171–172 for information on the evidence required). It enables you to recall things you have done and match them to the competencies in the PERs (see below). It is *your* responsibility to do this, not your supervisor's. Try to become familiar with the requirements and make a pencil mark next to each one you believe you have carried out competently – if you can show a date, or dates, and refer to your Practice Evidence Record, then your supervisor is more likely to remember it and may sign it off.

- **Do not lose them!** It is important to keep a record of signed competencies throughout the course and check it regularly with your tutor.
- **Keep your PERs in a safe place:** try to avoid leaving your PERs with your supervisor – this may seem sensible but often leads to disaster if you or he/she is absent, the book gets mislaid

or damaged, or the placement comes to an end followed by a long holiday.

- **Attendance record:** your study centre may require you to keep an attendance sheet that logs the times and dates of placement attendance. This needs to be signed regularly by your supervisor and kept by you.
- **Getting signatures:** in addition to your attendance record and PER competencies you will also need to obtain your supervisor's signature to authenticate (i.e. show that they are genuine) displays, observations and portfolio activities.

Cooperation and teamwork

No two training placements or supervisors will be the same. It is important, therefore, to settle as quickly as possible into new and different routines and practices. Gathering the placement information, as suggested on pages 7–9, should speed up this process.

Cooperating with other professionals and recognising their contributions are areas that are assessed through the PDP at the end of each placement. If you are a student who attends for one or two days a week, it can be difficult to pick up the threads of what has happened on the days you have been at your study centre. The opportunity to attend your placement for a block week will give you the chance to experience the full range of activities, including PE, music, cookery and other topic work that you may otherwise be missing.

As you are attending on the same days each week it may seem that you are always given the same jobs to do – Fridays usually involve washing paint pots! These jobs have to be done and, if they are carried out by other staff members or helpers on other occasions, then it is not unreasonable for you to be expected to do them too as part of your training.

It only becomes a problem if you are given tasks that are always – or often – away from the children, and you are not having the opportunity to carry out the requirements of the course. If this is the case you need to speak to your tutor, who may visit and discuss these issues with your supervisor.

Time management

There are often conflicting pressures on your time when working in early years settings. However well prepared a timetable is, something can always occur that upsets the smooth running of the day. Even when you are caring for one young baby in the parent's home, you will find it useful to follow these guidelines.

- **Prioritise your tasks:** it is a good idea to make a written list of the various tasks you have to complete in a particular session; then you can divide the tasks into essential and non-essential (but desirable) tasks.
- **Set targets:** try to set deadlines for completing certain tasks; you may be able to fit in a simple task – such as organising the creative play area – between other tasks. Be realistic in what you hope to achieve. Be aware that you may be interrupted in what you are doing and will need to return to it later.
- **Try not to become overwhelmed:** there will be some days when you wonder if you will ever complete any one task. Take a deep breath and try to put it all into perspective. As long as you are doing your best and have the children's welfare as your primary concern, try not to panic if you are running late!
- **Share your concerns:** your colleagues will understand the pressures (and the rewards) of working with children, and about the unpredictability of such work. By sharing your worries you can learn how to manage your time and routines more effectively.

Values and positive attitudes

Our values and attitudes towards others develop from early childhood. The way in which we are brought up and the behaviour we see around us will help us to form opinions and make choices about every aspect of our lives. The first values we absorb into our learning come from our early childhood experiences, particularly from our:

- parents or primary carers and family
- friends and their families

- early experiences in playgroup, nursery and school.

Children learn moral values by example and by imitation. If a child is made to feel secure and loved within their family, they will develop confidence and self-esteem, and find it easier to form close relationships with others. Children whose early life involves unhappy or very weak relationships with others often find it difficult to form close, lasting relationships when they are older. Attitudes are the opinions and ways of thinking that we have towards others and their beliefs. These attitudes are shaped by our values.

Examples of moral values are:

- truth
- socially acceptable behaviour
- love
- non-violence
- peace
- justice.

Our attitudes towards others are based on our beliefs and feelings about the world. Negative attitudes towards others may result from assumptions about people and their way of life, which may be very different from our own. Travellers, for example, have often been discriminated against within care settings because of these differences.

Positive attitudes towards children enable them to:

- feel good about themselves
- feel that they are valued
- develop high self-esteem.

It is not our task to try to change the values and attitudes of others, but we should challenge others if their behaviour shows discrimination. What is most important is that we act as **good role models** through our work with children, so that they can learn to imitate our behaviour and express positive attitudes towards others.

The poem in the box below by Dorothy Law Nolte describes the effect our values have on children's development.

Activity

Exploring your attitudes and values

Consider the following moral questions.

1 Should women go out to work when they have young children?

2 Should the armed forces accept gay men and women into their ranks?

3 Should it be against the law to smack a child? Should childminders and teachers have the right to smack a child if the parents consent?

4 Should gay couples (male or female) be allowed to adopt a child?

5 Should men take an equal share with women in bringing up their children?

In pairs, discuss each question in turn, making brief notes on the arguments for and against each question. Then, in the whole group, consider how each answer could affect your attitudes towards parents and children in the work setting.

Children learn what they live

If children live with criticism, they learn to condemn.

If children live with hostility, they learn to fight.

If children live with fear, they learn to be apprehensive.

If children live with pity, they learn to feel sorry for themselves.

If children live with ridicule, they learn to be shy.

If children live with jealousy, they learn to feel envy.

If children live with shame, they learn to feel guilty.

If children live with encouragement, they learn confidence.

If children live with tolerance, they learn patience.

If children live with praise, they learn appreciation.

If children live with acceptance, they learn to love.

If children live with approval, they learn to like themselves.

If children live with recognition, they learn it is good to have a goal.

If children live with sharing, they learn generosity.

If children live with honesty, they learn truthfulness.

If children live with fairness, they learn justice.

If children live with kindness and consideration, they learn respect.

If children live with security, they learn to have faith in themselves and in those about them.

If children live with friendliness, they learn the world is a nice place in which to live.

Dorothy Law Nolte

girl with the pretty dress'). Such labels devalue
children, restricting their sense of self-worth.
Always use the child's name.

- **Challenging discrimination:** if you see a
child teasing, insulting or hitting another child,
explain that such behaviour is hurtful. Criticise
the behaviour rather than the child; for example,
you could say: 'Kicking hurts. Carla is very upset
because it hurt,' rather than, 'You're very naughty.
Don't do that, I'm very cross with you.' This avoids
children feeling that you do not like them or that
they are worthless.

The responsibilities and the limits of your role in placement

You need to practise your skills with regard to certain
responsibilities; these responsibilities include the
following.

Confidentiality

Confidentiality is about trust and sensitivity to the
needs and the rights of others. You should always
treat all the information you are privileged to receive
within the work setting as confidential; avoid gossip
and stereotyping.

Anyone working with young children, whether in a
nursery setting, a school or in the family home, will
need to practise confidentiality.

Confidentiality is respect for the privacy of any
information about a child and his or her family.
In most instances you will be working under the
supervision of others, and it is likely that parents
will pass confidential information directly to a staff
member. However, there may be occasions on which
you are given information and asked to pass it on, or
that you may hear or be told confidential information
in the course of the daily routine.

You may be entrusted with personal information
about children, parents and staff, either directly
(being told or being given written information) or
indirectly (hearing staffroom discussions, parental

Activity

Exploring moral values

Working in pairs or small groups, identify and list
five moral values within the poem on the previous
page and, for each value, discuss how it can be
promoted within the care and education setting.
(One example could be the value of appreciation;
by praising children every time they have achieved
something, however small that thing may be, you
are demonstrating your appreciation for them as
individuals and promoting their self-concept – or
feelings of self-worth.)

Being a good role model

Children learn more from how they *see us act* than
they do from anything we may tell them. Children
directly copy what adults do, so it is important that
we nurture an environment that is free from any bias
and that encourages equality of opportunity. Being a
good role model involves the following aspects.

- **Non-verbal communication:** children pick up
signals about how we think, feel and act from
our body language, facial expressions, gestures,
pauses, etc. When listening to children, make sure
that your eyes are at their eye level, and give them
time to express themselves, making encouraging
sounds and smiling.
- **Using appropriate language:** how you talk to
children and respond to them are very important.
You need to be able to adapt your language
to the individual child and to be aware of any
communication difficulties.
- **Cooperating with others:** children need to see
that you are pleasant and that you can get along
with parents and other adults. Any conflicts
between members of staff, for example, should be
aired when in the staff room.
- **Showing respect:** learning how to pronounce
difficult names and listening to other people's
opinions are important in showing your respect
for others.
- **Avoiding stereotypes and labels:** avoid using
labels that result in children being stereotyped
(e.g. 'the boy with glasses', 'the Asian girl' or 'the

comments or children's conversations), and it is important that you do not repeat any of it at home or to friends.

There have been embarrassing – not to say unpleasant – incidents, sometimes resulting in students' placements being cancelled, through thoughtlessness. In small communities, such as schools or nurseries, it is easy for a parent or family member to overhear confidential information relating to daily events (e.g. an incident involving aggressive behaviour or swearing) or individual children (personal or family difficulties affecting the child concerned) if it is mentioned to a neighbour or the person you baby-sit for, even if it is through concern. The incidents may be discussed in your teaching sessions among your student group, but you should not identify the children concerned, and it must be agreed that they are not talked about beyond the group.

As long as you follow the guidelines, procedures and practices that apply to the work setting, you will not go far wrong.

Practising confidentiality

Children and their parents and carers need to feel confident that:

- you will not interfere in their private lives and that any information you are privileged to hold will not become a source of gossip. Breaches of confidentiality can occur when you are travelling on public transport, for example, and discussing the events of your day; always remember that using the names of children in your care can cause a serious breach of confidentiality if overheard by a friend or relative of the family
- you will ensure that any child or family's personal information is restricted to those who have a real *need to know* – for example, when a child's family or health circumstances are affecting their development
- you will not write anything down about a child that you would feel concerned about showing their parents or carers
- you understand when the safety or health needs of the child override the need for confidentiality; parents need to be reassured that you will always

put the safety and well-being of each child before any other considerations.

Commitment to meeting the needs of the children

All children should be treated with respect and dignity, and their needs must be considered as paramount. This means working within the guidelines of an equal opportunities code of practice, and not allowing any personal preferences or prejudices to influence the way you treat children.

Responsibility and accountability in the workplace

The supervisor, line manager, teacher or parent will have certain expectations about your role, and your responsibilities should be detailed in your job contract. (As a student, you should always consult your tutor if you are uncertain about anything, as you will not have a job contract.) As a child care practitioner, you need to carry out all your duties willingly and be answerable (or accountable) to others for your work. You need to know about the **lines of reporting** within a work setting and how to find out about your own particular responsibilities. If you are unsure what is expected of you – or if you do not feel confident in carrying out a particular task – then you should ask your line manager or your immediate supervisor for guidance.

Key term

Line of reporting – A vertical route in a hierarchy made up of individuals who report to or are responsible to the next most senior person.

Respect for parents and other adults

You need to respect the wishes and views of parents and other carers, even when you disagree with those views. You should also recognise that parents are usually the people who know their children best. In all your dealings with parents and other adults, you must show that you respect their cultural values and religious beliefs.

Communicate effectively with team members and other professionals

Being able to communicate effectively with team members, other professionals and with parents is a very important part of your role as a child care practitioner. You should always:

- be considerate of others and polite towards them
- recognise the contributions made by other team members; we all like to feel we are valued for the work we do; you can help others to feel valued by being aware of their role and how it has helped you fulfil your own role
- explain clearly to the relevant person any changes in routine or any actions you have taken; for example – as a nanny, always informing a parent when a child you are caring for has refused a meal or been distressed in any way, or reporting any behaviour problem or incident to your line manager in a nursery setting.

To meet the needs of all the children in a setting, the staff members must work effectively together as a team. The roles and responsibilities of individual team members will depend on the organisation of the work setting.

In your role as a nursery assistant you will be supporting the work of others. You will usually work under the direction, sometimes under the supervision, of a childcare practitioner or teacher, depending on the setting. There may also be professionals from other disciplines (e.g. medicine, social services, dentistry) who are involved with the families and children you work with. A special school or nursery that cares for children with physical disabilities will have a 'multidisciplinary' team; this may include teachers, childcare practitioners and assistants, trained special care assistants, physiotherapists, paediatricians and, possibly, social workers.

Effective teamwork is vital in such settings to ensure that:

- all concerned know their individual roles and responsibilities
- parents and primary carers know which team member can deal with any specific concerns.

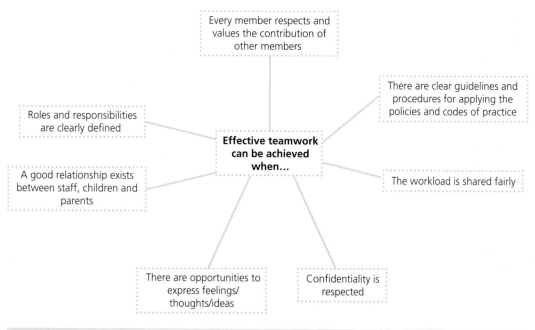

Every member respects and values the contribution of other members

There are clear guidelines and procedures for applying the policies and codes of practice

Roles and responsibilities are clearly defined

Effective teamwork can be achieved when...

The workload is shared fairly

A good relationship exists between staff, children and parents

There are opportunities to express feelings/ thoughts/ideas

Confidentiality is respected

Figure 1.3 Achieving effective teamwork

Knowing the limits of your role

Children are likely to treat you as any other adult on the staff – assuming that you can help them and are there to care for them as well as discipline them. This means that, by your behaviour, language and attitudes, you set an example for the children you are working with and caring for.

Being a good role model involves:

- showing consideration for others
- taking care over hygiene and appearance
- using appropriate language (you must address the children and adults politely and using the correct terms – avoid referring to the children as kids!)
- supporting other staff and parents, and
- following set procedures and policies.

Use of initiative is one of the aspects some students struggle with. It involves trying to anticipate (see in advance) situations and taking appropriate action.

- **Have confidence:** using initiative effectively requires confidence on your part and reassurance from your supervisor that you can (and should) deal with many incidents yourself if you happen to be the nearest adult.
- **Safety issues:** it is vital that you take steps on your own initiative when matters of safety are concerned (e.g. spilt sand or water, a child who is choking, a blocked fire exit).
- **Handling disputes:** additionally, you will be expected to deal with children's disputes and maintain behaviour according to your placement guidelines when you are supervising groups.
- **Being friendly – but not friends:** it is important to remember that your relationship with the children in your care is a professional one. You should always be friendly and approachable – but not try to take the place of the child's parents. At the same time, you should communicate with each child at a level that is appropriate to their stage of development and to their needs; you should not act as a child would when interacting with them. The same principle applies when you are communicating with parents. If the child of one of your friends attends your placement, you will both have to appreciate that there are then two

different relationships – the friendship one and the workplace one.

Remember: nobody will expect you to know everything at first. Staff members are there to help you to get the most out of each placement, and your tutor will discuss any concerns you may have. If you are unsure about any aspect of care, or how to speak with a parent, do not be afraid to ask your supervisor or college tutor.

Children's individual needs and the necessity for fairness and inclusive practice

Children's needs vary greatly. Apart from the basic needs that every child has – for food, drink, safety, shelter, warmth and protection from harm – each child will have **individual needs**. Short-term needs include:

- a child who has been unwell may have a short-term need for extra rest and attention to physical needs
- a child who has recently joined the setting will need more attention from his or key person while settling in.

Long-term needs include the following:

- a child who has visual or hearing difficulties may have several needs; for example, a child getting used to wearing glasses or using a hearing aid may need help and encouragement with managing the situation
- a child who has asthma may become frightened when breathless and will need reassurance and access to an inhaler at all times.

Fairness and inclusive practice

It is important that you recognise the differences between children and that you *value* those differences. Children should be encouraged not to feel anxious about people who are different from them. Many of the traditions practised within families from ethnic minorities are now adopted by

Western societies (e.g. baby massage with natural oils, and the carrying of babies in fabric slings). We all have a great deal to learn from one another.

Children may feel themselves to be different in other ways too, not simply by having a different cultural heritage. Children with special needs often feel that they are the odd ones out in a group setting – for example, if a child:

- wears glasses or a hearing aid
- has frequent bouts of asthma
- has a mobility problem
- has learning difficulties.

Case Studies Making assumptions

Sam, Jason, Laura and Fatima are playing in the home corner. The nursery teacher asks Sam and Jason to tidy away the train set and trucks, and asks Laura and Fatima to put the dolls and cooking pots away, as it is nearly story time.

The assumption here is that dolls and cooking utensils are 'girl' playthings, whereas trains and trucks are 'boy' playthings. The teacher is reinforcing this stereotype by separating the tasks by gender.

Paul's mother arrives at the school open day. She is in a wheelchair, being pushed by Paul's father. The teacher welcomes the parents and then asks Paul's father if his wife would like a drink and a biscuit.

This is a common feature of daily life for people who use wheelchairs. They are often ignored and questions are addressed to their companion, often because the other person is embarrassed by the unusual situation and fearful of making

a mistake. The assumption here is that the person in the wheelchair would not be able to understand and reply to what is said to them.

Harry's mother is a registered heroin addict who has been attending a drug rehabilitation programme for the last few months. Whenever Harry behaves in an aggressive way to other children or to staff, one staff member always makes a jibe about his home life: 'Harry, you may get away with that sort of thing where you come from, but it won't work here. We know all about you.'

This is an extreme and very unkind form of stereotyping. It is assuming that, because his mother is a drug user, Harry is somehow less worthy of consideration and respect. By drawing attention to his home life, the member of staff is guilty of prejudice and discriminatory behaviour. There is also a breach of the policy of confidentiality.

Avoiding stereotyping and labelling

It is important to avoid labelling or stereotyping people. A stereotype is a way of thinking that assumes that all people who share one characteristic also share another set of characteristics. Some examples are listed below.

- **Racism:** racism is the belief that some 'races' are superior to others – based on the false idea that different physical characteristics (like skin colour) or ethnic background make some people better than others.

- **Sexism:** sexism occurs when people of one gender (or biological sex) believe that they are superior to the other.
- **Ageism:** this occurs when negative feelings are expressed towards a person or group because of their age; in Western society it is usually directed towards older people.
- **Disablism:** this occurs when disabled people are seen in terms of their disability, rather than as unique individuals who happen to have special needs.

There are many other stereotypes, such as those concerning gay and lesbian groups, people from low socio-economic groups and those who practise a minority religion.

Stereotyped thinking can prevent you from seeing someone as an individual with particular life experiences and interests, and so lead to negative attitudes and to prejudice and discrimination.

Key term

Reflective practice – You should consider your actions, experiences or learning and their implications in order to suggest significant developments for future action, learning or practice. These are recognised cycles of reflective practice. Reflective practice can also show that you have performed exceptionally well.

Your own preferred learning style and developing study skills

I hear – I forget
I see – I remember
I do – I understand.

(Confucius c.551–479 BC)

We all have our own particular way of learning new information – our own preferred **learning style**. It does not have anything to do with how intelligent we are or what skills we have learned. It has to do with how the brain works most efficiently to learn new information. There are many different theories about learning styles.

What works best for *you* will not necessarily be the same as the approach used by other students, even those studying the same course. We are all unique as learners, although there are some patterns that emerge in any group of students. It is important to explore a whole range of approaches because that will enable you to find out what works best for you.

Your approach to learning may change as you develop new study skills, and many of us use different styles depending on the problem or task at hand. It is now widely accepted that the capacity to learn can be improved by:

- analysing how you do things
- being willing to try new things, and
- recognising what works best for you.

Different learning styles

Experts have identified three basic learning styles: **auditory**, **visual** and **tactile**.

Auditory

Auditory learners prefer to learn and remember by:

- talking out loud
- having things explained orally.

They may have trouble with written instructions; auditory learners may talk to themselves when learning something new.

Motto: If you hear it, you remember it.

If you are an auditory learner, you benefit:

- when information is presented in an oral language format
- from listening to lectures and participating in group discussions
- from obtaining information from audio tape
- when interacting with others in a listening/speaking exchange
- from talking aloud, when studying alone, to aid recall.

Visual

Visual learners prefer to learn and remember by:

- seeing what they are learning (visual details)
- writing down instructions; they may have trouble following lectures with no visual props
- studying alone in a quiet room.

Motto: You have to see it to believe it.

If you are a visual learner, you benefit from:

- teachers who use the whiteboard (or overhead projector) to list the essential points of a lecture, or who provide you with an outline to follow along with during the lecture
- information obtained from textbooks and class notes.

Tactile

Tactile (kinaesthetic) learners prefer to learn and remember by:

- doing activities that allow them to practise what they are learning about
- touching things in order to learn about them
- being physically active in the learning environment.

Motto: If you can touch it with your hands, you will remember it.

If you are a tactile learner, you benefit from:

- teachers who encourage demonstrations
- 'hands-on' student learning experiences
- jotting down key words, drawing pictures or making charts to help remember the information in the classroom.

Identifying your own preferred style

You probably will not fit neatly into any one category; most people have a mixture of learning styles.

Example: try thinking about the way in which you remember a phone number.

- Can you visualise (or see, in your mind's eye), how the numbers look on the phone? Or can you visualise the number on a piece of paper, 'seeing' it exactly as you wrote it down? (**visual learning style**)
- Can you 'hear' the number in the way that someone recited it to you? (**auditory learning style**)
- Do you 'let your fingers do the walking' on the phone? That is, your fingers dial the number without looking at the phone? (**tactile learning style**)

Learning strategies

While it is useful to know about personal learning styles, it is really our understanding of our learning *strategies* that makes us effective learners. The easiest way to think about learning strategies is to explore how you actually tackle a learning task (see Table 1.2).

Visual learners	Auditory learners	Tactile learners
• Use visual materials such as pictures, charts and maps • Use colour to highlight texts and own notes • Take notes or use handouts; look carefully at headings and patterns of topics • Brainstorm using illustrations, mind maps and models • Use multimedia where possible (computers, mind maps) • Study in a quiet place away from visual disturbances • Visualise information as a picture • Skim-read to get an overview before reading in detail	• Participate frequently in discussions and debates • Make speeches and presentations • Use a tape recorder if possible instead of (or as well as) making notes • Read text aloud • Create musical jingles and **mnemonics*** to aid memory • Discuss your ideas verbally • Dictate to someone else while they write your ideas down • Speak on to an audio tape and listen to your own ideas played back	• Take frequent study breaks • Move around to learn new things (e.g. read while using an exercise bike; model in clay to learn a new concept) • Stand up to work • Use bright colours to highlight reading material and turn it into posters or models • Skim-read before reading in detail

Table 1.2 Strategies for learning

* 'Mnemonic' is another word for a memory tool. Mnemonics are techniques for remembering information that is otherwise quite difficult to recall. A simple example is the '30 days hath September ...' rhyme for remembering the number of days in each calendar month.

Activity

Discovering your learning style

Answer the questions below, and then compare your answers with those of other students.

Do you do best in classes when teachers do a lot of writing at the whiteboard, provide clear handouts, and make extensive use of an overhead projector?	**V**
Does listening to audio tapes help you learn better?	**A**
Do you try to remember information by creating pictures in your mind?	**V**
Do you learn better when you have an actual object in your hands rather than a picture of the object or a verbal or written description of it?	**T**
Do you seem to learn best in classes where there are class discussions?	**A**
When trying to study, do you become distracted by activity around you?	**T**
Do you forget names but remember faces, or remember where you met?	**V**
In class, do you talk little but also dislike listening for too long?	**V**
Do you generally do well in classes in which there is a practical (task) component?	**T**
When trying to study, do you become distracted by untidiness or movement?	**V**
Do you learn best when you can move about and handle things?	**T**
Do you find yourself reading aloud or talking things out to gain better understanding?	**A**
In class, do you enjoy listening but are impatient to talk?	**A**
When trying to study, do you become distracted by sounds or noises?	**A**
In class, do you use a lot of body language (i.e. gestures and expressive movements)?	**T**
Do you take detailed written notes from your textbooks and in class?	**V**
When having problems on the computer, do you call the help desk or ask someone else?	**A**
When having problems on the computer, do you keep trying to do it or try it on another computer?	**T**
Key: A = auditory learner; V = visual learner; T = tactile learner	

If you answered Yes mostly to the questions with **V** in the column, you are probably a visual learner; if you answered Yes mostly to the questions with **A** in the column, you are probably an auditory learner; if you answered Yes mostly to the questions with **T** in the column, you are probably a tactile learner. You may find you answered Yes to a mixture of learning styles, which means you respond to a variety of teaching methods.

Study skills to help you complete your course

Organising and planning your time: getting the balance right

Any activity can seem preferable to working on an assignment or settling down to revision: tidying your room, staring at the wall, fetching 'just one more' small snack, or even doing the washing up!

However, when work is postponed regularly, deadlines and examination dates can increase feelings of disorganisation and panic, and can trigger a 'flight' response. It can become tempting to produce the minimum work possible, or even to abandon assignments completely. Excuses have to be invented, deadlines renegotiated, further assignments become due before the last ones are completed and, before long, the course begins to feel overwhelming and unmanageable. Of course, people can have very good reasons for finding their workload difficult to manage: child care or other family responsibilities, the need to earn money through part-time work, and unexpected traumas or illnesses can all increase pressure on students. However, if you are generally enjoying your course and finding the work stimulating and interesting, you are likely to want to find a way of organising your time so that you can keep a balance between your work, your social life and your other interests and commitments.

There are only so many hours in a week. Although keeping rigidly to a 'weekly planner' or timetable will not always be easy or desirable, it should help you to focus on what free time you have in a week, and which 'chunks' of it can be used for course work and revision.

Activity

Planning your time

1 Draw up a table, or print one out from a calendar program on a computer, showing the seven days of the week as headings and hourly blocks of time down the left-hand side (for example 8–9 am, 9–10 am through to 9–10 pm).

2 Now insert into the table:
   - your college or school timetabled commitments (i.e. your lectures and lessons)
   - any paid work, housework or child care/family commitments
   - travelling time
   - time you normally spend with friends/sports activities/other leisure pursuits
   - any 'unmissable' TV programmes (not too many!).

3 What 'chunks' of time have you left for studying?
   - In the day?
   - In the evening?
   - At weekends?

Do not forget that the half-term or end-of-term holidays can be a good time to catch up on assignments and revision. Remember to include these in your long-term calculations. However, having completed your planner, will you need to readjust any commitments to give you enough time to complete course work? How important will it be for you to spend some time studying in the day as well as in the evening?

Motivation during study periods

It is important to find a place where you can work without interruptions and distractions. Even if you have the luxury of a room and a desk of your own at home, you will probably need to consider using your school, college or public library for some study periods. Settling down to a period of study is easier if you:

- remove all distractions of hunger, noise, cold – and sociable friends!
- try not to study if you are feeling angry or upset
- keep a pad of paper or a jotter next to you as you work; when ideas or other things occur to you, you can note them down before you forget them
- give yourself realistic targets and decide for how long you will study before you start; try not to work for more than an hour without a short break; reward yourself for completing what you planned to do
- try to give yourself a variety of activities to work on
- have the phone number of someone else from your class or group handy in case you need to check what you need to do or want to discuss the best way to go about a task.

Compiling a portfolio

A portfolio is a collection of the different types of evidence that can be used to show successful completion of the course. Examples of evidence include:

- completed assignments, projects or case studies, including action plans and evaluations; these can be in written form or word-processed, although work in the form of video recordings, audio tape recordings, photographs, logbooks or diaries may also be acceptable where they contain evidence of the practical demonstration of skills – check with your teacher or tutor

- past records of achievement, qualifications, work experience or other evidence of 'prior learning'
- samples of relevant class or lecture notes, lists, personal reading records or copies of letters written (perhaps regarding work experience, to request information or advice, or related to job or higher education applications).

Equipment and materials

As soon as you know how many mandatory and optional units you will be taking for the course, it will be worthwhile taking advantage of any cheap stationery offers at high-street stores and equipping yourself with:

- A4 files, with subject dividers
- a hole punch
- file paper (plain and lined)
- plastic pockets or report files; these are not essential but you may feel better if finished assignments are presented neatly in a binder or pocket of some sort; however, do not enclose each individual sheet of an assignment within a plastic pocket – this is expensive, ecologically unsound and drives your teachers and assessors crazy when they have to remove sheets to make comments on your work!
- post-it index stickers can be useful to help 'flag up' important pieces of work in your completed portfolio
- small exercise books or notebooks, to act as logbooks or diaries.

If you are dyslexic or have another disability that prevents or makes it difficult for you to take notes in lectures, you might consider acquiring recording equipment to enable you to record lectures and play them back at another time.

Reading, note-taking and using a library

Textbooks such as this can offer you a basic framework for the ideas and information you need for the different subject areas covered in the course. Your lectures and classes will supply you with additional material. However, you will need to carry out your own reading and research, making your own notes and updating information in areas where there is constant change (such as child care legislation). It will be useful for you to find out how the national organisation of care and education services works in the area and in the community in which you live.

You cannot do this successfully without making full use of libraries (including their computers), newspapers and journals, television and film, and information produced by a range of national, local and voluntary organisations. If you have personal access to the internet, you may find such research decidedly easier, and this book contains many references to websites worth exploring. Make sure that you are shown how to use all the relevant facilities of your library, whether school, college or public.

Using the internet

Think before reaching for the mouse. Using the internet can be highly productive but it can also take up a lot of your time. Before you start, work out:

- what you need to know
- how much you need to know
- when you need the information by
- whether you have a sensible search strategy – so that you have a list of recommended sites or know the best way to use a 'search engine' such as Google or Yahoo!
- if you could find the information you need more easily in books or a journal.

Strategies for reading and note-taking

We have all had the experience of reading a sentence, paragraph, or even a whole page, without being able to remember what we have just read. To be of most use to you, reading will often need to be combined with note-taking.

Taking notes is time-consuming and requires *active* concentration. Students often worry if:

- they are spending too much time taking endless, detailed notes without really understanding what they will be used for
- they give up note-taking because they cannot seem to work out what to write down and what not; this can be a particular problem when taking notes in lessons and lectures.

Essentially, note-taking is a strategy for helping you to:

- think, understand and remember.

There are many situations in life when it is important to focus on the **key issues** or points being communicated.

Example: You may have to know exactly what to do if a child in your care has an asthma attack or needs adrenalin for a peanut allergy. You may have to explain these things quickly to another person, summarising essential information.

Deciding what to write down when you take notes is easier if you think about *why* you are taking notes. You may need to take different types of notes for different reasons. You will get better at working out methods of note-taking that suit you, the more you try out different approaches. It also helps to think about ways to store your notes so that they are easily accessible to you when you need them. If they are written or designed in such a way that you can make use of them again, you will be more likely to come back to them.

Mind mapping

If you work better visually or spatially rather than in writing, you can make graphic 'notes': flow charts, block designs, family trees, spider plans or other forms of **mind map**. These can be used for:

- generating ideas
- planning your work (e.g. for an observation or report)
- note-taking and – later on – revising.

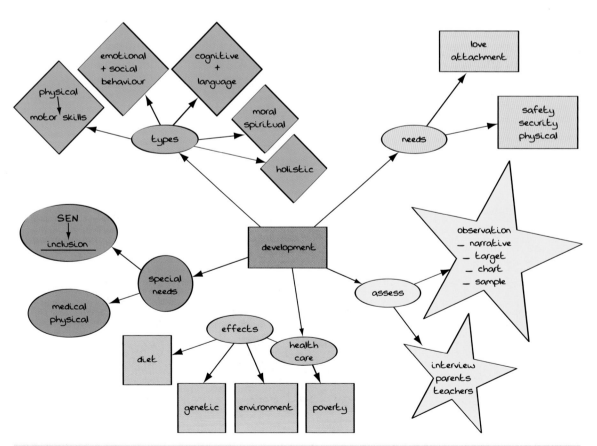

Figure 1.4 An example of a mind map

How to draw a mind map:

1 In the centre of your page draw a picture of, or name in words, your main topic or theme.
2 Draw branches from this main topic in thick lines (use different colours or patterns). Label your branches with key words and/or images.
3 Draw sub-branches from the main branches to represent sub-topics or to elaborate and extend your ideas. Again, use key words, phrases, images, pictures and colour. Use italics, underlining and capitals to highlight your work.

Let your ideas flow and develop. Add more detail to your mind map as ideas occur to you. However, the mind map is not meant to be an art form or elaborate doodle – more a way to focus your attention on the essential components of a piece of work, topic or report.

Underlining and highlighting

If you own the book or article you are taking notes from, highlighting, underlining and marking the margin with asterisks or other symbols can be a quick and effective method of skim-reading a text, focusing your attention on it and getting to grips with the material as a whole. Again, the most important part of this activity is that you are *concentrating* on what you are doing.

Writing assignments, observations and reports

Much of your *written* course work is set in the form of assignments and projects – although some is assessed through multiple choice question papers (MCQs) and short answer tests.

Planning and prioritising tasks

If you use a planner regularly (see page 19), it is easier to break up assignments, plans and observations into a series of smaller tasks, each of which you could aim to complete within a manageable time, such as an hour or two. Subdividing your course work in this way also allows you to **prioritise** the tasks. In what order are they best done? Which really needs to be done straight away? Make a list of small tasks in order of priority, with the time you estimate they will take and target dates for completion. Leave room on your action plan to amend these dates when and if your plan is modified.

Monitoring and revising your work

There are likely to be many points during the completion of a piece of course work when you will change direction or modify your original plan in some way. On your action plan, keep a note of:

- the reasons for changing your plans
- what new plans you have for the work.

Writing a bibliography

You will be expected to write a bibliography (a list of books, articles and other resources used) for each assignment or observation you submit. To do this properly, you need to make a note of the materials and references you use as you study. There is nothing worse than finishing an assignment and then spending valuable time hunting down the name of a book you read in the library but did not note the details of. As a general rule, you need to note:

- the title of the book or article (or website address)
- the author(s)
- the publisher
- the date of publication
- the place of publication.

Here are some examples.

Book: Bruce, T. (2011) *Early Childhood Education* (4th revised edition), London: Hodder Education.

Article: Bruner, J., Wood, D. and Ross, G. (1976) 'The role of tutoring in problem-solving', *Journal of Child Psychology and Psychiatry*, **17**, pp.89–100.

The **Harvard system of referencing** is most often used. The **references** *within* your text use the author's name and the date of publication. Then the full details of the book or article are listed – alphabetically – in the 'Bibliography' and/or 'References' list at the end of the assignment. Other sources of information or references in your work may come from the internet (give the website address and the date you accessed the site), workplace (acknowledge the source), television programmes, video or film (give the title and date) or friends, family and teachers (attribute information as accurately as you can).

Giving presentations and sharing information

There are many different ways of sharing information with others. Informal discussions can be useful if the group have a shared experience. Many colleges expect students to be able to give reports and presentations in order to share information. Learning the skills of presentation will be invaluable both in interviews and in your future career.

Preparation

You may be asked to give a presentation on some topic or area in your course. Before planning your presentation, research some PowerPoint talks that you think work well. Prepare the structure of the talk carefully and logically, as you would for a written report:

- Outline the objectives of the talk and the main points you want to make.
- Write out the presentation in rough, just as you would if preparing the first draft of an essay or report.
- Review the draft. Delete any irrelevant or superfluous information.
- Prepare and number cue cards – each with key words and phrases.
- Prepare any visual aids (OHPs or slides) and mark on your cue cards the visual aids that go with them.
- Rehearse your presentation to ensure that the words and the sequence of visual aids work together.

Making the presentation

Firstly, introduce yourself and then follow these guidelines:

- tell the audience what you are going to tell them
- then tell them
- at the end, tell them what you have told them.

Face the audience and speak clearly, pausing deliberately at key points. Try not to face the screen behind you when talking, and try not to fix your gaze on just one or two people – everyone in the room needs to feel included. It is better to keep your presentation short, in order to prevent information overload. In general, allow about two minutes for each PowerPoint slide or visual aid you use, but longer for any that you want to use for developing specific points. Remember to leave enough time at the end for discussion of the points raised. (You could prepare a question for the audience in case nobody asks a question!) If you feel very nervous about giving a presentation alone, ask if you could pair up with a fellow student to give a joint talk.

Participating in group discussions

Group discussions can be very useful. Listening to and responding to other people's ideas can help you to think through your own beliefs and ideas. Some people feel nervous when asked to contribute to a discussion; others enjoy debating issues and may end up dominating the whole discussion. You need to show respect for other people's views and to listen carefully when others are speaking. If you know the topic under discussion in advance, it is useful to find out as much as possible about it so that you can make a valuable contribution.

Punctuation and grammar

The main reason for the correct use of punctuation and grammar is so that your readers can focus on *what* you are trying to say rather than on *how* you are saying it. When people make grammatical mistakes or punctuation mistakes, these draw attention away from the content of the writing. The correct use of grammar and punctuation allows the reader to relax and take in what you are trying to communicate. When there are errors, it makes the reader focus on your grammar instead of what you are trying to communicate. It is not a good idea simply to rely on the 'spelling and grammar check' tool in Word documents, as the meaning of your sentences can be completely changed from your intended meaning. If you know that you have difficulties with grammar, punctuation and spelling – even though you may be able to write well – it is important to get help. Free, confidential help on improving writing skills is always available at college.

When you need to take a test or MCQ paper

When the day of a test arrives, give yourself plenty of time to check everything; check equipment, have breakfast, arrive on time but not too early. Try not to talk about the test with friends before you start. Have a last look at any brief notes or summaries you have made. As soon as you are allowed to, read the questions.

- Make sure you understand the test instructions.
- Ask for help if necessary.
- Take your time.
- Highlight key words and note down any key facts you know you will have to use at some point but may forget as the test proceeds.

 Progress check

Recording your own progress

Do you keep a record of all training days and staff development events you have attended?

Have you revisited your development plan – reviewed it and reflected on it?

Assessment practice

Your work role

As preparation for the Unit One Assignment, use the information in this chapter to compile a folder that provides information about:

- the duties and responsibilities of your own work role
- the importance of the first impressions that you make in the setting
- the ways in which you can show positive attitudes when working in a child care setting
- the ways in which you can ensure that your personal attitudes or beliefs do not obstruct the quality of your work
- the importance of keeping information about children and families confidential
- the importance of recognising your own learning style and using this knowledge effectively in your studies.

2 The developing child: Unit 2

This Unit focuses on patterns of development for each area and the factors that affect development. You will be introduced to ways of observing children so that you can support development through appropriate activities and care routines. You will also learn how to work with children when they move from one setting to another.

> ## Learning outcomes
>
> During this unit you will learn about:
>
> 1 The expected pattern of development.
>
> 2 The importance of careful observations and how they support development.
>
> 3 How to identify influences that affect children's development, such as background, health and environment.
>
> 4 How to use everyday care routines and activities to support development.
>
> 5 How to support children through transitions in their lives.

The expected pattern of development

It is important to keep in mind that every child is unique. By looking at the holistic (or integrated) development of children, we can view the child as a whole person – physically, emotionally, intellectually, morally, culturally and spiritually. Physical growth is different from physical development. *Physical growth* means that children grow in height and weight, whereas *physical development* means that children gain skills through being able to control their own bodies.

Learning about development

Children's physical development follows a pattern:

- **From simple to complex:** a child will stand before he can walk, and walk before he can skip or hop.
- **From head to toe:** physical control and coordination begin with a child's head and work down the body through the arms, hands and back and finally to the legs and feet.
- **From inner to outer:** a child can coordinate his arms using gross motor skills to reach for an object before he has learned the fine motor skills necessary to pick it up.
- **From general to specific:** a young baby shows pleasure by a massive general response (eyes widen, legs and arms move vigorously, etc.); an older child shows pleasure by smiling or using appropriate words or gestures.

The whole child may be looked at using six headings or aspects. You can remember these as together they make up the acronym **PILESS**:

- **P**hysical development
- **I**ntellectual development
- **L**anguage and communication development
- **E**motional development
- **S**ocial and behaviour development
- **S**piritual development.

Physical development

Physical development is the way in which the body increases in skill and becomes more complex in its performance. There are two main areas:

1 **gross motor skills**: these use the large muscles in the body and include walking, squatting, running, climbing, etc.

2 **fine motor skills**, which include:
- gross manipulative skills – *single limb movements, usually the arm, for example throwing, catching and sweeping arm movements*
- fine manipulative skills – *precise use of the hands and fingers for pointing, drawing, using a knife and fork, writing, doing up shoelaces, etc.*

There are wide variations in the ages at which children acquire physical skills, such as sitting, standing and walking. The rate at which children develop these skills will have an effect on all the other areas of development: for example, on the development of language, understanding, self-confidence and social skills. Once a child has learned to crawl, to shuffle on her bottom, or to be mobile in other ways, she will be more independent and be able to explore things that were previously out of reach. Adults will make changes to the child's environment now that she is mobile, by putting reachable objects out of her way and making clear rules and boundaries.

The senses of a newborn baby

Newborn babies are already actively using all of their senses to explore their new environment. They are:

- sight (or visual development)
- hearing
- taste
- touch
- smell.

Visual development

Newborn babies are very near-sighted at first, and they can focus best on things that are within 25 cm (10 inches) of their faces. This means that they can see well enough to focus on their mother's face when being held to the breast. Their vision is quite blurry outside this range but they can follow a light with their eyes and turn toward lights. Sometimes babies appear to have a squint as their eyes may move independently of each other. This is normal, as they are still gaining control of the eye muscles. Newborn babies prefer to look at:

- people's faces and eyes, especially those of their mothers
- bright colours – they will often reach for colourful objects
- light and dark contrasts and sharp outlines
- patterns, such as stripes or circles, rather than plain surfaces
- things that are moving: they will focus on and follow a moving ball with their eyes, a skill known as **tracking**.

Hearing

Babies develop a very acute sense of hearing while in the womb. Ultrasound studies have shown that unborn babies as early as 25 weeks' gestation can 'startle' in response to a sudden loud noise. Newborn babies can distinguish different voices and other sounds, and they can also determine from which direction a sound is coming. For example, if a small bell is rung above a newborn baby's head, he will turn his head in the direction of the sound and watch the object making the sound. Newborn babies prefer to listen to:

- **the human voice**, especially female voices. They usually recognise their own mother's voice from the start, since this is the voice they have heard, although muffled, throughout their time in the womb. Newborn babies become quiet when they hear their mother's voice, and they turn their head toward their mother when she speaks. After about a week or so, most newborn babies will prefer their father's voice to that of other men.
- **soft, melodic speech:** they can tell the difference between a calm, happy tone and an angry voice, and will respond with pleasure to a soft, lilting voice or may cry when they hear a loud, angry voice.

Hearing is an important part of speech development, so it is essential that babies are talked to. Parents and other adults automatically alter the pitch of their voices when talking to babies, and use a lot of repetition.

Touch

Newborn babies are very sensitive to touch. They love to be held close, comforted, cuddled, stroked, and rocked. Newborn babies prefer:

- **stroking of their skin:** this action helps newborn babies to sleep, and it helps to encourage closeness between baby and parent
- the feel of soft fabrics
- **skin-to-skin contact** with their parents, and being cuddled.

Babies who are fed but not touched or held often have problems with their physical and mental development. Gentle stroking is especially beneficial for premature babies. Research shows that it leads to increased weight gain, more alertness and activity, and an earlier discharge from hospital.

Taste

Newborn babies also have a well-developed sense of taste. They generally enjoy sweetness and dislike sour liquids. They can detect differences in the taste of their mother's milk, which can change depending on what the mother eats. Babies show that they find a particular taste unpleasant by screwing up their faces and trying to reject the taste from their mouth.

Smell

Newborn babies are sensitive to the smell of their mother, and they can tell it apart from that of other women. They are attracted not just to the smell of milk, but also to their mother's own unique body scent. Breastfed babies are more aware of their mother's smell compared with babies who are bottle-fed. This may be because breastfed babies spend more time in skin-to-skin contact with their mothers compared with babies who are bottle-fed. Babies will also turn away from a smell they find unpleasant.

Intellectual development

Intellectual (or cognitive) development is the development of the mind – the part of the brain that is used for recognising, reasoning, knowing and understanding. It involves:

- what a person knows and the ability to reason, understand and solve problems
- memory, concentration, attention and perception
- imagination and creativity.

Children learn through play. They need opportunities to:

- **Learn to predict:** children learn to predict that something is about to happen. For example, a baby learns to predict that food will soon appear if a bib is tied around his or her neck.
- **Learn the consequences of their actions:** children understand that they can bring about a result by their own actions. For example, a baby learns that if he or she cries, he or she will be picked up and comforted.
- **Ask questions:** as soon as they can talk, children ask questions to try to make sense of their world and gain information. For example, four-year-old children constantly ask the question 'Why?' whereas a child aged two-and-a-half years often asks 'Who?' and 'What?'
- **Understand concepts:** experiences with real objects help young children to understand concepts and to develop problem-solving skills. For example, mathematical concepts involve understanding number, sequencing, volume and capacity, as well as weighing and measuring.
- **Use repetition:** children learn by repeating activities over and over again. For example, they can learn a song or nursery rhyme by hearing it sung to them many times.
- **Use imitation:** children learn by copying what others do. For example, they learn how to write by copying letters, and in **role-play** children are copying the way they have observed others behave in certain situations.

Key term

Role-play – A form of pretend play when children engage in, explore and learn about the everyday roles that occur in their familiar experience: the roles carried out by their parents or carers and members of their community.

Figure 2.1 Driving a train: learning through role-play

Language and communication development

Language development is very closely linked with cognitive development, and a delay in one area usually affects progress in the other. Language development is the development of communication skills. These include skills in:

- receptive speech – what a person understands
- expressive speech – the words the person produces
- articulation – the person's actual pronunciation of words.

Babies are born with a need and a desire to communicate with others before they can express themselves through speaking. Learning how to communicate (to listen and to speak) begins with **non-verbal communication**, which includes:

- body language, such as facial expression, eye contact, pointing, touching and reaching for objects
- listening to others talking to them
- making sounds to attract attention
- copying the sounds made by others.

These skills develop as babies and young children express their needs and feelings, interact with others and establish their own identities and personalities.

Emotional, social and behavioural development

These three areas of development are very closely linked. Emotional development involves:

- the growth of feelings about, and awareness of, oneself
- the development of feelings towards other people
- the development of **self-esteem** and a **self-concept**.

Key terms

Self-esteem – The way in which you feel about yourself (good or bad) leads to high or low self-esteem.

Self-concept – How you see yourself, and how you think others see you; sometimes called self-image.

Social development

Social development includes the growth of the child's relationships with other people. **Socialisation** is the process of learning the skills and attitudes that enable the child to live easily with other members of the community.

The development of social and self-help skills

At as early as six months of age, babies enjoy each other's company. When they are together, they look at each other, smile and touch each other's faces. As their social circle widens they learn how to cooperate with each other when they play, and they begin to make friends.

Developing a sense of self and of belonging

Developing trust

Learning to separate from their parents

Playing with other children: sharing and taking turns

Being able to express their opinions and desires

Developing skills of caring for and looking after themselves (independence)

Using words to solve conflicts and develop control of emotions

Learning that it is okay to make a mistake

Developing confidence and self-respect

Developing respect for others and feelings of empathy

Figure 2.2 Social skills

What are social skills?

Children need to develop certain social skills (or ways of behaving) in order to fit in – and to get on well – with the people around them: see Figure 2.2.

Key terms

Behaviour – The way in which we act, speak and treat other people and our environment.

Empathy – Awareness of another person's emotional state, and the ability to share the experience with that person.

Socialisation – The process by which children learn what is expected of them in terms of behaviour and attitudes within society.

Spiritual and moral development

Moral and spiritual development consists of a developing awareness of how to relate to others ethically, morally and humanely. It involves understanding values such as honesty and respect, acquiring concepts such as right and wrong, and taking responsibility for the consequences of one's actions.

Case Study   Christophe

Christophe is new to The Ark nursery. He is two years old and has a brother, Olivier, who is four-and-a-half years old and has started attending pre-school. Christophe's family have recently moved to the UK from France. Monique, the mother, is fluent in English but speaks French to the boys at home, and has employed a French-Canadian au pair to collect the boys from the nursery two days a week. Antoine, the father, also speaks good English, but is very rarely at the nursery.

Case Study   Christophe (cont.)

The boys are both very lively. Olivier soon picks up English phrases and everyone is delighted and relieved at his speedy progress in becoming bilingual. However, Christophe is struggling with English words, and Monique reports that he has stopped speaking so much French. At nursery, Christophe does not say any recognisable words, and will instead 'grunt' answers or start crying. This makes it difficult for nursery staff to communicate with him – he just stares as they address him and does not respond to instructions at all. He can sometimes be quite destructive and refuses to tidy up after tipping over boxes. Staff members try to show him with actions, but Christophe rarely responds. However, apart from his obvious frustration when trying to communicate, Christophe loves to run around and laughs a lot as he watches other children, and joins in their games. He also joins in with different activities.

1. Why do you think Olivier finds the new language so much easier than Christophe does?
2. How has Christophe's difficulty in communicating impacted on other areas of his development?

Child development and The Early Years Foundation Stage (EYFS)

In the EYFS, all areas of learning and development are important and interconnected. Three areas are particularly crucial for igniting children's curiosity and enthusiasm for learning, and for building their capacity to learn, form relationships and thrive. These three areas, *the prime areas*, are:

- communication and language
- physical development, and
- personal, social and emotional development.

See Unit 10 for more detailed information on the EYFS.

The stages and sequence of holistic development from birth to 16 years

The following pages outline the main features of holistic child development, the ages shown being those at which the average child performs the specific tasks. Remember, however, that children develop at different rates, and some may be faster or slower to learn certain skills than other children.

Key terms

Dynamic tripod grasp – Using the thumb and two fingers in a grasp closely resembling the adult grasp of a pencil or pen.

Echolalia – The tendency of a child to echo the last words spoken by an adult.

Palmar grasp – Using the whole hand to grasp an object.

Pincer grasp – Using the thumb and fingers to grasp an object.

Primitive tripod grasp – Grasping objects by use of the thumb and two fingers.

Telegraphese – The abbreviation of a sentence such that only the crucial words are spoken, as in a telegram – e.g. 'Where daddy going?' or 'Shut door'.

Holistic development: The first month

Physical development

Gross motor skills	Fine motor skills
• The baby lies **supine** (on his or her back). • When placed on his or her front (the **prone** position), the baby lies with head turned to one side, and by one month can lift the head. • If baby is pulled to sitting position, the head will lag, the back curves over and the head falls forward.	• The baby turns his or her head towards the light and stares at bright or shiny objects. • The baby is fascinated by human faces and gazes attentively at carer's face while being fed or held. • The baby's hands are usually tightly closed. • The baby reacts to loud sounds but by one month may be soothed by particular music.

Communication and language development

- Babies need to share language experiences and cooperate with others from birth onwards. From the start babies need other people.
- The baby responds to sounds, especially familiar voices.
- The baby quietens when picked up.
- The baby makes eye contact.
- The baby cries to indicate need, e.g. hunger, dirty nappy, etc.
- The baby may move his or her eyes towards the direction of sound.

Intellectual development

Babies explore through their **senses** and through their own activity and movement.

Touch
- From the beginning babies feel pain.
- The baby's face, abdomen, hands and the soles of his or her feet are also very sensitive to touch.
- The baby perceives the movements that he or she makes, and the way that other people move them about through his or her senses.
- For example, the baby gives a 'startle' response if they are moved suddenly. This is called the '**Moro**' or startle reflex.

Sound
- Even a newborn baby will turn to a sound. The baby might become still and listen to a low sound, or quicken his or her movements when he or she hears a high sound.
- The baby often stops crying and listens to a human voice by two weeks of age.

Taste
- The baby likes sweet tastes, e.g. breast milk.

Smell
- The baby turns to the smell of the breast.

Sight
- The baby can focus on objects 25 cm (10 inches) away.
- The baby is sensitive to light.
- The baby likes to look at human faces – eye contact.
- The baby can track the movements of people and objects.
- The baby will scan the edges of objects.
- The baby will imitate facial expressions (e.g. he or she will put out their tongue if you do). If you know any newborn or very young babies, try it and see!

Holistic development: The first month (cont.)

Emotional and social development

- A baby's first smile in definite response to carer is usually around five to six weeks.
- The baby often imitates certain facial expressions.
- The baby uses total body movements to express pleasure at bath time or when being fed.
- The baby enjoys feeding and cuddling.
- In the first month, babies are learning where they begin and end, e.g. his or her hand is part of them but mother's hand is not.

Table 2.1 Holistic development: the first month

Holistic development from one to four months

Physical development

Gross motor skills	Fine motor skills
From four to eight weeks: • The baby can now turn from side to back. • The baby can lift the head briefly from the prone position. • Arm and leg movements are jerky and uncontrolled. • There is head lag if the baby is pulled to sitting position. From eight to 12 weeks: • When lying supine, the baby's head is in a central position. • The baby can now lift head and chest off a flat surface in prone position, supported on forearms. • There is almost no head lag in sitting position. • The legs can kick vigorously, both separately and together. • The baby can wave his or her arms and bring his or her hands together over the body.	• The baby turns her head towards the light and stares at bright or shiny objects. • The baby will show interest and excitement by facial expression and will gaze attentively at carer's face while being fed. • The baby will use his or her hand to grasp the carer's finger. • The baby moves his or her head to follow adult movements. • The baby watches his or her hands and plays with his or her fingers. • The baby holds a rattle for a brief time before dropping it.

Communication and language development

From four to eight weeks:

- The baby recognises the carer and familiar objects.
- The baby makes non-crying noises such as cooing and gurgling.
- The baby's cries become more expressive.

Holistic development from one to four months (cont.)

From eight to 12 weeks:

- The baby is still distressed by sudden loud noises.
- The baby often sucks or licks lips when he or she hears sound of food preparation.
- The baby shows excitement at sound of approaching footsteps or voices.

During the first three months:

- The baby listens to people's voices. When adults close to the baby talk in motherese or fatherese (a high-pitched tone referring to what is around and going on) the baby dances, listens, replies in babble and coo.
- The baby cries with anger to show they are tired, hungry, and to say they need to be changed.
- The baby is comforted by the voices of those who are close to them and will turn especially to the voices of close family members.

Intellectual development

- The baby recognises differing speech sounds.
- By three months the baby can even imitate low- or high-pitched sounds.
- By four months the baby links objects they know with the sound, e.g. mother's voice and her face.
- The baby knows the smell of his or her mother from that of other mothers.

Emotional and social development

Four to eight weeks:

- The baby will smile in response to an adult.
- The baby enjoys sucking.
- The baby turns to regard nearby speaker's face.
- The baby turns to preferred person's voice.
- The baby recognises face and hands of preferred adult.
- The baby may stop crying when he or she hears, sees or feels her primary carer.

Eight to 12 weeks:

- The baby shows enjoyment at caring routines such as bath time.
- The baby responds with obvious pleasure to loving attention and cuddles.
- The baby fixes his or her eyes unblinkingly on carer's face when feeding.
- The baby stays awake for longer periods of time.

Table 2.2 Holistic development from one to four months

Holistic development from four to six months

Physical development

Gross motor skills	Fine motor skills
• The baby is beginning to use a **palmar grasp** and can transfer objects from hand to hand. • The baby is very interested in all activity. • Everything is taken to the mouth. • The baby moves his or her head around to follow people and objects.	• The baby now has good head control and is beginning to sit with support. • The baby rolls over from back to side and is beginning to reach for objects. • When supine, the baby plays with his or her own feet. • The baby holds his or her head up when pulled to sitting position.

Communication and language development

- The baby becomes more aware of others so he or she communicates more and more.
- As the baby listens, he or she imitates sounds he or she can hear, and reacts to the tone of someone's voice. For example, the baby might become upset by an angry tone, or cheered by a happy tone.
- The baby begins to use vowels, consonants and syllable sounds, e.g. 'ah', 'ee aw'.
- The baby begins to laugh and squeal with pleasure.

Intellectual development

- By four months the baby reaches for objects, which suggests they recognise and judge the distance in relation to the size of the object.
- The baby prefers complicated things to look at from five to six months and enjoys bright colours.
- The baby knows that he or she has one mother. The baby is disturbed if he or she is shown several images of his or her mother at the same time. The baby realises that people are permanent before they realise that objects are.
- The baby can coordinate more, e.g. the baby can see a rattle, grasp the rattle, put the rattle in his or her mouth (they coordinate tracking, reaching, grasping and sucking).
- The baby can develop favourite tastes in food and recognise differences by five months.

Emotional and social development

- The baby shows trust and security.
- The baby has recognisable sleep patterns.

Table 2.3 Holistic development from four to six months

Holistic development from six to nine months

Physical development

Gross motor skills	Fine motor skills
• The baby can roll from front to back. • The baby may attempt to crawl but will often end up sliding backwards. • The baby may grasp feet and place them in his or her mouth. • The baby can sit without support for longer periods of time. • The baby may 'cruise' around furniture and may even stand or walk alone.	• The baby is very alert to people and objects. • The baby is beginning to use a **pincer grasp** with thumb and index finger. • The baby transfers toys from one hand to the other and looks for fallen objects. • Everything is explored by putting it in his or her mouth.

Communication and language development

- Babble becomes tuneful, like the lilt of the language the baby can hear (except in hearing-impaired babies).
- Babies begin to understand words like 'up' and 'down', raising their arms to be lifted up, using appropriate gestures.
- The baby repeats sounds.

Intellectual development

- The baby understands **signs**, e.g. the bib means that food is coming.
- From eight to nine months the baby shows that he or she knows objects exist when they have gone out of sight, even under test conditions. This is called the concept of object constancy, or the **object permanence test** (child psychologist Jean Piaget's theory). The baby is also fascinated by the way objects move.

Emotional and social development

- The baby can manage to feed herself using her fingers.
- The baby is now more wary of strangers, sometimes showing **stranger fear**.
- The baby might offer toys to others.
- The baby might show distress when his or her mother leaves.
- The baby typically begins to crawl and this means he or she can do more for him- or herself, reach for objects and get to places and people.
- The baby is now more aware of other people's feelings. For example, he or she may cry if their brother cries.

Table 2.4 Holistic development from six to nine months

Holistic development from nine to 12 months

Physical development

Gross motor skills	Fine motor skills
• The baby will now be mobile – may be crawling, bear-walking, bottom-shuffling or even walking. • The baby can sit up on her own and lean forward to pick up things. • The baby may crawl upstairs and onto low items of furniture. • The baby may bounce in rhythm to music.	• The baby's pincer grasp is now well developed and he or she can pick things up and pull them towards him or her. • The baby can poke with one finger and will point to desired objects. • The baby can clasp hands and imitate adults' actions. • The baby can throw toys deliberately. • The baby can manage spoons and finger foods well.

Communication and language development

- The baby can follow simple instructions, e.g. kiss teddy.
- Word approximations appear, e.g. hee-haw = donkey or more typically mumma, dadda and bye-bye in English-speaking contexts.
- The tuneful babble develops into 'jargon' and the baby makes his or her voice go up and down just as people do when they talk to each other. 'Really? Do you? No!' The babble is very expressive.
- The baby knows that words stand for people, objects, what they do and what happens.

Intellectual development

- The baby is beginning to develop images. Memory develops and the baby can remember the past.
- The baby can anticipate the future. This gives the baby some understanding of routine daily sequences, e.g. after a feed, changing, and a sleep with teddy.
- The baby imitates actions, sounds, gestures and moods after an event is finished, e.g. imitate a temper tantrum he or she saw a friend have the previous day, wave bye-bye remembering Grandma has gone to the shops.

Emotional and social development

- The baby enjoys songs and action rhymes.
- The baby still likes to be near to a familiar adult.
- The baby can drink from a cup with help.
- The baby will play alone for long periods.
- The baby has and shows definite likes and dislikes at mealtimes and bedtimes.
- The baby thoroughly enjoys peek-a-boo games.
- The baby likes to look at him- or herself in a mirror (plastic safety mirror).
- The baby imitates other people – e.g. clapping hands, waving bye-bye – but there is often a time lapse, so that he or she waves after the person has gone.
- The baby cooperates when being dressed.

Table 2.5 Holistic development from nine to 12 months

Holistic development from one year to two years

Physical development

Gross motor skills	Fine motor skills
At 15 months: - The baby probably walks alone, with feet wide apart and arms raised to maintain balance. He or she is likely to fall over and often sit down suddenly. - The baby can probably manage stairs and steps, but will need supervision. - The baby can get to standing without help from furniture or people, and kneels without support. At 18 months: - The child walks confidently and is able to stop without falling. - The child can kneel, squat, climb and carry things around with him or her. - The child can climb onto an adult chair forwards and then turn round to sit. - The child can come downstairs, usually by creeping backwards on her tummy.	- The baby can build with a few bricks and arrange toys on the floor. - The baby holds a crayon in palmar grasp and turns several pages of a book at once. - The baby can point to desired objects. - The baby shows a preference for one hand, but uses either. - The child can thread large beads. - The child uses pincer grasp to pick up small objects. - The child can build a tower of several cubes. - The child can scribble to and fro on paper.

Communication and language development

- The child begins to talk with words or sign language.
- By 18 months: The child enjoys trying to sing as well as to listen to songs and rhymes. Action songs (e.g. 'Pat-a-cake') are much loved.
- Books with pictures are of great interest. The child points at and often names parts of their body, objects, people and pictures in books.
- The child echoes the last part of what others say (**echolalia**).
- The child begins waving his or her arms up and down, which might mean 'start again', or 'I like it', or 'more'.
- Gestures develop alongside words. Gesture is used in some cultures more than in others.

Intellectual development

- The child understands the names of objects and can follow simple instructions.
- The child learns about things through trial and error.
- The child uses toys or objects to represent things in real life (e.g. using a doll as a baby, or a large cardboard box as a car or a garage).
- The child begins to scribble on paper.
- The child often 'talks' to him- or herself while playing.

Emotional and social development

- The child begins to have a longer memory.
- The child develops a sense of identity (I am me).
- The child expresses his or her needs in words and gestures.
- The child enjoys being able to walk, and is eager to try to get dressed – 'Me do it!'
- The child is aware when others are fearful or anxious for him or her as he or she climbs on and off chairs, and so on.

Holistic development from one year to two years (cont.)

Table 2.6 Holistic development from one year to two years

Holistic development from two years

Physical development

Gross motor skills	Fine motor skills
• The child is very mobile and can run safely. • The child can climb up onto furniture. • The child can walk up and down stairs, usually two feet to a step. • The child tries to kick a ball with some success but cannot catch yet.	• The child can draw circles, lines and dots, using preferred hand. • The child can pick up tiny objects using a **fine pincer grasp**. • The child can build tower of six or more blocks (bricks) with longer concentration span. • The child enjoys picture books and turns pages singly.

Communication and language development

- Children are rapidly becoming competent speakers of the languages they experience.
- The child overextends the use of a word, e.g. all animals are called 'doggie'.
- The child talks about an absent object when reminded of it; e.g. seeing an empty plate, they say 'biscuit'.
- The child uses phrases (**telegraphese**), 'doggie-gone' and the child calls him- or herself by name.
- The child spends a great deal of energy naming things and what they do – e.g. 'chair', and as they go up a step they might say 'up'.
- The child can follow a simple instruction or request, e.g. 'Could you bring me the spoon?'
- The child increasingly wants to share songs, dance, conversations, finger rhymes.

Intellectual development

- The child has improved memory skills, which helps his or her understanding of **concepts** (e.g. the child can often name and match two or three colours – usually yellow and red).
- The child can hold a crayon and move it up and down.
- The child understands cause and effect (e.g. if something is dropped, he or she understands it might break).
- The child talks about an absent object when reminded of it (e.g. he or she may say 'biscuit' when seeing an empty plate or bowl).

Holistic development from two years (cont.)

Emotional and social development

- The child is impulsive and curious about their environment.
- **Pretend play** develops rapidly when adults encourage it.
- The child begins to be able to say how he or she is feeling, but often feels frustrated when unable to express him- or herself.
- The child can dress him- or herself and go to the lavatory independently, but needs sensitive support in order to feel success rather than frustration.
- By two-and-a-half years the child plays more with other children, but may not share his or her toys with them.

Table 2.7 Holistic development from two years

Holistic development from three years

Physical development

Gross motor skills	Fine motor skills
• The child can jump from a low step. • The child can walk backwards and sideways. • The child can stand and walk on tiptoe and stand on one foot. • The child has good spatial awareness. • The child rides a tricycle, using pedals. • The child can climb stairs with one foot on each step – and downwards with two feet per step.	• The child can build tall towers of bricks or blocks. • The child can control a pencil using thumb and first two fingers – a **dynamic tripod grasp**. • The child enjoys painting with a large brush. • The child can use scissors to cut paper. • The child can copy shapes, such as a circle.

Communication and language development

- The child begins to use plurals, pronouns, adjectives, possessives, time words, tenses and sentences.
- The child might say 'two times' instead of 'twice'. The child might say 'I goed there' instead of 'I went there'. The child loves to chat and ask questions (what, where and who).
- The child enjoys much more complicated stories and asks for his or her favourite ones over and over again.
- It is not unusual for the child to stutter because he or she is trying so hard to tell adults things. The child's thinking goes faster than the pace at which the child can say what he or she wants to. The child can quickly become frustrated.

Holistic development from three years (cont.)

Intellectual development

The child develops symbolic behaviour. This means that:

- The child talks.
- The child enjoys pretend play – often talking to him- or herself while playing.
- The child takes part in simple non-competitive games.
- The child represents events in drawings, models, etc.
- Personal images dominate, rather than conventions used in the culture, e.g. writing is 'pretend' writing.
- The child becomes fascinated by cause and effect; the child is continually trying to explain what goes on in the world.
- The child can identify common colours, such as red, yellow, blue and green – although may sometimes confuse blue with green.

Emotional and social development

Pretend play helps the child to **decentre** and develop **theory of mind** (the child begins to be able to understand how someone else might feel and/or think).

- The child is beginning to develop a gender role as they become aware of being male or female.
- The child makes friends and is interested in having friends.
- The child learns to negotiate, to give and take, through experimenting with feeling powerful, having a sense of control, and through quarrels with other children.
- The child is easily afraid, e.g. of the dark, as he or she becomes capable of pretending. The child imagines all sorts of things.

Table 2.8 Holistic development from three years

Holistic development from four years

Physical development

Gross motor skills	Fine motor skills
<ul><li>A sense of balance is developing – the child may be able to walk along a line.</li><li>The child can catch, kick, throw and bounce a ball.</li><li>The child can bend at the waist to pick up objects from the floor.</li><li>The child enjoys climbing trees and frames.</li><li>The child can run up and down stairs, one foot per step.</li></ul>	<ul><li>The child can build a tower of bricks and other constructions too.</li><li>The child can draw a recognisable person on request, showing head, legs and trunk.</li><li>The child can thread small beads on a lace.</li></ul>

Holistic development from four years (cont.)

Communication and language development

- During this time the child asks why, when and how questions as he or she becomes more and more fascinated with the reasons for things and how things work (cause and effect).
- Past, present and future tenses are used more often.
- The child can be taught to say his or her name, address and age.
- As the child becomes more accurate in the way he or she pronounces words, and begins to use grammar, the child delights in nonsense words that he or she makes up, and jokes using words.

Intellectual development

- At about age four, the child usually knows how to count – up to 20.
- The child also understands ideas such as 'more' and 'fewer', and 'big' and 'small'.
- The child will recognise his or her own name when it is written down and can usually write it.
- The child can think backward and forward much more easily than before.
- The child can also think about things from somebody else's point of view, but only fleetingly.
- The child often enjoys music and playing sturdy instruments, and joins in groups singing and dancing.

Emotional and social development

- The child likes to be independent and is strongly self-willed.
- The child shows a sense of humour.
- The child can undress and dress him- or herself – except for laces and back buttons.
- The child can wash and dry his or her hands and brush their teeth.

Table 2.9 Holistic development from four years

Holistic development from five to eight years

Physical development

Gross motor skills	Fine motor skills
From five years: • The child can use a variety of play equipment – slides, swings, climbing frames. • The child can play ball games. • The child can hop and run lightly on toes and can move rhythmically to music. • The sense of balance is well developed. • The child can skip. Six and seven years: • The child has increased agility, muscle coordination and balance. • The child develops competence in riding a two-wheeled bicycle. • The child hops easily, with good balance. • The child can jump off apparatus.	• The child may be able to thread a large-eyed needle and sew large stitches. • The child can draw a person with head, trunk, legs, nose, mouth and eyes. • The child has good control over pencils and paint-brushes. He or she copies shapes, such as a square. • The child can build a tall, straight tower with blocks and other constructions too. • The child can draw a person with detail, e.g. clothes and eyebrows. • The child can write letters of alphabet at school, with similar writing grip to an adult. • The child can catch a ball thrown from one metre with one hand.

Communication and language development

• The child tries to understand the meanings of words and uses adverbs and prepositions. The child talks confidently, and with more and more fluency.
• The child begins to be able to define objects by their function, e.g. 'What is a ball?', 'You bounce it.'
• The child begins to understand book language, and that stories have characters and a plot (the narrative).
• The child begins to realise that different situations require different ways of talking.

Intellectual development

Communication through body language, facial gestures and language is well established, and opens the way into **literacy** (talking, listening, writing and reading).

• The child includes more detail in their drawings – e.g. a house may have not only windows and a roof, but also curtains and a chimney.
• The child will recognise his or her own name when it is written down and can usually write it him- or herself.
• Thinking becomes increasingly coordinated as the child is able to hold in mind more than one point of view at a time. **Concepts** – of matter, length, measurement, distance, area, time, volume, capacity and weight – develop steadily.
• The child enjoys chanting and counting (beginning to understand number). The child can use his or her voice in different ways to play different characters in pretend play. The child develops play narratives (stories), which he or she returns to over time. The child helps younger children into the play.
• The child is beginning to establish differences between what is real and unreal/fantasy. This is not yet always stable, so the child can easily be frightened by supernatural characters.

Emotional and social development

• The child has developed a stable **self-concept**.
• The child can hide their feelings once they can begin to control them.
• The child can think of the feelings of others.
• The child can take responsibility, e.g. in helping younger children.

Holistic development from five to eight years (cont.)

Table 2.10 Holistic development from five to eight years

Holistic development from eight to 11 years

Physical development

Gross motor skills	Fine motor skills
From eight to nine years: • The child can ride a bicycle easily. • The child has increased strength and coordination. • The child plays energetic games and sports. From ten to 11 years: • Children differ in physical maturity. Girls experience puberty earlier than boys do and are often as much as two years ahead of them. • The child's body proportions are becoming more similar to an adult's.	• The child can control his or her small muscles well and has improved writing and drawing skills. • The child can draw people with details of clothing and facial features. • The child is starting to join letters together in handwriting. • The child tackles more detailed tasks such as woodwork or needlework. • The child is usually writing with an established style – using joined-up letters.

Communication and language development

From eight to nine years:

• The child uses and understands complex sentences.
• The child is increasingly verbal and enjoys making up stories and telling jokes.
• The child uses reference books with increasing skill.

From ten to 11 years:

• The child can write fairly lengthy essays.
• The child writes stories that show imagination, and are increasingly legible and grammatically correct.

Intellectual development

From eight to nine years:

• The child has an increased ability to remember and pay attention, and to speak and express their ideas.
• The child is learning to plan ahead and evaluate what they do.

Holistic development from eight to 11 years (cont.)

- The child has an increased ability to think and to reason.
- The child can deal with abstract ideas.
- The child enjoys different types of activities – such as joining clubs, playing games with rules, and collecting things.
- The child enjoys projects that are task-orientated, such as sewing and woodwork.

From ten to 11 years:

- The child begins to understand the motives behind the actions of another.
- The child can concentrate on tasks for increasing periods.
- The child begins to devise memory strategies.
- The child may be curious about drugs, alcohol and tobacco.
- The child may develop special talents, showing particular skills in writing, maths, art, music or woodwork.

Emotional and social development

At eight or nine years old:

- The child may become discouraged easily.
- The child takes pride in their competence.
- The child can be argumentative and bossy, but can equally be generous and responsive.
- The child is beginning to see things from another child's point of view, but still has trouble understanding the feelings and needs of other people.

At 11 or 12 years old:

- The child may be experiencing sudden, dramatic, emotional changes associated with puberty (especially girls, who experience puberty earlier than boys).
- The child tends to be particularly sensitive to criticism.
- The child prefers to spend leisure time with friends and continues to participate in small groups of the same sex, but is acutely aware of the opposite sex.
- The child succumbs to peer pressure more readily and wants to talk, dress, and act just like friends.

Table 2.11 Holistic development from eight to eleven years

Holistic development from 12 to 16 years

Physical development

Physical development during adolescence is known as puberty. The age at which **puberty** starts varies from person to person, but on average it begins between nine to 13 in girls and ten to 15 in boys. Many physical changes occur during puberty.

Growth accelerates rapidly – often called a **growth spurt**. This usually happens in a particular order from outer to inner:
- the head, feet and hands grow to adult size first, then
- the arms and legs grow in length and strength, and finally
- the trunk (the main part of the body from shoulder to hip) grows to full adult size and shape.

Holistic development from 12 to 16 years (cont.)

This sequence of growth means that, for a brief period, adolescents may feel gawky and clumsy, as they appear to be 'out of proportion'. The average boy grows fastest between 14 and 15. Girls start earlier, growing fastest when 12 and 13. Girls also finish their growth spurt earlier, at 18, while boys need another two years before they finish growing aged 20.

Secondary sex characteristics develop: these are external traits that distinguish the two sexes, but are not directly part of the **reproductive system**; for example, the growth of pubic hair in both sexes, facial hair and deepened voice for males, and breasts and widened hips for females.

Primary sex characteristics also develop; these are the penis and sperm in males and the vagina and ovaries in females. During puberty, hormonal changes cause a boy's penis and testicles to grow and the body to produce sperm. Girls start to menstruate or have their monthly period. Both these events signal **sexual maturity** – the ability to reproduce.

The main features of physical development in puberty

In girls	In boys
The first external sign of puberty in most girls is usually breast development – often accompanied by a growth spurt.	The first external sign of puberty in most boys is an increase in the size of the testicles and then the penis. This is followed by the growth of pubic and underarm hair. At the same time, the voice deepens and muscles develop. Lastly, boys grow facial hair.
Breasts develop: at first, the nipples start to stick out from the chest (often called 'budding'). Behind the nipple, milk ducts begin to grow. Next, the flat, circular part of the nipple, the areola, rises and starts to expand. Glands that make sweat and scent develop beneath it. The breast begins to fill out, as fat is deposited around the nipple. Some girls feel a tingling sensation or have tender breasts. Initially the breasts stick out in a conical shape. As growth continues they gradually round off into an adult shape.	**Voice breaking**: testosterone causes the voice box – or larynx – to enlarge and the vocal cords to become longer. Sometimes, as the voice changes to become deeper, it may change pitch abruptly, or 'break' at times; the voice box tilts and often protrudes at the neck – as an 'Adam's apple'. (Many boys start to develop breasts in their teenage years, but this disappears as the testosterone levels increase.)
Body size and shape: grow taller. Hips widen as the pelvic bones grow. Fat develops on the hips, thighs and buttocks, and the ratio of fat to muscle increases. The waist gets smaller and the body develops a more curved shape.	**Body size and shape**: grow taller. Body takes on a new, more muscular shape as the shoulders and chest become broader and the neck becomes more muscular.
Menstruation: menstruation – having periods – is part of the female reproductive cycle that starts when girls become sexually mature during puberty. During a menstrual period, a woman bleeds from her uterus (womb) via the vagina. This lasts anything from three to seven days. Each period begins approximately every 28 days if the woman does not become pregnant during a given cycle. The onset of menstruation is called the menarche; it can occur at any time between the ages of nine and 16, most commonly around the age of 12–13. It means that the body is capable of **reproduction**.	**Chest hair** may appear during puberty – or some years later.
	Penile erections: these occur spontaneously, even from infancy, but during puberty they become more frequent. Erections can occur with or without any physical or sexual stimulation and can cause acute embarrassment.
	Sperm: once the testicles begin to grow they also develop their adult function – producing sperm. Mature sperm is present in the male body towards the end of puberty (most commonly between the ages of 13 and 15) and means that the body is capable of **reproduction**.

Holistic development from 12 to 16 years (cont.)

In both girls and boys

Pubic hair starts to grow around the genitals, and becomes coarse, dark and curly. In girls, pubic hair forms an upside-down triangle shape; in boys, the hair grows between the legs and extends up from the penis to the abdomen.

Hair grows in the armpits and on the legs.

Sweat: a different kind of sweat is now produced in response to stress, emotion and sexual excitement. It is produced by the apocrine glands, and occurs only in the armpits, the belly button, the groin area, the ears and the nipples. As bacteria break down the sweat it starts to smell strongly – known as BO (body odour).

Oil glands: oil-secreting glands in the skin can become overactive – this can cause skin to become greasier and can also cause acne.

Communication and language development

- During this period, children become increasingly independent and spend much of their day outside the home – at school or after-school activities, and with peers.
- The young person has a fast, legible style of handwriting.
- The young person communicates in an adult manner, with increasing maturity.
- The young person understands abstract language, such as idioms, figurative language and metaphors.
- The young person is able to process texts and abstract meaning, relate word meanings and contexts, understand punctuation, and form complex syntactic structures.

Intellectual development

Around this time, children experience a major shift in thinking from **concrete** to **abstract** – an adult way of thinking. Piaget described this as the **formal operational stage** of intellectual development. This involves:

- *thinking about possibilities* – younger children rely heavily on their senses to apply reasoning, whereas adolescents think about possibilities that are not directly observable.
- *thinking ahead* – children start to plan ahead, often in a systematic way; e.g. younger children may look forward to a holiday, but they are unlikely to focus on the preparation involved.
- *thinking through hypotheses* – this gives them the ability to make and test hypotheses, and to think about situations that are contrary to fact.
- *thinking about their own thought processes* – this is known as **metacognition**; a subcategory of metacognition is **metamemory**, which is having knowledge about your memory processes – being able to explain what strategies you use when trying to remember things (e.g. for an exam).
- *thinking beyond conventional limits* – thinking about issues that generally preoccupy human beings in adulthood, such as morality, religion and politics.
- They approach a problem in a systematic fashion and also use their imagination when solving problems.

Emotional and social development

- The young person may become self-conscious or worried about physical changes (e.g. too short, too tall, too fat, too thin).
- The young person develops a sexual identity; self-labelling as gay or lesbian tends to occur around the age of 15 for boys and 15½ for girls, although first disclosure does not normally take place until after the age of 16½ for both sexes.
- The young person often feels misunderstood.
- The young person can experience wide emotional swings (e.g. fluctuate between emotional peaks of excitement and depths of moodiness).
- The young person wants to become accepted and liked.
- The young person tends to identify more with friends and begins to separate from parents; they are less dependent on family for affection and emotional support.

Holistic development from 12 to 16 years (cont.)

Table 2.12 Holistic development from 12 to 16 years

Spiritual aspects of a child's development	
The first year	Even a tiny baby experiences a sense of self, and of awe and wonder, and values people who are loved by them. Worship is about a sense of worth. People, loved teddy bears, a daisy on the grass grasped and looked at (or put in the mouth!) are all building the child's spiritual experiences. This has nothing to do with worship of a god or gods. Spirituality is about the developing sense of relationship with self, relating to others ethically, morally and humanely and a relationship with the universe.
1 to 3 years	Judy Dunn's work suggests that during this period children already have a strongly developed moral sense. They know what hurts and upsets their family (adults and children). They know what delights them and brings about pleased responses. Through their pretend play, and the conversations in the family about how people behave, hurt and help each other, they learn how other people feel. They learn to think beyond themselves.
3 to 8 years	With the help and support of their family, of early years practitioners and the wider community, children develop further concepts like being helpful and forgiving, and having a sense of fairness. By the age of seven years, they have a clear sense of right and wrong – e.g. they realise that it is wrong to hurt other people physically.
8 to 11 years	By eight or nine years, children continue to think that rules are permanent and unchangeable because they are made up by adults, who must be obeyed and respected. They have a clear idea of the difference between reality and fantasy, and are highly concerned about fairness. By ten and 11 years, children understand that certain rules can be changed by mutual negotiation; often, they do not accept rules that they did not help make. They may begin to experience conflict between parents' values and those of their peers. These concepts become more abstract – such as justice, right, wrong, good versus evil, beauty and nature, the arts and scientific achievements.
12 to 16 years	Young people are able to think beyond themselves more and to understand the perspective of another. They are developing their own ideas and values, which often challenge those of home; they may deliberately flout rules or keep to them only if there is otherwise a risk of being caught.

Table 2.13 Spiritual aspects of a child's development

Age group	Physical development	Intellectual development	Communication and language development	Emotional and social development
Birth to 1 year				
1 to 3 years				
3 to 5 years				
5 to 8 years				
8 to 11 years				
12 to 16 years				

Table 2.14 Development chart

Assessment practice: stages of development timeline

Look at Table 2.14. Using the holistic development charts on pages 31–47, for each age group in Column 1, select three significant 'milestones' of development, using each category of development in Columns 2, 3, 4 and 5.

For example, for the age group **Birth to one year** (**physical development**) you could choose to include the following three milestones:
- At eight to 12 weeks, the baby can now lift head and chest off bed in prone position, supported on forearms.
- At four to six months, the baby is beginning to use a palmar grasp and can transfer objects from hand to hand.
- At nine to 12 months, the baby will now be mobile – may be crawling, bear-walking, bottom-shuffling or even walking.

The importance of careful observations and how they support development

Why observe children?

Parents, babysitters and child care workers automatically watch the children in their care.

They want to know that the children are safe, happy, healthy and developing well. Watching or observing closely can often reassure all concerned that everything is all right, but may also alert them to problems or illness. Any discussion about a child usually relates to what has been seen, heard or experienced, and leads to conclusions about his/her personality, likes and dislikes, difficulties, etc.

Anyone who works with children needs to develop the skill of observing them (sometimes to be written/recorded) to check that a child is:

- **safe** – not in any physical danger from the environment, from themselves or from others
- **contented** – there are many reasons why a child might be miserable; some may relate to physical comfort (e.g. wet nappy, hunger, thirst), emotional comfort (e.g. main carer is absent, comfort object is lost) or lack of attention and stimulation
- **healthy** – eats and sleeps well and is physically active (concerns about any of these aspects may indicate that the child is unwell)
- **developing normally** – in line with general expectations for his/her age in all areas; there will be individual differences but delays in any milestones (e.g. crawling/walking or speaking) may show a need for careful monitoring and, perhaps, specialist help; any particular strength or talent may also be identified and encouraged.

A series of observations – particularly if they are written or recorded in some way (e.g. photos) – can provide an ongoing record of progress, which can be very useful to parents and other professionals who may be involved with a child's care and education.

The importance of careful observations

Observations can provide valuable information about:

- individual children – their progress and how they behave in particular situations
- groups of children – the differences between individuals in the same situations
- adults – how they communicate with children and how they deal with behaviour
- what activities are successful and enjoyed by children.

What should be recorded?

There is some information that should be included in any observation, but other aspects will depend on the purpose of the observation. If it is to consider the child's fine motor skills then the detail will probably be different from one that is to find out about his/her social development – even if the same activity or situation is being observed. You should also record some *introductory* information (see below).

When you carry out a written observation it is usually because you want to find out something about an individual child or a group of children. This provides an **aim**, which should be identified at the start of your work. For example:

Aim: 'To see what gross motor skills Child R uses in a PE lesson and consider how confident he is on the apparatus.'

A clear aim explains what you want to find out and the activity or context that you have decided will best show you. This is better than saying you will watch Child R in a PE lesson. The aim you identify should affect what information you write in your introduction and in the actual observation.

As well as an aim, your observation should also have the following:

- date carried out
- start and finish times
- who gave permission
- where it took place (setting)

- number of children present
- number of adults present
- age of child/ages of children
- names or identification of children (remember confidentiality)
- method used (brief reason for choice)
- signature of supervisor or tutor.

How should it be recorded?

Your tutors will have their own preferences for how they want you to present your work but, generally, each observation should include the following sections: **Introduction**; **Actual observation**; **Evaluation**; **Bibliography**.

Introduction

In this section you must state where the observation is taking place (e.g. at the sand tray in a reception class) and give some information about what is happening (e.g. the children had just returned to the classroom from assembly). If there is any relevant information about the child, you might include it here (e.g. Child R has been ill recently and has missed two weeks of school). Include information that is relevant to your aim – it may be important to know whether he is of average build if you are dealing with physical skills, but not particularly relevant if you are dealing with imaginative play.

Actual observation

There are many different methods of recording and your tutors will help you decide which one is best – perhaps a 'chart' format, a checklist, or a written record describing what you see as it happens. Remember only to write what you see and, if appropriate, hear. **Do not write your judgements, opinions, assessments, and so on**. Make sure you include information about other children or adults involved, if it is relevant.

When recording your observation, remember to maintain **confidentiality** by only using a child's first name or initial, or some other form of identification (e.g. Child R). You may use 'T' or 'A' for 'teacher' or 'adult'.

Evaluation

An evaluation is an assessment of what you have observed. This section can be dealt with in two parts.

1 You need to look back at your recorded information and summarise what you have discovered. *Example*: 'Child R was looking around the classroom and fidgeting with his shoelaces during the story, and appeared bored and uninterested. However, he was able to answer questions when asked so he must have been listening for at least part of the time.' This is a *review* of what you saw.

2 You then need to consider what you have summarised, and compare your findings to the 'norm' or 'average' or 'expected' for a child of this age and at this stage of development. What have you, yourself, learned about this particular child/group of children, and how has this helped you to understand children's development more widely? Use relevant books to help you and make reference to them – or quote directly if you can find a statement or section that relates to what you are saying or the point you are making. Your tutor or assessor wants to know what you understand, not information s/he could read in a book, so use references carefully.

As observation of children can help carers to plan for individual needs, try to suggest what activity or caring strategy might be needed next. You may also, in this section, give your opinion as to reasons for the behaviour, and so on – but take care not to jump to conclusions about the role of the child's background, and never make judgements about the child or the child's family.

Bibliography

The bibliography is a list of the books you have used when reading and researching for information relating to your observation. See page 22 for information on referencing.

Techniques for observations

There are six different types of observation.

1 **Narrative**: perhaps the most common is the narrative or descriptive observation. This type attempts to record everything that happens, as it happens, with plenty of detail. Methods that fit into the 'narrative' framework are:
   - *descriptive/running record*
   - *detailed*
   - *target child*
   - *diary description*
   - *anecdotal record*
   - *aural recording and transcript (may be considered to fit into this category so long as the section focused upon and used for evaluation purposes is continuous and not a series of edited extracts)*
   - *video recording (as for tape and transcript).*

2 **Time sampling**: this is specific, selected information recorded at chosen time intervals. A chart format is most often used.

3 **Event sampling**: this involves specific actions, incidents or behaviour observed whenever they occur. A chart format is most often used.

4 **Diagrammatic**: these provide a visual and accessible display of collected information or, in the case or growth charts, information plotted in the context of identified 'norms'. They could take the form of:
   - *pie charts*
   - *bar graphs*
   - *flow diagrams*
   - *sociograms*
   - *growth charts.*

5 **Checklists:** this type of observation is carried out with a pre-prepared list of skills or competencies that are being assessed, and is often used for 'can do' checks in the context of a structured activity.

6 **Longitudinal study**: usually a collection of observations and measurements taken over a period of time using a variety of recording methods. (This method is particularly useful in contributing to evidence of a child's **learning journey** – an important part of the EYFS.)

Sharing observations

Most settings provide clear guidance (sometimes in a booklet or sheet written especially for students) about working with children. Some settings now also have an Observations Policy. As a student, you should also be given information that will help you understand what a particular setting is trying to achieve and how it does so. You will always need to gain **permission** to carry out an observation, and your placement supervisor may well wish to read your work. This is not only to check it through, but also out of interest, to find out more about the children, activity or safety aspects that you observed. Remember, information accurately observed by you can be just as valuable to the setting as that gathered by staff.

Cooperation between professionals requires sharing of information. However, in a work setting, observations and records must be kept confidentially and access given only to certain people – these may include the individual child's parents or legal guardian, supervisor, teacher or key person and other involved professionals (e.g. the health visitor).

Remember: Any information about a child may be shared only if the parent or legal guardian gives consent.

The importance of confidentiality and objectivity

Maintaining confidentiality is an important aspect of your role, but it is particularly important when carrying out observations, especially those that are written and recorded. For your own training and assessment purposes, the identity of the child and setting is not important. They must, therefore, be protected (see below). You are developing your observational and record-keeping skills as you learn more about children in general, children as individuals and the various work settings.

Objectivity in observations

When you record your observational findings you need to be as objective as possible. This means that you must record **factual information** – what you actually see and hear – rather than information you have already begun to interpret.

By including plenty of detail to describe what you see, you are providing yourself (and any reader) with a lot of information for analysis. For example, the first extract in the activity below presents a much fuller picture of the situation than the second, and may lead you to a different conclusion about G's interest and attention.

It is often difficult to describe facial expressions and actions accurately, which is why many students produce work in the style of Observation B rather than in the style of A.

 Progress check

How to maintain confidentiality in your observation

- Ensure you have permission for making an observation – from your supervisor and the parent/main carer (this is confirmed by an authorising signature).
- Use codes rather than names to refer to the individuals involved – you should never use a child's first name. An initial or some other form of identification (e.g. Child 1) is sufficient. (You may use 'T' or 'A' for 'teacher' or 'adult'.)
- Understand and abide by policies and procedures in the setting.
- Remember that photographic and recorded evidence can reveal identity, and should only be used with appropriate authority.
- Take extra care when sharing observations with fellow students – they may have friends or family involved in a work setting and could easily identify individuals.
- Never discuss children or staff from your work setting in a public place (e.g. when sitting on a bus or in a café).
- Never identify individuals when talking at home about your daily experiences (e.g. they could be neighbours' children).

Activity

Observations

Read the two brief examples below and identify where the observer has substituted a conclusion or interpretation for what was actually seen.

Observation A

... G is sitting on the floor with her legs crossed and her left hand in her lap. She is twiddling her hair with her right hand and staring at a picture on the wall display behind the teacher's head. She is smiling. The teacher says, 'G, what do you think will happen to the cat next?' G stops fiddling with her hair and looks at the teacher. 'I think it will hide,' she says and laughs as she turns to N next to her ...

Observation B

... G is sitting cross-legged on the floor in front of the teacher. She is fiddling with her hair and looking bored. The teacher asks her a question: 'G, what do you think will happen to the cat next?' G says, 'I think it will hide.' ...

Identifying the influences that affect children's development

There are very many factors that affect the healthy growth and development of children. These factors work in combination and so it is often difficult to estimate the impact of any single factor on holistic child development.

The child's background

- **Parental health and lifestyle**: Children who live with one or both parents who have a mental health problem, such as depression, sometimes suffer as their parents may lack the necessary support to deal with their condition. Also, some older children may find themselves in the role of carer for younger children.
- **Parents not available to their children**: This may occur when parents have substance misuse and are often absent both physically (because they are out looking for drugs) and emotionally (because they are intoxicated). Either way, they are not available to the child. Parents who work long hours may also be unavailable to their children.
- **Poor parenting skills**: Substance misuse is often, but not always, associated with poor or inadequate parenting. This can show itself in a number of ways, including physical neglect, emotional neglect or unpredictable parental behaviour: for example, lurching between 'too much' or 'not enough' discipline and mood swings – being very affectionate or very remote. This leads to inconsistent parenting that can be confusing and damaging to the child. Some parents have poor parenting skills, such as being unable to cook.

Economic influences

Poverty is the single greatest threat to the healthy development of children in the UK. Growing up in poverty can affect every area of a child's development: physical, intellectual, emotional, social and spiritual.

- **Accident and illness**: Children growing up in poverty are four times more likely to die in an accident, and have nearly twice the rate of long-standing illness of those living in households with high incomes.
- **Quality of life**: A third of children in poverty go without the meals or toys or clothes that they need.
- **Poor nutrition**: Living on a low income means that children's diet and health can suffer.
- **Space to live and play**: Poorer children are more likely to live in substandard housing and in areas with few shops or amenities, where children have little or no space to play safely.
- **Growth**: They are also more likely to be smaller at birth and shorter in height.
- **Education:** Children who grow up in poverty are statistically less likely to do well at school and have poorer school attendance records.
- **Long-term effects**: As adults they are more likely to suffer ill health, be unemployed or homeless. They are statistically more likely to become involved in offending, drug and alcohol abuse. They are statistically more likely to become involved in abusive relationships.

Reflective practice

Supporting parents and carers

The great majority of parents are concerned to do their best for their child, even if they are not always sure what this might be. How might ineffective parenting skills affect a child's development? Find out what support is available for parents in the community.

Health and welfare

Infection

During childhood there are many infectious illnesses that can affect children's health and development. Some of these infections can be controlled by childhood immunisations; these are diphtheria, tetanus, polio, whooping cough, measles, meningitis, mumps and rubella. Other infections can also have long-lasting effects on a child's health.

Diet

There are various conditions that may occur in childhood that are directly related to a poor or unbalanced diet:

- **failure to thrive** (or faltering growth) – poor growth and physical development
- **dental caries or tooth decay** – associated with a high consumption of sugar in snacks and fizzy drinks
- **obesity** – children who are overweight are more likely to become obese adults
- **nutritional anaemia** – due to an insufficient intake of iron, folic acid and vitamin B12
- **increased susceptibility to infections** – particularly upper respiratory infections such as colds and bronchitis.

Sleep

Sufficient sleep is essential for all aspects of children's development. Being tired all the time because of insufficient sleep at night can affect their ability to learn as well as causing emotional, social and behavioural problems.

Immediate and wider environment

Pollution

Pollution of the environment can have a marked effect on the health and development of children. The three main threats to health are **water pollution**, **air pollution** and **noise pollution**. Children are particularly vulnerable to air pollution. This is partly because they have a large lung surface area in relation to their small body size; this means that they absorb toxic substances more quickly than adults do and are slower to get rid of them. The effects of air pollution from factory chimneys, the use of chemical insecticides and car exhausts include:

- **lead poisoning** – children are particularly susceptible to lead poisoning, mostly caused by vehicle exhaust fumes. Even very low levels of lead in the blood can affect children's ability to learn.
- **asthma** – air pollution can act as a trigger for asthma and can make an existing condition worse. The incidence of asthma is much higher in traffic-polluted areas.

Housing

Poor housing is another factor that affects healthy holistic development. Low-income families are more likely to live in:

- **homes which are damp and/or unheated** – this increases the risk of infection, particularly respiratory illnesses
- **neighbourhoods which are densely populated**, with few communal areas and amenities – children without access to a safe garden or play area may suffer emotional and social problems
- **overcrowded conditions** – homeless families who are housed in 'hotels' or bed and breakfast accommodation often have poor access to cooking facilities and have to share bathrooms with several other families; often children's education is badly disrupted when families are moved from one place to another.

Accidents

Some accidents have lasting effects on a child or young person's healthy growth and development, and many are preventable.

Emotional and social influences

A child who is miserable and unhappy is not healthy, although he or she may appear *physically* healthy. Children need to feel secure and to receive unconditional love from their primary carers. Child abuse, although not common, is bound to affect a child's health and well-being, and can have long-lasting health implications.

Cultural influences

Each family and community has certain values, customs and beliefs (or culture) that affect the way children are related to, treated and encouraged to behave. Religion and spiritual beliefs are also part of this culture. The culture in which a child grows up will shape their emotional and social development. In some families there are marked differences in the way in which boys and girls are treated, and this too may affect the child's developing sense of identity.

Recognising and responding to concerns about children's development

Practitioners are ideally placed to recognise when a child's development is not following the expected norms. Often the parents will have expressed their own concerns and you need to respond to these.

At any point in their lives children may need extra support in nursery or school. This may be for any reason, at any time and for any length of time. Some developmental concerns are temporary (such as a hearing impairment that is corrected by an operation) and therefore only require temporary support.

✓ Progress check

Concerns about development

The following factors can all affect the way in which a child develops holistically.

- **Family circumstances**: Family breakdown – e.g. separation of parents or arrival of a new partner; a child being a carer for another family member; being looked after by the authority or recently having left care.
- **Social or emotional problems**: Bereavement; behavioural difficulties; being involved in a bullying situation or subject to some form of discrimination; periods of transition.
- **Disability or health needs**: Hearing or visual impairment; language and communication difficulties; autistic spectrum disorder; chronic illness leading to frequent hospitalisation; conditions requiring a surgical operation.

A child whose development is giving cause for concern will need to be supported. Practitioners should try to identify the child's particular developmental needs and respond quickly; the sooner the difficulty is identified, the more likely that the support offered will be effective. Parents or carers should be consulted so that the support needed can then be tailored to the individual child.

How to use everyday care routines and activities to support development

To achieve and maintain healthy growth and development (that is, physical, intellectual and emotional), certain basic needs must be fulfilled. Whenever you are caring for children, you should always treat each child as an individual. This means that you should be aware of their individual needs at all times. Sometimes a child may have special or additional needs. (For further information, see Unit 9.)

Meeting the physical and health needs of children

This includes:

- planning a healthy diet for children
- the importance of rest and sleep
- hygiene – caring for children's skin, hair and teeth
- the development of bowel and bladder control
- clothing and footwear
- fresh air and exercise.

Planning a healthy diet for children

During childhood we develop food habits that will affect us for life. By the time we are adults, most of us will suffer from some disorder that is related to our diet – for example, tooth decay, heart disease or cancer. Establishing healthy eating patterns in children will help to promote normal growth and development, and will protect against later disease. As an early years practitioner, you need to know what constitutes a good diet and how it can be provided.

A healthy diet consists of a wide variety of foods to help the body to grow and to provide energy. It must include enough of these **nutrients** – proteins, fats, carbohydrates, vitamins, minerals, and fibre – as well as **water**, to fuel and maintain the body's vital functions.

Children need a varied **energy-rich** diet for good health and growth. For balance and variety, choose from the five main food groups (see Table 2.15).

Food groups	Main nutrients	Types to choose	Portions per day	Suggestions for meals and snacks
Bread, other cereals and potatoes All types of bread, rice, breakfast cereals, pasta, noodles, and potatoes (beans and lentils can be eaten as part of this group)	Carbohydrates (starch), fibre, some calcium and iron, B-group vitamins	Wholemeal, brown, wholegrain or high-fibre versions of bread; avoid fried foods too often (e.g. chips). Use butter and other spreads sparingly	FIVE All meals of the day should include foods from this group	One portion 5 • 1 bowl of breakfast cereal • 2 tbsp pasta or rice • 1 small potato Snack meals include bread or pizza base
Fruit and vegetables Fresh, frozen and canned fruit and vegetables, dried fruit, fruit juice (beans and lentils can be eaten as part of this group)	Vitamin C, carotenes, iron, calcium folate, fibre and some carbohydrate	Eat a wide variety of fruit and vegetables; avoid adding rich sauces to vegetables, and sugar to fruit	FOUR/FIVE Include 1 fruit or vegetable daily high in vitamin C, e.g. tomato, sweet pepper, orange or kiwi fruit	One portion 5 • 1 glass of pure fruit juice • 1 piece of fruit • 1 sliced tomato • 2 tbsp of cooked vegetables • 1 tbsp of dried fruit – e.g. raisins.
Milk and dairy foods Milk, cheese, yoghurt and fromage frais (this group does not contain butter, eggs and cream)	Calcium, protein, B-group vitamins (particularly B12), vitamins A and D	Milk is a very good source of calcium, but calcium can also be obtained from cheese, flavoured or plain yoghurts and fromagefrais	THREE Children require the equivalent of 1 pint of milk each day to ensure an adequate intake of calcium	One portion 5 • 1 glass of milk • 1 pot of yoghurt or fromagefrais • 1 tbsp of grated cheese, e.g. on a pizza Under-2s – do not give reduced-fat milks, e.g. semi-skimmed – they do not supply enough energy

Food groups	Main nutrients	Types to choose	Portions per day	Suggestions for meals and snacks
Meat, fish and alternatives Lean meat, poultry, fish, eggs, tofu, quorn, pulses – peas, beans, lentils, nuts and seeds	Iron, protein, B-group vitamins (particularly B12), zinc and magnesium	Lower-fat versions – meat with fat cut off, chicken without skin, etc. Beans and lentils are good alternatives, being low in fat and high in fibre	TWO Vegetarians will need to have grains, pulses and seeds; vegans avoid all food associated with animals	One portion 5 • 2 fish fingers (for a 3-year-old) • 4 fish fingers (for a 7-year-old) • baked beans • chicken nuggets or a small piece of chicken
Fatty and sugary foods Margarine, low-fat spread, butter, ghee, cream, chocolate, crisps, biscuits, sweets and sugar, fizzy soft drinks, puddings	Vitamins and essential fatty acids, but also a lot of fat, sugar and salt	Only offer small amounts of sugary and fatty foods. Fats and oils are found in all the other food groups	NONE Only eat fatty and sugary foods sparingly, e.g. crisps, sweets and chocolate	Children may be offered foods with extra fat or sugar – biscuits, cakes or chocolate – as long as they are not replacing food from the four main food groups

Table 2.15 Food groups

How much food should children be given?

Children's appetites vary enormously, so common sense is a good guide to how big a portion should be. Always be guided by the individual child:

- do not force them to eat when they no longer wish to, but
- do not refuse to give more if they really are hungry.

Some children always feel hungry at one particular mealtime. Others require food little and often. You should always offer food that is nourishing as well as satisfying their hunger (see Table 2.16).

Meals and snacks

Some children really do need to eat between meals. Their stomachs are relatively small and so they fill up and empty faster than adult stomachs. Sugary foods should not be given as a snack, because sugar is an appetite depressant and may spoil the child's appetite for the main meal to follow. Healthy snack foods include:

- pieces of fruit – banana, orange, pear, kiwi fruit, apple or satsuma
- fruit bread or wholemeal bread with a slice of cheese
- milk or home-made milk shake
- sticks of carrot, celeriac, parsnip, red pepper, cauliflower
- dried fruit and diluted fruit juices
- wholegrain biscuits, oatcakes or sesame seed crackers.

Breakfast	Orange juice Weetabix + milk, 1 slice of buttered toast	Milk Cereal, e.g. corn or wheat flakes, toast and jam	Apple juice 1 slice of toast with butter or jam	Milk Cereal with slice of banana, or scrambled egg on toast	Yoghurt Porridge, slices of apple
Morning snack	Diluted apple juice 1 packet raisins	Blackcurrant and apple drink Cheese straws	1 glass fruit squash 1 biscuit	Peeled apple slices Wholemeal toast fingers with cheese spread	Diluted apple juice Chapatti or pitta bread fingers
Lunch	Chicken nuggets or macaroni cheese Broccoli Fruit yoghurt Water	Thick bean soup or chicken salad sandwich Green beans Fresh fruit salad Water	Vegetable soup or fish fingers/cakes Sticks of raw carrot Kiwi fruit Water	Sweet potato casserole Sweet corn Spinach leaves Chocolate mousse Water	Bean casserole (or chicken drumstick) with noodles Peas or broad beans Fruit yoghurt Water
Afternoon snack	Diluted fruit juice Cubes of cheese with savoury biscuit	Milk shake Fruit cake or chocolate biscuit	Diluted fruit juice Thin-cut sandwiches cut into small pieces	Hot or cold chocolate drink 1 small packed dried fruit mix, e.g. apricots, sultanas	Lassi (yoghurt drink) 1 banana 1 small biscuit
Tea or supper	Baked beans on toast or ham and cheese pasta Lemon pan cakes Milk or yoghurt	Fish stew or fish fingers Mashed potato Fruit mousse or fromage frais Milk or yoghurt	Baked potatoes with a choice of fillings Steamed broccoli Ice cream	Home-made beef burger or pizza Green salad Pancakes Milk	Lentil and rice soup Pitta or whole grain bread Rice salad Milk

Table 2.16 Providing a balanced diet

Iron, calcium and vitamin D in children's diets

Iron

Iron is essential for children's health. Lack of iron often leads to **anaemia**, which can hold back both physical and mental development. Children most at risk are those who are poor eaters or on restricted diets.

Iron comes in two forms, found either in :

1 foods from animal sources (especially meat), iron from which is easily absorbed by the body, or

2 plant foods, iron from which is not quite so easy for the body to absorb.

If possible, children should be given a portion of meat or fish every day, and kidney or liver once a week. Even a small portion of meat or fish is useful because it also helps the body to absorb iron from other food sources.

If children do not eat meat or fish, they must be offered plenty of iron-rich alternatives, such as egg yolks, dried fruit, beans and lentils, and green leafy vegetables. It is also a good idea to give foods or drinks that are high in vitamin C at mealtimes, as this helps the absorption of iron from non-meat sources.

Calcium and vitamin D

Children need calcium for maintaining and repairing bones and teeth. Calcium is:

- found in milk, cheese, yoghurt and other dairy products
- absorbed by the body only if it is taken with vitamin D.

The skin can make all the vitamin D that a body needs when it is exposed to gentle sunlight. See Figure 2.3 for sources of vitamin D and calcium.

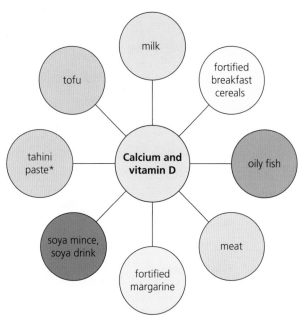

(* Tahini is made from sesame seeds; these may cause an allergic reaction in a small number of children.)

Figure 2.3 Sources of calcium and vitamin D.

Vitamin drops provide vitamins A, C and D. Children under the age of five should be given vitamin drops as a safeguard only when their diets may be insufficient.

Providing drinks for children

You need to offer children drinks several times during the day. The best drinks for young children are water and milk.

- **Water** is a very underrated drink for the whole family as it quenches thirst without spoiling the appetite; if bottled water is used it should be still, not carbonated (fizzy), which is acidic. More water should be given in hot weather in order to prevent dehydration.

- **Milk** is an excellent, nourishing drink. Reduced-fat milks should not normally be given to children under the age of five because of these milks' lower energy and fat-soluble content; however semi-skimmed milk may be offered from two years of age, provided that the child's overall diet is adequate.

Other drinks

All drinks which contain sugar can be harmful to teeth and can also take the edge off children's appetites. *Examples* are: flavoured milks, flavoured fizzy drinks, fruit squashes and fruit juice (containing natural sugar).

Unsweetened diluted fruit juice is the best drink – other than water or milk – for children, but should ideally be offered only at mealtimes. Low-sugar or diet fruit drinks contain artificial sweeteners and are best avoided.

Tea and coffee should not be given to children under five, as they prevent the absorption of iron from foods. They also fill children easily without providing nourishment.

Activity

The balanced daily diet

1. Look at the following daily diet.
   - Breakfast: a glass of milk + scrambled egg and toast
   - Mid-morning: a packet of crisps + a glass of blackcurrant squash
   - Lunch: a cheese and egg flan + chips + baked beans; apple fritters and ice cream + apple juice
   - Snack: chocolate mini-roll and orange squash
   - Tea: fish fingers + mashed potatoes + peas + strawberry milk shake

2. Arrange the portions or servings as shown in the example presented in Table 2.15 (i.e. the four food groups and one extra row for extra fat and sugar) and assess the nutritional content of the diet.

3. How could you improve the menu to ensure a healthy balanced diet?

Guidelines

Providing a healthy diet

- **Offer a wide variety of different foods**: Give babies and young children a chance to try a new food more than once; any refusal on first tasting may be due to dislike of the *new* rather than of the food itself.

- **Set an example**: Children will imitate both what you eat and how you eat it. Be relaxed, patient and friendly. It will be easier to encourage a child to eat a stick of raw celery if you eat one too! If you show disgust at certain foods, young children will notice and copy you.

- **Be prepared for messy mealtimes!** Present the food in a form that is fairly easy for children to manage by themselves (e.g. not difficult to chew).

- **Do not use food as a punishment, reward, bribe or threat**: For example, do not give sweets or chocolates as a reward for finishing savoury foods. To a child this is like saying, 'Here's something nice after eating those nasty greens.' Reward them instead with a trip to the park or a story session.

- **Give healthy foods as treats**: for example, raisins and raw carrots, rather than sweets or cakes.

- **Allow children to follow their own individual appetites** when deciding how much they want to eat. If a child rejects a food, never force-feed him. Simply remove the food without comment. Give smaller portions next time and praise the child for eating even a little.

- **Encourage children to feed themselves,** either using a spoon or by offering suitable finger foods.

- **Introduce new foods in stages**: For example, if switching to wholemeal bread, try a soft-grain white bread first. Involve the children in making choices as much as possible.

- **Teach children to eat mainly at mealtimes,** and avoid giving them high-calorie snacks (e.g. biscuits and sugary drinks) that might take the edge off their appetite for more nutritious food. Most young children need three small meals and three snacks a day.

- **Be imaginative with presentation**: For example, cut slices of pizza into interesting shapes. Use ideas from children's food manufacturers. Using these tactics can make mealtimes more fun.

- **Avoid adding salt to any food**: Too much salt can cause dehydration in babies and may predispose certain people to hypertension (high blood pressure) if taken over a lifetime.

- **Never give a young child whole nuts to eat – particularly peanuts**: Children can very easily choke on a small piece of the nut or even inhale it, which can cause a severe type of pneumonia. Rarely, a child may have a serious **allergic reaction** to nuts.

- **Respect individual preferences**: Some families prefer to eat with their fingers, while others use chopsticks or cutlery. Whatever tool is preferred, be patient – children need time to get used to them.

Establishing healthy eating habits

Some children can be choosy about the food they eat; this can be a source of anxiety for parents and for those who work with children. However, as long as children eat some food from each of the five food groups – even if they are the same old favourites – there is no cause for worry.

As an early years practitioner, you are ideally placed to ensure that **stereotyping** in relation to eating habits is not practised. Mealtimes and the choice of food can be used in a positive sense to affirm a feeling of cultural identity.

Special diets

Most children on special diets are not ill. Often they simply require a therapeutic diet that replaces or eliminates some particular nutrient in order to prevent illness. The diets listed in Table 2.17 are followed by children with specific needs.

Children on vegetarian diets

Children who are on a vegetarian diet need an alternative to meat, fish and chicken as the main sources of **protein**. These could include milk, cheese and eggs, pulses (lentils and beans).

Diabetes mellitus: diabetes mellitus occurs in 1 in every 500 children under the age of about 16 years, and results in difficulty in converting carbohydrate into energy due to underproduction of insulin. Insulin is usually given by daily injection and a diet sheet will be devised by the hospital dietician. It is important that mealtimes be *regular* and that some **carbohydrate** be included at every meal. Children with diabetes should be advised to carry **glucose** sweets whenever they are away from home in case of **hypoglycaemia** (low blood sugar).

Cystic fibrosis: the majority of children with cystic fibrosis have difficulty in absorbing fats; they need more protein and calories than children without the disease, and so require a diet high in fats and carbohydrates. They are also given daily vitamin supplements and pancreatic enzymes.

Coeliac disease: treatment for coeliac disease is by gluten-free diet and has to be for the rest of the person's life. All formula milks available in the UK are gluten-free, and many manufactured baby foods are also gluten-free. Any cakes, bread and biscuits should be made from gluten-free flour, and labels on processed foods should be read carefully to ensure that there is no 'hidden' wheat product in the ingredients list.

Galactosaemia: the child with galactosaemia cannot digest or use galactose – which, together with glucose, forms lactose, the natural sugar of milk. A list of 'safe foods' with a low galactose content will be issued by the dietician, and food labels should be checked for the presence of milk solids and powdered lactose, which contain large amounts of this sugar.

Obesity: a child who is diagnosed as being overweight will usually be prescribed a diet low in fat and sugar; high-fibre carbohydrates are encouraged (e.g. wholemeal bread and other cereals). The child who has to go without crisps, chips and snacks between meals will need a lot of support and encouragement from carers.

Children who have difficulties with chewing and swallowing: children with cerebral palsy can experience difficulties with either or both of these aspects of eating. Food has to be liquidised, but this should be done in separate batches so that the end result is not a pool of greyish sludge. Presentation should be imaginative. Try to follow the general principle of making the difference in the meal as unobtrusive as possible.

Table 2.17 Special diets

They also need to make sure that they are obtaining enough **iron**. As iron is more difficult to absorb from vegetable sources than from meat, a young child needs to obtain iron from sources such as:

- leafy green vegetables, such as spinach and watercress
- pulses (beans, lentils and chickpeas)
- dried fruit (such as apricots, raisins and sultanas)
- some breakfast cereals.

It is easier to absorb iron from our food if it is eaten *with* foods containing vitamin C, such as fruit and vegetables, or diluted fruit juices, at mealtimes; these make it easier to absorb the iron.

The vegan diet

A vegan diet completely excludes all foods of animal origin – that is, animal flesh, milk and milk products, eggs, honey and all additives that may be of animal origin. A vegan diet is based on cereals and cereal products, pulses, fruits, vegetables, nuts and seeds. Human breast milk is acceptable for vegan babies.

Variations in children's diets

Parents have a right to bring up their children according to their own beliefs and cultural practices. Sometimes, however, these preferences are difficult to accommodate within a group setting. Early years practitioners need to ensure that each child has their dietary needs and preferences recorded, and that every staff member knows how to follow these wishes. This is particularly important if a child has a **food allergy** or **intolerance**. Some nurseries have developed a system of personalised table placemats, which include the child's name and photo along with their specific dietary requirements.

Occasionally, children may arrive at the setting with sweets and packets of crisps. Both staff and parents need to work together to formulate a policy that gives consistent guidelines about what is allowed in the setting – and to ensure that every child is offered a healthy and nutritious diet when away from home.

Providing food in a multicultural society

The UK is the home of a multicultural and multi-ethnic society. Food is an important part of the heritage of any culture. Providing food from a wide range of cultures is an important way of celebrating this heritage. Children learn to enjoy different tastes, and to respect the customs and beliefs of people different from themselves.

The largest ethnic minority group in the UK belongs to the Asian community – about 1.25 million people. Asian dietary customs are mainly based on three religious groups: Muslims (or Moslems), Hindus and Sikhs.

Hindus

Orthodox Hindus are strict vegetarians as they believe in *Ahimsa* – non-violence towards all living beings – and some are vegans. Some will eat dairy products and eggs, while others will refuse eggs on the grounds that they are a potential source of life. Even non-vegetarians do not eat beef as the cow is considered a sacred animal. It is also unusual for pork to be eaten, as the pig is considered unclean. Wheat is the main staple food eaten by Hindus in the UK; it is used to make chapattis, puris and parathas. Ghee (clarified butter) and vegetable oil are used in cooking. Three festivals in the Hindu calendar are observed as days of fasting; these last from sunrise to sunset, during which Hindus eat only 'pure' foods such as fruit and yoghurt:

1 Mahshivrati – the birthday of Lord Shiva (March)
2 Ram Naumi – the birthday of Lord Rama (April)
3 Jan Mash Tami – the birthday of Lord Krishna (late August).

Muslims

Muslims practise the Islamic religion, and their holy book, the Koran, provides them with their food laws. Unlawful foods (called **haram**) include pork, all meat that has not been rendered lawful (halal), alcohol and fish without scales. **Halal** meat has been killed in a certain approved way and must be bought from a halal butcher. Wheat, in the form of chapattis, and rice are the staple foods. During the lunar month of **Ramadan**, Muslims fast between sunrise and sunset. Children under 12 and elderly people are exempt from fasting.

Sikhs

Most Sikhs will not eat pork or beef. Some Sikhs are vegetarian, but many eat chicken, lamb and fish. Wheat and rice are staple foods. Devout Sikhs will fast once or twice a week, and most will fast on the first day of the Punjabi month or when there is a full moon.

African-Caribbean diets

The African-Caribbean community is the second largest ethnic minority group in the UK. Dietary customs vary widely. Many people include a variety of European foods in their diet alongside the traditional foods of cornmeal, coconut, green banana, plantain, okra and yam. Although African-Caribbean people are generally Christian, a minority are Rastafarians.

Rastafarians

Rastafarians' dietary customs are based on laws, laid down by Moses in the Bible, which state that certain types of meat should be avoided. The majority of followers will eat only '**Ital**' foods, which are considered to be in a whole or natural state. Most Rastafarians are vegetarians and will not eat processed or preserved foods.

Jewish diets

Jewish people observe dietary laws which state that animals and birds must be killed by the Jewish method to render them **kosher** (acceptable). Milk and meat must never be cooked or eaten together, and pork in any form is forbidden. Shellfish are not allowed as they are thought to harbour disease. The most holy day of the Jewish calendar is Yom Kippur (the Day of Atonement) when Jewish people fast for 25 hours.

Food and festivals

There are often particular foods that are associated with religious festivals (e.g. mince pies at Christmas and pancakes on Shrove Tuesday). Providing foods from different cultures within an early childhood setting is a very good way of celebrating these festivals. Parents of children from minority ethnic groups are usually very pleased to be asked for advice on how to celebrate festivals with food, and may even be prepared to contribute some samples.

The social and educational role of food and mealtimes

Mealtimes can promote:

- hand–eye coordination – using cutlery and other tools
- sensory development – taste, touch, sight and smell
- language development – increased vocabulary
- development of concepts of shape and size, using different foods as examples
- learning through linked activities (e.g. cookery, weighing food, stories about food, where food comes from)
- independence – skills of serving food and taking responsibility
- listening skills
- courtesy towards others, and turn-taking
- sharing experience – a social focus in the child's day
- self-esteem – child's family and cultural background is valued
- self-confidence – through learning social skills, taking turns and saying 'please' and 'thank you'.

Sharing information with families

When parents register their child at nursery or school, they are asked to detail any special dietary requirements that their child may have. Some children may need special diets because of an underlying medical condition; others may require a vegetarian or vegan diet. It is important that all child care and education settings are aware of any particular allergies or problems with eating that a child may have. If a parent or carer expresses any concern to you about the food provided within your nursery or school, refer them to the person in charge, or the child's key person, for guidance.

The nutritional needs of babies

The way babies and children are fed is much more than simply providing enough food to meet nutritional requirements; for the newborn baby, sucking milk is a great source of pleasure, and is also rewarding and enjoyable for the mother. The ideal food for babies to start life with is breast milk, and breastfeeding should always be encouraged as the first choice in infant feeding. However, mothers should not be made to feel guilty or inadequate if they choose not to, or are unable to, breastfeed their babies.

Advantages of breastfeeding

- Human milk provides food constituents in the correct balance for human growth. There is no trial and error to find the right formula to suit the baby.
- The milk is sterile and at the correct temperature; there is no need for bottles and sterilising equipment.
- Breast milk initially provides the infant with maternal antibodies and helps protect the child from infection.
- The child is less likely to become overweight as overfeeding by concentrating the formula is not possible, and the infant has more freedom of choice as to how much milk she will suckle.
- Generally breast milk is considered cheaper despite the extra calorific requirement of the mother.
- Sometimes it is easier to promote mother–infant bonding by breastfeeding, although this is certainly not always the case.
- Some babies have an intolerance to the protein in cows' milk.
- The uterus returns to its pre-pregnancy state more quickly, by the action of oxytocin released when the baby suckles.

Advantages of bottle-feeding

- The mother knows exactly how much milk the baby has taken.

- The milk is in no way affected by the mother's state of health, whereas anxiety, tiredness, illness or menstruation may reduce the quantity of breast milk.
- The infant is unaffected by such factors as maternal medication. Laxatives, antibiotics, alcohol and drugs affecting the central nervous system can affect the quality of breast milk.
- Other members of the family can feed the infant. In this way the father can feel equally involved with the child's care and, during the night, could take over one of the feeds so that the mother can get more sleep.
- There is no fear of embarrassment while feeding.
- The mother is physically unaffected by feeding the infant, avoiding such problems as sore nipples.

How to support a mother who is breastfeeding

Many mothers give up breastfeeding when they return to full-time work. Others continue to breast-feed their baby fully by expressing their own milk and bringing it to the nursery or crèche for it to be given by bottle. This involves a considerable amount of planning and organisational skill. The baby's key worker should reassure the mother that her wishes will be respected, and that every effort will be made to support her in her preference for breastfeeding. As with bottle-fed babies in your care, you should ensure that you record the amount of feed taken, and note any changes or problems in feeding.

Bottle-feeding

Types of milk

Only commercially modified baby milks – known as formula milks – should be used for bottle-feeding babies from birth to one year old. The main types of formula milk for babies under six months are as follows.

First-stage formula milk: normally used for babies from birth; the protein content has more whey in it than casein, which reflects the balance of whey and casein in breast milk.

Second-stage formula milk: suitable for babies from birth, although usually promoted as being for 'hungrier' babies as it has a greater casein content, which is less easily digestible and is intended to keep the baby feeling fuller for longer: this is sometimes called 'follow-on' milk.

Soya formula: made from soya beans, which, like cows' milk, are modified for use in formula with added vitamins, minerals and nutrients. This is used for babies who are unable to tolerate cows' milk formula or whose parents are vegans. Babies should be given soya-based formula only on the advice of a health professional, such as a health visitor, GP or dietician.

Some other specialist formula milks are used for babies who have other special needs – for instance, pre-term babies.

Note: Ordinary cows' milk, condensed milk, dried milk, goats' milk, evaporated milk, or any other type of milk should never be given to a baby under 12 months old.

Giving a bottle-feed

1 Collect all the necessary equipment before picking up the baby. The bottle may be warmed in a jug of hot water; have a muslin square or bib and tissues to hand.
2 Check the temperature and flow of the milk by dripping it on to the inside of your wrist (it should feel warm, not hot or cold).
3 Make yourself comfortable with the baby. Do not rush the feed – babies always sense if you are not relaxed and it can make them edgy too.
4 Try to hold the baby in a similar position to that for breastfeeding and maintain eye contact; this is a time for cuddling and talking to the baby.
5 Stimulate the rooting reflex by placing the teat at the corner of the baby's mouth; then put the teat fully into the mouth and feed by tilting the bottle so that the hole in the teat is always covered with milk.
6 After about ten minutes, the baby may need to be helped to bring up wind; this can be done by leaning the child forwards on your lap and gently rubbing the back, or by holding the baby against your shoulder. Unless the baby is showing discomfort, do not insist on trying to produce a 'burp' – the baby may pass it out in the nappy.

Dummies

Babies are born with a strong sucking reflex and some babies are more 'sucky' than others. If a dummy is used before the baby is weaned, it should be sterilised in the same way as the teats of the bottles are sterilised. For older babies careful washing and rinsing are sufficient.

Safety point: To prevent accidental strangulation, *never* hang a dummy from a ribbon or string around the baby's neck, nor from a cot rail.

Good practice when bottle-feeding a baby

The National Children's Bureau states that babies who are bottle-fed should be held and have warm physical contact with an attentive adult while being fed. It is strongly recommended that a baby in a child care setting is fed by the same staff member at each feed. Babies should never be left propped up with bottles as this is dangerous and inappropriate to their emotional needs.

Guidelines on feeding a baby safely

- Always wash hands thoroughly when preparing feeds for babies.

- Never add sugar or salt to the milk, and never make the feed stronger than the instructions state – this could result in too high a salt intake, which can lead to severe illness.

- Always check the temperature of the milk before giving it to a baby. Try a few drops on your wrist; it should feel neither hot nor cold to the touch – in other words, you should not really feel it at all as it will be at body temperature.

- Do not use a microwave oven to warm the bottle as this may produce isolated hot spots. Expressed breast milk should not be microwaved because this breaks down the natural chemistry.

- Always check that the teat has a hole the right size and that it is not blocked.

- Never prop up a baby with a bottle – choking is a real danger.

- Always supervise siblings when feeding small babies.

Feeding problems

Babies often regurgitate small amounts of milk after a feed; this is known as **posseting** and is nothing to worry about. However, you should always inform the baby's parents if you are in a home setting, and your supervisor if you are in a group setting if you notice the following problems.

- **Vomiting**: if the baby brings up large quantities of the feed, this could be due to trapped wind but there could also be an underlying illness.
- **Refusal of a feed**: the baby may cry and draw her knees up to her chest – a sign of colic – or she may be hungry but unable to feed because of a problem with, for example, a blocked teat.

Always seek help if the baby you are caring for gives you cause for concern.

Weaning a baby – or starting on solid foods

Weaning is the gradual introduction of solid food to the baby's diet. The reasons for weaning are to:

- meet the baby's nutritional needs – from about six months of age, milk alone will not satisfy the baby's increased nutritional requirements, especially for iron
- develop the chewing mechanism; the muscular movement of the mouth and jaw also aids the development of speech
- satisfy increasing appetite
- introduce new tastes and textures; this enables the baby to join in family meals, thus promoting cognitive and social development
- develop new skills – use of feeding beaker, cup and cutlery.

For children from six to eight months of age, you can gradually increase the amount of solid foods you give. By 12 months, solid foods should form the main part of the diet, with breast or formula milk making up the balance (see Table 2.18).

Methods of weaning

Some babies take very quickly to solid food; others appear not to be interested at all. The baby's demands are a good guide for weaning; mealtimes should

Stage 1 Around 5–6 months	Stage 2 6–8 months	Stage 3 9–12 months
Mix a teaspoon of one of the following with the baby's usual milk (breast or formula): • vegetable purée – such as carrot, parsnip, potato or yam, or • fruit purée – such as banana, cooked apple, pear or mango, or • cereal (not wheat-based) – such as baby rice, sago, maize, corn-meal or millet. Offer this before or after one of the usual milk feeds, or in the middle of a feed, if that works better. If the food is hot, make sure you stir and cool it; test it before giving it to the baby.	Add other foods to the vegetable, fruit and cereal purées, such as: • purées of meat and poultry • purées of pulses such as lentils (dhal), hummus • full-fat milk products such as yoghurt or fromagefrais – unless advised otherwise by the health visitor or general practitioner (full-fat cows' milk can also be used for cooking only, e.g. in cheese sauce, but avoid giving cows' milk as a drink). Try to give cereals just once a day; start to add different foods and different tastes. By using family foods – mashing, or puréeing a small amount – you help to get the baby used to eating with the family.	Add a wider range of foods with a variety of textures and flavours: • finger foods such as toast, bread, breadsticks, pitta bread or chapatti, peeled apple, banana, carrot sticks, or cubes of cheese • pieces of meat from a casserole • 3–4 servings a day of starchy foods and fruit and vegetables – the vitamin C in fruit and vegetables helps our bodies absorb iron. If the baby is following a vegetarian diet, give two servings a day of pulses (e.g. red lentils, beans or chickpeas), or tofu.

Table 2.18 The three stages of weaning

never become a battleground. The Department of Health recommends that weaning should not be introduced until the age of six months. The health visitor will be able to offer additional advice on weaning. Even babies as young as six months have definite food preferences and should never be forced to eat a particular food, however much thought and effort have gone into the preparation. The best foods to start with are puréed cooked vegetables, fruit and ground cereals such as rice. Chewing usually starts at around the age of six months, whether the baby has teeth or not, and coarser textures can then be offered. The baby should be in a bouncing cradle or high chair – not in the usual feeding position in the carer's arms.

Methods of puréeing food:

- rub through a sieve using a large spoon
- mash soft foods such as banana or cooked potato with a fork
- use a mouli-sieve or hand blender
- use an electric blender (useful for larger amounts).

Food allergies and special diets
Cows' milk protein intolerance or allergy: babies who have an intolerance to cows' milk or an allergy

to it should be referred to a dietician, who may recommend a soya-based formula or a cows' milk-based formula that has been specially modified for babies with an allergy or intolerance.

Lactose intolerance: this is an intolerance to the sugar (lactose) found in milk. It is not an allergy, but babies will need to avoid milk; they may be given fermented milk products, such as yoghurt.

Gluten-free diet: babies who have the rare condition coeliac disease must not be given any foods that contain gluten. This is found in cereals (wheat, rye, barley and oats) and all foods made with them, such as bread, pastries, biscuits and cakes. Gluten-free alternatives must be given. Dieticians will advise parents, and useful advice is provided by the Coeliac Society (www.coeliac.co.uk).

Dairy-free diet: some babies with severe eczema may be advised to avoid dairy products such as milk, cheese and butter. Again, a dietician will give advice about a suitable diet.

Guidelines on weaning

- Try to encourage a liking for savoury foods.

- Introduce only one new food at a time.

- Be patient if the baby does not take the food – feed at the baby's pace, not yours.

- Do not add salt or sugar to feeds.

- Make sure that food is the right temperature.

- Avoid giving sweet foods or drinks between meals.

- Never leave a baby alone when she is eating.

- Limit the use of commercially prepared foods – they are of poorer quality and will not allow the baby to become used to home cooking.

- Select foods approved by the baby's parents.

Activity

Weaning a baby on to solid food

1 Prepare a booklet for parents on weaning. Include the following information:
   - when to start weaning a baby
   - what foods to start with
   - when and how to offer feeds
   - a weekly menu plan, which includes vegetarian options.

2 Visit a store that stocks a wide variety of commercial baby foods and note their nutritional content (e.g. protein, fat, energy, salt, sugar, gluten and additives). Make a chart that shows:
   - the type of food (e.g. rusks and cereals, savoury packet food, jars of sweet and savoury food)
   - the average cost in each category
   - the packaging – note particularly if manufacturers use pictures of babies from different ethnic backgrounds.

3 If possible, ask a parent who has recently used weaning foods what reasons they had for choosing one product over another.

Babies with special needs

Cleft lip and palate: feeding can be difficult in babies with this condition, as the gap caused by the cleft palate can cause milk to be regurgitated through the nose. Various specialist feeding bottles and teats can be used. A specially designed one-way valve and teat adjust milk flow to suit the baby's needs.

Down's syndrome: some babies with Down's syndrome may have feeding problems in the first few weeks. They need to be able to sort out the complicated coordination necessary to suck, swallow and breathe at the same time and they may splutter and choke a bit. Try holding the baby fairly upright to feed and check first that the tongue is not sticking to the roof of the mouth. For a baby to suckle and obtain adequate milk the teat must be on the tongue (not under it). Specially adapted teats are available to help babies who have difficulty feeding. Do not hurry the feed. Babies with Down's syndrome often feed very slowly, so do not stop too quickly. If the baby falls asleep in the middle of a feed, try tickling her cheeks, chin and feet.

When caring for babies with special needs, try to find out as much as you can about the particular condition by consulting the relevant websites.

Consulting parents and other carers about feeding preferences

Parents usually have very definite ideas about what feed their baby should be given – and how often. You need to be aware of their preferences and to make sure that their instructions are followed. It is good practice to keep a record of when and how much food or milk is taken by babies in your care.

The importance of rest and sleep

Rest and sleep are important for our health and well-being. By the end of the first year, most babies are having two short sleeps during the day – before or after lunch and in the afternoon – and sleeping through the night, although there is much variation between individual children. It is important to have 'quiet periods', even if the baby does not want to sleep.

When we sleep, we rest and gain energy for a new day. But sleep does more than that. When we dream, we process all the events of our daily life. After a night without enough sleep we often feel exhausted and irritable, but after a good night's sleep we feel rested, refreshed and full of energy. It is important to parents that their child sleeps through the night, as it influences the entire family's life and well-being.

Children need more sleep than adults because the brain is developing and maturing, and they are physically growing as well. Sleep is important to child health because:

- it rests and restores the body
- it enables the brain and the body's metabolic processes to recover (these processes are responsible for producing energy and growth)

- during sleep, growth hormone is released; this renews tissues and produces new bone and red blood cells
- dreaming is believed to help the brain sort out information stored in the memory during waking hours.

Children vary enormously in their need for sleep and rest. Some seem able to rush around all day with very little rest; others will need to 'recharge their batteries' by having frequent periods of rest. You need to be able to recognise the signs that a child is tired; these may include:

- looking tired – dark rings under the eyes and yawning
- asking for their comfort object
- constant rubbing of the eyes
- twiddling their hair and fidgeting with objects
- showing no interest in activities and in their surroundings
- being particularly emotional – crying or being stubborn
- withdrawing into themselves – sucking thumb and appearing listless.

Guidelines: establishing a routine for rest and sleep

Children will only sleep if they are actually tired, so it is important that adequate opportunity for activity and exercise is provided. Some children do not have a nap during the day but should be encouraged to rest in a quiet area.

When preparing children for a daytime nap, rest or bedtime sleep, you need to:

- treat each child uniquely; every child will have his or her own needs for sleep and rest
- find out all you can about the individual child's sleep habits; for example, some children like to be patted to sleep, while others need to have their favourite comfort object
- be guided by the wishes of the child's parents or carers; some parents, for example, prefer their child to have a morning nap but not an afternoon nap, as this fits in better with the family's routine
- reassure children that they will not be left alone, and that you or someone else will be there when they wake up
- keep noise to a minimum and darken the room; make sure that children have been to the lavatory beforehand – they need to understand the signals that mean it is time for everyone to have a rest or sleep
- provide quiet, relaxing activities for children who are unable, or who do not want, to sleep; for example, jigsaw puzzles, a story tape or reading a book.

Guidelines: establishing a bedtime routine for babies

Between three and five months, most babies are ready to settle into a bedtime routine.

- Give the baby a bath or wash, and put her in a clean nappy and nightwear.
- Take her to say goodnight to other members of the household.
- Carry her into her room, telling her in a gentle voice that it is time for bed.
- Give the last breast- or bottle-feed in the room where the baby sleeps.
- Sing a song or lullaby to help settle her, while gently rocking her in your arms.
- Wrap her securely and settle her into the cot or cradle, saying goodnight.
- If she likes it, gently 'pat' her to sleep.

The routine can be adapted as the baby grows. Advice from the Foundation for the Study of Infant Deaths (FSID) is that the safest place for a baby to sleep is in a cot in the parents' room for the first six months. After this time, the baby can safely be left in her own room.

Different views about sleep and rest

There are cultural differences in how parents view bedtime and sleep routines. In some cultures it is normal for children to sleep with their parents and to have a much later bedtime in consequence. Some families who originate from hot countries where having a sleep in the afternoon is normal tend to let their children stay up in the evening. Such children are more likely to need a sleep while in day care; as long as the overall amount of sleep is sufficient for the child, it does not matter. It is always worth discussing bedtime routines with parents when toddlers are struggling to behave well. Some areas have sleep clinics, managed by the health visiting service, to help parents whose children have difficulty sleeping.

Even after they have established a good sleep routine, children's sleep patterns can become disrupted between the ages of one and three years. There are thought to be a number of reasons for this, including developmental changes and behavioural issues.

Preventing sudden infant death syndrome

Sudden infant death syndrome (SIDS) is often called 'cot death'. It is the term applied to the sudden unexplained and unexpected death of an infant. The reasons for cot deaths are complicated and the cause is still unknown. Although cot death is the commonest cause of death in babies up to one year

old, it is still very rare, occurring in approximately two out of every 1,000 babies.

'Side' sleeping is not as safe as sleeping on the back, but it *is* much safer than sleeping on the front. Healthy babies placed on their backs are *not* more likely to choke. To prevent a baby wriggling down under the covers, place the baby's feet at the foot of the cot and make the bed up so that the covers reach no higher than the shoulders. Covers should be securely tucked in so that they cannot slip over the baby's head. Duvets or quilts, baby nests and pillows have the potential to trap air and may increase the risk of overheating.

How to put babies down to sleep

- Place babies on their back to sleep, with the feet near to the end of the cot to prevent the baby slipping under the covers ('feet to foot').
- Make sure the room is not too hot or too cold (it should be about 18–20°C). If the room is warm enough for you to be comfortable wearing light clothing, then it is the right temperature for babies.
- Do not overdress the baby – keep the head uncovered.
- Do not place the baby's cot in direct sunlight or near a radiator.
- Do not use duvets or quilts until the baby is over a year old.
- Do not smoke or let anyone else smoke near the baby.

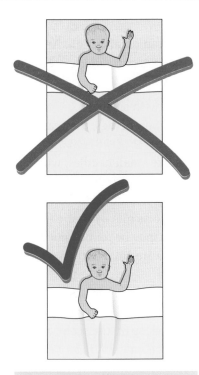

Figure 2.4 The feet to foot position

How to help children to sleep

When preparing children for the night-time sleep, you need to follow the guidelines above and also warn the child that bedtime is approaching (e.g. after the bath and story), and then follow a set **routine** as outlined in the accompanying guidelines.

Guidelines: a bedtime routine for children

- Take a family meal about one-and-a-half hours before bedtime. This should be a relaxing, sociable occasion.
- After the meal, the child could play with other members of the family.
- Make bath time a relaxing time to unwind and play with the child; this often helps the child to feel drowsy.
- Give a final bedtime drink followed by teeth cleaning. (Never withhold a drink at bedtime when potty training – see below.)
- Read or tell a story; looking at books together develops a feeling of closeness between the child and their carer.
- Settle the child in bed, with curtains drawn and nightlight on if desired, and then say goodnight and leave.

Promoting and maintaining good hygiene and hygiene routines

Unit 3 discusses hygiene routines in the child care setting.

Caring for babies' skin and hair

A baby's skin is soft and delicate, yet also tough and pliant. Young babies do not have to be bathed every day because only their bottom, face and neck, and skin creases get dirty, and the skin may tend to dryness. If a bath is not given daily, the baby should have the important body parts cleansed thoroughly – a process known as 'topping and tailing'; this limits the amount of undressing and helps to maintain good skin condition. Whatever routine is followed, the newborn baby needs to be handled gently but firmly, and with confidence. Most babies learn to enjoy the sensation of water and are greatly affected by *your* attitude. The more relaxed and unhurried you are, the more enjoyable the whole experience will be.

Guidelines: topping and tailing for babies

Babies do not like having their skin exposed to the air, so should be undressed for the shortest time possible. Always ensure the room is warm – no less than 20°C (68°F) – and that there are no draughts.

- Warm a large, soft towel on a not-too-hot radiator and have it ready to wrap the baby in afterwards.
- Wash your hands. Remove the baby's outer clothes, leaving on her vest and nappy. Wrap the baby in the towel, keeping her arms inside.
- Using two separate pieces of cotton wool (one for each eye; this will prevent any infection passing from one eye to the other), squeezed in the boiled water, gently wipe the baby's eyes in one movement from the inner corner outwards.
- Gently wipe all around the face and behind the ears. Lift the chin and wipe gently under the folds of skin. Dry each area thoroughly by patting with a soft towel or dry cotton wool.
- Unwrap the towel and take the baby's vest off, raise each arm separately and wipe the armpit

Guidelines: topping and tailing for babies (cont.)

carefully. The folds of skin rub together here and can become quite sore. Again, dry thoroughly and dust with baby powder if used.

- Wipe and dry the baby's hands.
- Take the nappy off and place in a lidded bucket.
- Clean the baby's bottom with moist swabs, then wash with soap and water; rinse well with flannel or sponge, pat dry and apply protective cream.
- Put on clean nappy and clothes.

Caring for children's skin and hair

As children grow and become involved in more vigorous exercise, especially outside, a daily bath or shower becomes necessary. Most young children love bath time and adding bubble bath to the water adds to the fun of getting clean.

Children should NEVER be left alone in the bath or shower, because of the risk of drowning or scalding.

Head lice

Head lice are a common affliction. Anybody can get them but they are particularly prevalent among children. Head lice:

- are tiny insects with six legs
- live only on human beings; they cannot be caught from animals
- have mouths like small needles, which they stick into the scalp and use to drink the blood
- are unable to fly, hop or jump
- are not the same as nits – nits are the egg cases laid by lice; nits may be found 'glued' on to the hair shafts; they are smaller than a pinhead and are pearly white
- are between 1 and 4 mm in size – slightly larger than a pin head
- live on, or very close to, the scalp, and do not wander down the hair shafts for very long
- are caught just by coming into contact with someone who is infested; when heads touch, the lice simply walk from one head to the other
- do not discriminate between clean and dirty hair, but tend to live more on smooth, straight hair.

Guidelines: Caring for children's skin and hair

- Wash face and hands in the morning. (Note: Muslims always wash under running water.)
- Always wash hands after using the toilet and before meals; dry hands thoroughly – young children will need supervision.
- After using the toilet, girls should be taught to wipe their bottom from front to back, to prevent germs from the anus entering the vagina and urethra.
- Wash hands after playing outside, or after handling animals.
- Nails should be scrubbed with a soft nailbrush and trimmed regularly by cutting straight across; never cut into the sides of the nails as this can cause sores and infections.
- Find out about any special skin conditions, such as eczema or dry skin, and be guided by parents' advice concerning the use of soap and creams.
- Children should have their own flannel, comb and brush, which should be cleaned regularly.
- Skin should always be dried thoroughly, taking special care of such areas as between the toes and the armpits; black skin tends to dryness and may need massaging with special oils or moisturisers.
- Babies' and young children's hair should ideally be washed during bath time using a specially formulated mild baby soap or shampoo. (Adult shampoos contain many extra ingredients, such as perfumes and chemicals, all of which can lead to irritation of children's delicate skin.)
- Hair usually only needs washing twice a week; children with long or curly hair benefit from the use of a conditioning shampoo, which helps to reduce tangles. Hair should always be rinsed thoroughly in clean water and not brushed until it is dry – brushing wet hair damages the hair shafts. A wide-toothed comb is useful for combing wet hair.

Guidelines: Caring for children's skin and hair (cont.)

- African-Caribbean hair tends to dryness and may need special oil or moisturisers; if the hair is braided (with or without beads), it may be washed with the braids left intact, unless advised otherwise.

- Rastafarian children with hair styled in dreadlocks may not use either combs or shampoo, preferring to brush the dreadlocks gently and secure them with braid.

- Regular combing and brushing will also help to prevent the occurrence of head lice.

Activity

Prevention and treatment of head lice

1. Find out how to prevent head lice.

2. Find out how to treat an individual child with head lice.

3. Prepare a fact sheet to give to parents that explains:
   - what head lice are and why children are particularly susceptible to them
   - how head lice can be prevented
   - the different methods of treatment and where to obtain them.

Care of children's teeth

Care of the first, 'milk', teeth is as important as for permanent teeth, since it promotes good habits and encourages permanent teeth to appear in the proper place. Every time the child eats sweet things, acid is produced which attacks the enamel of the tooth. Saliva protects the teeth from this and more saliva is produced during meals. The protective effect lasts for about half an hour so the more frequently the child eats sweets or sugary drinks, the more exposure to acid the teeth have. After the child's first birthday, they can be taught to brush their own teeth, but they will need careful supervision. You can help by following the guidelines presented here.

The use of dummies

Parents often have strong views about the use of soothers and dummies. These are only likely to be harmful to tooth development if they are used constantly and habitually, or if they are sweetened, which is likely to cause decay. Dummies should be sterilised regularly and changed if they have been dropped on the floor. Dummies should *never* be sucked by adults before giving to babies as this merely transfers bacteria from adult to child and can cause stomach upsets.

Guidelines: caring for children's teeth

- Babies under one year should have their teeth brushed with a soft brush once or twice a day using gentle toothpaste.

- Drinks should be given after meals, with water between meals. Bottles and cups should not contain fizzy or sweetened drinks, and fruit juice should be limited to mealtimes.

- Babies should not be allowed to have constant access to a bottle or cup.

- Babies between 12 and 15 months should be encouraged to drink from a cup.

- Teach children to brush their teeth after meals: show them how to brush up and away from the gum when cleaning the lower teeth and down and away from the gum when cleaning the upper teeth. (Younger children will need help in brushing the back teeth.)

- Crusty bread, crunchy fruit and raw vegetables, such as carrot or celery, help to keep teeth healthy and free of **plaque** – a substance that builds up on the teeth, attracting bacteria and causing tooth decay.

Guidelines: caring for children's teeth (cont.)

- Sweets may be given after meals, if at all.
- Take children to the dentist regularly so that they get used to the idea of having their mouth looked at.

Equipment for physical care

There is a wide variety of equipment that may be used when physically caring for children. Children will find it easier to be independent in their hygiene routines if they are provided with suitable equipment (e.g. a stool that enables them to reach the washbasin, or a child-sized toothbrush).

The development of bowel and bladder control

Children will not achieve control over their bowel or bladder function until the nerve pathways that send signals to the brain are mature enough to indicate fullness. This usually happens between two and three years of age, with most children achieving control by four years. Gaining control over these basic functions is a major milestone that relies on both psychological and physical readiness.

- Toilet training should be approached in a relaxed, unhurried manner. If the potty is introduced too early, or if a child is forced to sit on it for long periods of time, they may rebel and the whole issue of toilet training becomes a battleground.
- Toilet training can be over in a few days or may take some months. Becoming dry at night takes longer, but most children manage this before the age of five.
- There is no point in attempting to start toilet training until the child shows that he or she is ready, and this rarely occurs before the age of 18 months.

There are different opinions on using a potty or placing the child straight on the toilet. Privacy must be considered within the nursery setting and the potty placed in a cubicle if the child is used to a potty; however, if the toilet is 'child-sized' then they can be encouraged to use it. Aids such as clip-on seats and steps are available to enable children to use an adult-sized toilet and still feel safe – some children are anxious about falling down the toilet.

Guidelines: toilet training

Toilet training must be discussed with the parents and the decision on when to start agreed.

1 Parents must not feel pressured into toilet training their child; however, children do exhibit certain signs and behaviours that will indicate that they are developmentally ready to consider training – that is, they are likely to achieve control successfully and without too much difficulty – and parents may find this information helpful.

2 You should understand how to recognise the signs that children are ready to be toilet trained; these include:
  - ability to pull down pants
  - has bowel movements at regular times (e.g. after breakfast)
  - is willing to sit on the toilet or potty without crying or fuss
  - shows an interest in using it and will usually pass urine if placed on toilet/potty
  - has a word or gesture to indicate a wet or soiled nappy.

3 Anticipate when the child is likely to need the toilet – such as after meals, before sleep and on waking – and sit the child on the potty or toilet.

4 Give children praise on 'going' and have a practical and sympathetic attitude to 'accidents'.

5 Demonstrate that using the toilet is a normal activity that everyone does when they are old enough to manage it.

Dealing with accidents

Even once a child has become used to using the potty or toilet, there will inevitably be occasions when they have an 'accident' – that is, they wet or soil themselves. This happens more often during the early stages of toilet training, as the child may still lack the awareness or the control to allow enough time to get to the potty. Older children may become so absorbed in their play that they simply forget to go to the toilet.

You can help children when they have an accident by:

- not appearing bothered; let the child know that it is not a big problem, just something that happens from time to time

- reassuring the child by using a friendly tone of voice and offering a cuddle if they seem distressed
- being discreet; deal with the matter swiftly – wash and change them out of view of others and with the minimum of fuss
- if older children want to manage the incident themselves, encouraging them to do so, but always checking tactfully afterwards that they have managed
- always following safety procedures in the setting (e.g. wearing disposable gloves and dealing appropriately with soiled clothing and waste).

Case Study — Toilet training

Jack is 25 months old. He is an intelligent little boy, who is healthy in all areas of his development.

His mother, Monica, is a good friend of Priya, mother of Jasmine who is 22 months old and attends the same class as Jack. Jasmine loves to play with the older girls in pre-school when the classes join up, and has recently begun to potty train herself. She has had a couple of 'accidents' when distracted or excited, and still wears a nappy for nap times, but generally has been very successful. Monica brings Jack in one day and expresses her concern that he has no interest in using the potty – he will do so when asked, but rarely does anything but sit. Jack's

key worker reassures Monica that Jack will begin to use it in his own time, but she is unconvinced and decides to start putting him in pants. This starts off well – members of staff take Jack to use the potty regularly and he occasionally uses it. However, he never expresses a need to use the potty. Gradually, as the nursery gets busier, Jack has 'accidents' more frequently. This begins to distress him, especially when his own spare clothes run out and he has to use the nursery's stock.

1. Why do you think Monica is so concerned about Jack not using the potty?
2. What do you think nursery staff could do to minimise Jack's distress?

Other developmental areas and gaining control

As we have seen before, all the areas of development are closely linked with each other, and the stages of development reached in one area will have an effect on the way in which independence in toilet needs is reached.

Physical development: a child with a spinal injury or other physical disability may not receive

the messages to the brain that tell them that their bladder is full; independence is therefore restricted.

Cognitive and language development: children who have communication difficulties may need the support of a signed language such as Makaton or Signalong in order to signal their toilet needs.

Emotional and social development: if a child is feeling insecure or under stress, this may affect the rate at which they gain control over their bladder and bowel function. Sometimes, children who have previously been both dry and clean may begin to have more 'accidents'. This is known as regression and is usually a temporary response to an emotional upset (e.g. the birth of a sibling in the family).

Signs of illness or abnormality

When you help children to use the potty or the toilet, you should always be alert to any problems they may have. All observations should be reported to the child's parents, or, if this is not appropriate, to your immediate supervisor. Some of the signs to look for are:

- **diarrhoea** – some nursery-age children are prone to bouts of diarrhoea, which is not usually a sign of infection but a result of the immaturity of the nervous system affecting the speed of digestion
- **constipation** – a child may have difficulty and feel pain when passing a motion
- **pain when passing urine** – this may be caused by a bladder infection (cystitis) and will require treatment
- **rashes around the nappy and genital area** – nappy rash or thrush may cause red spots around the nappy area
- **bruising or other marks** – these could indicate abuse (see Unit 3 for further information).

Care of children's feet

Babies do not need shoes: the bones of the feet are not fully developed during the first year and can easily be damaged by shoes – and even socks – as these restrict the natural movement of the toes and feet, especially if they are too small. The feet of babies and young children grow very quickly, so that both socks and shoes can become too small in a matter of weeks. Although miniature versions of adult shoes are available in sizes to fit babies they should be discouraged; unfortunately, because of the availability of such products, there is a tendency to believe they are not harmful. Babies should be left barefoot as much as possible, especially once they become mobile, because their attempts to balance and efforts at walking strengthen and develop the supporting muscles of the foot, including the arch.

Children's footwear: parents and carers should always go to a shoe shop where trained children's shoe-fitters can help them choose from a wide selection of shoes. Second-hand shoes should never be worn as all shoes take on the shape of the wearer's foot.

Clothing for children

Parents and carers should expect children to become dirty as they explore their surroundings, and should not show disapproval when clothes become soiled. Clothes for children need to be:

- hard-wearing
- comfortable
- easy to put on and take off, especially when going to the toilet
- washable.

Underwear should be made of cotton, which is comfortable and sweat-absorbent.

Sleep suits – all-in-one pyjamas with hard-wearing socks – are useful for children who kick the bedcovers off at night. (Note: these must be the correct size to prevent damage to growing feet.)

Daytime clothes should be adapted to the stage of mobility and independence of the child; for example, a dress will hinder a young girl trying to crawl; dungarees may prove difficult for a toddler to manage when being toilet trained. Suitable daytime wear includes: cotton jersey tracksuits, T-shirts and cotton jumpers.

Outdoor clothes must be warm and loose enough to fit over clothing and still allow freedom of movement; a showerproof anorak with a hood is ideal as it can be washed and dried easily.

Choose clothes that are appropriate for the weather: for example, children need to be protected from the sun with wide-brimmed hats with neck shields; they need warm gloves, scarves and woolly or fleece hats in cold, windy weather, and waterproof coats and footwear when out in the rain.

Caring for children's clothes

When caring for clothes, you should:

- look at the laundry care labels on each garment and make sure that you are familiar with the different symbols

- check and empty all pockets before laundering
- be guided by the parents regarding choice of washing powder – some detergents can cause an adverse skin reaction in some children
- dry clothes thoroughly before putting them away
- label children's clothes with name tapes before they go into group settings.

Guidelines: changing nappies in a group setting

Nappy changing is an important time and you should ensure that the baby feels secure and happy. Chatting and singing should be built in to the procedure to make it an enjoyable experience. Each setting will have its own procedure for changing nappies. The following is an example.

- Nappies should be checked and changed at regular periods throughout the day.
- A baby should never knowingly be left in a soiled nappy.
- Collect the nappy and the cream needed. Put on apron and gloves. Ensure you have warm water and wipes.
- Carefully put the baby on the changing mat, talking to and reassuring him or her.
- Afterwards, dispose of the nappy and discard the gloves.
- Thoroughly clean the nappy mat and the apron with an antibacterial spray.
- Wash your hands to avoid cross-contamination.
- Record the nappy change on the baby's nappy chart, noting the time, whether it was wet or dry, whether there had been a bowel movement. Note any change you have observed – for example, in the colour or consistency of the stools – or if the baby had difficulty in passing the stool. Also note whether there is any skin irritation or rash present.
- Check nappy mats for any tears or breaks in the fabric and replace if necessary.
- **Never** leave a baby or toddler unsupervised on the changing mat.

The health and safety requirements when working with children from birth to age five years are covered in Unit 3. The principles of effective communication when working with families and their children are discussed in Unit 5.

The importance of routines

Key term

Routine – The usual way tasks or activities are arranged.

One aspect of children's need for love and security is the need for **routine** and predictability. This is why having daily routines is so important in all aspects of child care. By meeting children's need for routine, parents and carers are helping the child to:

- feel acknowledged
- feel independent
- increase self-esteem.

Routines – for example, around mealtimes and bedtimes – can be very useful in helping babies and toddlers to adapt both physically and emotionally to a daily pattern; this will suit both them and those caring for them. It will prove especially helpful during times of **transition** and change in their lives, such as starting nursery or moving house. If certain parts of the day remain familiar, they can cope better with new experiences. Having routines for everyday activities also ensures that care is consistent and of a high quality.

All settings that provide care and education for children have **routines** for daily activities. This does not mean that every day is the same; rather, it means that there is a recognised structure to the child's day – one that will help children to feel secure and safe. Such routines include:

- hygiene – changing nappies and toileting older children; ensuring there is a hand-washing routine after messy activities, and before eating and drinking
- health and safety – tidying away toys and activity equipment; making regular checks on equipment for hazards
- safety at home times and trips away from the setting – ensuring there is a correct ratio of adults to children, permission from parents and contact numbers, etc.
- meal and snack times – serving of meals and drinks under close supervision (see Unit 7)
- sleep and rest
- outdoor play.

Supporting hygiene routines and encouraging independence

All children benefit from regular routines in daily care. You need to encourage them to become independent by helping them to learn how to take care of themselves. Ways of helping children to become independent include:

- teaching them how to wash and dry their hands before eating or drinking
- making sure that they always wash and dry their hands after going to the toilet and after playing outdoors

- providing children with their own combs and brushes, and encouraging them to use them every day
- providing a soft toothbrush, and teaching children how and when to brush their teeth
- ensuring that you are a good role model for children – for example, when you cough or sneeze, always cover your mouth
- devise activities that develop an awareness in children of the importance of hygiene routines – for example, you could invite a dental hygienist or dental nurse to the setting to talk to children about daily tooth care
- make sure that children are provided with a healthy diet and that there are opportunities for activity, rest and sleep throughout the nursery or school day.

Planning routines to meet individual needs

Anyone looking after children should be able to adapt to their individual needs, which will change from day to day. You therefore need to be flexible in your approach and allow, whenever feasible, the individual child to set the pattern for the day – as long as all the child's needs are met. Obviously, parents and carers have their own routines and hygiene practices, and these should always be respected. (For example, Muslims prefer to wash under running water and Rastafarians wear their hair braided so may not use a comb or brush.)

Whenever you are caring for children, you should always treat each child as an individual. This means that you should be aware of their individual needs at all times.

- Sometimes a child may have special or additional needs.
- Children may need specialist equipment or extra help with play activities.
- Routines may need to be adapted to take into account individual needs and preferences.

In practice

Everyday routines for babies and young children

- Be patient – even when pressed for time, try to show children that you are relaxed and unhurried. Allow time for children to experiment with different ways of doing things.
- If you work directly with parents, encourage them to make a little extra time in the morning and evening for children to dress and undress themselves. Children could be encouraged to choose their clothes the night before from a limited choice (the choosing of clothes to wear is often fertile ground for disagreements and battles of will).
- Resist the urge to take over if children are struggling, since this deprives them of the sense of achievement and satisfaction of success.
- Show children how to do something and then let them get on with it. If they ask for help, they should be shown again. If adults keep doing things for children that they could do for themselves, they are in danger of creating 'learned helplessness'.
- Offer praise and encouragement when children are trying hard, not just when they succeed in a task.

Supporting children through transitions

A transition is a passage of change from one stage or state to another. Children naturally pass through a number of stages as they grow and develop. Often, they will also be expected to cope with changes such as movement from nursery education to primary school, and from primary to secondary school. You may have just made the transition from secondary school to a tertiary college or sixth form. Along with the excitement of a new course and possibly making new friends, you are likely to have felt some apprehension about the change to your life. This is likely to affect you more if you have experienced many changes in your life.

These changes are commonly referred to as **transitions**. Some children may have to cope with personal transitions that – unlike the transition to school at a certain age – are not necessarily shared or understood by all their peers.

You need to be able to identify transitions and understand what you can do to support children through them. Before we can fully understand the importance of transitions in children's lives, we need to explore the concepts of attachment, separation and loss.

Attachment

Attachment means a warm, affectionate and supportive bond between a child and his or her carer, which enables the child to develop **secure relationships**. When children receive warm, responsive care, they feel safe and secure.

- Secure attachments are the basis of all the child's future relationships. Because babies experience relationships through their senses, it is the expression of love that affects how they develop and that helps to shape later learning and behaviour.
- Children who are securely attached will grow to be more curious, get along better with other children and perform better in school than children who are less securely attached.
- With children who have a strong attachment to their parent or primary carer, the process of becoming attached to the **key person** is easier, not harder, than it is for children with a weaker attachment. Remember, though, that all parents find separation difficult, whether they have formed a strong attachment with their child or not.

Key term

Key person system – A system within a nursery setting in which care of each child is assigned to a particular adult, known as the key person. The role of the key person is to develop a special relationship with the child, in order to help the child to feel safe and secure in the nursery. The key person will also liaise closely with each child's parents.

Figure 2.5 Babies need to have a strong attachment with their primary carers

The role of the key person

Each family is given a key person at nursery who gets to know them well, and this helps everyone to feel safe. A baby or young child knows that this special person and the important people at home often do the same things for them:

- they help you manage through the day
- they think about you
- they get to know you well
- they sometimes worry about you
- they get to know each other
- they talk about you.

The Sure Start programme makes a distinction between the **key worker** role and the **key person** role. The term 'key worker' is often used in nurseries to describe how staff work, to ensure liaison between different professionals, and to enhance smooth organisation and record-keeping. The key person role is defined as a special emotional relationship with the child and the family.

Separation

Many of the times which are difficult for children have to do with separation. Going to bed is separation from the main carer and is often a source of anxiety in children. Some young children can be terrified as a parent walks out of the room. How children react to separation is as varied as children are themselves. For some children, each new situation will bring questions and new feelings of anxiety. Other children love the challenge of meeting new friends and seeing new things.

Loss

Children who have had to make many moves or changes may feel a sense of loss and grief. These changes may have a profound effect on their emotional and social development. Reasons for transitions include the following.

- **Divorce or separation:** children whose parents have separated or divorced may have to live and get along with several 'new' people (e.g. stepfathers, stepmothers, half-brothers and sisters).

- **Changes in child care arrangements:** children may experience many different child care arrangements (e.g. frequent changes from one nanny or childminder to another).
- **Children who are in local authority care –** either in residential children's homes or in foster care.
- Children whose families have moved house several times – for example, for employment reasons, or as Travellers.

How transitions may affect children's development and behaviour

Children who have experienced multiple transitions need to feel supported each time they enter a new setting. They may feel:

- **disorientated** – no sooner have they settled in one place and got to know a carer than they may be uprooted and have to face the same process again
- **a sense of loss** – each time they make a move, they lose the friends they have made and also the attachments they have formed with their carers
- **withdrawn** – children may withdraw from new relationships with other children and with carers, because they do not trust that the separation will not happen again.

As children become older, they start to cope better with being separated from their parents or main carers; however, the way they cope will still depend on their early experiences of separation and how earlier transitions were managed. Children who have had to change schools many times – maybe because of a parent's job being changed – often find it harder to settle in and make new friends and relationships.

How to support children through transitions

The first few days at a nursery or playgroup can be very daunting for some children. They may not have been left by their parents or primary carers ever

before, and some children will show real distress. You need to be able to recognise their distress and find ways of dealing with it. Children show their distress at being separated from their carer by crying and refusing to join in with activities. Parents too can feel distressed when leaving their children in the care of others; they may feel guilty because they have to return to work, or they may be upset because they have never before been separated from their child.

You can help a child to settle in by following the suggestions given below.

1 **Trying to plan for the separation**: nursery staff can help by visiting the child and their parents at home. This gives both parents and children the opportunity to talk about their fears and helps them to cope with them. When children know in advance what is going to happen and not happen, they can think about and get used to their feelings about it. Parents can be encouraged to prepare their child for the change by:
   - *visiting the nursery with their child so that they can meet the staff*
   - *reading books about starting at a nursery or going to hospital, and*
   - *involving their child in any preparation, such as buying clothing or packing a 'nursery bag'.*

2 Encouraging parents to stay with their child until the child asks them to leave: this does not mean that the parents should cling to their child. Children can always sense a parent's uncertainty. Although young children do not have a very good sense of time, parents and carers should make it very clear when they will be back (e.g. saying 'I'll be back in one hour').

3 Allowing the child to bring a comforter – for example, a blanket or a teddy bear – to the nursery. If it is a blanket, sometimes the parent can cut a little piece and put it in the child's pocket if they think there will be any embarrassment. Then the child can handle the blanket and feel comforted when feeling lonely. This object is often called a transitional object as it helps the child to make the transition from being dependent on family for comfort to being able to comfort him- or herself.

4 Having just one person to settle the child: hold and cuddle the child and try to involve him or her in a quiet activity with you (e.g. reading a story). Most child care settings now employ a key person who will be responsible for one or two children during the settling-in period.

5 Contacting the parent or primary carer if the child does not settle within 20 minutes or so. Sometimes it is not possible to do this, and you will need to devise strategies for comforting and reassuring the child. Always be honest with parents regarding the time it took to settle their child.

Figure 2.6 Child using a comfort object

Other transitions

Where children are facing other transitions or changes in their lives – such as bereavement or loss, or the arrival of a new sibling – their key person will need to be especially sensitive to their feelings and always take time to talk with them about how they are feeling. Opportunities should be provided for children to express their feelings in a safe and unthreatening environment. For example, some children may be encouraged to use play dough to release pent-up feelings of frustration; others may choose to use role-play.

Reflective practice

Thinking about your own behaviour

Reflect on your practice by asking yourself the following questions:

- Do I know why the child is behaving as he or she is?
- Have I considered the child's needs? Is he or she tired, hungry, or simply needing a hug?
- Have I talked with and listened to the child?
- Have I been consistent in dealing with unacceptable behaviour, and set a positive role model?
- Would it be appropriate for a child to say or do what I have just done?
- Is there anything I could change in the physical environment to create a more relaxed, comfortable environment, one that is conducive to meeting the child's needs?

Key terms

Transition – Any significant stage or experience in the life of a child that can affect his or her behaviour and/or development.

Transitional object – Often a soft toy or blanket to which a child becomes attached, a transitional object is used by a child to provide comfort and security while he or she is away from a secure base, such as mother or home.

Reflective practice

Comfort objects

Do you remember having a special comfort object? What did this object mean to you? Using examples from your settings, discuss how, in early childhood, such objects help to comfort young children coping with separation and transitions.

In practice

Helping children to settle in

This activity will help a child who is new to the setting to realise that he or she is not alone, and that other children also feel shy and alone at times.

- **Introduction**: choose a teddy and introduce him to the group, saying something like 'Teddy is rather shy and a little bit lonely. How can we help him to feel better?'
- **Discussion and display**: take photos of Teddy – using a digital camera if possible – with different groups of children, and in different places in the nursery (e.g. playing in the sand, reading a book, doing a puzzle), and use them later for discussion and display.
- **Circle time**: in circle time, pass Teddy round and encourage each child to say something to him – for example, 'Hello Teddy, my name is Lara' or 'Hello Teddy, I like chocolate ...'.
- **Taking teddy home**: each child takes it in turns to take Teddy home. Include a notebook and encourage parents to write a few sentences about what Teddy did at their house that evening. The children can draw a picture.
- **Story time**: read and act out the story of 'Goldilocks and the Three Bears', with the different-sized bowls, beds and chairs.
- **Cooking**: use a shaped cutter to make teddy-shaped biscuits or dough teddies.
- **Teddy bears' picnic**: arrange a teddy bears' picnic where each child brings in a favourite bear – 'What does your teddy like to eat?', 'Are there enough plates, biscuits and cups for all the bears?'
- You can probably think of many more teddy-related ideas that will help children gain a sense of belonging.

In practice

Transitions

How does your setting help children to cope with transitions? Does it have a settling-in policy? Find out how children new to the setting are helped to separate from their parents or carers.

Assessment practice (1)

Observing social needs

1. In your work placement, plan to observe an individual child's social needs during a whole session. Make a checklist that includes the following needs.
   - Interaction with other children: observe how the child plays – for example, does he or she play alone (**solitary play**), alongside others but not with them (**parallel play**), or actively with other children?
   - **Attention from adults:** does the child seek attention from one particular adult, or from any adult? Note the number of occasions a child seeks adult attention and describe the interaction.
   - **Self-help skills and independence:** observe the child using self-help skills (e.g. putting on coat to go outside, washing hands and going to the lavatory).

2. Identify the stage of social development the child is passing through and list the ways in which you can ensure that their social needs are met within the setting.

Assessment practice (2)

Transitions

1. Explain what is meant by the term 'transition'. Why is it important to be able to identify when a child is going through a transition?

2. Describe the different transitions that a child may experience. Give examples of how each type of transition might affect the child.

3. Explain how you could support a child through a transition phase.

3 Safe, healthy and nurturing environments for children: Unit 3

This Unit teaches you about the preparation and maintenance of a safe environment and how to safeguard children and adults through working practices. It also describes your role in managing conflict when working with children.

Learning outcomes

During this unit you will learn about:

1. How to prepare and maintain a safe environment and follow relevant policies and procedures.

2. How to implement working practices that safeguard children and the adults who work with them.

3. The role of the practitioner in working with children to manage conflict.

Preparing and maintaining a safe environment and following relevant policies and procedures

Health and safety legislation and policy aim to make sure that all workers, children and families are safe and protected from harm when in work or using services. You do not need to be an expert in this area, but you should be aware of the legal issues and national and local guidance relating to health and safety, and know where to go and who to ask for advice and support.

Health and safety legislation

The most relevant laws relating to health and safety in settings for children in the UK are listed in Table 3.1.

There are a number of documents giving guidance on safe practices when working with children and parents. The most relevant document is the *Guidance for Safe Working Practice for the Protection of Children and Staff in Education Settings* (2005). Although the focus is on those working in education, much of the guidance provides useful advice for practitioners working in a non-education setting.

Policies and procedures

Every child care and education setting will have **policy documents** covering such areas as:

- safety
- health and hygiene
- safety at arrival and departure times, and on outings
- prevention of illness and provision of first aid
- fire prevention
- staffing ratios and supervision.

In group settings, a member of staff is usually nominated as being responsible for health and safety. In a childminder's home or if you are working as a nanny, you can contact the local Childminding Association or nanny agency for information on health and safety.

Lines of responsibility and reporting

Your setting's health and safety policy will contain the names of staff members responsible for health and safety. All practitioners are responsible for health and safety in any setting.

Your responsibilities include:

- taking reasonable care for your own safety and that of others
- working with your employer in respect of health and safety matters

Health and safety legislation

Health and Safety at Work Act 1974

Employers have a duty to:
- make your workplace as safe as they are able to
- display a Health and Safety Law poster or supply employees with a leaflet with the same information. This is available from the Health and Safety Executive.
- decide how to manage health and safety. If the business has five or more employees, this must appear on a written Health and Safety Policy.

As an employee, you have a duty to:
- work safely. If you are given guidance about how to use equipment, you should follow that guidance. You should not work in a way that puts other people in danger.

Control of Substances Hazardous to Health Regulations 1994 (COSHH)

Things such as bleach or dishwasher powders, some solvent glues and other materials in your setting can be hazardous. You should have a risk assessment that tells you what these things are and what to do to minimise the risks involved. Any new person coming to the team must be made aware of what to do.

Fire Precautions (Workplace) Regulations 1997

Fire Officers must check all child care premises while they are in the first registration process. They will advise what is needed to make the workplace as safe as possible.
- Evacuation procedures should be in place, known to all the adults, and practised regularly using all available exits at different times, so that everyone can leave the building quickly and safely if an emergency occurs.
- Some exits may be locked to prevent children wandering away or intruders entering, but adults must, in the case of an emergency, quickly open them.
- Designated fire exits must always be unlocked and kept unobstructed. Fire extinguishers should be in place and checked regularly. A fire blanket is needed in the kitchen.

Reporting of Injuries, Diseases and Dangerous Occurrences Regulations 1995 (RIDDOR)

An accident book must be kept in which incidents that happen to staff are recorded. If an incident occurs at work that is serious enough to keep an employee off work for three or more days, employers will need to fill in the relevant paperwork and send the report to the Health and Safety Executive. They may investigate serious incidents and give advice on how to improve practice if needed.

Childcare Act 2006, Regulation of Care (Scotland) Act 2001 and National Standards

The Care Standards Act 2000 sets out 14 minimum standards that settings for children must meet. The different inspectorates – Ofsted (in England), HMIe (in Scotland), Estyn (in Wales) and ETI (in Northern Ireland) – are responsible for registering nurseries, childminders, playgroups, after-school clubs, crèches and play schemes.

Health and Safety (First Aid) Regulations 1981

Employers should make sure that at least one person at each session has an up-to-date first aid qualification and is the 'Appointed' first aider. In settings regulated by Ofsted, HMIe, Estyn or ETI there is also a requirement for a staff member to be trained in 'Paediatric First Aid'. Methods of dealing with incidents for adults and children are not the same, particularly where resuscitation is involved. Recommendations also change. For this reason, first aid qualifications must be renewed every three years.

Health and safety legislation (cont.)

Personal Protective Equipment at Work Regulations 1992

Under these regulations, employers must make sure that suitable protective equipment is provided for employees who are exposed to a risk to their health and safety while at work. This is considered a last resort, for the risk should be prevented wherever possible. In children's settings, the most important piece of personal protective equipment that is provided will be gloves, to be used when dealing with body fluids. Employees and learners should be made aware of the need to use these when changing nappies or dealing with blood spillage or vomit. Good hygiene protects both adults and children.

Food Handling Regulations 1995

If you prepare or handle food, even something as basic as opening biscuits or preparing food for a snack, you need to comply with Food Handling Regulations. These cover what might be seen as common-sense things:
- Washing your hands before preparing food
- Making sure the surfaces and utensils you use are clean and hygienic
- Making sure food is stored safely at the correct temperature
- Disposing of waste hygienically.

They also include knowledge of safe practices in the use of chopping boards, having separate sinks for hand washing and preparing foods, how to lay out a kitchen, and so on. There should always be people who have completed a Basic Food Hygiene certificate available to ensure guidance is properly carried out.

Table 3.1 Health and safety legislation

- knowing about the policies and procedures in your particular place of work – these can all be found in the setting's health and safety policy documents
- not intentionally damaging any health and safety equipment or materials provided by the employer
- reporting all accidents, incidents and even 'near misses' to your manager. As you may be handling food, you should also report any incidences of sickness or diarrhoea
- reporting any hazards immediately you come across them.

Apart from your legal responsibilities, knowing how to act, and being alert and vigilant at all times, can prevent accidents, injury, infections and even death – this could be in relation to you, your fellow workers, or the children in your care.

The emergency procedures followed in a range of settings

How to respond when a child or young person is ill or injured

The responsibility of caring for a child who becomes ill is enormous; it is vital that carers should know the signs and symptoms of illness and when to seek medical aid. When a child is taken ill or is injured, it is vital that the parents or guardians are notified as soon as possible. If a child becomes ill while at nursery, he or she may have to wait a while to be taken home; meanwhile:

- offer support and reassurance to the child, who may feel frightened or anxious
- always notify a senior member of staff if you notice that a child is unwell; that person will then decide if and when to contact the child's parents
- a member of staff – preferably the child's key person – should remain with the child all the time and keep them as comfortable as possible
- deal with any incident of vomiting or diarrhoea swiftly and sympathetically to minimise the child's distress and to preserve their dignity.

All child care settings have an exclusion policy that lets parents know when it is safe for their sick child to return to the nursery or group.

What to do in case of serious illness or injury

- **Call for help**: Stay calm and do not panic! Your line manager or designated first aider will make an assessment and decide whether the injury or illness requires **medical help**, either a GP or an ambulance. He or she will also **contact the parents** to let them know about the nature of the illness or injury.

- **Stay with the child** and comfort and reassure him or her.
- **Treat the injury or assess the severity of the illness** and treat appropriately. You are not expected to be able to diagnose a sudden illness, but should know what signs and symptoms require medical treatment.
- **Record exactly what happens** and what treatment is carried out.

What to do when an accident happens

If a child has had an accident, they are likely to be shocked and may not always cry immediately. They will need calm reassurance as **first aid** is given, together with an explanation of what is being done to them and why. Parents must be informed and the correct procedures for the setting carried out. If the child needs emergency hospital treatment, parental permission will be needed.

If you work in a setting with others such as a day care facility or school, there is likely to be a designated person who is qualified in first aid, and they should be called to deal with the situation.

Remember! It is essential that you do not make the situation worse. It is better to do the minimum to ensure the child's safety such as putting them into the **recovery position**. The only exception to this is if the child is not breathing or there is no heartbeat.

Recognising the need for urgent medical attention

A child who has sustained a serious injury or illness will need to be seen urgently by a doctor. Serious conditions include:

- a head injury or any loss of consciousness
- a wound that continues to bleed after first aid treatment is given
- fracture or suspected fracture, burns and scalds, foreign bodies

- life-threatening incidents: for example, seizures, poisoning, choking, **anaphylaxis**, loss of consciousness, respiratory and cardiac arrest.

How to get emergency help

- **Assess the situation:** stay calm and do not panic.
- **Minimise any danger to yourself and to others** – for example, make sure someone takes charge of other children at the scene.
- **Send for help:** notify a doctor, hospital, parents, etc. as appropriate. If in any doubt, call an ambulance: dial 999.
- Be ready to assist the emergency services by answering some simple questions:
  a) your name and the telephone number you are calling from
  b) the location of the accident – try to give as much information as possible (familiar landmarks such as churches or pubs nearby)
  c) explain briefly what has happened – this helps the paramedics to act speedily when they arrive
  d) tell them what you have done so far to treat the casualty.

What to do in the event of a non-medical incident or emergency

There are many different types of emergency (apart from a medical emergency when a person is seriously injured or ill), and it is important to know what procedures to follow; for example:

- if a child goes missing
- in case of fire
- if there is a security incident.

Missing children

Strict procedures must be followed to prevent a child from going missing from the setting. However, if a child *does* go missing, a procedure must be followed; for example:

1 The person in charge will carry out a thorough search of the building and garden.
2 The register is checked to make sure no other child has also gone astray.

3 Doors and gates are checked to see if there has been a breach of security whereby a child could wander out.

4 The person in charge talks to staff to establish what happened.

5 If the child is not found, the parent is contacted and the missing child is reported to the police.

Case Study — Missing from a nursery

A two-year-old girl walked out of her pre-school nursery one winter morning, leaving her coat behind, and crossed a busy road as she wandered half a mile to her home. The first that the nursery knew of her disappearance was when her furious father turned up demanding to know why he had found his tearful daughter struggling to open their garden gate.

Fortunately, potentially dangerous events like this are very rare, but they should be preventable.

1. How do you think that this could have happened?

2. Consider your own setting and assess whether it could happen there.

3. How could such incidents be prevented?

In case of fire

In the case of fire or other emergency, you need to know what to do to safely **evacuate** the children and yourselves. Follow these rules for fire safety:

- Smoking is not allowed in any child care setting.
- Handbags containing matches or lighters must be locked securely away out of children's reach.
- The cooker should not be left unattended when turned on.
- Fire exits must be clearly signed.
- Fire drills should be carried out regularly; registers must be kept up to date throughout the day.
- Fire exits and other doors should be free of obstructions on both sides.
- Instructions about what to do in the event of a fire must be clearly displayed.

- You should know where the fire extinguishers are kept and how to use them.
- Electrical equipment should be regularly checked for any faults.

Evacuation procedures

A plan for an escape route and the attendance register must be up to date so that everyone – children and staff – can safely be accounted for at the meeting point of safety. The attendance record must be taken by the person in charge when the building is evacuated. Clearly written instructions for fire drills and how to summon the fire brigade must be posted in a conspicuous place in the setting.

Security issues and violence

Early years settings and schools should be secure environments where children cannot wander off without anyone realising. But they also need to be secure so that strangers cannot enter without a good reason for being there. Occasionally you might encounter a problem with violence – or threats of violence – from a child's parents or carers. Your setting will have a policy that deals with this issue.

First aid for babies and children

Most employers expect specialised training and qualifications in first aid to be completed by employees, in line with legislation. There are now specialist courses, such as St John Ambulance's **Early Years First Aid** and the British Red Cross's **First Aid for Child Carers**. The Sure Start Childcare Approval Scheme for nannies requires candidates to hold a relevant Paediatric First Aid Certificate.

Once you have learned how to respond to an emergency you never lose that knowledge, and knowing how means that you could save a life one day.

First aid for an infant and a child who is unresponsive and breathing normally

A child's heart and/or breathing can stop as a result of lack of oxygen (e.g. choking), drowning, electric shock, heart attack or other serious injury. If an infant or child has collapsed, you need first to find out if he is conscious or unconscious.

1   **Can you get a response**? Check if conscious.
    * For an infant: *Call their name and try tapping them gently on the sole of their foot.*
    * For a child: *Call their name and try tapping them gently on their shoulders.*
2   If there is no response you need to **check for breathing**. *For both infants and children:*
    * **Open the airway:** *Place one hand on the forehead and* gently *tilt the head back. Then using your other hand lift the child's chin. Take a quick look and remove any* visible *obstructions from the mouth and nose.*
    * **Look, listen and feel** *for normal breathing: Place your face next to the child's face and listen for breathing. You can do this while looking along the child's chest and abdomen for any movement. You may also be able to feel the child's breath on your cheek. Allow up to ten seconds to check if the child is breathing or not.*
3   If the infant or child is unconscious but breathing normally, place him or her into **the recovery position** – see below.

The recovery position

If a child is unconscious this means that they have no muscle control; if lying on their back, their tongue is floppy and may fall back, partially obstructing the airway. Any child who is breathing and who has a pulse should be placed in the recovery position while you wait for medical assistance. This safe position allows fluid and vomit to drain out of the child's mouth so that they are not inhaled into the lungs.

Recovery position for an infant (from birth to one year approx.)

Cradle the infant in your arms, with his head tilted downwards to prevent him from choking on his tongue or inhaling vomit.

Recovery position for a child (from one year onwards)

1   Place arm nearest to you at a right angle, with palm facing up.
2   Move other arm towards you, keeping the back of the child's hand against their cheek.
3   Get hold of the knee furthest from you and pull up until foot is flat on the floor.
4   Pull the knee towards you, keeping the child's hand pressed against their cheek.
5   Position the leg at a right angle.
6   Make sure that the airway remains open by tilting the head back, then check breathing by feeling and listening for breath.

In practice

The recovery position

In pairs, practise placing each other in the recovery position you would use for a child.

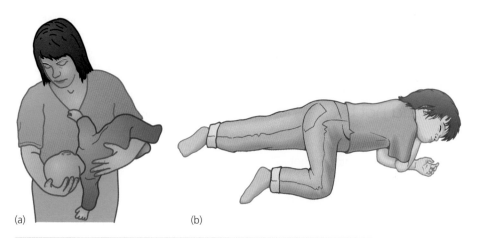

(a)   (b)

Figure 3.1 (a) The recovery position for an infant (b) The recovery position for a child

Continuous assessment and monitoring of an infant and a child while in your care

Remember your **ABC** and continue to monitor the infant or child in your care until you can hand over to a doctor or paramedic.

A is for AIRWAY: Check that the airway remains open. Always monitor a child while in the recovery position.

B is for BREATHING: Check that breathing is normal and regular.

C is for CIRCULATION: Check the pulse (*if you are trained and experienced*) **but ensure you take no more than ten seconds to do this:**

- *In a child over one year*: feel for the carotid pulse in the neck by placing your fingers in the groove between the Adam's apple and the large muscle running from the side of the neck.
- *In an infant*: feel for the brachial pulse on the inner aspect of the upper arm by lightly pressing your fingers towards the bone on the inside of the upper arm, and hold them there for five seconds.

Remember: Try to use your second and third fingers when taking a pulse. This is because both your first finger and your thumb have a pulse that can be confused with the casualty's pulse.

In practice

Taking the pulse

In pairs, practise taking each other's pulse – both the *radial* pulse – at the wrist – and the *carotid* pulse in the neck.

First aid for an infant or a child who is unresponsive and not breathing normally

An infant or child who is unresponsive and not breathing normally will need to be given CPR (cardio-pulmonary resuscitation). CPR is a combination of rescue breaths and chest compressions. This keeps the vital organs alive until the ambulance service arrives and starts advanced life support.

Send for help: If you have carried out the checks above and the child is not breathing normally, if you have someone with you, send them to **dial 999** for an ambulance immediately. If you are alone, give one minute of CPR – *then* call an ambulance. If the casualty is under one year, take the infant with you to call an ambulance.

CPR: Resuscitation for an infant who is not breathing (from birth to one year)

- **Open the airway** by gently tilting the infant's head back and lifting the chin.
- Give FIVE **rescue breaths** by placing your mouth over their **mouth and nose,** and blow gently for about one second, until you see the chest rise.
- Place two fingers on the centre of the infant's chest, and give 30 **chest compressions** by pressing down about a third of the depth.
- Then give TWO rescue breaths, followed by 30 chest compressions.
- Continue this cycle of breaths and compressions for one minute.

If not already done, **call for an ambulance** now and continue the above cycle until help arrives or the infant starts to breathe.

CPR: Resuscitation for a child who is not breathing (from one year onwards)

- **Open the airway** by gently tilting the child's head back and lifting the chin.
- Pinch the child's nose. Give FIVE **rescue breaths** by placing your mouth over their mouth and blow steadily until you see the chest rise.
- Place one hand on the centre of the child's chest and lean over the child. Give 30 **chest compressions** by pressing down about a third of the depth of the chest.
- Then give TWO rescue breaths, followed by 30 chest compressions.
- Continue this cycle of breaths and compressions for one minute.

If not already done, **call for an ambulance** now and continue the above cycle until help arrives or the child starts to breathe.

When to administer CPR

CPR should only be carried out when an infant or child is unresponsive and not breathing normally.

If the infant or child has any signs of normal breathing, coughing or movement, **DO NOT** begin to do chest compressions. Doing so may cause the heart to stop beating.

How to administer CPR using an infant and a child manikin

The techniques of giving CPR should never be practised on a child. Infant and child manikins are designed to give a very close experience to the 'real thing' and should always be used to practise on.

Choking

Choking is when a child struggles to breathe because of a blockage in the airway. Children under three years are particularly vulnerable to choking because their airways are small and they have not yet developed full control of the muscles of their mouth and throat.

What causes it?

Usually, choking in small children is caused by a small foreign object blocking one of the major airways. This may be a small toy they have put in their mouth and inadvertently swallowed, or a small piece of food they have not chewed properly.

Symptoms

Choking often begins with small coughs or gasps as the child tries to draw in breath around the obstruction or clear it out. This may be followed by a struggling sound or squeaking whispers as the child tries to communicate their distress. The child may thrash around and drool, and their eyes may water. They may flush red and then turn blue. However, if a small item gets stuck in a baby or toddler's throat, you may not even *hear* them choking – they could be silently suffocating as the object fills their airway and prevents them from coughing or breathing.

If a child is choking, **ACT QUICKLY!**

1 **First check inside the child's mouth**: if the obstruction is visible, try to hook it out with your finger, but do not risk pushing it further down. *If this does not work …*
   - *For a baby: lay the baby face down along your forearm, supporting her head and neck with your hand. The baby's head should be lower than her bottom.*
   - *For an older baby or toddler: sit down and put the child face down across your knees with head and*

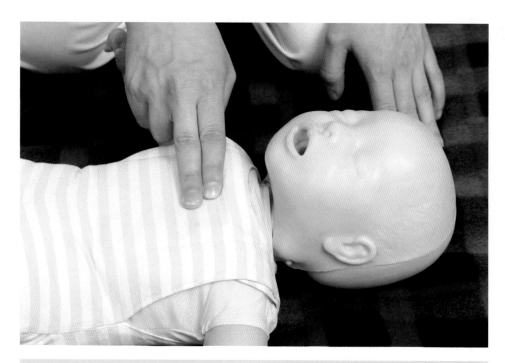

Figure 3.2 An infant resuscitation manikin

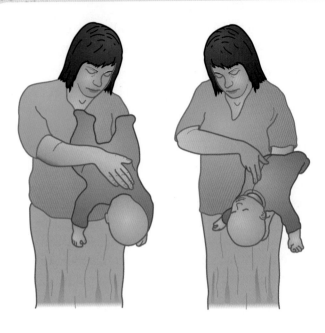

Figure 3.3 How to treat an infant or child who is choking

arms hanging down. Keep the child's head lower than the chest.

2 **Give five back blows** between the shoulder blades with the heel of your hand.

3 **Turn the child over**, check the mouth again and remove any visible obstruction.

4 Check for breathing.

5 If the child is not breathing, give **five 'rescue breaths'** (see ABC of resuscitation).

6 If the airway is still obstructed, give **five chest compressions**.

7 If the child is still not breathing, **repeat the cycle** of back slaps, mouth-to-mouth breathing and chest compressions.

After two cycles, if the child is not breathing, **dial 999 for an ambulance**.

(*Never* hold a baby upside down by the ankles and slap its back – you could break its neck.)

Bleeding: Cuts, grazes and nosebleeds

Even tiny amounts of blood can seem like a lot to a child. Any bleeding may frighten children because they are too young to realise that the blood loss will stop when clotting occurs. When a child loses a large amount of blood, he or she may suffer shock or even become unconscious.

Minor cuts and grazes

- Sit or lay the child down and reassure them.
- Clean the injured area with cold water, using cotton wool or gauze.
- Apply a dressing if necessary.
- Do not attempt to pick out pieces of gravel or grit from a graze. Just clean gently and cover with a light dressing.
- Record the injury and treatment in the **Accident Report Book** and make sure the parents/carers of the child are informed.

Nosebleeds

1 Sit the child down with her head well forward.

2 Ask her to breathe through her mouth.

3 Pinch the fleshy part of her nose, just below the bridge.

4 Reassure her, and tell her not to try to speak, cough or sniff as this may disturb blood clots.

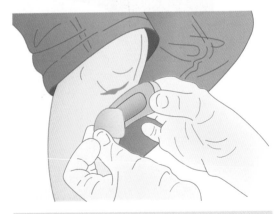

Figure 3.4 Treating a graze

5 After ten minutes, release the pressure. If the nose is still bleeding, reapply the pressure for further periods of ten minutes.

6 If the nosebleed persists beyond 30 minutes, seek medical aid.

Severe bleeding

When a child is bleeding severely, your main aim is to stem the flow of blood. If you have disposable gloves available, use them. It is important to reduce the risk of cross-infection.

1 **Summon medical help**: dial 999 or call a doctor.
2 Try to stop the bleeding:
   - **apply direct pressure to the wound**; wear gloves and use a dressing or a non-fluffy material, such as a clean tea towel
   - **elevate the affected part** if possible.
3 **Apply a dressing**. If the blood soaks through, *do not* remove the dressing, apply another on top, and so on.
4 Keep the child warm and reassure them.
5 *Do not* give anything to eat or drink.
6 Contact the child's parents or carers.

If the child loses consciousness, follow the ABC procedure for resuscitation.

Note: always record the incident, and the treatment given, in the Accident Report Book. Always wear disposable gloves if in an early years setting, to prevent cross-infection.

Minor burns and scalds

Burns occur when the skin is exposed to direct heat or to chemicals, for example fire, sunburn, friction, acid, bleach or garden chemicals. **Scalds** occur when the skin is exposed to hot fluids, for example boiling water, steam or hot fat.

1 **Cool down the area** by running it under cool water for at least ten minutes or until the pain eases – or soak in cold water for ten minutes. This will prevent the burn from getting worse.
2 **Gently remove any constricting articles** from the injured area before it begins to swell.
3 **Lightly cover the burned area** with a sterile dressing – or you can use cling film, a clean plastic bag or cold, wet cloth (but not wrapping). This will help to protect the sore skin from further irritation and infection.
4 Stay calm and watch for any **signs of shock**. If the child loses consciousness, open the airway, check her breathing and be prepared to begin rescue breaths.

DO NOT

- use adhesive dressings
- apply lotions, ointments or grease to burn or scald
- break blisters or otherwise interfere.

Sprains and strains

Follow the **RICE** procedure:

R – **rest** the injured part

I – apply **ice** or a cold compress

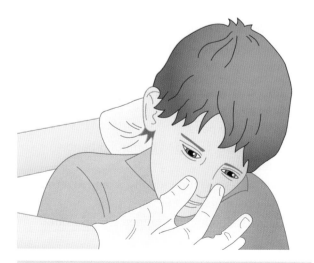

Figure 3.5 Treating a nosebleed

Figure 3.6 Treating a minor burn or scald

C – **compress** the injury

E – **elevate** the injured part.

1 Rest, steady and support the injured part in the most comfortable position for the child.
2 Cool the area by applying an ice pack or a cold compress. (This could be a pack of frozen peas wrapped in cloth.)
3 Apply gentle, even pressure by surrounding the area with a thick layer of foam or cotton wool, secured with a bandage.
4 Raise and support the injured limb, to reduce blood flow to the injury and to minimise bruising.

Understand your role and responsibility in reporting and recording accidents

Reporting to parents

All accidents, injuries or illnesses which occur to children in a group setting must be reported to the child's parents or primary carers. If the injury is minor – e.g. a bruise or a small graze to the knee – the nursery or school staff will inform parents when the child is collected at the end of the session; or they may send a notification slip home if the child is collected by someone else. The parents are notified about:

● the nature of the injury or illness
● any treatment or action taken
● the name of the person who carried out the treatment.

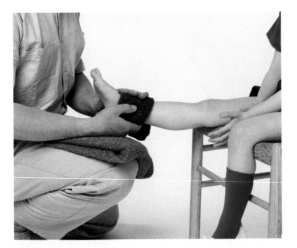

Figure 3.7 Elevate and apply a cold compress

In the case of a major accident, illness or injury then the child's parents or primary carers must be notified as soon as possible. Parents need to know that the staff are dealing with the incident in a caring and professional manner and to be involved in any decisions regarding treatment.

Accident Report Book

Every workplace is, by law, required to have an Accident Report Book and to maintain a record of accidents. Information recorded includes:

● name of person injured
● date and time of injury
● where the accident happened, e.g. in the garden
● what exactly happened, e.g. Kara fell on the path and grazed her left knee
● what injuries occurred, e.g. a graze
● what treatment was given, e.g. graze was bathed and an adhesive dressing applied
● name and signature of person dealing with the accident
● signature of witness to the report
● signature of parent or guardian.

One copy of the duplicated report form is given to the child's parent or carer; the other copy is kept in the Accident Report Book at the early years setting.

If you are working in the family home as a nanny, you should follow the same reporting procedure, even though you do not have an official Accident Report Book.

The first aid box

Every place of work must, by law, have an accessible first aid box with the following recommended basic contents:

● 20 individually wrapped sterile adhesive dressings – in assorted sizes
● two sterile eye pads
● six individually wrapped triangular bandages
● six safety pins
● six medium-sized individually wrapped sterile wound dressings
● two large individually wrapped sterile wound dressings
● three extra-large individually wrapped sterile wound dressings

- two pairs of disposable gloves
- one pair of blunt-ended scissors.

Large nurseries and schools may have more than one first aid box and the contents will vary according to individual needs; for example, a nursery setting will have a larger number of small adhesive dressings or plasters.

- The first aid box must be a strong container which keeps out both dirt and damp.
- It should be kept in an accessible place, but one that is out of reach of children.
- All employees should be informed where the first aid box is kept and it should only be moved from this safe place when in use.
- Supplies must be replaced as soon as possible after use.

Some first aid boxes also contain a small first aid manual or booklet.

 Progress check

First aid Revision Quiz

Choose the one correct answer to each of the following questions:

1. A child has a nosebleed. You should first:
   a) have her tilt her head back until it stops
   b) have her lean forward and pinch the bottom of her nose shut
   c) place ice on the bridge of her nose
2. The ABCs of first aid resuscitation are:
   a) Airway, Blood and Circulation
   b) Airway, Breathing and Circulation
   c) Airway, Breathing and Compressions
3. Strains and sprains should be treated initially by the RICE procedure:
   a) Rest, Ice, Compress and Elevate
   b) Rest, Ice, Compress and Examine
   c) Raise, Ice, Compress and Examine
4. What does the recovery position do?
   a) makes it easier to perform rescue breathing
   b) makes the casualty feel more comfortable
   c) keeps the tongue from blocking the throat
5. Which one of the following is true?
   a) Butter on a burn will help to heal it.
   b) Breathing into a paper bag will help the victim of a panic attack.
   c) A poisoned casualty should be encouraged to vomit.

6. A five-year-old child has a bad cut to the hand. What is the first thing you should do?
   a) Place your hand over their hand to apply pressure.
   b) Tell them to raise and put pressure on the area until you get your gloves out of the first aid box.
   c) Call 999 straight away.
7. A child in your care has scalded herself with a cup of hot coffee. The correct first aid measure is to:
   a) Cover the scalded area with a clean, non-fluffy dressing.
   b) Reassure the child and notify his parents.
   c) Immerse the scalded area in cold water.
8. When dealing with a bleeding wound, you should wear disposable gloves:
   a) if the child is, or you think may be, HIV positive
   b) every time a child is treated
   c) if the child has haemophilia
9. A child who you know has asthma is becoming breathless. You must first:
   a) Put the child in the recovery position.
   b) Dial 999 and ask for an ambulance.
   c) Sit the child down and reassure them.
10. A child has fallen over and grazed his knee. What would you use to clean a graze?
   a) soap and water applied with a sponge
   b) antiseptic and cotton wool
   c) antiseptic wipes

Answers to the quiz are on page 282.

How to identify risks in the setting

Children need a safe but challenging environment. Practically every human activity involves a certain degree of risk, and children need to learn how to cope with this. For example, when a child first learns to walk, he or she will inevitably fall over or knock into things. This is a valuable part of their learning and a natural part of their development.

Children who are sheltered or overprotected from risk and challenge when young will not be able to make judgements about their own strengths and skills, and will be poorly equipped to resist peer pressure in their later years. Also, a totally risk-free environment lacks challenges and stimulation; this leads inevitably to children becoming bored and displaying inappropriate behaviour. Simply being *told* about possible dangers is not enough: children need to see or experience the consequences of not taking care. An important aspect of teaching children about risk is to encourage them to make their own **risk assessments** and think about the possible consequences of their actions. Rather than removing objects and equipment from the environment in case children hurt themselves, adults should teach children how to use them safely. It is important to strike the right balance: protecting children from harm while allowing them the freedom to develop independence and risk awareness.

The risk assessment process

Risk assessment is a method of preventing accidents and ill health by helping people to think about what could go wrong and devising ways to prevent problems. The flow chart in Figure 3.8 shows how to carry out a risk assessment.

The most important factor in preventing accidents is you!

↓

Look for hazards

↓

Decide who might be harmed and how

↓

Weigh up the risk: a risk is the likelihood that a hazard will cause harm

↓

Decide whether existing precautions are enough

↓

If not, decide what further precautions are required to reduce the risk

↓

Record your findings

Figure 3.8 How to carry out a risk assessment

What is the difference between a risk and a hazard?

In the child care setting a hazard may be a substance, a piece of equipment, a work procedure or a child's condition. Examples of hazards in early years settings are shown in Table 3.2.

Hazards in child care settings	
Toys and play equipment	Chemical hazards, such as cleaning materials and disinfectants
Biological hazards, such as airborne and blood-borne infections	The handling and moving of equipment and of children
Unsupervised children	Security of entry points and exits
Administration of medicines	Visual or hearing impairment of children

Table 3.2 Hazards in child care settings

Hazards in child care settings

Key terms

Hazard – A source of potential harm or damage, or a situation with potential for harm or damage.

Risk – The possibility of suffering harm or loss; danger.

Risk assessment – The assessments that must be carried out in order to identify hazards and find out the safest way to carry out certain tasks and procedures.

Risk is defined as the chance or likelihood that harm will occur from the hazard. The likelihood is described as 'the expectancy of harm occurring'. It can range from 'never' to 'certain' and depends on a number of factors.

Example 1: A door

The main entrance to a nursery or primary school may present a **hazard**. The **risks** are that:

- a child might escape and run into the road, or go missing, or
- a stranger might enter the building.

The likelihood of the **hazard** of the entrance/ door posing a **risk** will depend on a number of factors:

- the security of the entrance – can it only be opened by using a key pad or entry phone system, and is the door handle placed high up, out of a child's reach?
- policies and procedures being known to parents and other visitors, for example at collection times.

Example 2: A damaged or uneven floor surface

This may present a **hazard**. The **risk** is that someone may trip over and become injured.

The likelihood of the **hazard** of the damaged floor posing a **risk** will depend on a number of factors:

- the extent of the unevenness or damage
- the number of people walking over it
- the number of times they walk over it
- whether they are wearing suitable footwear
- the level of lighting.

Safe working practices: Protecting children from common hazards

All areas where children play and learn should be checked for hygiene and safety at the start of every session and again at the end of each session – but do be alert at all times. Look at your setting's written **policy** for health and hygiene issues. Find out from your manager how to clean toys and other equipment, and remember that many objects (plastic toys and soft toys) end up in children's mouths, which is a way of passing on and picking up an infection.

Remember that *you* could also be a risk to children's health. For example, if you have a heavy cold or have suffered from diarrhoea or vomiting within the previous 24 hours, you must not attend for work as you could pass on a serious infection to the children.

The indoor and outdoor setting should be made as accident-proof as possible. Remember that playing should be fun and is an important part of growing up. Your role is to make sure that it stays fun and does not lead to a serious accident.

The following guidelines apply both to the home setting and to nursery and other group settings:

Guidelines: for playing safely indoors

- Try to keep very young children out of the kitchen, even when an adult is there.
- Put them in a playpen or high chair if there is no alternative; or you could try putting a stair gate in the doorway.
- Put safety film over glass doors and beware of children playing rough-and-tumble games near glass doors or low windows.
- Encourage children not to play on the stairs or in the main walkways in group settings.

In a flat or maisonette

- Always supervise children on balconies – they may be tempted to climb up or over the railings.

Playing with toys

- Keep toys and other clutter off the floor so that no one trips up; use a toy box such as a large, strong cardboard box.
- Choose toys suitable for the child's age and stage of development. Keep toys for older children away from younger brothers or sisters to prevent them from choking on small parts. Follow the manufacturer's instructions.
- Check the toys in family homes and group settings. Go through the toy box regularly and clear out any broken and damaged toys. Do not hand them on to jumble sales or charity shops, where they could cause injury to another child.

Guidelines: for playing safely outdoors

If there is a garden or outdoor play area:

- Make sure the children cannot get out on their own: block up gaps in the fence and keep the gates locked.
- Set up garden toys properly and check they are stable with no loose nuts and bolts.
- Have something soft under climbing frames – regularly watered grass is fine, but dried earth can be as hard as concrete.
- Watch children at all times in the paddling pool and empty it straight away after use.
- Remember, small children can drown in just a few inches of water.
- Cover, fence off or fill in the garden pond to keep small children away.

Playgrounds are good places for children to run around and play, but some are safer than others. You should always:

- Teach children to use the equipment properly – make sure they understand your instructions; for example, teach children never to run in front of or behind children using swings.
- Keep a close eye on very young children at all times.
- Avoid old, damaged or vandalised equipment which could hurt a child.
- Keep to playgrounds with safety surfaces.
- Check for rubbish such as broken glass or even syringes, particularly if young people or adults meet there. (If these problems persist, contact the playground owners.)
- Watch out for nearby hazards such as roads and streams.
- Provide appropriate supervision for children, being especially vigilant when caring for children with additional needs, for example, those with mobility problems or a visual impairment.
- Whenever children are **playing with or near water** – even indoors at the water play area – they must be supervised at all times.

Guidelines: Safety and hygiene – checking equipment regularly

- **Floors and surfaces**: floors and surfaces must be checked for cleanliness.
- **Plastic toys**: throw out any plastic toys that have cracks or splits in them, as these cracks can harbour germs; also check for splits and cracks when you clean them; plastic toys such as Duplo bricks should be washed weekly.
- **Metal equipment**: check tricycles, pushchairs and prams for rust and/or broken hinges or sticking-out screws, etc.
- **Wooden equipment**: check wooden blocks or wheeled carts for splinters and rough edges; remove any that are damaged, and report this to your supervisor.
- **Dressing-up clothes and soft toys**: all toys and play equipment should be cleaned at least once a week. This includes dressing-up clothes and soft toys – and you should always remove from the nursery any toy that has been in contact with a child who has an infectious illness. Particular care should be taken to keep hats, head coverings and hairbrushes clean, in order to help prevent the spread of head lice.
- **Water tray**: water trays should be emptied daily, as germs can multiply quickly in pools of water.

Guidelines: Safety and hygiene – checking equipment regularly (cont.)

- **Sandpit**: check that sandpits or trays are clean, and that toys are removed and cleaned at the end of a play session; if the sandpit is kept outside, make sure it is kept covered when not in use.

- **Home area**: the home area often contains dolls, saucepans and plastic food; these need to be included in the checking and in the regular wash.

- **Ventilation**: adequate ventilation is important to disperse bacteria or viruses transmitted through sneezing or coughing. Make sure that windows are opened to let fresh air in to the nursery – but also make sure there are no draughts.

- **Outdoor play areas**: these should be checked before any play session for litter, dog or cat faeces, or any other object that could cause children harm.

Your role in preventing accidents

There are different views on whether the environment should be made 'toddler-proof' by removing all potentially dangerous items and ensuring adult supervision at all times, or whether by helping children to develop skills, including self-control, they can be encouraged to recognise and manage a degree of risk appropriate to their capabilities. The following guidelines will help you to ensure that children in your care are protected from some common hazards.

Preventing burns and scalds	Preventing poisoning
<ul><li>Never carry a hot drink through a play area or place a hot drink within reach of children.</li><li>Make sure the kitchen is safe for children – kettle flexes coiled neatly, cooker guards used and saucepan handles turned inwards.</li><li>Make sure the kitchen is inaccessible to children when no one is in it.</li><li>Never smoke in child care settings, and keep matches and lighters out of children's reach.</li></ul>	<ul><li>Make sure that all household chemicals are out of children's reach.</li><li>Never pour chemicals or detergents into empty soft drink or water bottles.</li><li>Keep all medicines and tablets in a locked cupboard.</li><li>Use childproof containers.</li><li>Teach children not to eat berries or fungi in the garden or park.</li></ul>
Fire safety	**Preventing falls**
<ul><li>In the case of fire or other emergency, you need to know what to do to evacuate the children and yourselves. You should also always practise fire safety.</li><li>Remember that no smoking is allowed in any child care setting.</li><li>Keep handbags containing matches or lighters securely away, out of children's reach.</li><li>The nursery cooker should not be left unattended when turned on.</li><li>Fire exits and other doors should be free of obstructions on both sides.</li><li>Ensure you know where the fire extinguishers are kept and how to use them.</li><li>Regularly check electrical equipment for any faults.</li></ul>	<ul><li>Babies need to be protected from falls – close supervision is needed. All children will trip and fall at some time, but children should not be put at risk of serious injury.</li><li>Never leave a baby unattended on a table, work surface, bed or sofa.</li><li>Make sure young children cannot climb up near windows – and ensure window catches are used.</li><li>Always clean and dry a floor where children are playing.</li><li>Make sure that clutter is removed from floors.</li><li>Make sure you know how to use safety equipment, such as stair gates, reins and harnesses, adjustable changing tables and car seats.</li><li>Use safety gates when working in home settings.</li></ul>

Table 3.2 Protecting children in your care from common hazards

Maintaining and promoting the personal safety of the child

Children who play closely together for long periods are more likely than others to develop an infection – and any infection can spread quickly from one child to another and to the adults who care for them.

Good hygiene will help to prevent infection and the spread of disease. Being clean also increases self-esteem and social acceptance, and helps to prepare children in skills of independence and self-caring.

Here, as elsewhere, you should be a good role model with your personal hygiene and by wearing the right clothes. You should help children to develop good **personal hygiene routines** – for example, by encouraging children to keep their face clean by using a clean flannel.

Teach children how and when to wash their hands

The chief way of preventing the spread of infection is through the washing of hands. Regular hand washing should be practised and promoted within all early years settings. You need to teach children **how** to wash and dry their hands, and make sure they always wash their hands:

- **before eating and drinking**
- **after going to the toilet**
- **after playing outdoors**
- **after handling pets or other animals**
- **after blowing their nose**.

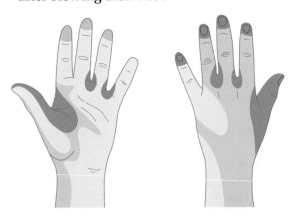

Figure 3.9 Parts commonly missed when washing hands: red = parts commonly missed; orange = parts sometimes missed; cream = parts rarely missed.

Teach children how to play safely

Children need a safe environment, so that they can explore, and thus learn and grow. As they develop, children need to learn how to tackle everyday dangers so that they can become safe adults. You have an important role – not only in ensuring that children are kept as safe and secure as possible but also in teaching them to be aware of safety issues. Every opportunity should be made to teach children about different aspects of keeping themselves – and others – safe. Above all, children should be taught the following.

1 **Road safety**: how and when to cross roads safely (even *with* adults holding on to them)
2 **Fire safety**: never to play with matches, lighters, cigarettes, sparklers, etc.
3 **Water safety**: not to play near ponds and rivers (ideally teach young children how to swim)
4 **Food safety**: how germs spread, and the importance of hand washing
5 **Play safety**: for example:
    - *to carry things carefully*
    - *never to run with anything in their mouths – this includes sweets and other food*
    - *never to run while carrying a glass, scissors or other pointed objects; if a child falls he can stab himself with something as simple as a pencil*
    - *never to throw sand*
    - *to take turns when using bikes, slides and climbing frames.*

Always give reasons for the safety message:

- 'You mustn't throw sand because you'll hurt your friend.'
- 'Never run into the road, because you could be hit by a car.'
- 'Don't run with a stick in your hand as it would hurt you if you fall.'

When teaching young children about safety, you will need to find ways to communicate with each child according to their needs – for example, by the following means.

1 **Repetition:** children learn best by doing or practising things – over and over again – but first you have to make the activity enjoyable.

2 **Adapting** your approach, according to the message you're trying to convey – for example, making sure that *all* children in the group can join in and benefit from the activity.

3 **Modifying the message:** children with hearing difficulties, for example, will need both children and adults to face them so that they can see any signs, and lip-read if the hearing loss is severe.

4 **Using real life examples:** children remember what they have seen and/or experienced themselves – so, if a child has had sand thrown in his eyes, this would be a good moment to teach other children about the dangers of throwing sand.

Practise sun safety

Strong sun can easily burn the skin. For people with fair skin, the more sun that you are exposed to, the more likely you are to get skin cancer later on in life. Sunburn is especially bad; it hurts a lot at the time, and sunburned children may be especially prone to skin cancer later in life. Follow these guidelines.

- Keep children out of the sun between 11 am and 2 pm. This is the time to let them read, do some drawing, watch a video or play with toys and games.
- Cover the children up. It is better to wear some clothes than nothing at all. The most protection comes from clothes that are loose, long-sleeved and made of tightly woven materials (like T-shirts).
- Provide floppy sun hats. Try to shade the head, face, neck and ears.
- Coat children with sun cream. Choose a high sun protection factor (SPF), as anything less than factor 8 gives little protection. Sun cream will not last all day, so apply more from time to time, especially if the children are in and out of water.

Note: Babies under six months old should be kept out of direct sunlight altogether. Written permission to use sun cream on a child is required from parents or guardians.

Keep children safe during meal and snack times

One of the most common accidents in babies and children under five is choking. Babies are most at risk from choking when left unsupervised either eating or playing. Young children are most at risk of choking when they are tired or crying, or when they are running around. Half of all cases of choking in children under four years involve **food**. (Only 6 per cent of cases are due to toys.)

- *Never* leave a child propped up with a bottle or feeding beaker.
- *Always* supervise babies and young children when eating and drinking. If a toddler goes to the toilet – or leaves the table for any reason – during meal or snack time, make sure an adult accompanies him or her. (Accidents in nursery settings have occurred when a child chokes silently on food when no adult is present.)
- *Never* give peanuts to children under four years old as they can easily choke on them or inhale them into their lungs, causing infection and lung damage.
- Make sure you know what to do if a child is choking (see the first aid section on page 89).

Food hygiene

In promoting the health of young children it is important that you understand the basics of food hygiene as they generally apply to you in the early years setting. Your role may involve serving children's food and drinks, and supervising them when they are eating and drinking. Often you will have to prepare simple snacks for the children. You need to be confident that you are doing everything in your power to provide children with food and drink that is safe to eat and free from illness-causing bacteria. As you progress in your career, you may become more involved in food preparation and will then be required to attend an accredited food hygiene course.

Young children are particularly vulnerable to the bacteria that can cause food poisoning or gastroenteritis. Bacteria multiply rapidly in warm, moist foods, and can enter food without causing it to look, smell or even taste bad. So it is very important to store, prepare and cook food safely, and to keep the kitchen clean.

Guidelines: food hygiene

- When serving food and clearing away after meals and snacks, you should observe the rules of food hygiene.
- Wash your hands using soap and warm water, and dry them on a clean towel.
- Wear clean protective clothing.
- Ensure any washing up by hand is done thoroughly in hot water, with detergent (and use rubber gloves).
- Cover cups/beakers with a clean cloth and air-dry where possible.
- Drying-up cloths should be replaced every day with clean ones.
- Never cough or sneeze over food.

The prevention of food poisoning

Storing food safely

- Keep food cold. The fridge should be kept as cold as it will go without actually freezing the food (1–5°C, or 34–41°F).
- Cover or wrap food with food wrap or microwave cling film.
- Never refreeze food that has begun to thaw.
- Do not use foods that are past their sell-by or best-before date.
- Always read instructions on the label when storing food.
- Once a tin is opened, store the contents in a covered dish in the fridge.
- Store raw foods at the bottom of the fridge so that juices cannot drip onto cooked food.
- Thaw frozen meat completely before cooking.

Preparing and cooking food safely

- Always wash hands in warm water and soap, and dry on a clean towel, before handling food and after handling raw foods, especially meat.
- Wear clean protective clothing that is solely for use in the kitchen.

- Keep food covered at all times.
- Wash all fruits and vegetables before eating. Peel and top carrots, and peel fruits such as apples.
- Never cough or sneeze over food.
- Always cover any septic cuts or boils with a waterproof dressing.
- Never smoke in any room that is used for food.
- Keep work surfaces and chopping boards clean and disinfected; use separate boards for raw meat, fish, vegetables, etc.
- Make sure that meat dishes are cooked thoroughly.
- Avoid raw eggs; they sometimes contain *Salmonella* bacteria, which may cause food poisoning. (Also avoid giving children *uncooked* cake mixture, homemade ice creams, mayonnaise or desserts that contain uncooked raw egg.) When cooking eggs, the egg yolk and white should be firm.
- When reheating food, make sure that it is piping hot all the way through, and allow to cool slightly before giving it to children. When using a microwave, always stir and check the temperature of the food before feeding children, to avoid burning from hot spots.
- Avoid having leftovers – they are a common cause of food poisoning.

Keeping the kitchen safe

- Teach children to wash their hands after touching pets and going to the toilet, and before eating.
- Clean tin openers, graters and mixers thoroughly after use.
- Keep flies and other insects away – use a fine mesh over open windows.
- Stay away from the kitchen if you are suffering from diarrhoea or sickness.
- Keep the kitchen clean – the floor, work surfaces, sink, utensils, cloths and waste bins should be cleaned regularly.
- Tea towels should be boiled every day and dishcloths boiled or disinfected.
- Keep pets away from the kitchen.
- Keep all waste bins covered, and empty them regularly.
- Keep sharp knives stored safely where children cannot reach them.

How to keep children safe on outings

Any outing away from the children's usual setting – for instance, trips to farms, parks and theatres – must be planned with safety and security issues as a top priority. Many schools now employ an Educational Visit Coordinator to oversee the safety of school trips. Each setting must consider the following points.

Planning: You may need to visit the place beforehand and discuss any particular requirements – for example, what to do if it rains, or specific lunch arrangements.

Contact numbers: A copy of the children's contact information should be taken on the outing and the person in charge should regularly check the names of the children against the day's attendance list.

Permission: The manager or head teacher must give permission for the outing, and a letter should be sent to all parents and guardians of the children.

Informing parents: Parents should be informed of what is involved on the outing; what the child needs to bring (e.g. packed meal, waterproof coat) – emphasise *no* glass bottles and *no* sweets, spending money if necessary (state the advised maximum amount).

Supervision: Arrange adequate adult supervision. There should always be trained staff on any outing, however local and low-key. The adult:child ratio should never exceed 1:4. If the children are under two years old or have special needs, then you would expect to have fewer children per adult. Swimming trips should be attempted only if the ratio is one adult to one child for children under five years old. The younger the children, the more adults are required, particularly if the trip involves crossing roads, when an adult must be available to hold the children's hands.

Transport: if a coach is being hired, check whether it has seat belts for children. By law, all new minibuses and coaches must have seat belts fitted, and minibus drivers have to have passed a special driving test.

Safety at arrival and departure times

Any early childhood setting or school should be secure so that children cannot wander off without anyone realising. There should also be a policy that guards against strangers being able to wander in without reason. Many child care settings now have door entry phones, and staff wear name badges. It is a matter of courtesy and security for all visitors for them to give advance notice of their visit.

At home time, staff *must* ensure that the child is collected by the appropriate person. If parents know that they will not be able to collect their child on a particular occasion, they should notify the setting, giving permission for another **named person** to collect their child. The child's **key person** should, where possible, be responsible for handover when the child arrives and when he or she leaves the setting.

The importance of road safety

Some facts about children and road safety:

- Every week, on average, nine children under the age of six years are killed or seriously injured on roads in the UK.
- Children under five years cannot judge how fast vehicles are going or how far away they are.
- If hit by a car travelling at 40 mph, four out of five child pedestrians will die. If hit by a car travelling at 30 mph, four out of five will survive. Children's survival rates increase even more the lower the speed of the car.
- The peak time for child casualties is weekdays, 3 pm to 5 pm, coinciding with the end of the school day. Friday is the peak day for child casualties.

Educating children about road safety

Educating children about safety on the roads should begin at a very early age, the best method being by example. Children need to learn about road safety in the same way as they learn any new skill: the message needs to be repeated over and over again until the child really has learned it. Every local authority employs a Road Safety Officer, and the Royal Society for the Prevention of Accidents (RoSPA) runs campaigns for children of all ages.

When walking on the pavement, parents and carers should:

- set a good example, as young children will copy adults
- hold the child's hand and put reins on a younger child if he or she is not strapped in a pushchair
- not allow the child to run ahead
- look out for and encourage the child to be aware of hidden entrances or driveways crossing the pavement
- make sure the child walks on the side of the pavement away from the traffic
- not let the child out alone or even with an older child
- always use a zebra or light-controlled crossing, or a school crossing patrol, if there is one.

'Walking bus' schemes, which allow children to walk to and from school safely in supervised groups, can also help children learn how to negotiate roads safely.

Children should wear light-coloured clothes or luminous armbands – or both – when out at dusk or when walking on country roads without pavements.

The Green Cross Code
The Green Cross Code is a very good method of teaching road safety to young children.

Safety when travelling by car

The UK law states that children of all ages must be safely fastened in an appropriate car seat. This applies to a newborn baby, as well as a teenager. The driver of the car is responsible for making sure that everyone is wearing a seat belt.

Implementing working practices that safeguard children and the adults who work with them

Child protection is a part of safeguarding and promoting welfare. It means protecting children from physical, emotional or sexual abuse or neglect. It also means helping children to grow up into confident, healthy and happy adults. Although child abuse is not common, it is important to recognise that there are, and will always be, children who are victims of abuse in one way or another.

Safeguarding procedures

All settings working with children provide the following:

- a policy – reviewed annually – that sets out the responsibilities for practitioners for the protection of children under the age of 18
- training on safeguarding for all those working in – or involved with – the setting
- a named senior staff member with responsibility for safeguarding arrangements

The Green Cross Code

1. Think first. Find the safest place to cross then stop.

2. Stop. Stand on the pavement near the kerb.

3. Use your eyes and ears. Look all around for traffic and listen.

4. Wait till it is safe to cross. If traffic is coming, let it pass.

5. Look and listen. When it is safe, walk straight across the road.

6. Arrive alive. Keep looking and listening for traffic while you cross.

Figure 3.10 The Green Cross Code

- a duty to inform the Independent Safeguarding Authority of any person involved with the setting who is a threat to children
- arrangements to work with the Local Safeguarding Board
- procedures that include risk assessment within the setting to ensure that the policy works in practice
- the Criminal Records Bureau (see below) checks on all adults who have regular unsupervised access to children under the age of 18.

 Progress check

A safeguarding policy

Find out about the policy and procedures in your workplace relating to child protection and safeguarding.

Types of child abuse

The categories of child abuse are:

- physical abuse
- emotional abuse
- neglect
- sexual abuse.

Physical abuse

Physical abuse, or non-accidental injury (NAI), involves someone deliberately harming a child. This may take the form of:

- bruising – from being slapped, punched, shaken or squeezed
- cuts – scratches, bite marks, a torn frenulum (the web of skin inside the upper lip)
- fractures – skull and limb fractures from being thrown against hard objects
- burns and scalds – from cigarettes, irons, baths and kettles.

Often the particular injuries can be explained easily, but you should always be suspicious if a child has any bruise or mark that shows the particular pattern of an object (e.g. a belt strap mark, teeth marks or the imprint of an iron). Also look out for behavioural disturbances in the child, such as aggressiveness towards others or a withdrawn attitude.

Emotional abuse

Emotional abuse occurs when a child consistently faces threatening ill-treatment from an adult. This can take the form of verbal abuse, ridiculing, mocking and insulting the child. It is difficult to find out how common this form of abuse is, because it is hard to detect. However, signs of emotional abuse include:

- withdrawn behaviour – child may not join in with others or may not appear to be having fun
- attention-seeking behaviour
- self-esteem and confidence are low
- stammering and stuttering
- tantrums beyond the expected age
- telling lies, and even stealing
- tearfulness.

Emotional neglect means that children do not receive love and affection from the adult. They may often be left alone without the company and support of someone who loves them.

Neglect

Physical neglect occurs when the adult fails to give their child what they need to develop physically. They often leave children alone and unattended. Signs of physical neglect include:

- being underweight for their age and not thriving
- unwashed clothes, which are often dirty and smelly
- a child may have poor skin tone, dull, matted hair and bad breath; a baby may have a persistent rash from infrequent nappy changing
- being constantly tired, hungry and listless or lacking in energy
- frequent health problems, and prone to accidents
- low self-esteem and poor social relationships – delay in all areas of development is likely because of lack of stimulation.

Sexual abuse

There is much more awareness today about the existence of sexual abuse. Sexual abuse means that the adult uses the child to gratify their sexual needs. This could involve sexual intercourse or anal intercourse. It may involve watching pornographic material with the child. Sexual abuse might also mean children being encouraged in sexually explicit behaviour or oral sex, masturbation or the fondling of sexual parts. Signs of sexual abuse include the following:

- bruises or scratches as in NAI or physical injury
- itching or pain in the genital area
- wetting or soiling themselves
- discharge from the penis or vagina
- poor self-esteem and lack of confidence
- may regress and want to be treated like a baby
- poor sleeping and eating patterns
- withdrawn and solitary behaviour.

Your role in reporting suspected abuse

You need to be aware of the indicators of child abuse as outlined above. However, it is important not to jump to conclusions. If you have any cause for concern, you should always talk to your immediate superior or to the head of the nursery or school. Every child care setting has a **policy** for dealing with suspected child abuse.

If you suspect child abuse in the **home setting**, then you should contact your local Social Services or the National Society for the Prevention of Cruelty to Children (NSPCC).

If a child tells you he or she has been abused, you should:

- reassure the child, saying that you are glad that they have told you about this
- believe the child; tell the child that you will do your best to protect them, but do not *promise* that you can do that
- remember that the child is not to blame, and that it is important that you make the child understand this
- do a lot of listening; do not ask questions
- report your conversation with the child to your immediate superior
- write down what was said by the child as soon as possible after the conversation.

Some facts about child abuse

All sections of society produce adults who abuse or neglect children. It is very dangerous to form stereotypes about the kind of people who might violate a child's rights or about the situations that could lead to child abuse or neglect.

As evidence gathers on the subject of child protection, it is becoming apparent that the abusive or neglectful person is almost always known to the child (e.g. a parent, a family member, a friend of the family, a carer or cohabitee).

- Premature babies and children from birth to four years of age are most likely to be abused or neglected.
- Separation of the mother and the baby for a period of time after birth can be associated with child abuse or neglect.
- Children who cry a great deal are much more likely to be abused or neglected.
- Children who do not enjoy eating are more likely to be abused or neglected.
- Stepchildren are vulnerable.
- Children with disabilities are more likely to be abused or neglected.
- Children who are boys when parents wanted girls, or girls when parents wanted boys, are more likely to be neglected.

Children at risk of abuse

Child abuse occurs in all different social groups of people from all walks of life. It is often believed that only parents are to blame or, in the case of sexual abuse, that strangers are to blame. However, children can become victims of abuse by anyone, whether parents, relatives, neighbours, family friends, acquaintances or strangers. Even those people who are entrusted to care for children – such as teachers, child care providers, church workers or foster parents – may abuse children. Abusers may be male or female. Their age may vary and could even include children and adolescents. There is no one profile of someone who abuses and there are many reasons why adults abuse children.

Certain factors within the family home can mean that children are at a higher risk of being abused.

- **Drug or alcohol abuse** by parents can lead to children being put at risk, even if the parents are not actually mistreating them; such abuse is a familiar trigger for **violence** in the home and can also lead to parents having a disordered lifestyle, which can leave children in danger.

- **Mental illness**: although this does not prevent individuals from being good parents, it can sometimes move a child up the scale from being one in need to one at significant risk of harm.

The role of the practitioner in working with children to manage conflict

Understanding children's behaviour

Behaviour is the way in which we act, speak and treat other people and our environment. Children whose early social and emotional development is positive are more likely to make friends, settle well into school and understand how to behave appropriately in different situations. They have strong self-esteem and a sense of self-worth, but also have a feeling of empathy for others. They understand what the boundaries are, and why they are necessary. Behaviour has a significant impact on current and later success for children, in terms of their social skill development and education.

Causes of positive and negative behaviour

It is well known that behaviour is commonly affected by certain factors. There are some factors that stem from the children themselves:

- illness
- accident and injury
- tiredness.

Other factors result from their situations:

- arrival of a new baby
- moving house
- parental separation or divorce

- change of carer – either at home or in a setting
- loss or bereavement
- change of setting – such as transition from home to nursery or nursery to school.

Effects of positive and negative behaviour

Individual children will respond to these situations differently, but *regression* is common (usually temporary) when they revert to behaviour that is immature for them. Events that they do not understand will leave them confused, leading to frustration and aggressive outbursts, or they may blame themselves, which could result in withdrawn behaviour and the development of inappropriate habits through anxiety.

Generally, any factor that causes stress may result in the child:

- needing more comfort and attention
- being less sociable
- being unable to cope with tasks that they would normally manage
- being subject to mood swings
- being unable to concentrate (this includes listening to instructions) and less able to cope with challenging situations and difficulties.

Behaviour is very closely linked to self-esteem – children who feel bad about themselves may not behave appropriately. The poem reproduced in Unit 1 (page 10) sums up the positive and negative ways in which adults can contribute to children's development and behaviour.

The role of the practitioner in managing behaviour

The setting's policies and procedures for promoting positive behaviour

Every setting should have a behaviour policy. This should be specific to the aims and needs of the setting and include guidelines for promoting positive behaviour of both children *and* adults involved with the setting. A behaviour policy will help all staff to learn how to promote positive behaviour, by explaining that children need to develop positive skills and attributes:

- self-respect and self-esteem
- consideration and **empathy** for others
- social skills such as negotiation and problem-solving.

Key term

Empathy – The ability to understand and share the feelings of another.

The policy should also include guidance in two important areas:

1 promoting appropriate behaviour in the children in the setting
2 discouraging inappropriate behaviour in the setting.

Specific procedures for staff to follow which help in achieving these aims should also be included, such as:

- **Being a positive role model**: showing the children what is appropriate behaviour in the setting, by setting a positive example in your own behaviour.
- **Showing respect** to children and other adults: by the way you listen, your facial expression, your body language and by what you say.
- **Praising children**: when they have shown positive and appropriate behaviour – for example, when they have been helpful to another child.
- **Organising the environment**: to make it easier for children to understand why they need to be patient or to take turns.
- **Intervening calmly**: to stop children hurting each other or behaving in an unsafe way.
- **Setting boundaries:** Support the learning of children to understand what sort of behaviour is acceptable and what is not.
- **Giving a simple explanation or alternative**: to the child who is finding it difficult to observe boundaries.

The policy should also detail the strategies that will definitely *never* be used in the setting and also explain why; for example:

- Adults will not hit or shake children – this is against the law. It is a misuse of your adult strength and is contrary to the ground rules for children's behaviour.
- Adults will not use verbal humiliation or insults – this would undermine children's self-esteem and would be an example of inappropriate behaviour.

In practice

Behaviour policy

Find out about the policy and procedures in your setting. Why is it important for settings to have a behaviour policy?

Behaviour linked to the ages and stages of development

The following stages are, of course, only loosely linked to the ages shown. As with any normative measurements, they only serve as a rough guide to help understand children's behaviour and how best to respond to it. Much will depend upon children's experiences and the way they have been helped to develop good relationships.

Aged one to two years

At this age, children:

- have developed their own personalities and are sociable with close family and friends
- still become shy and anxious when parents or carers are out of sight
- are developing their speech, and can attract attention by calling out or crying
- can become possessive over toys, but can often be distracted to something else
- are discovering that they are separate individuals
- are self-centred (see things from their own point of view)

- are gaining mobility, improving their ability to explore their surroundings – this results in conflicts, often regarding safety
- begin to understand the meaning of 'No', and firm boundaries can be set
- can be frustrated by their own limitations, but resist adult help (perhaps saying 'me do it').

Aged two to three years

Children now:

- are developing greater awareness of their separate identities
- are not yet able to share easily
- are developing their language abilities; they begin to communicate their needs and wishes more clearly and to understand 'in a minute'
- can still be distracted from the cause of their anger
- have tantrums (usually when parents or main carers are present) when frustrated – possibly caused by their efforts to become self-reliant (such as feeding or dressing themselves) or having ideas that the adult does not want them to carry out
- experience a range of feelings – being very affectionate and cooperative one minute and resistant the next
- are aware of the feelings of others and can respond to them.

Aged three to four years

Children at this age:

- are very aware of others and imitate them – especially in their play; their developing speaking and listening skills allow them to repeat swear words they hear
- are more able to express themselves through speech and, therefore, there is often a reduction in physical outbursts; however, they are still likely to hit back if provoked
- can be impulsive and will be less easily distracted
- become more sociable in their play and may have favourite friends
- can sometimes be reasoned with and are just becoming aware of the behaviour codes in different places or situations
- like and seek adult approval and appreciation of their efforts.

Aged four to five years

Children now:

- can behave appropriately at mealtimes and during other 'routine' activities and may begin to understand why 'Please' and 'Thank you' (or their equivalents) are important
- are able to share and take turns, but often need help
- are more aware of others' feelings and will be concerned if someone is hurt
- are becoming more independent and self-assured, but still need adult comfort when ill or tired
- will respond to reason, can negotiate and be adaptable, but can still be distracted
- are sociable and becoming confident communicators able to make more sense of their environment; there will continue to be conflicts that they cannot resolve on their own and with which they will need adult help
- can sometimes be determined, may argue and show aggression.

Aged five to six years

Children at this age:

- understand that different rules apply in different places (such as at home, school, grandparents' house) and can adapt their behaviour accordingly
- are developing control over their feelings – they argue with adults when they feel secure and need to feel there are firm boundaries in place
- will respond to reason and can negotiate, but are less easily distracted – anger can last longer and they need time to calm down
- are able to hide their feelings in some situations
- can cooperate in group play, but are not yet ready for team games
- may show off and boast (for example, when they celebrate an achievement)
- will continue to need adult support to resolve conflicts
- will share and take turns, and begin to have an understanding of what is 'fair' if given an explanation.

Aged six to eight years

Children now:

- can quickly adapt behaviour to suit the situation
- can play games with rules
- can argue their viewpoints
- are growing in confidence and becoming independent
- are developing some moral values and understanding of 'right' and 'wrong'
- can be friendly and cooperative
- can control how they feel much of the time but there are still times when they want to do things their way and quarrels develop.

Linking behaviour to child development

When assessing children's behaviour, it is important to bear these developmental stages in mind and to view the behaviour in the context of overall development. Here are two examples.

1 It is well known that **tantrums** are a common, even an expected, feature of a two-year-old's behaviour. There is bound to be some cause for concern, however, if they are a regular feature of a six-year-old's behaviour. However, some adults have unrealistic expectations of children and express surprise when inappropriate behaviour occurs.

2 A five-year-old becomes fidgety and whines during a Christmas pantomime. The adults will view the occasion as a treat and may feel resentment that their child is complaining, but it is reasonable that a five-year-old should lose concentration, and be unable to sit still for a lengthy period or understand all of what is going on.

The benefits of encouraging and rewarding positive behaviour

Positive behaviour management is about using positive rather than negative approaches to encourage children to behave appropriately. Promoting positive behaviour involves:

- setting clear boundaries, which are applied in a calm and consistent way
- encouraging children to make their own choices about behaviour – and to understand the negative consequences if they choose inappropriate behaviour
- setting 'positive' rules rather than 'negative' ones. Negative rules tend to begin with the word 'Don't', and tell children what they must not do, but do not guide them as to what they may or should do.

Skills and techniques for supporting and encouraging positive behaviour

In trying to understand behaviour, it is helpful to note whether there are particular incidents or situations that seem to trigger inappropriate behaviour. Some of these can be avoided altogether by minor changes in routine or approach, but others, such as siblings teasing each other, will occur frequently; children therefore need to be given strategies and support to be able to cope with them effectively. It is important never to reject the child but only what the child has done (for example, 'That was an unkind thing to say' rather than 'You are unkind').

The A-B-C of behaviour

Antecedent: what happens before, or leads up to, the observed behaviour.

Behaviour: the observed behaviour – what the child says and how he or she acts (this is any behaviour, both positive and negative).

Consequence: what happens following the observed behaviour.

Part of your role as a practitioner is to observe children's behaviour, whether or not you make a written record, so that you can contribute to discussions about a child's behaviour and develop good practice in managing unacceptable aspects. In your work setting you should try to see not only how other staff and parents deal with incidents, but also which methods seem to be effective with which children.

Observing and recording behaviour

Event sample

An **event sample** is a useful way of recording negative behaviour as and when it occurs. This method involves creating a chart to note:

- the time
- the context (location, activity)
- the people involved
- actions and language of the child or children
- actions and language of the adult
- child's response to adult/other children
- any other relevant information.

This provides the A-B-C information and helps to identify what, or who, may have led to each incident. You may find that:

- particular pairings or groupings of children present problems
- some form of bullying is occurring
- there is confusion about what is expected – unclear rules
- large-group times – register, story, assembly – are often the 'trouble' times
- the child responds positively to one form of discipline or adult more readily than to another.

Your findings can help staff to understand when inappropriate behaviour is likely to occur and extra support, perhaps a talk with the child about what would be acceptable behaviour, or closer supervision can be given. They may also highlight differences in the way the staff deal with it and which may be confusing for children. Adults can then meet and work out how best to help the child.

Time sample

A time sample can be even more useful and provide information, not only about the inappropriate

behaviour but also about the occasions when a child has behaved well.

This method involves creating a similar chart but a record of what is happening is made at regular intervals – every 30 minutes, or whatever seems appropriate and practical. This method enables you to see if the positive behaviour was noticed, appreciated and praised or rewarded. If it was overlooked, the child may use inappropriate behaviour to gain attention – of any kind!

Recording and sharing the information

Recording and sharing the information with other staff and parents helps everyone to agree on a realistic and practical course of action. Similar observations can be repeated at a later date to monitor progress and review strategies.

Serious incidents (for example, biting) should be recorded and reported to parents of the children involved. Parents of each child (or children) must be assured that these incidents are dealt with seriously and appropriately otherwise there is a risk that they will take issue with each other. They should be given information which explains what happened so that they:

- do not feel the need to question their child; and
- are aware of the full facts rather than their child's viewpoint.

Confidentiality is vitally important, although the children themselves will probably name names!

Providing an effective role model

Children learn about positive behaviour – such as sharing and saying 'thank you' – by watching others. They can also learn about inappropriate behaviours – such as being unwilling to share and swearing – from watching adults. You need to act as a positive role model for children. You can do this by modelling positive behaviour. Children will try to copy your behaviour, so you need to show positive behaviour at all times.

Involving children in decision-making

Children can be involved in helping to devise basic classroom rules, which can then – if wanted – be posted on the wall; an example is given below.

Case Study — Golden rules for positive behaviour

Staff at a nursery drew up a short set of Golden Rules, after discussing them with the children:

- We take care of our things.
- We share with each other.
- We walk inside.
- We listen when someone is talking.
- We are kind to each other.

They illustrated the Rules with photos of children behaving appropriately and also showed the relevant Makaton symbols.

How to manage behaviour: goals and boundaries

If children are to understand what is regarded as acceptable behaviour at home, in the work setting and in society, then they must be given very clear **guidelines**. Work settings will have a policy relating to behaviour and discipline, which all staff should follow and which is regularly reviewed. The policy will explain the rules that are applied and how children will be helped to understand, and learn to keep, them. In most cases the rules are simple and reflect the concerns for safety and for children to be considerate of others and their environment. They should be appropriate for the age and stage of development of the children and for the particular needs of the work setting.

Goals are the forms of behaviour that are encouraged, and cover physical, social and verbal aspects. They should be realistically set for the child's age and stage of development.

Examples of goals for a child aged four to five years are to:

- say 'please' and 'thank you'
- share play equipment

- tidy up
- be quiet and listen for short periods (e.g. story or register time).

Boundaries are the limits within which behaviour is acceptable – they identify what may, and may not, be done or said. Children need to understand the consequences of failing to act within those boundaries. It is important that the boundaries are appropriate for the age and stage of development.

Examples of boundaries for children aged four to five years are:

- they may play outside – but must not tread on the flowerbeds
- they may watch television – but only until tea is ready
- they may use the dressing-up clothes – if they put them away when they have finished.

In practice

Promoting children's positive behaviour

Check that you know what the policies and procedures are for promoting positive behaviour in your work setting. Describe the boundaries and rules used in your setting to promote positive behaviour, and explain why staff should apply these consistently and fairly.

Promoting positive behaviour

It is helpful to set '**positive**' rules rather than 'negative' ones.

Negative rules tend to begin with the word '**Don't**' and tell children what they must **not do** but give them no guidance as to what they may or **should do**.

Consistency in applying the boundaries is important, especially in the work setting where children need to relate to several adults. They will check that the rules have not changed and that they still apply whichever adult is present.

If you are supervising an activity, the children will expect you to apply the same rules as other staff. It undermines your own position if you allow

Figure 3.11 Children need to know what behaviour is expected of them; they need boundaries

inappropriate behaviour and another staff member has to discipline the children you are working with.

Managing behaviour

First of all it needs to be agreed in a work setting what behaviour is inappropriate, and then some decisions made as to how staff will manage it when it does arise. These should take account of **individual needs**, as children will respond in their own ways. Here are two examples:

1 In a school setting, staying in at playtime is punishment for some children but, for those who have poor social skills and find the playground rather intimidating, it can be a relief.
2 Some children enjoy tidying and helping the teacher because they might get more individual attention.

Theories about behaviour

1 **Albert Bandura** developed a **'social learning'** theory, which states that children learn about social behaviour by *watching* and *imitating* other people, especially those they admire. Children will learn negative behaviour as well as positive behaviour, so the presence of good role models is very important.
2 **B.F. Skinner** developed a **'behaviourist'** theory, which states that children's behaviour is shaped by adults through *positive* and *negative reinforcement*.

These two theories have influenced current practice for managing and modifying (shaping or reforming) behaviour.

There are three main aspects of **behaviour modification**.

1 **Identifying positive** and **negative behaviour** – deciding what behaviour is to be encouraged and what is to be discouraged.
2 **Rewarding positive behaviour** – encouraging and promoting it through reward. There are different forms of reward:
   • *verbal praise* (e.g. *'Well done'*)

- *attention – this could be non-verbal (e.g. smile of approval, a nod)*
- *stars or points (for older children) leading to certificates or for group/team recognition*
- *sharing success by having other staff and parents told*
- *own choice of activity or story*
- *tangible rewards such as stickers.*

These work on the principle of **positive reinforcement** – based on the idea that if children receive approval and/or a reward for behaving acceptably they are likely to want to repeat that behaviour. If one child is praised (e.g. for tidying up) others are often influenced to copy or join in so that they, too, will receive praise and attention. For young children the reward must be *immediate* so they understand the link between it and the positive behaviour. It is of little value to promise a treat or reward in the future. Similarly, star charts and collecting points are not appropriate for children younger than five years old.

3 **Discouraging negative behaviour** (according to this approach):

- **whenever possible such behaviour should be ignored** *(bearing in mind safety or injury), although not if attention is drawn to it (perhaps by another child) as the message sent then is that it is acceptable*
- *giving* **attention and praise** *to another child who is behaving acceptably*
- **distracting the child's attention** *(particularly appropriate with younger children) or removing him/her to another activity or group*
- **expressing disapproval** – *verbally and/or non-verbally through body language, facial expression (frowning) and shaking of the head*
- **imposing a punishment** – *withdrawal of a privilege (e.g. watching a favourite television programme).*

These work on the principle of **negative reinforcement** – based on the idea that children will avoid repeating an unpleasant experience. If they behave inappropriately and earn the disapproval of an adult, or receive some sort of punishment, they will be less likely to repeat that behaviour. As they learn from watching others, older children may be deterred (put off) from behaving inappropriately by seeing someone else receive discipline. This approach encourages the adult to act immediately so young children understand the link between the unacceptable behaviour and the adult's response to it.

Remember: Physical, or corporal, punishment is **illegal** in work settings and never allowed under any circumstances. This includes pulling a child by his/her elbow or arm, or grabbing him/her by the wrist. Intervention, to protect the child, others or property, should involve *minimal physical restraint*.

Using rewards

There are different forms of reward (see this page and the previous page). There are problems associated with rewards in that some children may behave in a particular way purely to receive the reward rather than from an understanding of the need to consider safety, others and their environment or enjoying what they have achieved for its own sake. The *type* of reward also needs to be considered; for example, is it desirable for children to be given sweets as rewards? Some parents may have strong views about this.

Rewards might work in the short term, but do not always succeed in the long term. They might even undermine lifelong learning by encouraging children to seek reward, rather than be disposed to learn because something is interesting.

Case Study — Using rewards

In an infant school a new head teacher introduced the regular practice of listening to children read to her. This involved children being sent individually to her office where she would reward them with a jelly bear if they read well or tried hard. One mother was surprised, when talking to her daughter about the school day, that she was upset to have read to her class teacher instead of to the head teacher. The girl explained that everyone was asking to read to the head teacher and she was not chosen – so she missed out on a jelly bear!

Case Study Using rewards (cont.)

The parent was alarmed, firstly that sweets were being given as a reward without parents knowing, and secondly that children were not rewarded by the experience itself and the head teacher's appreciation of children's efforts.

Strategies for managing conflict and inappropriate behaviour

Inappropriate behaviour conflicts with the accepted values and beliefs of the setting and of society. Inappropriate behaviour may be demonstrated through speech, writing, non-verbal behaviour or physical abuse and includes:

- attention-seeking
- aggression (both physical and verbal) towards others
- self-destructive behaviour or self-harming.

Attention-seeking

Children will do just about anything to get the attention they crave from parents and carers. This is often shown through *disruptive* (making noises, not responding to an instruction) or *aggressive* behaviour and needs managing as identified below. Sometimes children who are trying to please can be just as disruptive. Those who desperately want adults to notice them will call out, interrupt, ask questions and frequently push in front of other children to show something they have made or done.

Case Study A lack of consistency

Callum is in nursery class. He is an energetic, popular and sociable boy, aged two-and-a-half years. The room leader, Joanne, has a particular soft spot for Callum as she was a friend with his mum before he started at the nursery. Lately, Callum has begun to disrupt the class by running around during quieter times and meal times. He has recently dropped his afternoon nap at his mum's request, and is very noisy and boisterous when the other children are trying to sleep. Joanne is usually in the office during this naptime after lunch, and leaves Fiona in charge of the running of the room. Fiona adopts a firm line with Callum. She takes him aside, gets down to his level and tells him clearly why he cannot make noise and run around, and what behaviour she expects from him. She also takes the opportunity to go with him to find quiet games to play while the others are asleep. This works well for a little while, but usually Callum needs a few reminders before he accepts. Occasionally, as a treat, he is allowed to go and play outside with the pre-school children (if they have room for him) but Fiona will not allow this unless Callum is behaving well.

However, Fiona has noticed that when Callum is being disruptive and Joanne is in the room, she adopts a different approach. First Joanne will tell him to stop, but when he does not respond, she leaves the room – taking him with her to 'help' her run errands, saying to the other staff members that he is bored and that is why he is not behaving well. Fiona views this as rewarding inappropriate behaviour, and finds that after it has happened a few times, Callum becomes increasingly difficult to control, and becomes easily upset and tearful. He stops responding so positively to Fiona's technique, and requires one-to-one attention at a time when staff members are trying to settle ten other children for their naps, as well as supply play for the few children who, like Callum, no longer have daytime naps.

1. What do the staff need to do to rectify this situation?
2. Why do you think that Callum is now becoming upset easily?
3. Do you think that Callum's 'treat' of running errands is making him happy in the long run?
4. Why is it unfair on children when there is inconsistency in discipline techniques?

Strategies for dealing with attention-seeking behaviour

Children who seek attention challenge patience but with some reminding about turn-taking, and clear expectation that they will do so, they can learn to wait for their turn. It is important to give attention when they have waited appropriately so that they are encouraged to do so again. Practitioners could try the following strategies:

- whenever possible ignoring attention-seeking behaviour, unless their attention is drawn to it (perhaps by another child) as the message sent then is that it is acceptable to behave in that way
- giving attention and praise to another child who is behaving acceptably
- distracting the child's attention (particularly appropriate with younger children) or removing him or her to another activity or group
- expressing disapproval – verbally and/or non-verbally through body language, facial expression (frowning) and shaking of the head
- using a *sanction* – withdrawal of a privilege (such as removing a toy or activity).

Physical aggression

This usually results from strong feelings that are difficult to control. Whatever the cause – and it may be provocation – the adult should deal with it calmly and ensure that the needs of all the children involved are met. A child who has lost control frightens herself and the other children.

Strategies for dealing with aggressive behaviour

Time out: This involves the child who has been aggressive being taken to an identified place away from the incident – a corner or chair. 'Time out' allows for a calming-down period and for other children to be reassured. This method can work but needs positive follow-up by a staff member to explain that the behaviour was unacceptable, explain why and suggest how the child might have behaved otherwise; for example, asked instead of snatched, or listened to the apology for the model being broken. Unless this is done there is a danger that the chair (or area) becomes known to the children as the 'naughty chair' and staff begin to use it as a way of 'grounding' a child who is causing annoyance without really addressing the issues. Many adults do not like to use this approach for this reason. (See below, page 116, **The use of sanctions** for more strategies for dealing with inappropriate behaviour.)

Case Study — Aidan's behaviour

Aidan had recently started in the reception class and displayed inappropriate behaviour in many different ways and situations. On arrival in the playground in the mornings, with both his parents and younger sister, he would walk around poking and kicking other children. This caused anger among other parents, upset among the children and ill feeling towards his parents, who would shout at him before grabbing him, holding him by the hand and telling him off loudly. The staff discussed this with the parents and it was agreed that, in the short term, Aidan should be brought to school ten minutes later than everyone else. Every morning the father would deliver him to the classroom door with the instruction, 'Behave'.

Aidan always said that he would; however, he did not really understand what 'behave' meant in terms of his own actions. His teacher made a point of reminding him, throughout the day, of what behaviour was expected and explained what that meant for him; for example, 'When I ask you to "sit nicely", this means sitting still without touching any other child or anything.' It was also an opportunity to reinforce the rule for other children. Improvement was very gradual. Only one aspect of behaviour was

Case study — Aidan's behaviour (cont.)

dealt with at a time. He was given one-to-one support when available and observations were recorded to monitor progress and plan future strategies.

1. How did Aidan's teacher help him to change his behaviour?

2. In pairs produce some simple rules for four- to five-year-olds in a reception class that give clear guidance about what they should do – rather than what they should not do. For example, DO walk sensibly in the classroom (instead of DO NOT run in the classroom).

How to respond when a child bites

Try to think why the child has bitten. Ask the following questions to help you to understand why it has happened:

- When and where did it happen?
- Who with?
- What happened before?
- What happened afterwards?
- How do you think the child feels?
- Many settings develop a 'biting policy' and produce a leaflet with guidelines to support both parents and practitioners.

Strategies for dealing with a child who bites

- Comfort and take care of the child who has been bitten, in a 'low-key' calm way. Tell the bitten child, 'That must be sore, let's get a cold cloth.'
- To the biter, say firmly, but gently, 'It's not OK to bite, because biting hurts. If you want to bite, you can bite a biscuit or a toy, but I can't let you bite Martha.'
- Encourage the biter to 'make amends' in some way – to help get the cold cloth or a teddy for comfort.

Reflective practice

Sharing experiences

Discuss how staff in your setting deal with inappropriate behaviour. Do you feel that the methods used are generally effective?

Temper tantrums

These are usually associated with two-year-olds but can occur in older children. In fact, many people would not describe tantrums as inappropriate behaviour in toddlers. They may happen particularly when a child is ill or tired, but often build from a confrontational incident when he or she is asked to do something, or not to do something, and a battle of wills begins! Temper tantrums often involve shouting and crying, refusal to cooperate and mounting anger – shown through kicking, hitting, screaming, stamping – and, on occasions, self-harm. In younger children tantrums can be over very quickly but in older ones can take longer to reach a peak and longer to calm down afterwards.

✓ Progress check

Managing the behaviour of a child who bites

- Try to offer positive attention and affection to the 'biter' throughout the day.
- Provide snacks and drinks regularly.
- Make sure there is more than one of a favourite toy so there is a smaller chance of the child becoming frustrated.
- Arrange the room to make space for play.
- Show the child how to negotiate and take turns.
- Be aware of any changes taking place at home, and help the child to deal with these by talking sensitively with them about it.

✓ Progress check

Dealing with tantrums

- **Try to avoid them** – if you can anticipate them, try distracting the child with a game or another activity.
- **Try to ignore them** – apart from safety concerns, try to give as little attention as possible during the tantrum.
- **Be consistent** – if children think, from past experience, that the adult will not keep the boundary firmly, they will continue to tantrum; clear boundaries are essential.

Progress check (cont.)

- **A firm hug** may help the child feel secure and under control until the child calms down – this is useful in situations where you cannot walk away.
- **Talk about them** – this may help older children to express their feelings calmly.
- **Provide experiences and activities** that the child finds interesting; this usually helps children to become involved in positive ways.
- **Do not give in and let the boundary go** – this almost certainly leads to *more* rather than *fewer* tantrums because children are confused by inconsistency.

Self-destructive behaviour

This includes head-banging and forms of self-mutilation (e.g. tearing out hair, excessive nail-biting causing pain and bleeding). It usually signals some emotional difficulty that needs expert intervention. Staff and parents need to discuss their concerns and agree a common approach based on the advice they are given.

Unacceptable language

This includes swearing and name-calling that often result from children repeating what they have themselves heard. Sometimes they are unaware that it is unacceptable in one setting but not another. In these cases they need to be told firmly not to say those words 'here' – you cannot legislate for language they may use at home or criticise their families. Some children will deliberately use unacceptable language to shock or seek attention. In these cases you should state the rule calmly and firmly.

Name-calling

Name-calling must always be challenged and dealt with firmly, particularly if it is discriminatory (regarding race, creed, disability, family background, appearance, etc.). Explain that it is hurtful and that we are all different. This behaviour is best combated through good example and through anti-discriminatory practices in the work setting, which will help children to value other people as individuals.

The use of sanctions

A sanction is designed to discourage inappropriate behaviour. To be effective however, it must also protect the practitioner's relationship with the child and safeguard the child's self-esteem. Examples of sanctions to be used with young children include:

- A non-verbal signal: for example, a frown or shake of the head can be very effective.
- A minute's withdrawal (timed with a timer to ensure fairness) from the activity or group.
- Time out: It is important that 'time out' is used appropriately, and only when essential (see below).

When children misbehave, the adult responsible at the time should deal with it and, whenever possible, issue rebukes and sanctions in private. Children should always receive a warning before a sanction is imposed, to give them the chance to cooperate.

Time out

Time out involves removing the child from whatever they are doing and insisting that he or she sits in a safe place for a period of time, perhaps reading a book. The supervising adult in these circumstances should:

- **ignore the child, offering no eye contact or conversation**: This gives the child time to calm down – to think and reflect on his or her behaviour.
- **time the Time Out**: The length of time out should ideally match the age of the child; for example, for a three-year-old child use three minutes.
- **invite the child to return**: The child should be invited to return after the Time Out, and to agree to behave appropriately if he or she wants to rejoin the wider group.
- **praise the child**: If the child then behaves appropriately in the next few minutes, the adult should offer approval and praise.

Key term

Sanction – A course of action that can be used if necessary to make people obey a rule or behave in a particular way.

Referring inappropriate behaviour to others

Sometimes the behaviour management strategies outlined above fail to be effective, or are only effective for a short period of time. If inappropriate behaviour is linked to the child's development, is temporary and capable of being managed within the setting, then there is no need to refer to a professional.

When to refer

Practitioners may need to refer the following types of inappropriate behaviour:

- behaviour that is inappropriate for the child's stage of development: e.g. a child over four years old who continues biting, or an older child who hits other children or is physically aggressive in other ways
- self-harming behaviour
- bullying.

There are other professionals who may be called upon to help all those involved. It is useful for senior practitioners to attend meetings which allow everyone to contribute information about a child; these will help to create an overall view of progress, development and behaviour and it is here that recorded observations will be especially useful. It is important to follow correct procedures for reporting incidents.

Professionals who may become involved include the following:

- **Health visitors** work primarily with children up to five years and their families, checking for healthy growth and development.
- **Play therapists** have specialist training and work with children through play to help them feel emotionally secure.
- **Paediatricians** are doctors who specialise in the care of children up to the age of 16, to check for normal development and diagnose difficulties.
- **Educational psychologists** assess children who have special needs, and give advice, particularly for those with emotional and behavioural difficulties.
- **Child psychiatrists** work with children and their families to help them to express their thoughts and feelings.

(Assessment for this Unit is set externally in the form of a multiple choice question paper.)

4 Children and play: Unit 4

The Charter of Children's Rights (1989) states that every child in the world should have the right to play. Play is not the same as recreation or relaxation. Play is about high levels of learning, while recreation is about relaxing and not thinking very hard. See more on play in Unit 8.

The importance of play to development

What is play?

Through play, children bring together and organise their ideas, feelings, relationships and their physical expression. It helps them to use what they know and to make sense of the world and people they meet. Play brings together:

- ideas and creativity
- feelings
- relationships
- physical coordination
- spiritual development.

During play, children:

- begin to make sense and take control of what is happening in their world
- get ready for the future
- think about things that have happened.

There are different ideas about how to develop play, but although there are wide cultural variations, all children seem to develop and learn through play, including children with severe disabilities.

Children who do not play find it difficult to learn (e.g. children in the Romanian orphanages were held back in learning about objects, ideas, feelings, relationships and people).

Your role will be important in providing opportunities that support and extend children's play.

Theories of play

Ideas about play are influenced by thinkers from the past and thinkers from around the world. A theory is something that helps us to explain and answer 'Why?' It helps us to look at the role of play in a child's development. The different theories of play emphasise different aspects. They all help us to learn more about children's play.

Friedrich Froebel (1782–1852)

Froebel was a forester and mathematician. He was the first person to write about the importance of the play in development and learning. He started a community school, where parents were welcome at any time. He trained his staff to observe and value children's play.

Froebel has had a profound influence on early childhood education and care. He:

- thought it was important to talk with parents and learn with them how to help children learn through their play
- designed a set of wooden blocks (Gifts), which are still used in early childhood settings today. He also designed many other kinds of play equipment (Occupations) and Movement Games

(action songs and finger play rhymes and dancing) through which children learn by doing

- considered that relationships with other children were as important as relationships with adults, and he had a strong belief in the value of imaginative and symbolic play
- encouraged pretend play, and play with other children
- thought both indoor and outdoor play to be important
- helped children to make dens in the garden and to play with natural materials such as sand, water and wood
- believed that teachers should be sensitive and approachable, and that they should have qualities that the children could respect and imitate
- called his schools 'kindergartens' (for children aged two to eight years). Kindergarten means 'children's garden' in German. Even today there are kindergartens all over the world.

Maria Montessori (1880–1952)

Maria Montessori was an Italian doctor who worked in the poorest areas of Rome in the 1900s. She did not believe that pretend play was important. She thought children wanted to do real things (e.g. not *play* at being cooks but to actually do some cooking). However, she did like Froebel's play equipment, and she designed more (didactic materials) to help children learn, for example, about shapes, weight, colour, size and numbers.

Montessori believed the following:

- All children have absorbent minds, and the way in which children learn is different from the way in which an adult learns. She believed that children absorb information from the environment. Initially this learning is unconscious, but after the age of three the child absorbs information consciously. The ability to absorb language and to learn motor skills is initially without formal instruction but later children use language to question.
- Children experience sensitive periods during which they are particularly receptive to developing specific skills. A child will develop a particular interest in one specific skill or action, which they will repeat time and time again.

- Children should be guided by a trained adult to use equipment until they can use it confidently on their own and independently.
- A Montessori teacher plays a very different role from that of a teacher in mainstream school provision. The teacher, who is known as the directress, is seen to guide or direct the children, putting them in touch with their environment so that they can learn for themselves.

Montessori called her schools Children's Houses, and these are still to be found all over the world.

Rudolf Steiner (1861–1925)

Rudolf Steiner encouraged play through natural materials, such as clay, beeswax, silk scarves for dressing up and wooden blocks that are irregularly shaped.

He believed that singing and dancing were important, and that stories give children ideas for their play. For Steiner, education is an artistic process. There must be a balance between artistic, creative and practical experiences on the one hand, and academic activities on the other.

Steiner believed that children pass through three specific phases, as follows:

1 **The Period of Will** (birth to seven years) – where the active aspect predominates. Within this period there are three stages: birth to three years – the main features are walking, speech and the ability to think in words; three to five years – the development of the imagination and memory is important; five years onwards – the stimulation for play tends to come less from external objects but more from ideas generated within the children.
2 The **Period of the Heart** (seven to 14 years) – the feeling phase. The child is now ready for formal learning, although the role of the imagination is still very important.
   The **Period of the Head** (14 years onwards) – the cognitive phase. The adolescent phase is considered to be the period of thinking. At this stage children develop a healthy idealism, and may be very sensitive about their feelings.

Steiner's schools are called Waldorf Schools and are now the largest independent school system in the world, with many of the schools situated in North America and Australia.

Margaret McMillan (1860–1931)

Margaret McMillan (and her sister, Rachel) fought for the education of young children, to emphasise physical care and development. They campaigned and were successful in introducing free school meals under the Provision of School Meals Act 1906, and they introduced regular medical inspections for schoolchildren by opening the first clinic especially devoted to school children in 1908. McMillan believed that:

- children cannot learn if they are undernourished, poorly clothed, ill, with poor teeth, poor eyesight, ear infections, rickets, etc. (Recent reports emphasise that poor health and poverty are challenges still facing those who work with families in the UK today.)
- children learn by exploring, and they achieve their whole potential through play; she placed an emphasis on craft and water activities, singing and model-making
- outdoor play and being taught in the fresh air are important; gardening was a regular activity
- hygiene and cleanliness are very important; McMillan considered it to be her role to educate parents about how children should remain clean and hygienic
- the role of the 'home' in supporting a child's learning capability is very important
- it is very important to have trained teachers, and she opened a special training school for the teachers in her schools. Children were taught in small groups, and McMillan expected teachers to be imaginative and inventive
- very close **partnership with parents** is important: she encouraged parents to develop alongside their children, with adult classes in hobbies and languages made available to them.

The British nursery school, as envisaged by McMillan, has been admired and emulated across the world. McMillan Nursery schools have gardens, and are communities that welcome both parents and children.

Ideas about play from around the world

In Western Europe and the USA, children are often given toys to play with. Sometimes they are very expensive to buy. In other countries, specially designed toys may not be part of the way of life, and children will play mainly with natural materials, such as stones, twigs, sand, water and mud, and make their own pretend play.

In some cultures, adults think it is not a good idea to play with children. They let children play together and older children play with younger children (for example, Maori children in New Zealand). Other cultures believe that adults (usually mothers) ought to play with their children and teach them through their play.

How children become involved in their play and activities

Some theories emphasise the importance of childhood play because it encourages children to practise things they need to do later on in life. It helps them with the physical coordination of their bodies, objects and people.

Learning through practice play

There are two sides to practice play.

1 **The biological side of practice play**: studies of young animals playing show that, for example, lion cubs playing together quite naturally begin catching and chewing. This helps them to learn what they need to know later in order to hunt for their food and survive.
2 **The social/cultural aspect of practice play**: even newborn babies are very aware of other people. Children imitate people who are important role models for them.

The importance of play in supporting all aspects of development

Knowing the way that play progresses as children grow older helps adults to plan appropriate play materials and play opportunities for different children according to their stage of development.

This is called knowing about progression in the development of play.

Play, feelings and self-esteem

There is a popular idea that learning through play means always having fun. Certainly, children will have plenty of fun as they learn through play. However, children also learn about sad and angry feelings. They are challenged to learn about difficult things such as:

- death
- being separated from people they love
- being hurt.

Some theories emphasise the importance of children's feelings. These are 'psychoanalytic' ideas about why children play. The play scenarios children create deal with their feelings of happiness, sadness, anger, and so on, in an emotionally healthy way. Although this helps any child, therapists particularly emphasise sad and angry feelings through play for the children they work with. Research shows that emotional health is helped through play, and leads to children developing positive self-esteem and resilience.

Play helps socially acceptable behaviour

Other theories show that children learn to think of others through their play. They learn to behave in ways that are socially acceptable as they play. This helps them to understand how other people feel and to develop morally (to value and respect others, and to care about other people). This is called **theory of mind**.

Play helps thinking and ideas (concepts) to develop

Unit 10 has detailed information on important theorists in child care and education.

There are three important theories about how play helps children to have ideas and learn to think. They are all useful for adults working with young children. Two of these theories emphasise social/cultural learning.

Both Vygotsky's and Bruner's theories show that other people are important in developing a child's play.

1 **Lev Vygotsky** was a psychologist in the 1930s who found that children do their best thinking when they play with others. This is because play helps them to feel in **control** of their ideas, and to make sense of things that have happened. Play helps children to **think ahead**.

2 **Jerome Bruner** believes that play helps children to learn how adults do things in their culture. Adults observe children as they play and break things down into easily manageable steps for them. This is called **scaffolding the learning**.

3 **Jean Piaget**'s theory emphasised both biological and social/cultural learning. It is the most famous theory. Piaget emphasised that children are active learners. They learn through their senses (seeing, touching, hearing, smelling, tasting) and through their own movement.
   - *Sometimes children will **play alone**.*
   - *Sometimes they will **play with others** (children or adults).*
   - *Children are like scientists, exploring their world and working at different levels about the world.*
   - *Children go through stages of play (see below). Although each of the stages builds on the one before, they also overlap. Modern research shows some children do things earlier, and some later, than others.*

Piaget's stages of play

1 **Babyhood (birth to 18 months)**: play involves sensorimotor behaviour (the senses and movement).

2 **The early years of symbolic play (18 months to five years):** play involves making something stand for (represent) something else.

3 **The school years (five to eight years):** children move from play to taking part in games. They are able to play more cooperatively. The rules of games are quite different from the rules of play. In games the rules are given; in play children make up the rules as they go along.

Play and the development of conversation skills

Children experiment with language during play and use words to express their thoughts and ideas, to solve problems and to communicate their wishes.

Play and the development of physical coordination

Children vary and develop at different rates. This depends partly on their biological stage. It also depends on where they grow up and what play opportunities and materials they are given. A child who has played with wooden blocks since toddler times might well be building towers that are castles by the age of four years. A child who has not had these experiences is unlikely to do this.

This shows that what children learn is influenced by how adults help their development. This is why **observing all children** as they play is important.

The stages of play

It used to be thought that there were four stages of social play:

1 solitary play
2 parallel play
3 associative play
4 cooperative play.

Recent research shows that children do not develop as if they are climbing up a ladder. Instead, brain studies show that their play develops like a network. Sometimes they will play alone (solitary play). Sometimes they will play with others (parallel, associatively or cooperatively). These aspects of play are discussed on pages 122–127.

The chosen aspect of play will partly depend on their age, but it will also depend on their mood, others around them, where they are, and whether they are tired, hungry or comfortable.

It is certainly easier for toddlers and young children to play together in parallel, associatively or cooperatively if they are in a pair (two children). Larger groups are more of a challenge for young children. Gradually, three or four children might play cooperatively together. This tends to develop from three or four years of age.

Play and the development of physical coordination

Playing alone (solitary play)

From six months onwards
Solitary play is play that is undertaken alone, sometimes through choice and at other times because the child finds it hard to join in, or because of his or her developmental stage.

- In the first stage of play, beginning at about six months, babies play alone. Babies and toddlers need time and space to play alone, but often appreciate having others around them as they do so.
- Playing alone gives personal space and time to think, get to know yourself and like yourself.
- When toddlers play alone, they seek interesting experiences, but need support when frustrated.
- Children of all ages engage in solitary play sometimes; playing alone enables older children

Physical ability	Gross motor skills	Fine motor skills
Sit (usually 6–9 months)	• Play with feet (put them in mouth) • Cruise around furniture	• Play with objects using a pincer movement (i.e. finger and thumb) • Transfer toys from one hand to the other • Enjoy dropping objects over the side of the high chair and look to see where they have gone • Play with objects by putting them into the mouth • Enjoy 'treasure baskets' (natural objects and household objects) Provide: • Cups, boxes, pots of different sizes

Physical ability	Gross motor skills	Fine motor skills
Crawl (usually 9–12 months)	• When sitting, the baby leans forward and picks up objects • Enjoy playing by crawling upstairs or onto low furniture • Love to bounce in time to music	• Pick things up with a pincer movement (finger and thumb) • Pull objects towards themselves • Can point at toys • Clasp hands and love to copy adults' actions in play • Love to play by throwing toys on purpose • Hold toys easily in hands • Put objects in and out of pots and boxes Provide: • Push and pull toys
Walk (but with sudden falling into a sitting position) (12–15 months)	• Can manage stairs with adult supervision • Can stand and kneel without support	• Begin to build towers with wooden blocks • Make lines of objects on the floor • Begin using books and turn several pages at a time • Use both hands but often prefer one • Lot of pointing • Pull toys along and push buttons Provide: • Board books and picture books with lines • Big empty cardboard boxes • Messy play with water paints and sand (be alert for physical safety)
Walk confidently (usually 18 months)	• Can kneel, squat, climb and carry things, can climb on chairs • Can twist around to sit • Can creep downstairs on tummy going backwards	• Pick up small objects and threads • Build towers • Scribble on paper • Push and pull toys • Enjoy banging toys (e.g. hammer and peg drums) Provide: • Large crayons and paper for drawing
Jump (usually 2 years)	• Can jump on the spot and run, and climb stairs two feet at a time • Kick but not good at catching ball • Enjoy space to run and play (trips to the park) • Enjoy climbing frames (supervised)	• Draw circles • Build tall towers • Pick up tiny objects • Turn the pages of books one at a time • Enjoy toys to ride and climb on • Enjoy messy play with water paints and sand pits Provide: • Duplo, jigsaws, crayons and paper, picture books, puppets, simple dressing-up clothes, hats, belts and shoes
Hop (usually 3 years)	• Jump from low steps • Walk forwards, backwards and sideways • Stand and walk on tiptoe • Stand on one foot • Try to hop • Use pedals on tricycle • Climb stairs one foot at a time	• Build taller and taller towers with blocks • Begin to use pencil grip • Paint and make lines and circles in drawings • Use play dough, sand for modelling, paint • Hold objects to explore Provide: • Enjoy trip to the park, walks, library, swimming • Enjoy cooking, small world, gluing, pouring, cutting

Physical ability	Gross motor skills	Fine motor skills
Skip (usually 4 years)	• Balance (walking on a line) • Catch a ball, kick, throw and bounce • Bend at the waist to pick up objects from the floor • Climbing trees and frames • Can run up and down stairs one foot at a time	• Build tower with blocks that are taller and taller • Draw people, houses, etc. • Thread beads • Enjoy exercise, swimming, climbing (climbing frames and bikes) Provide: • Jigsaws, construction toys, wooden blocks, small world, glue and stick, paint, sand, water, clay, play dough, dressing-up clothes and home area play • Cooking (measuring, pouring and cutting)
Jump, hop, skip and run with coordination (usually 5 years)	• Use a variety of play equipment (slides, swings, climbing frames) • Enjoy ball games • Hop and run lightly on toes, and can move rhythmically to music • Well-developed sense of balance	• Sew large stitches • Draw with people, animals and places, etc. • Coordinate paint brushes and pencils, and a variety of tools • Enjoy outdoor activities (skipping ropes, football – both boys and girls enjoy these) • Make models, do jigsaws
Move with increased coordination and balance (usually 6–7 years)	• Can ride two-wheel bicycle • Hops easily with good balance • Can jump off apparatus at school	• Build play scenarios with wooden blocks • Draw play scenarios in drawings and paintings • Hold pencil as adults do • Enjoy ball games • Enjoy vigorous activity (riding a bike, swimming) (Note: children should never be forced to take part, unless they want to) • Enjoy board games and computer games • Often (but not always) enjoy work being displayed on interest tables and walls (Note: children should never be forced to display their work)

Table 4.1 Play and the development of physical coordination

to concentrate and practise their skills (e.g. when constructing a model).
- It is important to protect the child's play space and toys from interference by other children.
- Children should be allowed to experience 'ownership' of toys and not be pushed to share before they are ready.

Example: A child might play alone – for example, with a doll's house – because they want to play out a story that they have in their head. Having other children join the play would stop them being able to do this.

Figure 4.1 Babies sometimes like to play alone

Figure 4.2 Parallel play

Onlooker behaviour

From about eight months to three+ years:
Onlooker 'play' is the passive observation of the play of others without actual participation. Before children begin to play with each other, they go through a brief stage of looking-on behaviour:

- Children will stop what they are doing to watch and listen to what other children are doing.
- Older children may also watch others play if they are new to the group and do not yet feel ready to enter into the play.
- Even a child who is already secure in a group may engage in onlooker behaviour – taking a passive interest in what their friends are doing, but not joining in.

Stages of social play: children play together

Parallel play

Parallel play develops from two to four+ years, and describes what happens when children play alongside each other but quite separately and without communicating with each other. Onlooker behaviour evolves into parallel – or side-by-side – play, which includes a lot of imitation and conversation back and forth between the players.

- During this stage, children like to have exactly the same toys as their peers do, but their own play space.

- They are no longer content to play alone, but they are also not ready for the demands of sharing toys or taking turns.
- Older children also enjoy parallel play with their friends.

Example: Two children might both put dolls to bed in the home area. They do not take much notice of each other.

Associative play

Associative play develops between the ages of three-and-a-half and five+ years. This is when two or more children actively interact with one another by sharing or borrowing toys, while not doing the same things. Children playing at the parallel stage will begin to become aware of other children. They will often begin to communicate through talking to each other or by becoming aware of each other's games and by explaining to each other what they are doing:

- Gradually one child will become involved in the other child's play; this is known as **associative** (or partnership) play.
- Language becomes much more important, imagination increases and dramatic themes begin to come into the play; this category of play may seem to be cooperative, but this is not the case – at this age, children are still too egocentric to have true cooperation.

Example: Two children might play so that one is the cook in the cafe and the other is the waitress. They do not seem to care that they have no customers.

Figure 4.3 Associative play

Cooperative play

Cooperative play happens from the age of four-and-a-half years onwards, and is when children begin to 'play' together – to share their play. They become more sociable and take on roles in the play. Children begin to be aware of the needs and the roles of their peers and gradually the play can become complex:

- Rules are sometimes devised and some cooperative play will be revisited over several days.
- Cooperative play continues throughout middle childhood, where it evolves into more stylised games with rules.
- In the early stages of cooperative play, the rules are not as important as the sense of belonging to a group and working towards a common goal.

Figure 4.4 Cooperative play

Example of early (or simple) cooperative play: One child might be the baby and the other might be the parent, as they play going to the shops. They talk about their play ideas: 'You say "mum" and I say "yes, darling."'

Example of later (or complex) cooperative play: A group of children between three and five years old have been on an outing in the local market. When they return, the adult sets up a market stall. Some children become customers and buy things. Others sell things. John has a hearing impairment and uses sign language. Jack understands his sign to give him three oranges. Other children talk as they play: 'You come and bag these apples.'

✓ Progress check

Matching stages of play

Read through the section in the book on 'Stages of play' and match the following descriptions to the stage of play and the approximate age when children tend to play in this way.

Stages of play:
- Solitary play
- Onlooker or spectator play
- Parallel play
- Associative play
- Cooperative play.

Four children are making biscuits. They decide how to measure out the ingredients and how to mix them together, sharing the tasks between them. They take turns and there is plenty of discussion.

Stage of play:

Approximate age:

Two children are sitting next to each other on the floor. Each is playing with wooden blocks and is totally absorbed, but not taking any notice of each other.

Stage of play:

Approximate age:

A baby is sitting on the floor, selecting items from a treasure basket containing natural and everyday objects.

Progress check (cont.)

Stage of play:

Approximate age:

Two children are playing with a farm set. A third child stops what he is doing and watches them intently for a while.

Stage of play:

Approximate age:

A group of children are playing at the sand tray. They are starting to talk to each other, explaining to each other what they are doing.

Stage of play:

Approximate age:

Types of play and appropriate activities for learning, and how to provide them

The areas and types of play

The terms 'structured play' and 'free play' are rather old-fashioned ways of describing the way children learn through play. Research is showing that we need to think about these in a modern way.

Free play

Children lead their own play, and adults leave them to it. They might make a play scenario with toy cars, for example, and pretend they are playing garages.

Adults provide:

- play materials
- play opportunities, both indoors and outdoors.

Children choose what to do and are given plenty of free time to develop their play.

Structured play

Research is showing that there are two kinds of structured play, as described below.

Directly structured play

Adults guide and lead the play. The adult might set up a shop and show the children how to play in it, introducing shop vocabulary (words about shopping) and guiding the play story that develops.

Indirectly structured play

The adult structures the environment indoors and outdoors. The materials offered to the children are chosen and organised carefully. Children have plenty of time for play. The adult observes the children as they play, and joins in following the children's play scenario ideas. The adult does not take over but follows the children's ideas.

This is a bit like the way a conversation between people goes along. One person speaks and the other listens; then the other person replies.

Indirectly structured play means that adults have to be sensitive to the child's play ideas. The adult is very important because they add ideas to help the child's play develop.

Creative play

Children must not be expected to 'make something'. Creative play is about experimenting with materials and music. It is not about producing things to go on display, or to be taken home; for example, when children are involved with messy finger play with paint, nothing is left at the end of the session once it has been cleared away.

Adults can encourage creative play by offering children a range of materials and play opportunities in dance, music, drawing, collage, painting, model-making and woodwork, sand (small-world scenarios), water (small-world scenarios) and miniature garden scenarios.

Creative play helps children to express their feelings and ideas about people, objects and events. It helps children to:

- be physically coordinated
- develop language
- develop ideas (concepts)
- develop relationships with people
- be more confident, and it boosts their self-esteem.

Drama and imaginative (or pretend) play

This is where children make play scenarios – for example, about a shop or a boat, a garage, an office or a swimming pool.

The important thing to remember about pretend play is that there will be nothing left to show anyone when the play finishes. Pretend play scenarios do not last. This is why it is difficult to explain to parents the importance of pretend play.

Some adults take video or photographs of children during their play, to try to capture it on film. They want to value pretend play as they do all the other learning that children do.

What to look out for in pretend play

- Children use play props – for example, they pretend a box is a fridge, or a stick is a spoon, or a daisy is a fried egg.
- They role-play and pretend that they are someone else (e.g. the shopkeeper).
- When they pretend play together, cooperatively, this is called socio-dramatic play.
- Young children pretend play everyday situations: getting up, going to sleep, eating (just as Peppa Pig and George Pig® do on television and in books.
- Gradually children develop their pretend play scenarios to include situations that are not everyday events, and that they may only have heard about but not experienced. This is called fantasy play. They might pretend to go to the moon or go on an aeroplane. It is not impossible that these things will happen to them.
- Superhero play develops when they use unreal situations, like Superman or Power Rangers or cartoon characters.
- Children use imaginative play to act out situations that they have definitely experienced, like going to the supermarket.
- For example, a group of children made a swimming pool out of wooden blocks. One of them pretended to be the lifeguard and rescued someone drowning. All the children had visited a swimming pool so this pretend play was based on a real experience.

EYFS 2012

Pretend play links with the EYFS Profile and is part of all six areas of learning. See Chapter 8, page 208, for more information. Pretend play also links with all areas of a child's development:

- emotional development
- social development
- language development
- cognitive (thinking) development
- physical development.

Spontaneous play

Spontaneous play is particularly rewarding as it often arises from a child's interest at the time. It can also be stimulated by natural events – for example, a playground full of puddles after a rainstorm – or by an experience a child has had and wants to share with you – for example, the arrival of a new baby or a new family pet. Spontaneous play can also arise from planned activities – for example, during an activity with wooden blocks, when children make their own decisions about how they use the blocks, perhaps arranging them as seats to pretend they are travelling on a train.

Heuristic (discovery) play

Heuristic play is the term used to describe children playing and exploring natural materials using all of their senses. (The word 'heuristic' means 'helping to find out or discover'.) The concept was developed by Elinor Goldshmied, a child psychologist, from her work watching children and the way they gained knowledge of the world around them.

Heuristic play is rooted in young children's natural curiosity. As babies grow, they move beyond being content to simply feel and ponder objects, to wanting to find out what can be *done* with them. Toddlers have an urge to handle things: to gather, fill, dump, stack, knock down, select and manipulate in other ways. Kitchen utensils offer this kind of activity and can occupy a child for surprising stretches of time.

When toddlers make an enjoyable discovery – for instance when one item fits into another, or an interesting sound is produced – they often repeat the action several times to test the result. This strengthens cognitive development as well as fine muscle control and hand–eye coordination. Treasure basket play was also developed by Elinor Goldshmied to promote heuristic play.

 In practice

Observing a baby with a natural treasure basket

Babies learn about their environment using all their senses – touch, smell, taste, sight, hearing and movement. A treasure basket is a collection of everyday objects chosen to stimulate the different senses. Babies have the chance to decide for themselves what they want to play with, choosing in turn whichever object they want to explore.

Choose a sturdy basket or box – one that does not tip over easily.

Fill the basket with lots of natural objects or objects made from natural materials so that the baby has plenty to choose from. For example:

• fir cones	• large seashells	• loofah
• fruit (e.g. apple, lemon)	• brushes	• woollen ball
• wooden pegs	• small baskets	• feathers
• large pebbles	• gourds	• pumice stone

Make sure that everything you choose for the basket is clean and safe. Remember that babies often want to put everything into their mouths, so you need to check that all objects are clean and safe.

Make sure the baby is seated comfortably and safely, with cushions for support if necessary. Sit nearby and watch to give the baby confidence. Only talk or intervene if the baby clearly needs attention.

You should check the contents of the basket regularly, cleaning objects and removing any damaged items.

 In practice (cont.)

Write an observation of the activity, noting the following:
- the length of time the baby plays with each item
- what he or she does with it
- any facial expressions or sounds made by the baby.

Physical play and exercise

Physical play promotes a child's health. It links with all other areas of a child's development. The brain works better if children have plenty of fresh air and exercise. That is why both indoor and outdoor play are very important.

Through physical play children learn to challenge gender stereotypes. Boys and girls can enjoy playing ball games (e.g. football play scenarios, running and climbing). Children need to be encouraged in these activities. It helps if they wear clothes and shoes that allow freedom of movement. Children also:

- learn through their **senses**
- coordinate their **movements**
- develop their **muscles**
- learn about pace and keeping going (**stamina**)
- learn how to use space in a **coordinated** way
- learn to challenge **gender stereotypes**.

Manipulative play

Children need plenty of opportunities to play using manipulative skills. This particularly encourages children to use their hands, which are very important in human development.

Boys and girls can enjoy manipulative play.

EYFS 2012

Manipulative play links with the EYFS Framework, with the area of learning called Physical Development. See Chapter 10 for more information on the EYFS.

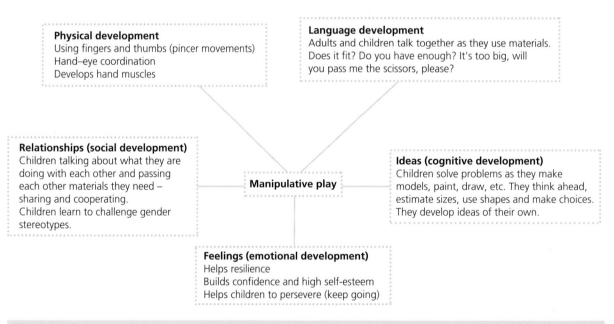

Physical development
Coordinates movements (fine motor and gross motor)
Develops muscles
Develops stamina
Helps children to use space in a coordinated way
Learn through the senses
Learn through movement

Language development
There are endless opportunities, e.g. adults need
to give children words they need (vocabulary),
such as fast, slow, up, down, nearly, a good landing.

Relationships (social development)
Children who play physically learn to be
sensitive and aware of others, to give
them enough space, take turns and share.
They cooperate with each other so that
they can all have fun together.
During rough-and-tumble play, they bond
with each other emotionally.
This physical play is usually for short
periods and can often end quickly, and
sometimes in tears!

**Ideas (cognitive development) e.g. children
develop understanding of :**
timing
awareness of space
reasons why things happen, e.g. if I jump
from the second step I need to push off
harder and to bend my knees when I
land. otherwise I will fall.

Physical play

Feelings (emotional development)
When a child falls over but gets back on the climbing frame,
they are becoming resilient.
When children shout 'Look at me I am high up', as they climb,
It builds their confidence and gives them high self-esteem.
Children who have plenty of time for free movement in a safe physical
environment have opportunities to become adventurous.

Figure 4.5 Aspects of physical play

Physical development
Using fingers and thumbs (pincer movements)
Hand–eye coordination
Develops hand muscles

Language development
Adults and children talk together as they use materials.
Does it fit? Do you have enough? It's too big, will
you pass me the scissors, please?

Relationships (social development)
Children talking about what they are
doing with each other and passing
each other materials they need –
sharing and cooperating.
Children learn to challenge gender
stereotypes.

Ideas (cognitive development)
Children solve problems as they make
models, paint, draw, etc. They think ahead,
estimate sizes, use shapes and make choices.
They develop ideas of their own.

Manipulative play

Feelings (emotional development)
Helps resilience
Builds confidence and high self-esteem
Helps children to persevere (keep going)

Figure 4.6 Aspects of manipulative play

✓ Progress check

Understanding key terms in play

1. Match the category of play in column one with the example in column two.

Category of play	Example
1. Physical play	A. Child using a brush and paint on paper
2. Fantasy play	B. Three children are playing in the home area; one is the shopkeeper and the other two are customers
3. Exploratory play	C. Child pretending to be a fire-fighter
4. Manipulative play	D. Child playing outdoors on a climbing frame and slide
5. Creative play	E. Baby playing with treasure basket which contains natural and everyday objects
6. Pretend or imaginative play	F. Children playing with beakers and wheels at the water tray
7. Heuristic play	G. Child threading beads onto a lace
8. Socio-dramatic play	H. Child pretending he is flying to the moon on a broomstick

2. Using the headings from Column 1, think of two more examples of activities which correspond to each type of play – (except for heuristic play).

3. When you have finished, place the sheet in your Unit 4 work file.

Case Study — Making a waterfall

Andrew enjoyed playing at making a waterfall in the water tray by pouring water out of a bottle from as high as he could reach up. Other children joined in.

Adults can develop this play by setting up more bottles and having two water trays, to prevent the activity from becoming too crowded. They can set up the paddling pool outside to use as a big water tray, and let children use the hosepipe to fill it. Put guttering in the paddling pool to act as a water chute and provide jugs to pour water down the chutes. Spare clothes are needed in case children get wet. It is important to keep the floors indoors safe from becoming slippery with too much water. Always keep a mop and bucket near a water activity.

Planning activities for play in a range of settings and provision

When planning play activities, adults should consider the points made in Figure 4.7.

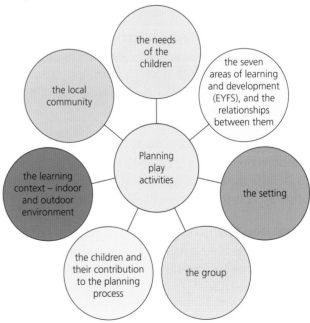

Figure 4.7 Planning play activities

For information on the EYFS, see below, page 191.

How to plan

The best planning comes from knowing the children really well. This develops from using the **observations** adults make of children to plan the next step in their play.

Children need a variety of activities or experiences, using a range of resources, to enable them to learn and make progress in all areas of development. Planning what will be offered helps children to use a range of resources and materials. It encourages a 'balanced' day.

Having made decisions about what to provide it is then necessary to plan each activity/experience and consider the following factors:

- aim or purpose
- time needed/group size
- preparation in advance
- preparation at the time
- space/resources/safety
- suitability for age/stage of development
- supervision/adult role
- adaptation for a child with a special need
- consideration of equal opportunities issues
- opportunities for monitoring and assessing individual children.

Aim or purpose

As for observations, a clear aim is preferable to one that is too wide or vague – for example, 'To develop fine manipulative skills through putting a straw in a carton of drink' or 'To develop listening skills through a "sound" lotto game'.

Almost all activities have many benefits and will help development in more than one area. It is a good idea to identify the main purpose and mention briefly other aspects that are also likely to be involved.

Time needed/group size

Most settings have a daily routine which fosters opportunities for free-flow play. These include opportunities for:

- refreshment, sleep or rest
- outdoor or energetic activity
- assembly or group time, and

- start and finish times for sessions (these may vary for individual children in a nursery setting).

Knowing how long you are going to need to carry out an activity from start to finish for a group is very important. It helps to decide when it can be done and, if all children are to have the opportunity to do it, how many 'sessions' will be needed. Generally, the younger the children, the fewer you would have in a group – perhaps for a 'messy' activity such as finger painting you may work with pairs or perhaps just one child. You need to allow time for clearing away, especially if the tables or the area are needed for another activity. Similarly, the children themselves may need to wash ready for lunch or get dressed for going outside/home.

Preparation/resources
In advance:

- The first step is to find out the setting's current topic and planning, and discuss with your supervisor what activity might be appropriate.
- You should then plan the activity, show the plan to your supervisor and, if it is suitable, agree when you may implement it. This should avoid a similar one being carried out by someone else the day before! At this stage you can ensure that the space you need (e.g. the book corner or the water tray) will be available. An activity that uses 'permanent' equipment (e.g. Lego, Stickle Bricks, puzzles) will need setting up – space, layout of equipment, seating if applicable. However, one that uses 'consumable materials' (i.e. ones that are used up and need replacing, such as paper, paint, glue) requires more consideration.
- Make a comprehensive list of what you need – this should be detailed. For example, not just 'six sheets of paper' but six sheets of A3, black, sugar paper (i.e. state size, colour, type).
- Check that your selected resources are available (another staff member may have reserved the last of the gold paper for a particular display or activity, so do not just go and help yourself!) and collect them in plenty of time. Some may need further preparation – for example, cutting to a smaller size or particular shape, arranging in pots or tubs for easy access, and so on.

- Check that:
  - *(for very young children) there are no tiny pieces*
  - *materials are clean*
  - *materials are undamaged*
  - *there are no toxic substances/contents.*
- For preparation relating to food and cooking activities see Unit 8, pages 209–211.

At the time:

- **Always allow time for preparation on the day** – arrive early if necessary. Your supervisor will have made arrangements for you to take the agreed number of children at the agreed time. If you are not ready, someone else has to supervise those children and/or find them an alternative activity.
- **Remember to protect tables**, surfaces, children and their clothing appropriately.
- **Prepare sufficient quantities of paint, paper**, and so on, for the group size identified and have them conveniently to hand – you cannot leave a group of young children alone while you go to fetch more paper from the stock cupboard or to mix up more paint!
- When planning your activity think about how you will introduce it – what will be your starting point? You might show the children the equipment and ask them about it, or remind them of a previous related experience.

Suitability for age/stage of development

Although you can use books to help you understand what is the 'expected' or 'norm' ability for the age range you are working with, it is more important to base your own planning on what you can see and have experienced in your particular work setting. If you have used your placement time effectively you will have helped with activities planned by other staff members and become familiar with the resources and with the children. Remember that children should be **active learners** and your plan should provide them with 'hands on' experience. Avoid activities that involve colouring in work sheets or 'sticking' ones that do not allow children to select their own materials and choose how to use the space.

Supervision/adult role

Your activity – perhaps a physical one involving large apparatus – may require more than one adult supervising. In this case it is important not only to check that there are sufficient adults available but also that any other adult knows your activity's aim and what is involved. If you have written a clear plan then it can be shared more easily. Try to think ahead about any aspects of your plan that may involve an adult in offering practical help to all children or an individual child.

Adaptation for a child with a special need/ consideration of equal opportunities

As you will be planning for children in your work setting you will be aware of any children with special needs – whether the difficulty results from a physical condition, a sensory impairment, a learning disorder, or a behavioural or emotional problem.

Take notice of the strategies used by other staff members to allow access to all activities and equipment. This may be as straightforward as ensuring that you make left-handed or 'dual-handed' scissors available, or more challenging in adapting space and materials for a child whose leg is in plaster.

Try to think about adaptations for children with sensory impairment:

- Visually impaired children will depend heavily on hearing and touch so try to adapt resources or provide extra ones to support their learning (e.g. samples of materials mentioned in stories like 'The Three Little Pigs' – straw, sticks and bricks).
- Hearing-impaired children will also benefit from learning through touch, but will need visual aids too – perhaps puppets or figures to demonstrate parts of a story or clear pictures sequenced to help with a cooking or construction task.

Always make sure that you have the children's attention, touching a visually impaired child on the arm so it is clear she needs to listen, and ensuring that when talking or giving instructions to a hearing-impaired child, she is able to see the speaker's face (see section on effective communication, in Unit 5).

Think about the equal opportunities issues dealt with in Unit 1 (e.g. gender and cultural stereotyping) and make sure that your resources promote **positive images**.

Opportunities for monitoring and assessing individual children

Your activity will offer opportunities for observing how children use equipment, listen to any instructions, talk about what they are doing and interact with each other. At the end of an activity make a note about any aspects that presented difficulties, caused frustration or were not sufficiently challenging. Make a note also of those in which the children were particularly successful. This helps staff to keep records, report progress to parents and plan for individual children's future needs.

Evaluating your plan

As well as recording the points mentioned above in relation to the children, you need to consider your own learning. You should try to judge how suitable your activity was and how it might be improved or altered. You can also reflect on your own ability to prepare, explain, support children and maintain behaviour. Refer to all the factors you had to consider, and identify which ones 'worked' (were appropriate) and which were less successful.

Example: would it have been more effective with thicker paint, coloured paper, fatter brushes? Did you allow enough/too much time? Was the cutting task too fiddly for the children to manage independently? How could it have been improved? Do not be too dismayed if an activity seems to be a disaster, but make sure you understand *why* and *what* went wrong!

Planning activities to meet children's needs

Daily planning allows staff to meet the individual needs of children by responding to children's emerging skills and interests. When deciding what activities and experiences will be offered to children, staff in a work setting must consider safety, space, children's ages and stage of development, supervision, and availability of resources. Most work settings plan activities around well-chosen themes or topics. These are usually relevant to the children themselves and, perhaps, the time of year; common ones are 'Ourselves', 'Autumn', 'Festivals' (e.g. Christmas, Diwali, Hanukkah, Chinese New Year), 'Growth' and 'Nursery Rhymes'.

The role of risk and challenge in play

Play England states that:

'All children both need and want to take risks in order to explore limits, venture into new experiences and develop their capacities, from a very young age and from their earliest play experiences.'

Everyday life always involves some degree of risk and children need to learn how to cope with this. Being *told* about possible dangers is not enough – children need to *see* or *experience* the consequences of not taking care. Children who learn early on to make their own rational decisions instead of simply doing what they are told to do by others will be in a better position to resist the pressures they will inevitably face as adolescents and adults. Children who have been over-protected will probably lack the ability to make rational decisions, and this could lead to them putting themselves at risk.

Taking small risks has a positive impact on a child's physical, intellectual, social and emotional development:

- **Physical development**: Children learn how to move safely and to develop their coordination and balance. Physically challenging activities that involve safe risk-taking help children to build and extend their strength and fitness levels. Vigorous activities such as completing an obstacle course or running will also help to reduce obesity.
- **Intellectual development**: Children learn how to negotiate, to solve problems and to make choices.
- **Emotional and social development**: Children build resilience and social competence from taking risks when working or playing with others. Being able to make decisions from a range of choices is an important life skill that helps them to gain confidence and have good self-esteem.

Unacceptable risk and challenge in children's play

Safe and unsafe risks

Practitioners have a duty of care to keep children safe from harm. The need to support and extend children's abilities and learning about safe risk-taking has to be balanced with protecting them from harm. All experiences have some level of risk attached to them.

A **safe risk** means that:

- the benefits from the experience far outweigh the risk of possible harm
- the consequences of the potential risk are likely to be minor or insignificant
- the adults think carefully about the risks, know the children well and have taken appropriate action to minimise the risks.

Example: If a child in your group is not ready – either physically or emotionally – to try a particular climbing experience, the relative risk that is to be found in any climbing activity would shift to being a dangerous – or **unsafe** – risk. In this situation, you would need to support the child physically as he or she climbs or to provide an alternative climbing experience to match the child's abilities.

Figure 4.8 Children enjoying the challenge while climbing and swinging

The importance for children of managing risk and challenge for themselves

Children's lives are often strictly controlled by adults, with after-school activities, playing in competitive sport teams and doing extra homework. Today, very few children walk or ride bikes to school, or are allowed to play freely in their local neighbourhoods. It is now even more important that practitioners provide children with opportunities to:

- make choices and engage in problem-solving and diverse creative experiences
- participate every day in physical unstructured and planned activities
- learn how to cope socially and emotionally as a member of a group.

Supporting children to manage risk and challenge

Practitioners need to explain the value of challenging play to parents and involve them in developing policies on risk management. This helps parents to feel informed and positive about risky play and will allay any concerns they may have about the activities that are provided for their children. They also need to:

- **Be good role models**: by showing safe and sensible behaviour you can help children to understand how to behave outdoors and inside.
- Teach children about **personal safety**, risks and the safety of others.
- Support children in **problem-solving** and making choices.
- **Encourage children to make their own risk assessments**: children need to be encouraged to

assess the risks of an activity and to think about the possible consequences of their actions. For example, when building with wooden blocks, children need to be helped to see how their building can be made stable and less likely to fall. This is more effective than telling children they can only build so many blocks high.

Reflective practice

Managing risks and challenges

Think about the way in which risk and challenge are managed in your setting.

- Have you encouraged a child to assess the risks involved in a particular activity, and to work out for themselves how to manage the risk? Did you have to intervene to support the child?
- Have you encouraged a child to try a more challenging activity?
- Have you helped a child to talk through potential problems during a play activity?
- How could you improve the way in which you support children to understand and assess risks?

Keeping children safe as they learn through play

Physical safety

Children who play in a physically safe environment are more likely to develop confidence, self-esteem and self-reliance. They are in a can-do situation. In modern life it is often dangerous for children to play outside in the street. It is therefore very important that when children attend group settings they can be physically safe.

Children with disabilities may find it more challenging to play, and will need careful help from others.

Safety should always be borne in mind when working with young children so that accidents are prevented. This is called risk assessment because adults are thinking ahead about possible physical danger to children. It is important to check materials such as pens, crayons and felt pens for the safety mark. Remember, children put objects into their mouths as part of the way they learn.

In practice

Safety in play

- Worn equipment should be mended or replaced.
- Equipment should be checked for splinters, sharp edges or peeling paint.
- At the end of each day all aprons should be checked and wiped clean.
- Tables need to be disinfected.
- Floors need sweeping and washing once the rooms have been tidied.
- Carpets should be cleaned with a vacuum.

Setting up materials and equipment

- Check large apparatus such as climbing frames and trucks for safety catches and safety surfaces. Do the children have enough space to move about safely?
- Heavy objects should not be on shelves in case they fall on children.
- All fire exits must be kept clear at all times.
- Doors must not be left half open, especially if there are children with visual impairments, as they could bump into them.
- Objects on shelves should not stick out at a child's head height in case they bump their heads.

Emotional safety

Children need to feel emotionally safe or they will not be confident enough to play. They need to play with or near an adult, especially if they are just settling in or they have been upset.

They may need to have a special friend with them in order to feel secure enough to play confidently.

Social safety

When children quarrel they often begin to shout at each other and even fight. Shouting means they are trying to put their feelings into words. Adults can help them by saying something like, 'I think you are angry. What shall we do about it? Do you want the bike? When Mary has finished with it she will give you a turn.'

If children become very quiet they might be blocking the drains or something adults do not want them to do. Children need to be supervised carefully. It is important for adults never to sit with their back to the group, either indoors or outdoors.

If children rush about and become overexcited, it is sometimes best to join their play and help them to develop a storyline. Sometimes they may have lost their play ideas in the excitement.

Violence and play

In some settings, both war play and guns are banned. The thinking here is that this discourages children from becoming violent. Some adults think that children need to learn about the terribleness of violence in ways that are emotionally safe. Others think that children learn how to stop violence through play about violence.

In this approach, adults usually allow war play as long as these emotional safety rules are kept:

- Children can play war only with children who have agreed to join this play scenario.
- They cannot pretend to shoot at or pretend to kill children or adults who are not playing this war scenario.
- They must stop if children decide they want to leave the play, or they do not like it.

Adults usually join the play to help children think about pain, hurting people and the sadness of losing people they love, not having food to eat, being tired, being rough.

Reflective practice

'We Don't Play with Guns Here'

Playing with 'guns' or other weapons is especially popular with boys around the age of four who want to be Superman or another fighting hero. Discuss the following points of view:

- War play is important to children's development. Playing powerful games can give children a sense of control at a time in their lives when other things around can make them feel powerless and weak. Giving children the message that 'guns' are bad or to be avoided is irresponsible and unrealistic.
- War play says to children that adults think using violence to solve problems is OK. War play can also support prejudice against some children, e.g. if 'the baddies' are from a different ethnic group or culture.

Dealing with sad and frightening events in play

Children will see things on television and in videos that show wars, starvation, etc. They might want to use these ideas in their play scenarios as a way of helping them to understand these events.

Children often think about monsters, giants, witches, ghosts, and creatures from outer space. It is best if adults do not introduce these ideas into children's play. Children are usually **emotionally safe** if they do this for themselves. This is because if they create the monster, then the monster is under their control. They can decide how the monster behaves and when to stop the play.

Feeling in control is important for children's emotional safety when they play with danger and fear. This is why **hospital play** is often important for children before and after a visit.

A new baby in the family also brings fears, such as 'Am I still loved?' and **play scenarios** help children to deal with this fear.

Promoting anti-discriminatory play

Children need to be helped not to develop ideas which are discriminatory or which **stereotype** people (think of other people in narrow ways).

Play scenarios – for example, where Eskimos (now called Inuits) are stereotyped as still living in igloos, might lead children to think that is how such people live nowadays.

Children see gender stereotypes on television and in videos. Boys and girls will imitate well-known characters in accordance with gender stereotypes. This often leads to superhero play – for example, boys may be Superman and girls may be Catwoman.

This can be dealt with by helping children to decide as they play – for example, what does Superman eat for breakfast? When does he shop for his food? Who irons his shirts?

The role of the adult in providing activities and supporting children

Adults need to choose play materials carefully and to create:

- play opportunities
- time to play
- space for play indoors and outdoors
- places for dens, physical play, manipulative play and creative play
- play props and clothes for dressing up and role-play
- an adapted play environment for children with disabilities.

Adults who provide **open-ended** materials create more play possibilities for children. You should provide:

- recycled junk materials (string, boxes, wood)
- natural materials (clay, woodwork, sand, water, twigs, leaves, feathers)
- traditional areas (home area, wooden blocks, work shop area with scissors, glue, etc.).

Choosing materials and equipment to give children play opportunities

Children learn about play from natural and recycled materials, as well as specially designed toys and equipment.

Natural materials

These should be attractively presented. They are important for children living in a modern world. Plastic is everywhere; natural materials help children to learn about sand, water, wood and clay. These show children how they can find materials for themselves. They can be cheap to provide.

Recycled materials

These cost nothing to provide. Margarine tubs, bottle corks and plastic bottles, for example, need to be set out in attractive containers, easy to reach and use. Children need enough space and table room for creative play with these materials.

Commercially made equipment

This can be expensive and needs to be chosen carefully. Look at Unit 3, which emphasises the safety of equipment, non-toxic materials and cleanliness. Equipment is often pre-structured, which means that children can only use it in a narrow way. Open-ended equipment that can be used in a variety of ways is better value for money (e.g. wooden blocks, Lego®, Duplo®).

Children benefit if there are plenty of these so that they can build exciting models. It is best to have all the same brand of wooden blocks, or Lego® or Duplo®, then these can be added to over the years.

In practice

Equipment for play
- Check equipment for safety marks.
- Can it be cleaned easily?
- Can it be mended easily or are there replacement parts?
- Is it open-ended so that it can be used in many different ways (e.g. doll's house, farm, home area equipment, wooden blocks)?

Planning the indoor and outdoor areas

It is best not to change the room around too often because children take some time to find out where things are, both indoors and outdoors. Adults need to know about the child's development in play so that they, in their planning, can provide what is needed for play. Important points to consider when providing for children's play are:

- things should be set out so that they are interesting, with enough variety to keep stimulating the play
- the layout of the room should take account of different children's cultural experiences and heritage
- there should be specially adapted equipment for children with disabilities

- adults should think carefully about what materials to set out, and how to present them in order to encourage play.

The materials that adults set up indoors should (whenever possible) be available outdoors in any group setting (see the EYFS Guidance document). This means that children can learn as much outdoors as they do indoors. Examples include the following.

1 **Climbing frames**: these need to be carefully designed to offer children plenty of challenges as safely as possible. One side of the frame might have evenly spaced rungs for children who are less experienced in climbing. The other side might have unevenly spaced rungs, which need more thinking by the child.

2 **Tarmac**: an outdoor area needs some tarmac or tiled area so that in wet weather it is possible to run or walk about without muddy feet tramping back indoors.

3 **Wild area**: many gardens now have a wild area, which has plants that encourage butterflies, moths and birds. A bird table is also a source of great interest.

4 **Grass**: outdoor areas also need grass where children can find worms, make daisy chains and blow dandelion clocks. A grassy slope can also provide rough-and-tumble play and roly-poly possibilities on a fine day.

5 **Paddling pools**: these are suitable for fine days. When providing a pool, remember:
   - *the pool must be constantly supervised; there should always be towels near it so that children do not become cold*
   - *to protect children's skin from sunburn – follow your setting's policy*
   - *that there are cultural sensitivities with regard to children taking off their clothes when using a pool; this needs to be carefully discussed between staff and parents before introducing children to a paddling pool*
   - *some children do not like to be splashed and this needs to be respected; perhaps there can be ten minutes at the end of a session for 'splashy times' so that children who enjoy this can stay on in the pool and other children can get out if they want to; in this way children learn to respect each other's feelings.*

6 **Digging patches**: some outdoor areas provide digging patches and a vegetable planting area. Younger children tend to dig, carry earth about, find worms and tip water into holes (often two- to three-year-olds). Older children (often aged three to five years) begin to understand the process of digging, planting, watering and growing. This shows in their play – they want to play farmers or gardeners, and a sandpit is often where they will choose to do this.

7 **Bikes, carts and other wheeled equipment**: bikes are often the source of conflict among children. Some children always want to ride them. For this reason many settings now provide carts and different types of bikes and trikes, which two or three children can ride on and on which they can pull each other around. These are very useful in encouraging children to help each other so that they become a team. Adults often make special zones in the outdoor area where children can use bikes without knocking other people over.

The Early Years Foundation Stage (EYFS)

The EYFS Framework (2012) applies to children from birth to five years of age. During this Foundation Stage, children might be attending a playgroup, pre-school, nursery school, nursery class, day care setting, reception class or private nursery, or be with a childminder or nanny. The EYFS explains how and what children will be learning to support their healthy development. Children will be learning skills, acquiring new knowledge and demonstrating their understanding through **seven areas of learning and development**.

Children should mostly develop the **three prime areas** first. As introduced in Unit 2, these are:

- Communication and language
- Physical development; and
- Personal, social and emotional development.

These prime areas are those most essential for children's healthy development and future learning.

As children grow, the prime areas will help them to develop skills in **four specific areas**. These are:

- Literacy
- Mathematics
- Understanding the world; and
- Expressive arts and design.

Children in the EYFS learn by playing and exploring, being active, and through creative and critical thinking which takes place both indoors and outside.

Well-planned play, both indoors and outdoors, is an important part of the EYFS; it helps children to reach the early learning goals by the time they enter Year 1, Key Stage 1 of the National Curriculum.

Providing well-planned play for the EYFS

The following pages look more closely at seven different types of play provision and at the way they link to the six areas of learning and development in this Key Stage. These areas are:

1 wooden block play
2 sand and water play
3 home area
4 dressing-up clothes
5 small-world play
6 clay, dough and mud patches
7 painting and drawing.

Wooden block play

Indoors
Wooden blocks are best if they are free standing. They never wear out and can easily be reconditioned (sanded). There are three kinds of blocks:

1 unit blocks
2 mini hollow bricks
3 large hollow bricks.

All of these link with each other. To use wooden blocks, children need:

- enough space to build
- to play with the blocks away from 'traffic' of people walking through the area
- to have the blocks set out on shelves with outlines of shapes showing each type of block, so that children know where different types of blocks should be stored – children need to see them and to choose which they will use
- a complete set of blocks (and not to lose any!); they should be easily tidied away
- to have blocks available each day.

Outdoors
Blocks could also be milk crates or wooden boxes, which can be stored outside along the wall and used each day. Children can make stepping stones and build with them.

Safety
Children must not build too high unless supervised (except when using soft foam blocks), in case blocks fall on them. Look at the section on general safety on page 143 to see whether you have missed things you need to remember when you are working with wooden blocks with the children.

Progression in block play
At **one to two years**: children mainly build towers and put blocks in rows.

At **two to three years**: children make enclosures, towers get taller and they put blocks in rows. Balance is important now. They sometimes call their models something (e.g. a house).

At **three to five years**: children begin to put together a variety of patterns. They begin to create play scenarios with more complicated stories. They make many patterns and quite difficult balancing is achieved. They are interested in how to balance and build blocks.

At **five to seven years:** the stories and buildings become very complex and are highly coordinated.

Personal, social and emotional development
Interested, excited, motivated to learn
Try out new ideas and activities
Select blocks they want to use without help and feel valued
Sensitive to others; share and take turns
Make good relationships with other children and adults

Communication, language and literacy
Talk as they build
Listen to each other
Make up play scenarios with stories
Make comments and ask questions
Increase vocabulary about blocks (it's taller; could you pass me the cylinder, please?)

Problem-solving, reasoning and numeracy
Use number ideas
Use maths language: talk about shapes and sizes of blocks
Solve practical problems – is this too tall?
Space awareness about blocks

Knowledge and understanding of the world
Find out about materials – wooden blocks, foam blocks
Ask questions about how to do things with blocks
Think about how wooden blocks are made from trees
Building and constructing with blocks

Physical development
Use blocks with confidence and safety
Use a range of wooden blocks, hollow and unit blocks to develop fine and gross motor skills
Balance blocks with increasing control
Aware of space and of other using the block play area

Creative development
Explore shape, form, texture and space of wooden blocks
Use senses and movement to explore blocks
Use imagination to make play scenarios
Design and make constructions (children use their own ideas)

Figure 4.9 Wooden block play

Construction

Construction is similar to block play except that all the pieces connect with each other, whereas blocks balance. Ideally, a variety of construction sets should be available (e.g. Lego®, Duplo®, Stickle Bricks®, Construct-O-Straws®). However, it is important that whatever sets you have should contain enough pieces to interest a group of children. Younger children find Duplo easier than Lego because the pieces are larger and easier to hold as they develop muscle control in their hands. By then they have developed their pincer movement and enjoy practising using it.

Sand and water play

Indoors

Sand can be offered in a commercial sand tray, in seed boxes from a garden shop or in washing-up bowls on tables. It can be poured on to a plastic mat and used as a 'beach' experience with shells, buckets, spades and pebbles. The mat can be rolled up at the end of the session and the sand poured into a sand tray to use again.

- There should always be both wet and dry sand on offer (e.g. dry sand in bowls on tables, or wet sand in a sand tray).
- Provide jugs, scoops, funnels, sponges, small-world scenarios, farms, tubes, spades, small buckets and rakes.
- Miniature gardens can be made by adding twigs, moss, and leaves.

Outdoors

Sand and water play outside is similar to indoors. However, the following equipment can also be used outdoors:

- hoses
- watering cans
- water-washable paint for use on the tarmac (using buckets of water and giant brushes)
- large, covered sand pit where several children can play.

Safety

- Make sure that sand and water play is carefully supervised.

- Be alert, as children can drown in very shallow water, get sand in their eyes or slip on wet floors.
- Outdoor sand pits need covers to keep animals and insects out.
- Place the indoor water tray near to the sink (because it is heavy and in case people slip).
- Change the water every day.
- Always sweep the floor after sand play.
- Use a mop to ensure floors are not slippery after water play.

Progression in sand and water play

At **one to two years**: children begin by pouring and carrying water and sand, and by putting these materials in and out of containers.

At **three to five years**: children begin to enjoy practical problems, and to solve them as they develop their learning (e.g. how to make a strong jet of water, how to make sand keep its shape).

At **five to seven years**: children's play scenarios have more of a story than before. They use a variety of play people and cooperate more with other children.

Figure 4.10 Water play

Home area

Indoors

The home area is one of the most important areas in early childhood settings. The home area should ideally have:

- some things in it that are like those in the child's home (e.g. cups, cooking pots)
- some things that are from other cultures (e.g. a wok, chopsticks)
- a proper place for everything, and children should be encouraged to tidy up carefully
- a large dresser – with hooks for cups, and cupboards to store dishes and saucepans
- big, middle-sized and small dolls, representing children of different cultures
- a cooker (this can be homemade – e.g. from a cardboard box)
- wooden boxes, which can be used as beds, tables, chairs
- food can be pre-structured (plastic fruit), transformable (dough), real food (a salad)
- clothes can be kept in a chest of drawers, labelled with pictures and words
- magazines, notepads and writing implements can be put by the telephone, and perhaps a bookcase with books
- adaptations for children with disabilities (e.g. a child who is a wheelchair user will need a low table so that they can use the bowls and plates).

Outdoors

- The home area outside is a den. Children at home enjoy playing in outside dens.
- Old furniture can be used outside to make a home area. An old airer (clothes horse) with a sheet or blanket over it makes good walls.
- Children can make pretend food using sand, water and messy materials.
- A rug can be put in the den and furniture can be made by collecting spare cardboard boxes (e.g. they can become tables or beds for dolls).
- Cushions can make seats or beds.
- A box on its side can become a cupboard with flaps as the cupboard doors.

- Cups and saucers can be made out of old yoghurt pots and margarine containers.

Safety

Wooden equipment should be checked regularly for rough edges and splinters.

Cutlery must be carefully introduced. Ask your supervisor for advice.

Glass and china break easily and should not be used in the home area.

Progression in home area play

At **one to two years**: children carry materials – pots, pans, dolls, etc. – about; put them in and out of boxes, prams; put them in rows.

At **two to three years**: they begin to make play scenarios, often about food.

At **three to five years**: more of the story develops, about a wider range of events and people.

Dressing-up clothes

Indoors and outdoors

- Children wear dressing-up clothes indoors, but enjoy wearing them outdoors too.
- The clothes need to be simple and flexible in use.
- A basic cape, some basic hats (including 'uniform' hats such as a fire-fighter's helmet), scarves and drapes, sari, tunic, shoes and baggy trousers help children in role-playing. They need to reflect different cultures.
- Fastenings should be varied to give children different experiences of connecting clothes together (e.g. zips, buttons, tying bows, buckles and Velcro).
- The clothes need to be hanging on a rack, with separate boxes for shoes and hats. A large safety mirror at child height is useful.

Safety

There should be no strings, ribbons or purses on strings around the neck, which might strangle a child.

Beware of children tripping over clothes that are too long.

Figure 4.11 Playing in a den

Make sure children wear suitable footwear (e.g. no high heels when playing on climbing frames or running out of doors).

Clothes should be washed regularly.

Progression in dressing-up clothes play

At **one to two years**: children wear hats and shoes.

At **two to three years**: children wear hats, shoes, capes and scarves.

At **three to five years**: children are more adventurous – they begin to wear whole outfits and want more accuracy to look right for the role they play.

Small-world play

Garages, farms, zoos, space scenes, domestic, hospitals, boats and castles all feature in small-world play.

Indoors

- Children can easily create play scenarios with pretend people, and make up imaginative stories using small-world materials to help them. These are best set out on a floor mat or carpet, or in a sand tray (see 'Sand and water play').

Figure 4.12 Dressing up (as a knight)

- Miniature gardens make a good play scene; these can be made in seed trays from garden centres and put on tables.
- Children can make their own gardens and make up stories using them – pots of moss, gravel, twigs, pebbles and feathers.
- They can also make paths, trees, grass and hills.
- Older children begin to use doll's houses, garages and castles.

Safety

Check that the pieces are not so small that a younger child might choke on them.

Progression in play

At **one to two years**: children mainly put toys in rows and make constructions.

At **two to four years**: they make more complex constructions (e.g. a house; simple everyday stories).

At **four to six years**: children use play scenarios (e.g. going shopping) and make up a story with different people (e.g. hospital scenes, outer space, garage scenes).

Clay, dough and mud patches

Indoors

Children often do not make anything in particular because this is creative play. There is no need to have any sort of result or finished product. It is important not to force children into this.

Storing clay

Clay can be brown or grey. It is stored by rolling it into a ball, the size of a large orange, pressing a thumb into it, pouring water into the hole, and covering the hole full of water with clay. It should then be stored in a bin with a well-fitting lid.

Outdoors

A mud patch for digging is a popular area outdoors. Spades and rakes with short handles are useful. Children love to bury things and fill holes with water. They enjoy planting flowers and vegetables.

Figure 4.13 Small-world play

Safety

Dough must be made using salt and cream of tartar if it is to be stored and used more than once.

Deter children from putting the dough in their mouths. Be extra vigilant with children who have coeliac disease as they must not consume any gluten (present in ordinary flour).

Progression in play

At **one to three years**: children bash and bang clay.

At **three to five years**: they learn to pinch, pull and roll it as well:

- they can make shapes
- they choose their tools or use their hands more carefully
- they begin to design and make models, which they sometimes like to keep and display, but not often.

Figure 4.14 Playing with dough

Painting and drawing

Indoors

For drawing: children need a variety of materials to draw with (fat and thin felt pens, chubby crayons, pastels, chalks, charcoal and pencils). They also need paper of different sizes, textures, shapes and colours; paper should be attractively set out and stored on shelves or in boxes or trays.

For painting: provide a variety of paints – freshly mixed every day – and brushes, clean water, non-spillable paint containers, and pots to mix colours.

- Children need a range of paintbrushes (thick, middle and thin), ideally made from good-quality hog's hair. Poor-quality brushes lead to poor-quality paintings and are frustrating to use.
- Flat tables are easier for younger children to use than easels.
- Children should choose which paper and tools to use.
- A well-designed paint dryer, which stacks paintings while allowing them to dry, is ideal, but you can spread paintings out on the floor under a radiator – or hang with pegs to dry from a washing line.
- Mixing colours: it is best only to provide primary colours (red, blue and yellow paints) and to make shades by adding white or black to lighten or darken the colours:
  - *red + blue = purple*
  - *red + yellow = orange*
  - *blue + yellow = green*
  - *red + white = pink*
  - *all colours mixed together = brown*
- Children can mix their own colours if these are presented in large tins in the middle of the table, with a spoon in each tin. Patty pan pallets can be used for mixing, and water can be scooped with a small ladle from a large bowl in the centre into small, easily manageable jugs. In this way, children can pour small amounts, and learn to mix the colours and shades of paint they need with a paintbrush.
- Children need encouragement to wear aprons. Those they step into using their arms first are the most popular, as aprons over the head can be frightening for very young children.

- If children want to keep their paintings or drawings they need to be kept in a safe place. They might like to see them displayed on the wall. They must have the right to say if they do not want this.
- Painting is a messy activity, which is probably why it is not always done in the home. Protect the floor, easels and tables with newspaper.
- Young children should always be given the opportunity to express themselves through painting, undisturbed by adults. Adults should never interrupt, ask questions about the child's painting or make their own suggestions; these actions will discourage creativity and may stop the children from valuing their own work.
- Many children are not interested in the product of their paintings. At this stage they are interested in the process.

Safety

Children should be discouraged from walking around with pencils or brushes in their mouths – in case they fall and injure themselves or someone else.

Mop up any major water spills quickly to avoid floors becoming slippery.

How to encourage exploration and investigation through play

Babies and young children learn about their world through their senses and by exploring objects around them. Their interaction with a wide range of objects helps them to develop the basic concepts of shape, colour, size, weight, texture, sound and many others. Providing children with interesting objects in their environment is an important way to encourage curiosity, experimentation and problem-solving skills.

Providing interest objects

Safety must be the first consideration. *Avoid* objects that:

- are damaged (unless they are natural objects)
- are made from toxic materials
- are too fragile to be handled

Figure 4.15 Painting

- are too heavy
- have small pieces.

Choose objects that:

- are appropriate for the age/stage of children
- link to a topic/theme or concept
- are sufficiently robust for children to handle
- can be investigated through the senses.

If you choose to provide objects that may be delicate (e.g. a wasps' nest, pine cones or shells) then it is important to set some guidelines for handling them. If they really are too fragile then allow children to use magnifying glasses to look at them or to touch the object while it is under the control of an adult. Even quite young children will understand this if they are given an explanation.

Using simple pictorial signs (e.g. of a hand with a tick through it or a hand with a large cross through it) to indicate whether objects may be handled or not will be clearer than a written sign saying 'Do not touch'.

Objects from the past can stimulate children's interest and help them develop an understanding of history. For example, collections of electrical appliances – irons, kettles, toasters, radios, etc. – can be used to help them relate their grandparents' and parents' lives to their own experiences.

Objects that represent everyday aspects of other cultures can provide the same links. Encouraging children to bring objects from home is an ideal way of maintaining positive links with their families, raising self-esteem and valuing their home life.

Ideas for collections of objects

- **Natural objects**: leaves, nuts, seeds, flowers, twigs, pieces of bark, stones, pebbles, shells.
- **Shiny objects**: safety mirrors (card), spoons, foil wrappers, 'silver' or 'gold' items.
- **Different materials**: soft ones (e.g. velvet, fur (artificial), cotton wool, velour, towelling); rough ones (e.g. sandpaper, sacking, brick, brushes with stiff bristles).
- **Items connected with a season**: for example, clothing, related activities (buckets and spades, sunglasses or umbrellas, etc.).

- **Items from home connected to a theme**: baby toys, photos, favourite books, etc.

Providing inclusive play opportunities

Children aged **two to three** years:

- are easily frustrated, but they can concentrate well if they are allowed to make choices and decide what they do; otherwise, their concentration will last for only a few minutes
- enjoy using wheeled trucks to sit in and be pulled along, and to sit on and scoot with feet on the ground
- will not share easily with other children, so there need to be enough boxes, hats, toy cars, tea set pieces, wooden blocks, and so on, or there will be fights.

For children aged **three to five** years:

- they will use the area without so much adult support; even so, adults will need to make sure that children feel confident as they move about indoors and outdoors
- they enjoy using tricycles with pedals; a few children may manage to use two-wheeled bicycles
- a child who is a wheelchair user can join in wheeled play in the zone where children have space to go fast and feel freedom of movement together
- it is important to think about progression in play, so that you challenge children to learn through their play
- there need to be zones where children have enough space to use wheeled toys safely
- other areas need to be available where children can play without these so that they do not have to worry about being knocked over; this means dividing the outdoor area into wheeled truck zones and other areas where children are not allowed to take wheeled trucks or bikes.

 Useful resources

Play England
Promotes free play opportunities for all children, and works to ensure that the importance of play for children's development is recognised: www.playengland.org.uk.

5 Communication and professional skills within child care and education: Unit 5

Effective communication is the cornerstone of work in all early years settings. Being able to communicate well helps in forming positive relationships with colleagues, children and their families.

Learning outcomes

During this unit you will learn about:

1. How to develop effective communication skills to work with children and adults in a variety of settings.

2. How to use your developing knowledge and skills to improve your practice and set appropriate targets to develop professionally.

3. How to investigate employment opportunities and routes of progression.

How to develop effective communication skills

You need to be able to communicate effectively with a wide range of other people:

- children
- children's parents, families and carers
- colleagues and managers
- different professionals (e.g. teachers, doctors, nurses, social workers).

These may be **one-to-one** interactions, with a child or a parent, or **group** interactions, such as activities with children, case conferences and staff meetings.

Developing communication skills

The most important skill that will improve communication is that of being approachable, and of being a 'good listener'. Some people are easy to talk to, while others seem to put up a barrier. There are people who possess these skills naturally, but do not despair if you are not one of them! It is possible to learn the skills that will improve your ability to communicate with other people: see Figure 5.1.

Respect for other people's beliefs and views

We all have different ideas about how we conduct our lives. It is inevitable that each early years practitioner will encounter many people with vastly different backgrounds, beliefs and outlooks on life. Regardless of your own views, you should always respect the views of others. This involves:

- not passing judgement on the way other people live
- avoiding stereotyping people on the basis of age, gender or ethnicity (or colour)
- not trying to impose your views onto others.

Only if people feel that their individual values and beliefs are respected will they develop the confidence to express themselves freely and to make choices.

seeking feedback, paraphrasing and reflection

respect for other people's beliefs and views

establishing boundaries by managing expectations

conveying sincerity

showing interest in the individual

conveying understanding

using appropriate body language

conveying warmth

active listening

Figure 5.1 Skills needed for good communication

Case Study · A communication problem

Sumayah is two years old, and new to the nursery. Her family are originally from Pakistan but she was born in the UK. Sumayah's father is fluent in English and her mother has a good understanding but sometimes finds it difficult to articulate what she wants to say. Susie is Sumayah's key person. She gets on well with the family, and appears to have a positive relationship with Sumayah, who has been very happy attending nursery three days a week. However, Helen, a nursery assistant, is uncomfortable when one day Susie makes reference to Sumayah's mum as being 'a Paki' in general conversation.

Later in the same month, Sumayah is given a pork sausage by accident at lunchtime, despite the fact that her family is Muslim and do not eat pork. The staff on duty notice the error too late and feel guilty. Helen asks Susie if they should fill out an incident form before telling the family. Susie says, 'Oh, I wasn't even going to tell Sumayah's mum! She hardly understands anything anyway, and Sumayah enjoyed that sausage. Anyway, if they're going to live in this country, they have to expect that their children will become English.' Helen is left feeling uncomfortable with concealing information from Sumayah's mum and does not know what to do.

1. What do you think Helen should do?
2. What are the main issues arising from this scenario which need to be addressed?
3. Susie finds it difficult to communicate with Sumayah's mum. How might this impact on the level of care which Sumayah receives? How can Susie be supported to improve communication?

Establishing boundaries

All organisations operate within some set of boundaries or limits, which determines the extent of their willingness and ability to respond. People generally feel very uneasy and anxious if they are unsure about exactly what is expected of them. Think about situations at school or college when *you* felt uncomfortable in a lesson or lecture – perhaps because you were not sure if you were going to be chosen to answer a question. If you had been fully prepared, you would not have felt quite so anxious. Establishing boundaries within early years settings might include:

Figure 5.2 (a) An open posture encourages communication; (b) A closed posture inhibits communication

- an explanation of policies and procedures (e.g. arrangements on trips and outings)
- acceptable behaviour and ways of dealing with unacceptable behaviour
- your role in preserving confidentiality.

Showing interest in the individual

It is vital to try to establish a **rapport** with children and their parents, and with work colleagues. This can be achieved by:

- being patient and showing that you have time to listen to their views
- listening carefully to them
- trying to remember their names, likes, dislikes and personal preferences
- asking relevant questions and not suddenly changing the subject
- using **body language** effectively.

Using appropriate body language

How you sit and use gestures will make a great difference to your interactions with others. To put someone more at ease, adopt an **open posture**: sit with your arms apart, hands open, legs uncrossed and slightly apart, leaning forward – with your body fully facing the other person. This shows that you are ready to communicate and that you are interested in what the other person has to say.

Key term

Body language – Body language is also known as non-verbal communication. It includes facial expressions, eye contact, tone of voice, body posture and motions, and positioning within groups. It may also include the way we wear our clothes or the silence we maintain.

Active listening

On the whole we are poor listeners. Research shows that we tend to listen in 30-second spurts before losing attention. We tend only to hear items that we are interested in and not attend to others. If we are bored and we dislike the speaker's personality, mannerisms, accent or appearance, we may 'switch off' and follow more interesting thoughts of our own. Active listening, the listening required in any relationship with children, calls for concentration;

Communicating with parents and carers

You will find that there are many occasions when you are responsible for passing information clearly to parents. But parents will want to talk, as well as listen, to you. You will need to develop listening skills. Try to set a particular time for parents so that they do not take your attention when you are involved with the children. For some parents this can be very difficult to arrange, especially if they are working.

In practice

Guidelines for communicating well with parents

- Maintaining eye contact helps you to give your full attention to a parent.
- Remember that your body language shows how you really feel.
- Try not to interrupt when someone is talking to you. Nod and smile instead.
- Every so often, summarise the main points of a discussion, so that you are both clear about what has been said.
- If you do not know the answer to a parent's question, say so, and that you will find out. Then, do not forget to do this!
- Remember that different cultures have different traditions. Touching and certain gestures might be seen as insulting by some parents, so be careful.
- If the parent speaks a different language from you, use photographs and visual aids. Talk slowly and clearly.
- If the parent has a hearing impairment, use sign language or visual aids.
- When you are talking together, bear in mind whether this is the parent's first child or whether they have had other children already.
- Remember that if the parents have a child with a disability, they may need to see you more often to discuss the child's progress.
- If the parent has a disability, make sure that when you sit together you are at the same level.
- Occasionally, parents might become upset and will shout at you. If this happens, do not shout back. Simply talk quietly and calmly, and show that you are listening to them.
- Never gossip.

Communicating with children

How parents and other significant adults speak to children is extremely important. When talking with children, we tend to:

- emphasise key words
- slow our speech down
- repeat phrases if the child has not understood
- add gestures and expressions to help them understand the meaning.

This is an example of 'scaffolding' children's learning. When talking with babies, adults often talk in 'motherese' or 'parentese'; this means they speak slowly, in a higher-pitched voice than usual, and use a lot of repetition (e.g. 'cootchie, cootchie coo'). Many people use this sort of 'baby talk' unconsciously when talking to very young babies – and often to their pets too!

Good communication helps children develop confidence, feelings of self-worth and good relationships with others. It also helps them grow into adults who have good feelings about themselves and others.

Communication must be a **two-way process**. It is not just about you telling children something or giving advice, but rather listening to their viewpoints and accepting their emotions.

Non-verbal communication: how children communicate without words

From birth, babies are primed to learn; they learn about **body language** and non-verbal cues by observing and imitating other people. One of the first conscious facial expressions learned by a baby is the **smile**; this is because adults tend to smile at infants a great deal. Other baby body language includes:

- kicking and waving arms to show happiness
- turning away – and even shuddering – from an unpleasant taste

- banging on a high chair to get attention
- peering around the sofa to persuade the adult to play a game of hide and seek.

The range of gestures and expressions used before verbal communication takes over expands as the child becomes more mobile and inquisitive.

Toddlers

Examples of body language used by **toddlers** include:

- pointing
- touching
- reaching out a hand
- making eye contact
- shaking or nodding the head
- pushing something or someone away
- pulling something or someone closer.

Although this sort of body language is used with adults and with other children, it tends to be more obvious and forceful with other toddlers:

Example: If Cara, aged two, wants the toy that Anna is playing with, she will probably simply walk over and take it away from her!

Children aged three years to school age

Children show the same sort of non-verbal behaviour as before, but they develop their communication further by adding in **words**. For example, they may:

- point to a toy and ask to play with it rather than simply taking it
- move towards someone who is hanging back and invite him or her to come and join in their play
- hug other children and squeal excitedly
- sulk and pout to show their disappointment or anger.

Children still rely a great deal on body language – as do adults – but they are now able to combine verbal *and* non-verbal methods to express themselves and get what they want.

Interpreting children's body language

Young children often express themselves physically when they do not have enough words to say what they want or need. When children are frustrated or excited their body language takes over; for example:

- A child attempting to tell a lie will have trouble making eye contact; they may hang their head, or otherwise appear unsure of themselves.
- A child who is feeling frustrated or misunderstood may cry, hit out at others, or show some other expression of aggravation and frustration.
- A child who is very excited about a forthcoming event may jump up and down or rush around.

How you can help

You need to pay close attention to your *own* non-verbal messages and adapt them accordingly to best meet the needs of children. You can help children by:

- **making eye contact**: give your attention to the child, and use a friendly facial expression; this will make the child feel that he or she is important to you and that you are respectful of his or her needs
- **teaching them how to manage their emotions**, control their impulses and express feelings of anger with words
- **talking them gently through** the experience when they have just had a tantrum
- **questioning the child sensitively** – try to find out what he or she was feeling. You could ask: 'Did you feel sad?', 'Were you frightened?' or 'Were you angry?' Children need to be taught how to 'label' and manage their feelings – especially anger
- **get down to their level:** If the child has been aggressive – punching, biting or kicking others – try to prompt the child to think about how she would feel if someone else had done the same thing to them.

In practice

How to communicate with children

1. Make **eye contact** and show that you are listening - it is very difficult to have a conversation with someone who never looks at you! When talking with very young children, it is usually necessary to stoop down to their level or to sit at a table with them.

2. **Listen carefully** to the child's own spoken language and use it as a basis for conversation – very young children tend to use one or two words to mean any of a number of things; e.g. 'drink' can mean 'this is my drink', 'I want a drink', 'Where is my drink?' or 'You have got a drink'.

3. **Repeat** the child's words in a correct form, or a complete sentence. This checks understanding and provides the child with an accurate model for the future. For example, young children often use speech such as 'feeded' instead of 'fed', 'runned' instead of 'ran'. In checking what they mean the adult should use the correct term – Child: 'I feeded carrots to my rabbit'. Adult: 'Oh, you fed your rabbit some carrots.'

4. **Be a good role model**, speak clearly yourself and use correct grammar and patterns of speech.

5. **Use open-ended questions**: Encourage children to speak by asking 'open' questions which require an answer in phrases and/or sentences rather than a simple 'yes' or 'no'; e.g. 'Tell me about your party' instead of 'Did you have a good time at your party?' This opens up opportunities for the child to talk about a range of different things or one single event of his/her own choice – you can always ask more questions as the conversation progresses to check the information, supply additional vocabulary and correct grammar.

6. **Use prompts**: These invite the child to say more, to share ideas and feelings. They also tell the child that you are really listening and interested, that her ideas are important, and that you accept her and respect what she is saying. *Examples of prompts*: 'Oh, I see.' 'Tell me more.' 'That's interesting.'

7. **Listen attentively**: Get rid of distractions and pay attention to what the child is saying.

At times, adults may need to stop whatever they are doing and listen to the child. It is difficult to pay close attention to what the child is saying if you are busy trying to read at the same time.

8. **Respond sensitively**: Remember the importance of **non-verbal communication**. Watch out for when a child seems upset or looks sad: you could say, 'You seem upset – do you want to tell me about it?'

9. **Say 'Please' and 'Thank You' to children**: Children deserve the common courtesies that we – as adults – use with each other. Children will learn by imitating the speech and behaviour of adults.

10. **Use kind words to help promote self-esteem**: Kind words give children more self-confidence and help them to behave better, try harder and achieve more. They communicate love and respect, and also create an atmosphere in which problems can be discussed openly and understandings can be reached. *Example:* The child has spilt her orange juice on the floor. You could say, 'Don't be so clumsy! Just look at the mess you made.' But it would be better to say: 'Here's a cloth. Please wipe the juice up,' and later, 'Thank you for doing such a good job of cleaning the floor.'

11. **Do not use unkind words**: Unkind words make the child feel bad, and they prevent good communication. Avoid unkind words which:
    - *ridicule* the child: e.g. 'You're acting just like a baby.'
    - *shame* the child: e.g. 'I'm so ashamed of you.'
    - *label the child*: e.g. 'You're a naughty boy.'
    Unkind words, spoken without thinking of their results, make the child feel disliked – and result in low self-esteem. More importantly, unkind words do not help; they only make matters worse.

12. **Always be positive:** Tell children what to do instead of what not to do. *Examples:*
    - Instead of 'Don't slam the door!' try 'Please shut the door quietly.'
    - Instead of 'Don't spill your drink!' try 'Try holding your beaker with both hands.'

Figure 5.4 Getting down to the same level as the child promotes effective communication

How children learn to communicate

As you may expect, young children *understand* more than they can *express* themselves. They may be able to follow simple instructions (especially if they are accompanied by a gesture e.g. pointing) such as 'Give daddy a kiss' or 'Fetch your teddy' long before they can use sentences themselves. They learn new words – initially names of objects and important people – by listening carefully and copying. Many words which have unstressed syllables – such as 'important' and 'computer' – are learned as 'portant' and 'puter' because these are the sounds that they are able to hear easily.

Speaking and listening activities in group settings

These range from individual conversations between adult and child to whole class/group 'news' times. In addition there are many games and activities which provide ideal opportunities for children to use and practise their speaking and listening skills. For very young children sharing rhymes – traditional nursery, finger and action – songs and books with an adult are both valuable and enjoyable.

As language develops and listening skills develop, older children will be able to play games which involve 'active' listening such as:

- **'What (or who) am I?'** This involves the adult (or a child – perhaps with help) giving clues until the animal/person/object is identified. 'I have sharp teeth. I have a long tail. I have a striped coat. I eat meat. What am I?' Answer: a tiger or a tabby cat.
- **Taped sounds** – these can be environmental (kettle boiling, doorbell, someone eating crisps) or related to a particular topic (farm animals, pet animals, machines) or of familiar people's voices.
- **Recorded voices** – Reception or Year 1 children record their own voices giving clues about themselves but without saying who they are. 'I have brown eyes. I have two brothers. I have a Lion King lunchbox. I have short, dark hair. Who am I?' This activity is best done with a small group so they are not guessing from among the whole class! They find it difficult not to say their own names but love hearing themselves and their friends. The enjoyment factor makes it valuable and ensures concentrated listening once the excitement has died down.
- **Feely box** – use varied objects for children to feel (without being able to see) and encourage them to describe the shape, size, texture, surface etc. This can be topic-related e.g. fruit or solid shapes, and is a very good activity for extending children's vocabulary.
- **'Snowball'** games which involve active listening and memory – 'I went to market and I bought ….'. There are many versions of this. It can be used for number (one cabbage, two bananas, three pencils, etc.), to reinforce the alphabet (an apple, a boat, a crane, etc.) or topic-related (food items, transport items, clothing, etc.).
- **Circle activities** in which children and adult/s sit in a circle and a 'special' object is held by the person who is speaking. Rules are that only the person holding the object is allowed to speak – the object is passed around in turn or to whoever wants to say something (adult supervision needed!). Alternatively a large ball can be rolled across the circle and the person rolling the ball makes his/her contribution (this can be on a theme – favourite foods/colours/games, etc.) and the person who receives the ball makes the next contribution.

These activities encourage children to take turns, to use language to express their thoughts, feelings and ideas and to gain confidence as communicators. The circle activities are particularly good for encouraging shy or withdrawn children who may not otherwise get a chance to speak.

Multi-agency working

Multi-agency working is about different services, agencies and teams of professionals and other staff working together to provide the services that fully meet the needs of children and their parents or carers. Practitioners share a sense of team identity and are generally line-managed by the team leader, though they may maintain links with their home agencies through supervision and training. Features of multi-agency teams include the following:

- There is a dedicated team leader.
- There is a good mix of education, health, social care, youth justice and youth work staff.
- The people who work in the team think of themselves as team members; they are recruited or seconded into the team, either full- or part-time.
- The team engages in work with universal services and at a range of levels – not just with individual children, but also small-group, family and whole-school work.
- The team is likely to share a base, though some staff may continue to work from their home agencies.
- There are regular team meetings to discuss case working as well as administrative issues.

One example of a multi-agency team is a BEST (see below).

Behaviour and Education Support Teams (BESTs)

These are multi-agency teams bringing together a complementary mix of professionals from the fields of health, social care and education. The aim of a BEST is to promote emotional well-being, positive behaviour and school attendance, by identifying and supporting those with, or at risk of developing, emotional and behavioural problems. BESTs:

- work with children aged five to 18, their families and schools, to intervene early and prevent problems developing further

Figure 5.5 Different professionals included in a BEST team

- work in targeted primary and secondary schools, and in the community, alongside a range of other support structures and services
- have a minimum of four or five staff members, who between them have a complementary mix of education, social care and health skills in order to meet the multifaceted needs of children and their parents.

Figure 5.5 shows the professionals included in a typical team.

Schools with BESTs include those with high proportions of pupils with, or at risk of developing, behavioural problems, usually demonstrated in levels of exclusion and attendance.

Another example of multi-agency working is **Early Support** – services for disabled children in early years. Early Support is the central government mechanism for achieving better-coordinated family-focused services for very young disabled children (aged under three) and their families. Families receive coordinated support through key worker systems, better sharing of information between agencies, family support plans and family-held records.

How to communicate with other professionals in a multi-agency approach

Being able to communicate effectively with team members, other professionals and with parents is a very important part of your role as a practitioner. You should always:

- be considerate of others and polite towards them
- recognise the contributions made by other team members; we all like to feel we are valued for the work we do. You can help others to feel valued by being aware of their role and how it has helped you fulfil your own role
- explain clearly to the relevant person any changes in routine or any actions you have taken; for example, as a nanny, always informing a parent when a child you are caring for has refused a meal or been distressed in any way, or reporting any behavioural problem or incident to your line manager in a nursery setting.

Being part of a team

To meet the needs of all the children, the staff members must work effectively together as a team. The roles and responsibilities of individual team members will depend on the organisation of the work setting. In your role as a learner you will be supporting the work of others. You will usually work under the direction (or sometimes supervision) of a nursery nurse or teacher, depending on the setting. There may also be professionals from other disciplines (medicine, social services, dentistry, etc.) who are involved with the families and children you work with. A special school or nursery that cares for children with physical disabilities will have a multidisciplinary team. This team may include teachers, nursery nurses and assistants, trained special care assistants, physiotherapists, paediatricians and, possibly, social workers.

Effective teamwork is vital in such settings to ensure that:

- everyone knows their individual roles and responsibilities
- parents and primary carers know which team member can deal with any specific concerns.

 Progress check

Communication in a multi-agency approach

Each profession has its own jargon and set of rules. You do not need to know about these in depth, but should always be willing to learn from other professionals and to respect the contribution of others working with children and families. You need to:
- be clear about your own role
- be aware of the roles of other professionals
- be confident about your own standards and targets, and
- be respectful of those that apply to other services.

The importance of confidentiality

As we have seen in earlier units, confidentiality is very important when working in early years settings. You will often be entrusted with personal information about children and their families – especially if you appear friendly and approachable – and it is important that you do not abuse this trust. You should never gossip about parents or their children, and never discuss one parent with another.

In many instances you will be working under the supervision of others and it is likely that parents will pass confidential information directly to a more senior staff member. However, there may be occasions on which *you* are given information and asked to pass it on, or that you may hear or be told confidential information in the course of the daily routine. You may be entrusted with personal information about children, parents and staff, either directly (being told or being given written information) or indirectly (hearing staffroom discussions, parental comments or children's conversations), and it is important that you do not repeat any of it at home or to friends. The incidents may be discussed in your teaching sessions among your student group but you should not identify the children concerned and it must be agreed that they are not talked about beyond the group.

Sharing information

Some information *does* have to be shared, but only with your line manager. For example, if you suspect there may be a safeguarding or child protection issue, this should be shared with your line manager in strictest confidence. Parents need to be aware of this policy from the outset of your partnership so that they understand that, although they may tell you things in confidence, you may have to share the information with your line manager. It is not fair to encourage parents to talk about confidential things with you unless they first understand this. Some information has to be shared with the whole staff team, such as information about diet, allergy and if the child is being collected by someone else. Make sure parents are clear about the sort of information that *cannot* be confidential.

Case Study — Lisa

Lisa is a student on the CACHE Level 2 Child Care and Education course and her first placement is in a private nursery. She enjoys most of the work at the nursery, but is unsure how to react when children show inappropriate behaviour – such as name-calling, biting and pulling the hair of other children. Her supervisor has arranged to hold a special evening session on problem behaviour and has encouraged Lisa to attend if she can.

Lisa usually catches the same bus as a fellow student, Natasha, who is working at a nearby primary school. One day, Lisa pours out all her pent-up feelings of frustration to Natasha on their journey home. She is particularly anxious about Abigail, a three-year-old child who has started biting the other children in her group, and tells Natasha that Abigail has a young, inexperienced mother whose partner has recently left her for another woman. She says she feels sorry for the mother, but that there is no excuse – in her book – for any child to bite another child, and she thinks the mother is to blame.

Also on the bus that afternoon, sitting directly behind Lisa and Natasha, was Abigail's auntie. She realises it is her niece being talked about and is very upset. She does not say anything to Lisa, but decides to phone the nursery manager to complain when she gets home. When Lisa arrives at the nursery the following day, she is called in to see her supervisor about the incident and soon realises that she has made a dreadful mistake.

1. Which fundamental principle has Lisa ignored by her behaviour on the bus?
2. Give three examples of information that Lisa spoke about to Natasha.
3. Would the situation be any different if Lisa and Natasha were the only people on the bus, and if so, how?

Using developing knowledge and skills to improve practice and set appropriate targets to develop professionally

Develop knowledge, skills and understanding

The opportunities for learning when working with children are endless. You will increase your knowledge and skills every day through interacting with children and their carers or parents. It is important to take every opportunity to learn more – to increase your skills and understanding. For example, parents and carers will soon recognise when someone has learned about the common pattern of development in their child's age group. They will also appreciate when someone has taken the trouble to learn more about their child's particular condition or home background. You will also learn a lot from colleagues and training opportunities, and should always be willing to share any knowledge you have gained.

Personal and professional development

There are many skills involved in working with and caring for children that all adults need. These include:

- experience and the support to reflect and learn from experience
- confidence and the ability to respond in the best possible ways to individual children
- really knowing about the child, trusting that knowledge and the judgements that are based on it
- being prepared to learn from the child – for example, by listening to what a child tells you and observing what they do.

Working in the field of child care and education can be physically and emotionally exhausting, and professionals will need to consolidate their skills and develop the ability to be **reflective** in their practice. You also need to be able to give and receive feedback; this is a skill that needs to be practised in order for it to be effective for both parties.

The importance of setting targets

Setting targets – or goals – as part of a personal development plan will help you to get more involved in your learning. Remember, your targets are *personal* – they may be quite different from those of others in your class. Learning targets can help you to:

- decide what is most important to you in your learning
- fit your studies in with your other commitments
- decide on how you will study
- become an active learner
- reflect on your own practice
- think about your personal and professional development.

Your learning targets should:

- include a **timescale** to show when they should be completed; you could identify a final goal and then break down the steps towards achieving that goal into **short-term, medium-term** and **long-term targets**
- identify **success criteria** – to show how you will know when have achieved a target
- be **realistic**
- be **relevant to you**.

Setting appropriate targets
SMART targets
Each member of a team needs to know exactly what is expected of them. These expectations are called targets or 'objectives'. The targets that are most likely to be achieved are those which are 'SMART'.

SMART is an **acronym** for:

Specific: The targets must be easy to understand and say exactly what you want to happen.

Measurable: Success can be measured by checking back carefully against the instructions that have been given.

Achievable: The targets can be reached with reasonable effort in the time you are allowed.

Relevant: The targets must be appropriate, building on previous strengths and skills.

Time-related: The targets have clearly set deadlines and are reviewed frequently.

 **Progress check**

Using SMART targets

Look at the following scenarios and see how SMART targets can help individuals and teams to plan and to achieve their objectives.

Scenario 1: Paula has been asked if she would organise a display for the nursery room. The only instructions she has been given are:

'Paula, can you put up a nice, colourful display in the nursery room, please?'

Scenario 2: At a different nursery, Mark has also been asked to organise a display. On Wednesday, he was given these instructions:

'Next Monday we need to create an interactive display for the nursery room. It will be on the theme of Autumn. We've already collected some pine cones and autumn leaves, and we also have some good posters, but I'd like you to plan what else we need and let me have a list of resources by tomorrow lunchtime.'

Reviewing, updating and amending targets for professional skills

It is important to review the targets identified in your Personal Plan at regular intervals. Sometimes you may find that the targets set were unrealistic, either in timescale or in the amount of work involved. An important part of planning and evaluating your plan is knowing when and why to review and amend your targets.

Using targets for personal and professional development

- Write down in two or three sentences what you hope to achieve through your course and how you see it helping you in the future.
- What do you want to be able to do, think, feel, understand or know?
- How would this learning be recognised by others?
- What are the steps you need to take to reach the end result?
- Now write your Personal Plan (see below) and learning targets based on these ideas and using the information in this Unit as a guide.

Your personal development plan

A personal development plan will:

- help you to take responsibility for your own career and professional development
- motivate you to develop your own skills
- help you to be aware of your strengths and weaknesses
- help you to decide what training might be required to fulfil your future plans.

There are five main steps to creating a personal development plan:

1 **Think about your skills, strengths and weaknesses**: Before you can decide which areas you need to develop, you need to identify the skills you already have.
2 **Decide which areas you need to develop**: Think about what you need to do to become more competent in your present work role.
3 **Create the plan**: Think about how you can achieve your objectives, whether you need training, to shadow a colleague or take on a different role. This then should be given a timescale for the achievements of the objectives. Ensure you set yourself SMART targets (see above).
4 **Discuss your plan with others**: It is important to discuss your plan with colleagues, managers etc. as they may offer advice and support or have suggestions in which you can gain experience or knowledge.

5 **Implement the plan**: If you have researched well and your plan is realistic then your plan should be straightforward, although you may find that a course you were going to attend has changed dates, for example, and then you would need to change your plan and the timescale given.

How your personal experiences contribute to your professional development and affect your practice

Your personal development includes your own 'growth' as a person:

- Your experiences at work and at home can change your attitudes, priorities and ambitions.
- Changes in home circumstances influence decisions you make about your work, such as the hours you work, where you work and the level of responsibility you take on. If you are without family responsibilities you may welcome the extra challenge of a training course to develop your career. However, if you have to strike a balance between career and home life, and additional time is not available for training, then this might seem a burden.
- Sometimes a personal interest will influence the course of your professional development. You may, personally, become interested in working with children with physical difficulties – perhaps you have become involved with the disabled child of friends – and would like to find a job in that field. The opportunity to gain experience or training would benefit you both personally and professionally.

An important part of your personal development is self-awareness. **Self-awareness** means:

- knowing who you are and what you enjoy doing
- being able to recognise your skills, strengths and weaknesses
- being able to recognise your effect on other people.

Key areas for self-awareness include our personality traits, personal values, habits, and emotions.

Self-awareness helps you exploit your strengths and cope with your weaknesses. The process of being self-aware can be uncomfortable when you realise that something you have done or said has had a negative impact on someone else. However, unless we face such self-awareness we can never really develop and improve our practice. What is important here is that you have a network of colleagues that you can call upon for support and guidance should you require it. Self-awareness is also crucial for developing good interpersonal skills and building effective relationships with children and their families. Additionally, being self-aware allows you to identify your own **learning needs** and the ways in which those learning needs can be met – and then it is involved in your **evaluation** of whether those needs have been met.

Evaluating your own performance

Self-evaluation is important because it helps you to improve your own practice and to modify plans to meet the learning needs of the children. You can best evaluate your own performance by reflecting on your practice.

Reflective practice

You should get used to reviewing and reflecting on your experiences as part of your everyday learning. In this way, each experience – whether positive or negative – will contribute to your development and personal growth. Ways to reflect include:

- setting yourself some goals or targets when you start studying, and using your tutor's and your placement supervisor's feedback to monitor your progress
- working out what you have achieved and what you still need to work on
- making a record of your thoughts and reflections to help you to keep track of your ideas and see how far they have developed over a period of time
- recording your thoughts on any difficulties or challenges you are facing
- talking things through with another person, such as another student or a trusted friend
- asking yourself questions about what you did and thinking about how you could have done it better
- using evidence to support or evaluate any decision – for example, observations or lecture notes.

Write it down! It is a good idea to develop the habit of recording your reflections. This will help you to extend your skills in reflective practice.

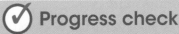
Progress check

Reflective practice

Using **reflective practice** will help you to review and evaluate your own practice. General and specific reflective questions will help to organise this evaluation. For example:

General questions:
- Was my contribution to the planning meeting or activity appropriate?
- Did I achieve my targets? If not, was it because the targets were unrealistic?
- What other methods could be used?
- How can I improve my practice?
- Who can I ask for advice and support?

Specific questions:
- How can I help a child to settle into the classroom again after his hospital stay?
- What is making a child behave inappropriately at mealtimes?

Reflective practice

Reviewing your learning activities

You may be asked to plan an activity to implement in your work setting, such as a story-telling session using props or a painting activity. Choose one activity that you have carried out with a group of children and then record your answers to the following questions:

1. How suitable was the activity for the group of children?
2. How successful were you in planning the task? Did you consider the following factors: safety, space, children's ages and stage of development, supervision and availability of resources?
3. How did the children respond during the activity? Were you able to maintain their interest?
4. How might you improve the activity if you did it again? What would you do differently and why?
5. Write a short summary of the activity – perhaps using a format for Observations (see page 51) – and use your findings to help you prepare for the next activity.

Using feedback to identify areas of your practice that need development

Feedback is structured information that one person offers to another, about the impact of their actions or behaviour – in other words, how you are doing in your study or work role. It is vital to the success of most workplace tasks, and is an activity we engage in on a daily basis. Feedback should not be confused with *criticism*, which is often an unprepared reaction to people who are not behaving in the way you want them to; criticism can make the recipient feel undervalued or angry – both unproductive emotions.

The information you hear when receiving feedback from others may be new – and even surprising. You may react with strong emotion. Good feedback is an offer of information, not a diagnosis of your character or potential, so you should not react angrily or take it too personally.

Receiving feedback can:

- help you become aware of how you are getting on – the good and the bad, what is working and what is not
- give you some ideas to help you plan your own development, in order to reach your full potential
- give you a 'reality check' – you can compare how you think you are, with what other people tell you.

Feedback from a number of different people helps you make a balanced decision about the information you are hearing. (Remember – not everyone has good feedback skills; you are likely to get a mixed quality of feedback, some perceptive and supportive, some critical and unspecific.)

Apart from the feedback you receive through formal appraisals of your performance, you may receive other forms of feedback, such as:

- **informal observations** by colleagues, or by the children in your care
- **mentoring**: a mentor supports you by modelling good practice and guiding you to look critically

at your own practice and to decide how it can be improved

- **questionnaires**: these are useful in obtaining feedback from parents and carers about the setting.

In practice

Guidelines for receiving feedback

1. **Ask questions**: state what you want feedback about. Be specific about what you want to know. Give the speaker time to think about what they want to say.
2. **Listen**: listen attentively – do not interrupt or digress. Ask for clarification if you are not sure you have understood what you have heard. Try not to be defensive or to reject the information. You need to listen, but not necessarily to agree. Take notes of what is said.
3. **Check**: check what you have heard. Repeat back what they have said and ask for examples of what the speaker means. Give your reactions to the feedback or ask for time to think about it if necessary. Ask for suggestions on what might work better.
4. **Reflect**: feedback is information for you to use – it is not a requirement to change. If you are unsure about the soundness of the feedback, check it out with other people. Work out the options open to you and decide what you want to do. It is up to you to **evaluate** how accurate and how useful the feedback is.

How to keep a placement diary

The Practice Evidence Diary for this CACHE Level 2 course is very important. Your tutor will explain how to complete the practical tasks in the diary – all of which relate directly to the **Practice Evidence Records** (PERs), which you will use to show competence in your placements.

The Practice Evidence Diary will give you the opportunity to demonstrate your skills in evaluation and reflection. It will also give you the opportunity to show your understanding of the practical skills you have gained in placement.

See Unit 6 for more information on keeping a placement diary and Practical Evidence Records.

Accessing support to make improvements to your practice

Support from your tutor

Work with an appropriate person, such as your tutor or trainer, to give your opinions and develop an individual plan that includes:

- **targets** that clearly show what you want to achieve in your learning, work or personal life, and how you will know if you have met these
- the **actions** you will take (action points) and dates for completing them (deadlines) to help you meet each target
- how to get the support you need, including who will review your progress and where and when this will take place.

Your tutor or trainer will help you to discuss your progress; he or she will enable you to reflect on *what* you learned, *how* you learned, and *what* has gone well and what has not gone so well. You should also aim to:

- **Identify the targets** you have met, by checking your plan to see if you have done what you set out to do.
- **Identify your achievements**: Check what you need to do to improve your performance (the quality of your work, and the way you work).
- **Use ways of learning** suggested by your tutor or supervisor, making changes, when needed, to improve your performance.

Support from your placement supervisor

You should find a time to talk to your placement supervisor, who will be able to help you in reviewing your progress. It may not always be possible to talk to him or her during their visit to your placement; you may need to make an appointment to see them after the session has finished.

Other resources

There are many books that will help you to plan and implement activities with young children. Your local library, school or college library and your placement usually offer a range of books and magazines on a wide range of early education topics.

Investigating employment opportunities and routes of progression

Employment opportunities in the public, voluntary and private sectors

You will have worked hard to obtain the Level 2 Award/Certificate/Diploma in Child Care and Education and can then look forward to

THE PUBLIC SECTO R		
Local Education Authority	**Local Government Services**	**Health Authority**
Areas of work	**Areas of work**	**Areas of work**
Nursery schools	Family Centres	Health visiting in the community
State nurseries	Children's Centres (run by Social Services)	Hospitals
Infant, lower and primary schools	Holiday Playschemes	Hospital crèches and nurseries
Schools for children with special needs		Adventure Centres and One O'clock Clubs
Types of job	**Types of job**	**Types of job**
Nursery trained teacher	Nursery assistant in Family	Health visitor assistant in clinics and in clients' homes
Nursery assistant	Centres and Children's Day	
Classroom assistant	Care Nurseries	Play assistant in hospital children's units
Special needs classroom assistant	Playworker in Holiday Playschemes and Adventure Centres	Nursery assistant in crèches and nurseries

THE VOLUNTARY SECTOR	
Areas of work	**Types of job**
Pre-school playgroups	Nursery assistants
After-school clubs	After-school club assistants
Holiday playschemes	Holiday playscheme workers
Nurseries	Playworkers
THE PRIVATE SECTOR	
Areas of work	**Types of job**
Day nurseries	Nursery assistants
Nursery schools	Playworkers or ski nannies
Crèches (in workplaces, shopping centres or sports and leisure centres)	Mother's help (looking after children and doing housework)
Holiday companies: e.g. ski chalets, watersports, cruise ships, hotels	Au pair – usually unqualified in child care; often young people from abroad who live with a family and offer child care services
Families	Nanny – usually qualified in child care; may live with the family or live out

Table 5.1 Working in the public, voluntary and private sectors

developing your career with children. This is called professional development and is important because it:

- enables you to develop greater knowledge and understanding in connection with your work
- offers opportunities to improve skills or gain new ones
- can enable you to experience new situations
- can prepare you for different roles and responsibilities.

The range of professional development available

You may decide to progress to the **CACHE Level 3 Diploma in Child Care and Education** or a **Playwork** course. Some aspects of professional development are dealt with through in-service **training courses**, often organised and paid for by your employer. You may receive the training from a member of your own staff or visit a college or recognised training organisation on a part-time basis. Courses can cover anything from dealing with a particular medical condition to developing ways of improving assessment and record-keeping. It is also important to keep abreast of all the changes in child

care practice by reading the relevant journals, such as *Nursery World, Early Years Educator (EYE), Child Education* and *Professional Nanny*.

Employment opportunities

CACHE Level 2 qualifications provide a stepping stone to Level 3 qualifications. They show that you have a good knowledge and understanding, and the ability to perform various well-defined tasks with some direction and guidance. The knowledge and skills that you learn are applicable to the following jobs, where you will be working under supervision: see Figure 5.6.

How to find out about career progression through career advisers

Local careers advice

- Your **Jobcentre** or **Jobcentre Plus** – for vacancy information in your area. Find in your local phone book or visit www.jobcentreplus.gov.uk.
- **Local colleges** – for details about their training courses and how to enrol.
- Local **Careers Service** – for help with career information and local job or training opportunities.

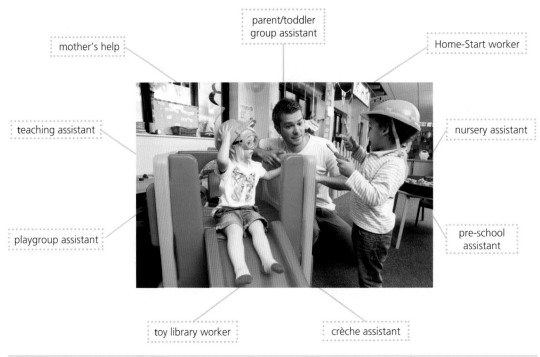

Figure 5.6 Possible employment opportunities

- **Local employers** – nurseries, pre-schools, playgroups, playwork schemes – and ask about job vacancies.

National sources of help with jobs and careers

The Teaching Agency is responsible for the recruitment, supply and initial training and development of teachers. It also supports the recruitment and development of early education and child care workers, special educational needs coordinators and education psychologists, and oversees the regulation of the conduct of teachers: www.education.gov.uk/teachingagency.

National Careers Service has advisers to offer careers information, advice and support to 13–19-year-olds between 8am and 10pm seven days a week: www2.cxdirect.com

The National Day Nurseries Association promotes quality child care and early years education. Its website profiles people who have chosen to work in child care and education: www.ndna.org.uk.

The Pre-School Learning Alliance runs its own courses, and publishes information on pre-school work and training: www.pre-school.org.uk.

The National Childminding Association provides information on training and childminding generally: www.ncma.org.uk.

4Children (formerly Kid's Club Network) provides information on jobs and training in out-of-school child care and playwork: www.4children.org.uk.

Daycare Trust gives information and advice on child care issues: www.daycaretrust.org.uk.

Skills Active gives information on a career in playwork: www.skillsactive.com.

Ofsted (Office for Standards in Education, Children's Services and Skills) – for advice on requirements for working in early years, child care and playwork, including registration of childminders: www.ofsted.gov.uk.

Directgov for search service for jobs, training, careers, child care and voluntary work (provided by Jobcentre Plus): www.jobseekers.direct.gov.uk.

Preparing for your careers guidance interview

Arrange a careers guidance interview, or interview with a careers guidance adviser as early as possible in the year you are due to complete your course, as you may get information or advice you want to think about or investigate.

- Identify your abilities, interests, skills and values, using a variety of methods. Discuss this with your careers adviser.
- Review your careers guidance action plan, if you have one, with your careers guidance adviser or tutor as early as possible, to give yourself time to think about options or change your mind.
- Use a computer-aided guidance program, available in schools and colleges, and from careers officers. It is more helpful if you can discuss any outcomes with an adviser, but you can usually use them as often as you want for ideas.
- Look at careers books or leaflets in your learning resources centre, library, or careers offices.
- Attend any careers fairs or conventions, higher education fairs and similar events for ideas, information or job opportunities. Prepare before you go: look at the programme, decide who you want to talk to, and think about questions you want to ask.
- Take copies of your CV (curriculum vitae) to hand out. Make sure you have a pen and paper with you, so you can take notes.
- Do an aptitude test, if appropriate, which will need to be completed with a careers adviser.

- Keep your Progress File (if you have been given one by your school or college) up to date, and keep any documents or records showing your activities, interests and achievements. These will be useful in preparing for any interviews, and will remind you about useful background information for CVs and application forms.
- Keep a record of all temporary or part-time jobs you have done, and any references from employers. Keep copies of any applications to courses or jobs.
- Check that you know about money issues, such as opening a bank account, loans and credit cards, managing debt, money for further learning in colleges or universities or learning while working, benefits or other money issues. Information is available from tutors, careers advisers and welfare rights advisers.

 Progress check

Working as a child care practitioner

- Make a list of what you consider to be the most important qualities a child care and education practitioner should possess.
- Explain what type of professional development a child care and education practitioner might expect in his/her first year of employment.
- Create your own list of ten 'top tips' that you think would be helpful to a child care and education practitioner about to begin his/her first job.

6 The child care practitioner in the workplace: Unit 6

This Unit involves your *practical* work with children. You will learn about the professional standards of the practitioner and how to apply these. You will also get the opportunity to observe the ways in which children develop, and to carry out planned play activities.

Learning outcomes

During this unit you will learn about:

1. The professional standards of the practitioner.

2. How to observe development across a minimum of two of the following age ranges: birth to three years, three to seven years, seven to 12 years and 12 to 16 years.

3. How to carry out planned play/activities.

4. How to use effective communication skills and contribute to positive relationships.

The professional standards of the practitioner

You have a responsibility to work to the required professional standards of a child care practitioner. These are discussed more fully in Units 1 and 5 and include the following:

- regular attendance and good time-keeping
- appearance: appropriate dress code
- interpersonal skills
- cooperation and teamwork
- confidentiality
- record-keeping
- reflective practice.

All child care practitioners should work within a framework that embodies sound values and principles. The CACHE Statement of Values is a useful tool for checking that you are upholding important child care values.

CACHE Statement of Values

You must ensure that you:

- Put the child first by:
  - *ensuring the child's welfare and safety*
  - *showing compassion and sensitivity*
  - *respecting the child as an individual*
  - *upholding the child's rights and dignity*
  - *enabling the child to achieve his or her full learning potential.*
- Never use physical punishment.
- Respect the parent as the primary carer and educator of the child.
- Respect the contribution and expertise of staff in the child care and education field, and other professionals with whom they may be involved.
- Respect the customs, values and spiritual beliefs of the child and his or her family.
- Uphold the Council's Equality of Opportunity Policy.
- Honour the confidentiality of information relating to the child and his or her family, unless its disclosure is required by law or is in the best interests of the child.

Reflective practice

Do you think some people are naturally good child care practitioners? Or are training and qualifications always necessary? Do you think there are any special qualities and skills that are necessary to work in an early years setting or school? Share your thoughts in a small group or with another learner.

Identify and provide evidence that shows your competence in a range of set tasks

Unit 6 contains four parts, which you must complete in order to achieve the Unit. These are:

1 Placement Summary
2 Practice Evidence Records (PERs)
3 Practice Evidence Record Diary
4 Professional Development Profiles (PDPs).

Placement Summary

This provides an accurate record of your work placements. You should fill in the record when you have completed each practical placement and ensure that the placement supervisor signs for each placement. Your tutor will then sign the Placement Summary at the end of your course. It is very important that you keep this record up to date and provide accurate information.

Practice Evidence Records (PERs)

When you receive your *Candidate Handbook* at the start of the course, take a look at the **PERs** at the end of the book – but do not be alarmed by them! Your tutor will explain what is required of you on placement and will also tell you about the PDPs. The PERs contain statements that describe the skills and tasks you must be able to perform competently in your practical placement. The statements are linked to the learning outcomes in the relevant units and also show links to the National Occupational Standards in Children's Care, Learning and Development.

- PERs describe the skills and tasks that you must show you are able to carry out competently (capably and effectively).
- You must show your competence in practical skills in both core age ranges (one to three years 11 months, and four to seven years 11 months).
- There may also be the opportunity to gain experience with babies (birth to one year) and with older children (eight to 16 years).
- When you are in your placement you will learn how to do practical things (e.g. set out play

materials, supervise outdoor play, prepare snacks), but the underpinning knowledge – in this book – explains why they are done that way.

Your placement supervisor, tutor or teacher will sign each practice evidence statement when they are satisfied that you are competent in the particular task or skill described.

Practice Evidence Record Diary Tasks

You will also be expected to complete **Practice Evidence Record Diary Tasks**. Your tutor or teacher will explain how to complete the diary, which can also form a useful part of your portfolio when you continue your career with children. The diary will provide evidence of your ability to evaluate and **reflect** upon your practice through a given task. Each task will have a sheet to be filled in. You are not expected to produce large amounts of written material as these tasks are not assignments and do not have to be referenced. The diary consists of tasks that ideally you will complete in your work placement. The diary must be completed to achieve a Pass grade for your practical unit (Unit 6).

Professional Development Profiles (PDPs)

There are nine sections in a PDP. You need to gain a Pass in each section to achieve a satisfactory PDP. If you do not achieve a satisfactory PDP, you will be **referred**. Each placement supervisor will complete a final PDP towards the end of your placement, indicating a Pass or Refer, and will provide comments for each statement. You should make sure that you discuss the outcome with your supervisor and ask how you can improve your work, particularly if you are referred.

In order to achieve an overall Pass in the PDPs you need to complete **two** PDPs satisfactorily (a Pass in each of the nine sections). Each PDP must be completed over a period of at least 20 days, unless it was achieved in a birth to one year environment. If, at the end of your course of study, you have not achieved a Pass in the required number of PDPs, you will be required to undertake an additional training placement of 25 days for each outstanding PDP.

Remember: You will receive plenty of support from your tutor and your placements to enable you to complete the necessary paperwork.

Maintaining a professional approach to your work

Unit 1 describes your role and responsibilities. Although your duties will vary from placement to placement (and often even from week to week), the core standards provide a framework for your practice. Together with the standards described above, you should try to develop the skill of reflective practice. The following case study should be familiar to anyone working in a nursery setting.

Reflective practice

Settling in

Read the following case study and then – in your group – discuss the questions below.

George, aged two-and-a-quarter, has been coming to Stepping Stones nursery for three weeks. Every time his mother leaves him there he becomes very tearful and withdrawn. George's mother, Laura, is very rushed in the mornings as she also has a baby aged ten months who has to be delivered to a childminder so that Laura can get to work. It usually takes about an hour until George starts to join in the activities with the other children. His key person, Paul, spends most of that first hour trying to interest George in various activities but is beginning to feel that nothing will ever work and admits that he finds it very frustrating. His room supervisor suggests that Paul try a number of different ways to ease the situation and also to keep a record of what seems to work well and to try to analyse why.

1. Why do you think it takes George so long to settle at the nursery?
2. What sort of activities do you think might be useful to provide for George?
3. Paul has been encouraged by his supervisor to reflect upon – or evaluate – his practice with George. What would be the best way to record these reflections – and why?

The value of interpersonal skills when working with children in a range of settings

Key term

Interpersonal skills – These are the skills you use when you interact with other people, and include your capacity to listen carefully, to show empathy and understanding, and to communicate effectively.

The following interpersonal skills are all very important when working with children:

- **Listening**: Attentive listening is a vital part of the caring relationship. Sometimes a child's real needs are communicated more by what is left unsaid than what is actually spoken. Facial expressions, posture and other forms of body language all give clues to a child's feelings. A good carer will be aware of these forms of non-verbal communication.
- **Comforting**: This has a physical side and an emotional side. Physical comfort may be provided in the form of a cuddle at a time of anxiety, or by providing a distressed child with a reassuring, safe environment. Touching, listening and talking can all provide emotional comfort.
- **Empathy**: This should not be confused with sympathy. Some people find it easy to appreciate how someone else is feeling by imagining themselves in that person's position. A good way of imagining how a strange environment appears to a young child is to kneel on the floor and try to view it from the child's perspective.
- **Sensitivity**: This is the ability to be aware of and responsive to the feelings and needs of another person. Being sensitive to others' needs requires the carer to anticipate their feelings – for example, the feelings of a child whose mother has been admitted to hospital or whose pet dog has just died.
- **Patience**: This involves being patient and tolerant of other people's methods of dealing with problems, even when you feel that your own way is better.

- **Respect**: A carer should have an awareness of a child's personal rights, dignity and privacy, and must show this at all times. Every child is unique, so your approach will need to be tailored to each individual's needs. Respect also includes being non-judgemental and avoiding stereotypes.
- **Warmth and friendliness**: A caring relationship is a two-way process. You do not have to actively *like* the child you are caring for, but warmth and friendliness help to create a positive atmosphere and to break down barriers.
- **Acceptance is important**: You should always look beyond any disability or disruptive behaviour to recognise and accept the person.
- **Self-awareness**: A carer is more effective if he or she is able to perceive what effect his or her behaviour has on other people. Being part of a team enables us to discover how others perceive us, and to modify our behaviour in the caring relationship accordingly.
- **Coping with stress**: Caring for others effectively in a full-time capacity requires energy, and it is important to be aware of the possibility of professional burnout. In order to help others, we must first help ourselves: the carer who never relaxes or develops any outside interests is more likely to suffer burnout than the carer who finds his or her own time and space.

The importance of self-management in maintaining a professional approach

During the course you will become familiar with your role and responsibilities. These will vary from one placement to another. A student who cannot be relied on to turn up on time, or who does not conform to the standards for hygiene and dress code, cannot expect to be trusted as a professional in the workplace. Self-awareness and self-management are important factors in professionalism. For example, if you know that you have a tendency to leave everything until the last minute and are often late for appointments, make a conscious decision to change your ways. You will find it easier to be professional in your approach if you regularly spend some time planning and preparing for each placement.

 In practice

Getting to know your practical placement

Before starting each placement, try to fill in the relevant answers to the questions below. You will then feel more confident about policies and procedures within each setting.

Name and address of placement	
Name of supervisor or teacher	
Telephone numbers	
What are the opening hours and what hours will I be working? Should I turn up earlier than these times?	
How do I find out about codes for entry gates?	
What should I wear? (e.g. special sweatshirt, name badge, flat shoes, etc.)	
What should I do if I know I am going to be late?	
Location of fire exits and fire extinguisher	
Procedure in event of fire or fire drill	

In practice (cont.)

Where should I put my coat, bag, mobile phone, etc?

Location of setting's policies: health and safety, food hygiene, confidentiality, etc.

Where are the children's records kept?

How do I find out about children's special dietary requirements?

How do I find out about children's special or additional needs?

What do I do if I am unwell and cannot attend?

What should I do if I have sickness and/or diarrhoea?

Where do I go for my breaks/lunch/tea, etc.?

Where are the spare toilet rolls, disposable gloves and other necessities kept?

Where do I find the mop and bucket to clear any spills?

Where are the paints and where should I mix them?

Where is the First Aid Box and the Accident Report Book?

Who is the named first aider?

The importance of effective communication skills in the workplace

Unit 5 describes the importance of effective communication skills – and how to communicate with children and adults.

Progress check

Communicating with parents

Using the information in Units 5 and 11 and your practical experiences, answer the following questions:
- Why is it important to exchange information with parents?
- What types of information are required by parents, and how does the work setting communicate it to them?
- What types of information are required from parents and how can this information be recorded?
- List THREE factors that might prevent information being passed on to the parents.

Providing a positive role model and interacting positively with children

Positive attitudes towards children enable them to:
- feel good about themselves
- feel that they are valued
- develop high self-esteem.

It is important that we act as positive role models through our work with children, so that they can learn to imitate our behaviour and express positive attitudes towards others.

For more information on being a positive role model, see Unit 1.

An inclusive approach to practice

By using the principle that inclusion is a **right** for all children, early years settings should try to ensure that **every child**:
- has an equal chance to learn and develop
- participates equally in activities

- is given the opportunity to communicate in their preferred format
- has his or her individual needs known and met
- feels safe and knows that he or she belongs
- is valued as a unique individual, and
- feels strong and confident about his or her identity.

✓ Progress check

Identifying prejudice, stereotypes, and discriminatory behaviour

Read the following scenarios (A to E) and then – for each one:
- Write down any examples of stereotyping or discriminatory behaviour you have identified.
- Discuss the possible reasons for such behaviour.
- Discuss what action could or should be taken to promote fairness and inclusive practice.

A. Alice has just started school and is very proud of her new reading glasses. At playtime, a group of other children force her into a corner of the playground and start chanting, 'Goggle-eyes, goggle-eyes, you can't catch us,' and then run away shrieking with laughter.

B. A group of parents have complained to the primary school teacher about the inclusion of Naveen, a child with cerebral palsy on the grounds that it will 'hold the other children back'.

C. A parent raises objections to her three-year-old son, Sam, spending so much time dressing up and playing in the home area, on the grounds that it will 'make him gay'.

D. Two children refuse to play with a black doll because they say it is 'dirty'.

E. Paul is a seven-year-old who has developmental dyspraxia; this causes him to have difficulties in PE lessons. One day he arrived home from school with a big scratch on his face, saying that the other boys in the class were bullying him because he is no good at sports. His mother says that the others ignore him when he asks to join in games and that they call him names because of his lack of ability.

Observing development

See Unit 2 for further information on observing children and the methods used.

The trend towards babies and infants being cared for in settings other than their own homes has led to the need for parents and other caregivers, including child care practitioners, to gather information – formally and informally – and to share it for the benefit of the children. The most important reason for carrying out observations and assessments is to ensure that the needs of individual children are met. Record-keeping and assessment have always been good practice in early years settings, and there is also a legal requirement to demonstrate the process.

✏ In practice

Observing children during physical activity

Select one child to observe during a period of physical activity, e.g. a gym or dance class, outdoor play with climbing equipment, or ball games. Devise a checklist (see Unit 2 for guidelines on making observations) to record the child's use of:
- **gross motor skills**: e.g. running, squatting, climbing, etc., and
- **fine motor skills**: e.g. throwing and catching a ball, picking up equipment and carrying objects etc.

Write a conclusion to show how the particular session of physical activity benefited the individual child; note if there were ways that the session could be extended to improve the development of these skills.

Observing children sensitively

Recording information about children and their interests, beliefs, discoveries and ideas can assist early years practitioners to plan for routines, transitions, and play and learning experiences. This information, together with knowledge and an awareness of child development, builds an understanding of the 'whole' child. All observations

How to contribute to positive relationships

It is important to establish appropriate and effective relationships with all the people you encounter in your work. Relationships begin before a baby is born. They begin with the care and attention that babies receive while they are in the womb. **Bonding** is the term that is commonly used to describe the strong attachment between a baby and the important people in the baby's life. It used to be thought that babies really only bonded with their mothers but research shows that babies can bond to a number of important or significant people. Babies can form an attachment with a variety of others: see Figure 6.1.

Maintaining positive relationships with children

In line with the **CACHE values**, you need to ensure that the child is at the centre of your practice – that his or her needs are **paramount**.

Treat children with respect

- Give only essential directions and **allow children to make choices**.
- Set **appropriate directions** which are realistic and consistent.

- Ask **open-ended questions** to encourage language development.
- **Avoid labelling** children.
- Be **warm** and **positive** in a way which affirms children.

Value and respect children and young people

- **Listen** to them.
- **Do not impose your own agendas** on them.
- **Do not single** out a child for special attention.
- Ensure that children **maintain control over their own play.**
- Be friendly, courteous and **sensitive to their needs.**
- Praise and **motivate** them; display their work.
- Speak to the child not at the child; with young children, this means getting down to their level
- Respect their **individuality**.
- Develop a sense of **trust and caring** with each child.

Physical contact with babies and children

Babies and very young children need physical contact – they need to be held and cuddled in order to develop emotionally. Hugging a baby, comforting a child when they are upset, putting a plaster on them, changing their wet pants – all these are ways

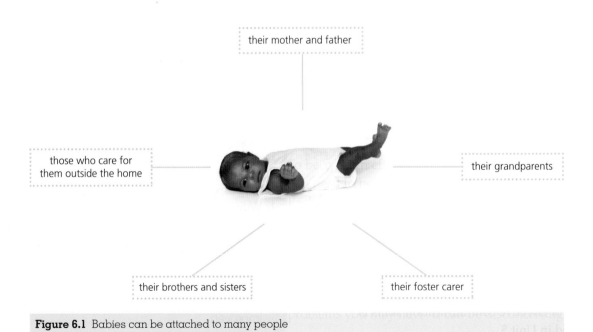

their mother and father

those who care for them outside the home

their grandparents

their brothers and sisters

their foster carer

Figure 6.1 Babies can be attached to many people

in which adults care for young children every day. However, there is a growing concern among child care professionals about *touching* children in their care. Researchers say that there is anxiety and uncertainty about what is acceptable and what is not acceptable when it comes to innocent physical contact with children. If teachers and other child care professionals are no longer allowed to offer comforting hugs – or sometimes even to put on a plaster or sun cream – their relationship with the children they look after will certainly suffer.

Your setting should have a **code of conduct** that will give clear guidelines on appropriate physical contact with the children in your care. What is appropriate physical contact with a baby or toddler, such as hugging them when upset or sitting them on your lap to explain something, will not be seen as appropriate with an older child.

Maintaining a professional attitude

Your relationship with the children in your care is a professional one; see Unit 1 for guidance on maintaining a professional attitude with children.

Case Study — A problem relationship in the nursery

Kate is a key person for six children in a day nursery. On Wednesdays, four of her key children attend nursery. One of the children, Jodie, has recently started at the nursery and was difficult to settle. Her mother spent a lot of time accompanying her and getting to know the staff, particularly Kate, to whom she warmed immediately and who struck up a trusting, professional relationship with her to help the family with their transition from using a childminder as efficiently as possible. As a result, Jodie relies heavily on Kate's presence in the room and will cry if she is handed over to another staff member in the morning.

Jodie has been used to one-to-one care for the first two years of her life. Throughout the day, she becomes tearful during noisy play and group activities. Outside, while the other children run around, Jodie holds Kate's hand and sucks her thumb, watching the other children in silence. Kate encourages Jodie to run around with her and the other children, but Jodie is not keen and Kate soon gives in, sitting on the garden bench with Jodie on her lap. The nursery manager sees this happen for a few days and reminds all the staff that they should not be sitting down when outside with the children; this is an active time for them, and they should be promoting physical play.

Other staff members begin to feel the strain as Jodie demands Kate's time and she neglects her other key children. Kate feels bad, but does not know what to do. One day, Kate is off work. Jodie spends the day following another staff member around, is very tearful and will not settle for her lunchtime nap. In the afternoon, she becomes so upset that her mum has to be called to take her home.

Note: Kate has a close bond with Jodie, which is a positive aspect of the relationship between key person and child. However, it is not a healthy bond, and Jodie is the person who seems worst affected.

1. Can you list:
   a) the reasons why this is not a healthy bond in a nursery setting
   b) how it is affecting Jodie negatively
   c) what the consequences might be for her.
2. Who is affected by Kate's 'favouritism'? Think about outside the nursery setting as well. How is each of the people in your list affected?
3. What could Kate have done differently to avoid this happening?
4. What actions could be taken now by Kate, the Room Leader, and the nursery manager to solve the problem?

7 Working with children from birth to five years: Unit 7

During this Unit you will learn about how to plan and support environments for children aged from birth to five years. This will involve you working with other professionals and being part of a team that establishes relationships with parents. You will consider the diverse needs of babies and young children and how to meet them.

Learning outcomes

During this unit you will learn about:

1. How to plan and support environments for children from birth to age five years.

2. How to contribute to working with parents as part of a team.

3. How to recognise the importance of working with other professionals.

4. How to meet the diverse needs of babies and young children.

Planning and supporting environments for children

Children and their families need an environment that is not only safe, healthy and hygienic, but also reassuring and welcoming. To provide for all children's needs (i.e. their physical needs, intellectual and language needs, emotional and social needs), the early years environment should:

- take account of each child's individual needs, and provide for them appropriately
- be stimulating – it should offer a wide range of activities that encourage experimentation and problem-solving
- provide opportunities for all types of play.

The differences between settings

In Unit 1, the range of settings was described. The way in which a safe, nurturing environment is provided will vary according to the type of setting. Examples include the following.

- **The home environment**: children who are cared for at home (by a nanny) or in a childminder's home (a **home learning environment**) may not have access to special child-sized equipment or the wide range of activities that can be provided in a purpose-built nursery setting. (*Private sector*)
- **Pre-school or playgroups**: staff may have to clear away every item of equipment after each session because the hall or room is used by other groups – for example, when the sessions take place in a village hall. (*Mostly private or voluntary sector*)
- **Purpose-built nurseries, workplace crèches and infant schools**: these usually have child-sized chairs, basins, lavatories and low tables. Such provision makes the environment safer and allows children greater independence. (*Mostly public – or state – sector, but workplace crèches are usually private*)

How to promote a healthy, hygienic and safe environment

The regulatory requirements for settings that have children aged under 16 in the setting for more than two hours a day are detailed in Ofsted's National Standards. They include the requirements shown in Table 7.1.

It is your responsibility as a practitioner to help to ensure the safety of the children in your setting. Your manager will be responsible for providing equipment and premises that comply with safety requirements – and also for making sure that all repairs and inspections of equipment are carried out by suitably qualified people.

Regulatory requirements in children's settings	
Clean and well maintained	Appropriate rest tables
Adequate ventilation: locks and toughened glass on windows	Outdoor and indoor surfaces should be stable, non-slippery and easily cleanable
All areas well lit for full visibility	Clear telephone communication, with emergency numbers available
Plugs covered and current breakers for all electrical equipment	Appropriate outdoor space with suitable equipment: soft area under climbing equipment
Adequate space and storage	Welcoming: access points must be kept clear, unlocked and made known to all children and adults, including visitors, in the case of an emergency evacuation
Adequate security: all external doors and gates locked and coded as appropriate; handles and door locks out of reach of children	Appropriate kitchen and laundry facilities
Appropriate temperature: 15–18°C; babies' rooms 20–22°C	Safe and appropriate play equipment
Safe and adequate supply of hot, cold and drinking water	Appropriate toilet facilities
Sole use of premises during session	Safe outings and use of transport
Safe supply of gas and electricity	Awareness of fire safety: regular fire drills, etc. Smoke alarms and emergency equipment available. Fireguards in front of fire and radiators covered
Appropriate supervision: the legal requirements of registered settings are: Under 2 years: 1 adult to 3 children Over 2 and under 3 years: 1 adult to 4 children 3–5 years: 1 adult to 8 children School Reception class (full day): 1 adult to 13 children	Appropriate plants
Adequate insurance	

Table 7.1 Regulatory requirements in children's settings

The importance of promoting children's welfare in a range of settings

Maintaining the environment so that it is safe, hygienic, reassuring and attractive is part of *everyone's* role, wherever children are being cared for.

In a nursery setting

Jobs may be shared out on a **rota** basis (e.g. cleaning toilets, preparing snacks, washing and sterilising equipment). However, it is every individual's responsibility to deal with any health and/or safety hazard that arises. This may be something quite straightforward, such as mopping up a spillage, or more serious, such as clearing away glass from a broken window. Immediate steps should be taken to make the surrounding area safe by clearing away fragments, keeping children away and then reporting the situation to the appropriate person.

In the home

Whether working with a childminder or in the child's home, you are expected to be alert to any potential hazards in the child's environment – for example, stairs without safety gates, access to outside, family pets, sharp corners on tables.

Where children are able to see that the care of their environment is important and shared between all adults, they are provided with **positive role models** to influence their own attitudes.

Children learn about themselves, others and the world through play. As adults, it is our responsibility to make sure play is as safe as possible. You have an important role in ensuring that the environment where children play, learn and are cared for is as safe as possible.

Providing reassuring and secure surroundings for young children

You can help to promote a **sense of belonging** by:

- greeting children individually by name and with a smile when they arrive
- marking their coat pegs with their names and their photographs
- naming their displayed work
- ensuring that their cultural backgrounds are represented in the home corner, in books, displays and interest tables
- providing routines for children – children like their environment to be predictable; they feel more secure and comfortable when their day has some sort of shape to it; most early years settings have a daily routine, with fixed times for meals, snack times and outdoor play.

In practice

Helping children to feel valued

Children and their families need to feel that they matter and that they are valued for themselves. You can help by doing the following:

- Establish a good relationship with parents; always welcome and listen to them.
- Squat or bend down to the children's level when you are talking with them.
- Praise, appreciate and encourage children.
- Be responsive to children's needs.
- Use positive images in the setting.
- Provide support for children who may be experiencing strong feelings (e.g. when settling in to a new nursery, or when they are angry or jealous).
- Encourage children who use them to bring in their comfort objects (e.g. a favourite teddy or a piece of blanket).
- Encourage the development of self-reliance and independence.
- Ensure that children who have special needs are provided with appropriate equipment and support.

Reflective practice

Welcoming children into the setting

Think about the way you welcome children into your setting:

- Do you look interested when a child or young person is talking to you?
- How do you make sure that the child knows you are listening and that you consider that what he or she has to say is important to you?
- Do you recognise and understand the ways in which body language is used by both you and the child?

Think of the ways in which you could improve how you welcome a child into the setting. You could use a Reflective Diary to record your reflections.

Adapting environments to meet the diverse needs of children

Children with particular needs should have the same opportunities for playing and learning as other children. Early years settings may need to adapt their room layout to improve access – for example, for children who use wheelchairs or for children with visual impairment. They may need to work with parents to find out how the child can be encouraged to participate fully with other children within the nursery or school. Any setting must take into account the particular needs of each child – in addition to the basic care needs of all children. This might involve:

- providing ramps for wheelchair users
- providing thick pencils and brushes for children with poor fine motor skills
- positioning children so that they learn effectively – for example, by making sure the light falls on the adult's face, so that a child wearing a hearing aid is able to lip-read and a child with a visual impairment can use any residual eyesight to see facial expressions
- adapting standard equipment – for example, by having a tray on the table so that objects stay on the table, and a child with a visual impairment does not 'lose' objects that fall off
- providing the opportunity to learn sign languages – for example, Makaton or PECS (see Unit 9, pages 233–234)
- helping children to maintain good posture, appropriate muscle tone and ease of movement, and promoting skills in independent mobility
- helping children to manage eating and drinking; there is a wide range of specialist aids for eating and drinking, such as angled spoons and suction plates
- promoting relaxation and support to help children manage stress and anxiety; some settings use a sensory room, but a quiet, comfortable area will benefit all children.

Planning environments

The physical layout of the environment

Creating a comfortable, child-friendly environment means planning both the **physical layout** and the **organisation of activities**. It involves:

- considering health and safety before anything else – for example, fire exits and doors should be kept clear at all times
- ensuring that the environment is secure: this means ensuring that safety and security measures are used so that children cannot wander off without anyone realising, and also so that

strangers cannot enter without a good reason for being there
- giving children the maximum space and freedom to explore; rooms should be large enough to accommodate the numbers of children and be uncluttered
- ensuring that the room temperature is pleasant – neither too hot nor too cold (between 18°C and 21°C)
- making maximum use of natural light; rooms should be bright, airy and well lit
- enabling access to outdoors; this should not be restricted to certain times and seasons
- ensuring displays are clearly visible and interest tables are at child height where possible, and include items that can be safely handled and explored
- available space being divided appropriately to suit the range of activities offered.

There are certain aspects of arranging the space that are decided already by some fixed features. These include the following.

- **The position of electric sockets**: this will dictate, to a certain extent, where you can site the computer, and where you can use a television/video recorder. Remember, it is dangerous to have wires and leads trailing across the floor. There may need to be similar consideration for audio/tape players.
- **Washable flooring** is likely to be near the sinks and taps, therefore messy activities – such as water play, painting and clay modelling – need to be arranged in this area.
- **Carpeted area**: quieter activities and the book 'corner' will be best suited to a carpeted area, although a natural light source is important. Equipment should be stored close to the area where it will be used – construction resources and 'small world' may be in tubs or crates near a large carpeted floor space where children can spread out. Pencils, paper, puzzles and table-top games need to be near tables and chairs.

The needs of *adults* working with children should also be provided for; adults need to feel comfortable to work effectively. For example:

- furniture should be arranged to allow supervision without excessive walking

- materials should be stored conveniently and be easily accessible
- furniture should be designed to be flexible – easy to rearrange
- equipment provided should be designed to avoid excessive lifting (e.g. nappy-changing units with steps, or cots with drop sides – travel cots are sometimes chosen for ease of storage, but these can cause backache in practitioners as the child has to be lifted from floor level)
- seating for adults – gliders, settees, and rockers are perfect for bonding with babies; there should also be chairs that are low, yet scaled to fit adults, so staff can interact at the child's level.

Furniture

Chairs must be stable and allow children to have their feet on the floor so that they feel comfortable and secure. This firm base strengthens control of their upper bodies. Height-adjustable tables are also useful in a setting with varying sizes of children. In addition:

- they can be altered for a child who is standing or sitting for a particular activity
- they are useful in after-school settings or for children with special needs (some tables are kidney-shaped, allowing the practitioner to reach each child easily).

The **furniture** in any early years setting should:

- be appropriately child-sized – in all dimensions
- comply with safety standards with regard to materials
- be well designed to suit its intended purpose or function
- be stable, but not too heavy – this allows items to be moved to create flexibility in layout
- be hard-wearing
- be easily washed/cleaned
- have safe 'corners' (rounded or moulded) and edges
- be attractive – perhaps through use of colour.

Provision of equipment

Always remember that you, the practitioner, are the child's most valuable resource. (One of the principles that underpins the EYFS is that 'Warm, trusting relationships with knowledgeable adults will support children's learning more effectively than any amount of resources.') Most early years settings provide a wide variety of equipment, as listed below.

- **Sand**: wet and dry, and equipment in boxes on shelves nearby, labelled and with a picture of contents; these may be 'themed' (e.g. things with holes in/clear plastic/red items).
- **Water**: activities that require water or hand washing should be near the sink and with aprons nearby. Equipment can be stored as for sand.
- **Clay and play dough**: cool, airtight storage; selection of utensils for mark-making, moulding, cutting.
- **A quiet area**: for looking at books and reading stories, doing floor puzzles; ideally carpeted and with floor cushions.
- **Puzzles, small blocks and table-top games**: stored accessibly close to tables and carpeted area.
- **Technology**: computer, weighing balance, calculators, tape recorders, etc.
- **Cookery**: with measuring equipment, bowls, spoons and baking trays.
- **Art work**: with tabards/aprons, brushes, paints and other materials within easy reach.
- **Domestic play**: with dolls, cots, telephones, kitchen equipment, etc.
- **Make-believe play**: box of dressing-up clothes – these should be versatile and have simple fastenings.
- **Small-world toys**: animals, cars, people, farms, dinosaurs, train and track, etc.
- **Construction**: blocks for building, small construction blocks (e.g. Duplo, Mobilo, Stickle Bricks); a woodwork area.
- **Writing/graphics**: with a variety of paper and different kinds of pencils and pens.
- **Workshop**: with found materials (e.g. cardboard from boxes, egg boxes), glue, scissors, masking tape, etc.
- **Interest table**: with interesting objects for children to handle.
- **Growing and living things**: fish aquarium, wormery, growing mustard and cress, etc.; ensure conditions suit (e.g. away from direct sunlight).

A variety of **outdoor** play equipment is needed, as listed below.

- **Outdoor space**: with safe equipment for climbing and swinging, a safety floor surface, wheeled toys, balls and bean-bags.
- **Garden**: plants and a growing area, a wild area to encourage butterflies, a mud patch for digging.

- **Supervision is important** and separate areas indoors can be divided at child height so that children can focus attention and not be distracted, yet still be overseen by an adult. Storage units, low-level screens and display surfaces can all be used to divide space effectively without 'shutting off' some activities. The 'role-play' area can get quite noisy and needs to be set up away from similar activities – 'small-world' play, train track, construction, etc. In school settings, particularly, where there will be more 'directed' and 'structured' activities, this can lead to rising noise levels and cause disruption.

The different ways to display children's work

Work settings would be dull and uninteresting places without displays. They can give a lot of information to children, parents and visitors about the setting's values and curriculum. Displays are created for a range of purposes and, sometimes, for different audiences. Most settings have a notice or display board for parents and carers, usually sited near the entrance. This is used to update general information and news about usual routine and forthcoming events. Often there will be named photographs of staff members and, perhaps, the week's menus.

Most displays reflect the activities and learning that take place.

- Some will be used as **learning resources** – alphabet and number friezes, days of the week, word banks (lists of commonly used words to consolidate reading and support writing, particularly in school settings), children's birthdays, and so on – and remain on display indefinitely.
- Others will be of **work done by the children** themselves, showing their ideas, of their own or about a topic or different materials (e.g. string painting, finger painting, collage). These displays show that we value all the children's efforts.

Creating attractive displays needs careful consideration and can be time-consuming. Factors to take into account include:

- size of space available
- themes/materials/colour schemes of adjacent displays

- location of space (some are very tricky, having thermostat controls or pipes in awkward places, or involve going round corners!)
- availability of materials
- age and stage of development of children – this affects content and also what kinds of labels, titles or lettering you use.

Different types of display

Wall display

The most usual type of display found in early years settings is a straightforward wall display. Boards of varying shapes and sizes are often placed on otherwise plain walls so that displays can be created and changed frequently to provide interest.

Window display

The use of windows for displays is also common. Paint (with a little washing-up liquid added so it can be washed off easily) is used to create colourful window displays – often of well-known characters from cartoons, stories or television, or of animals or seasonal pictures. Sometimes pieces of art or craft work may also be attached to windows, particularly if the materials lend themselves to having light behind them (e.g. 'stained glass' windows or tissue paper pictures). Remember that the sunlight will fade the colours after a short time.

'Mobile' or 'hanging' display

Mobile or hanging displays can be used effectively, especially in very large rooms. Hanging or suspending shapes or pictures from a hoop or the ceiling needs careful thought. For them to be at an appropriate height for the children may cause difficulties for staff! Also you may have to consider security or alarm systems that can be set off by moving objects. Such displays can be useful in identifying particular areas of a work setting (e.g. story characters over the book area, solid or flat shapes over the maths or numeracy area).

Table-top display

Table-top displays (sometimes referred to as **interactive displays**) give you the opportunity to use objects or artefacts that will engage the children's interest. Interest objects should be attractively and appealingly displayed to encourage children to interact with them. Posing a question (e.g. 'How many blue shapes can you find?') will invite children to use the display as an extra activity (if working with very young children then you must explain what they might do and, perhaps, take them to the display and handle the objects with them). These displays are often accompanied by an upright board or display space, which can be used for interesting pictures, photographs or posters and your own titles to add interest. Older children may appreciate related fact and story books to use for research.

Figure 7.1 A display about wood

The basic physical and health needs of children from birth to five years

To achieve and maintain healthy growth and development (that is, physical, intellectual, social and emotional), certain basic needs must be fulfilled. These basic needs are:

- food
- shelter, warmth, clothing
- cleanliness
- fresh air and sunlight
- sleep, rest and activity
- love and consistent and continuous affection

- protection from infection and injury
- stimulation
- social contacts
- security.

It is difficult to separate these basic needs in practical care, as they all contribute to the holistic development of a healthy child. (The care of children from birth to age five is covered in Unit 2.)

Health and safety requirements

The health and safety requirements when working with children from birth to age five years are described in Unit 3.

Contributing to working with parents as part of a team

Promoting and maintaining relationships with families

Parents or guardians and their families occupy a central position in children's lives. They provide their child with what they need to develop and grow, and are the people who know their child the best.

Your role: you must never try to take over this central role inappropriately. Instead, listen to parents and families as the true 'experts' in their own children's care.

Parents and guardians start off in an unequal relationship with child care staff. Some get very anxious – they may never have been separated from their child before, or may speak a different language from that used in the child care setting.

Your role: you need to be able to see things from their point of view and do everything possible to make them feel welcome.

A crucial part of making families feel welcome and part of the child care setting is respecting their traditions and child care practices.

Your role: always listen to any specific wishes, and comply with them whenever possible.

There are differences between the relationship that a parent has with their child and the relationship you have with that child.

Your role: try to keep a little distance, while working in a warm, sensitive way. You should not develop a deeply emotional attachment.

What carers, parents and guardians *do* all have in common is their desire for the best for the child.

Your role: the best approach is to think of yourself as a resource and source of support for parents. You can offer ideas, but must not insist on, or be judgemental about, the way that they bring up their children. Share information about children's development and progress openly with their parents or guardians. This encourages a spirit of collaboration, which will ensure that the child gets the best and most consistent care. It also builds trust between the early years practitioner and parents or guardians.

The importance of shared care between the setting, the home and the family

Working with parents and carers is an essential aspect of work with children. You can strengthen and build on this responsibility so that parents experience an increase in enjoyment of their children and an understanding of child development. Remember that it takes time and regular communication to build positive relationships with parents that are founded on mutual trust and respect. (You can learn more about the importance of sharing care in Unit 11.)

The principles of effective communication when working with families and their children

The guidelines given in Unit 5 will help you to follow the principles of effective communication. See also Unit 11, Supporting children and families.

The role of the key person

The advantages of having a **key person** are that children feel happier and more secure. They also gain in confidence and independence skills; this enables them to explore and to try out new things. Having a key person in group settings is particularly important for babies and young children; but even when children are older and can hold special people in mind for longer, there is still a need for them to have a key person to depend on in the setting, such as their teacher or a teaching assistant.

A key person:

- helps the baby or child to become familiar with the setting and to feel confident and safe within it
- develops a genuine bond with children and offers a settled, close relationship
- meets the needs of each child in their care, and responds sensitively to their feelings, ideas and behaviour
- talks to parents to make sure that the child is being cared for appropriately for each family.

Figure 7.2 The relationship between a child and key person is very important

The key person's relationship with parents

Some parents may worry that the close emotional relationship their child has with a key person in the setting might undermine their own relationship with their child. They should be reassured that nobody can take their place in their child's life. Studies in **attachment** have shown that babies and young children in 'group' care benefit greatly from having their own familiar key person. Careful records of the child's development and progress are created and shared by parents, the child, the key person and other professionals as necessary.

Nurseries and other group settings should ensure that:

- staffing rotas are based on when a key person is available for each child
- there is a *second* key person for children so that when the main key person is away there is a familiar and trusted person who knows the child well
- there is planned time for each key person to work with parents so that they really know and understand the children in their key group
- as children move between settings, they are helped to become familiar with their new key person
- a key person does not become over-attached to a child; also they should reassure parents who worry that children may be more attached to staff than to them.

In the private sector, nannies and childminders are also expected to fulfil the key person role for the children in their care.

The lines of reporting and recording to management in a professional manner

It is vital that all practitioners know the **lines of reporting** and how to obtain clarification of their own role and responsibility. If you do not feel confident in carrying out a particular task, either because you do not fully understand it or because you have not been adequately trained, then you have a responsibility to state your concerns and ask for guidance. (See also Unit 1, page 12 for guidelines on reporting and recording to management.)

Diverse family backgrounds and the importance of valuing different lifestyles

The many different family structures are described in Unit 11.

Good child care provision should be holistic, covering all areas of learning and development, including cultural diversity. Many settings already have cultural activities, such as celebrating well-known festivals from around the world like as Diwali and Chinese New Year. It is important to avoid making any assumptions about the families of the children in your settings. Settings need to value diversity – in every sense – ethnicity, gender, religion, food customs, etc. Take time to talk to children and their families, and find out about any cultural similarities and differences in family life, customs, food and clothes. This information will help to inform planning for your daily sessions.

 In practice

Valuing and promoting cultural diversity

- Provide a range of activities, which celebrate these differences (for example, make children aware of what is involved in celebrations of religious festivals such as Diwali and Chinese New Year, as well as Christmas and Easter, whether or not there are children in the setting who celebrate these occasions).
- Promote a multicultural approach to food provision; for example, parents could be invited into the setting to cook authentic national and regional dishes – Caribbean food, Yorkshire pudding as a dessert, Welsh barabrith, Irish stew, Asian sweets, etc.
- Encourage self-expression in solo and in group activities; for example, by providing 'tools' for cooking and eating from other cultures such as woks, chopsticks, griddles.
- Celebrate the diversity of language; use body language, gesture, pictures and actions to convey messages to children whose home language is not English.

The importance and role of parents in children's lives

There are many reasons why it is valuable to involve parents or carers in the work setting:

- Parents are the first and primary educators of their children.
- Parents know their children better than anyone else.
- Children benefit from the extra attention, particularly one- to-one help.
- A range of different skills can be brought to the work setting, such as music, sewing, drawing, cooking, etc.
- Parents and carers who do not share the same language or culture as the work setting can extend the awareness and knowledge of staff and children about the way other people live, cook and communicate.
- Parents and carers can help by sharing lots of books with children from an early age, and by hearing and helping their child read when they start school.
- Involving parents and carers in the play and learning experiences of their children can help to counteract any negative feelings parents may have about education systems, arising perhaps from memories of their own school days.

Meeting the needs of parents in a variety of settings

You need to be aware of the wide variety of parenting and family approaches. Families have a range of approaches to problems and in some cases these may contradict what is expected in an early years setting or school; for example, a child might be smacked at home, but be expected not to hit while in nursery. Children may be made to stay at the table until they have finished their dinner at home, but an early years setting may allow children to choose what they eat, and how much. The best approach to difficulties like these is to try to build bridges between home and the setting, while accepting that there are differences. Staff and parents can explain to a child that there is a different expectation or rule in nursery, for example.

A key person, in response to a parent who does not want the child to play outside on a cold day, might first show sympathy and understanding, then explain the policy on free flow, and finally meet the parent's needs to some extent by undertaking to ensure that the child is really well wrapped up, and by arranging a further discussion, if necessary, to explain the nursery's approach.

Full-time employment: Some parents and carers who are in full-time employment may have a different attitude towards their child settling into the setting from those who have chosen to place their child in a nursery or playgroup on a part-time basis to widen the child's experience.

Individual needs: Every situation and family must be treated individually and the family's needs met through a flexible approach; for example, parents who are dealing with a large family or with disabled family members will have different priorities from a lone-parent family with one child.

Transition to school: Schools often have to deal with children who have had no experience of early childhood education or nursery care, as well as with those who have been in day nurseries from a few months old. Some parents whose children have been in full-time day care find the school's 'staggered' intake – when children attend on a part-time basis at first – both unnecessary and inconvenient, especially if they work. However, most children take time to adapt to a full school day, as this includes a long lunchtime period with less supervision than they are used to, and no facilities for an afternoon rest.

Referral by Social Services: When children have been placed in a child care setting on the advice of a social worker, there may be some resentment from carers. They may feel that their rights and responsibilities have been overridden. It is important that a positive relationship between carers and the setting is established as soon as possible, with a clear understanding that the interest of the child or young person is everyone's main concern. In these situations there will usually be regular meetings involving parents and carers, staff and other professionals to discuss the child's progress. Children will be invited to attend, as their opinions are important to any decision made.

Parents and carers who may not want to become involved

Many parents will want to become involved in their child's setting, especially if there is an open, welcoming atmosphere and a place to meet other parents. However, there will always be some parents who do not want to participate.

There could be a number of reasons for this reluctance. These include:

- working full-time or having other daytime commitments
- feeling that they have nothing of value to contribute
- not being interested in spending time with other people's children
- lacking confidence or feeling shy.

It is important that parents do not feel pressured into becoming involved. You should always respect parents' decisions and not assume that this shows a lack of interest in their children.

Some early years settings have a drop-in facility for parents that helps support those feeling isolated and experiencing problems, while a family support group, with a skilled family worker on hand, can help people with parenting skills and other issues.

Key principles of legal frameworks to support working with children and children's welfare

All settings that provide care and education for children must be registered with the appropriate authority:

The Early Years Register: All early years practitioners – such as childminders, day nurseries, pre- schools and private nursery schools – providing for children from birth to the 31 August following their fifth birthday (known as the early years age group) must register on the Early Years Register and deliver the Early Years Foundation Stage (EYFS) in England,the Foundation Phase in Wales, the Early Years Framework in Scotland or the Foundation Stage in Northern Ireland.

The EYFS is the statutory framework for the early education and care of children in the early years age group. The EYFS includes requirements for the provision of young children's welfare, learning and development that all providers must meet, as well as good practice guidance.

General Childcare Register (GCR): The GCR has two parts:

- *Compulsory part*: Providers of child care for children from 1 September following their fifth birthday (for example, the end of the Foundation Stage) up to the age of eight, and where at least one individual child attends for a total of more than two hours in any one day, are required to register on the compulsory part of this register, unless they are exempt. Care that is provided in the child's home is exempt from compulsory registration.
- *Voluntary part*: Providers of child care to children aged eight and over, or care that is exempt from compulsory registration, can now choose to be registered on the voluntary part of the register if they meet the requirements.

The different inspectorates – Ofsted (in England), HMIe (in Scotland), Estyn (in Wales) and ETI (in Northern Ireland) – are responsible for regulating and inspecting all settings with children under the age of 16 for more than two hours each day.

How to recognise the importance of working with other professionals

As an early years practitioner, you will work alongside other professionals – either in your own setting or in the wider early years community. Multi-agency working enables different services and professionals to join forces in order to prevent problems occurring in the first place. It is an effective way of supporting children and families with additional needs, and helps to secure improved outcomes. Integrated working involves everyone who works with children, whether part-time or full-time. Any member of the children's workforce (such as an early years practitioner, a nurse, teacher, youth worker, sports coach, social worker) needs to understand the importance of working together in an integrated way and to build it into their everyday practice. Integrated and multi-agency working is also collectively known as partnership working.

Key terms

Integrated working – When everyone supporting children works together effectively to put the child at the centre, meet their needs and improve their lives.

Multi-agency working – Practitioners from different sectors and professions within the workforce are brought together to provide integrated support to children and their families; for example a 'team around the child'.

The importance of working with other professionals

Before multi-agency working became the accepted way of working, the parents of a child with special or additional needs would probably face many different appointments with several different people, none of whom would have spoken to each other and all of whom would expect the parents to give a detailed breakdown of their child's disability. Multi-agency working is designed to cut across this by bringing together professionals with a range of skills to work across their traditional service boundaries.

As an early years practitioner, you will work closely with your colleagues in the setting and will liaise with parents of the children in your care. You may also be involved in the network of relationships between staff at the setting and other professionals from outside agencies. These include the following.

- **Health service professionals**: doctors, health visitors, paediatricians, physiotherapists, occupational therapists, school nurses, speech and language therapists, psychologists, play workers, hospital play specialists and play therapists.
- **Social service professionals**: social workers, specialist social workers in mental health, sensory disabilities, physical disabilities, children and families.

- **Local education authority professionals**: support teachers, special needs advisers, specialist teachers, education welfare officers.
- **Charities and voluntary organisations**: for example, Portage workers, National Autistic Society, RNIB (Royal National Institute for the Blind), NDCS (National Deaf Children's Society), SCOPE (about cerebral palsy) and many others. There are many other local support groups, including Gingerbread, which works on behalf of lone parents, and Contact A Family, which provides independent information, advice and support to parents of children with disabilities or special needs.

The key principles of partnership working are openness, trust and honesty, agreed shared goals and values, and regular communication between partners.

The role of different professionals who may work with children and their families

As you are working with children, you may already know other professionals in your setting who provide support for children and their families. Each will have a clearly defined role and responsibilities within their own profession.

Key term

Portage workers – Education support workers who visit families of pre-school children in their homes. Portage workers are specially trained in understanding and promoting child development and come from a variety of other professions, ranging from nurses or other health professionals to school teachers.

The role of multi-agency professionals is further discussed in Unit 9.

How to meet the diverse needs of babies and young children

Earlier in this Unit you will have learned how to meet the diverse needs of children through the provision of a safe and reassuring environment. You also need to know how children can be safeguarded – or protected – through multi-agency work.

The protection of all children and the role of multi-agency work

Inter-agency child protection

You may have heard about children being *'on the child protection register'* but technically they should be described as having an **inter-agency child protection plan**. The plan is implemented in the following way:

Initial assessments are undertaken by specialist children's social workers in response to referrals made by schools, doctors, nurses and early years settings, for example. The initial assessment informs the decision of what to do next. Possible decisions include:

- **Offering services to support the child and family**, if it is judged that the child is not at immediate risk of harm but is at risk of poor developmental outcomes.
- **Urgent action to protect the child from harm** – for example, applying for a Court Order to take the child into care. Social workers cannot take children away from their parents – only the courts can direct this. However, a police officer can take a child into police protection in an emergency.
- **Holding a strategy discussion**. This would happen where the assessment indicates that the child may be suffering significant harm. Other professionals who know the child and family, such as GPs, health visitors, teachers and early years practitioners, may be invited to this discussion. Specialist police officers must always be represented in strategy discussions. Where appropriate, a **child protection conference** will be arranged.

It is important to remember that staff in early years settings and schools should not investigate possible abuse or neglect. The role of the early years practitioner is to refer concerns to children's social care, to contribute to the initial assessment and to attend meetings as requested.

The initial assessment can lead to:

- further work and assessment being undertaken by specialist children's social workers – this is called the **Core Assessment**
- help being offered to the child and family on a voluntary basis, usually coordinated under the **Common Assessment Framework (CAF)**
- a Child Protection Conference being convened – key staff working with the family, along with the child's parents, will be invited to this conference; the meeting will be organised by an independent chairperson who has not previously been involved in the case in any way, and who reports to the Director of Children's Services.

Child Protection Conference

The Child Protection Conference seeks to establish, on the basis of evidence from the referral and the initial assessment, whether the child has suffered ill-treatment, or whether his or her health or development has been significantly impaired as a result of physical, emotional or sexual abuse, or neglect. A professional judgement must be made about whether further ill-treatment or impairment is likely to occur.

It is possible to hold a Child Protection Conference pre-birth if there are significant concerns that the newborn baby will be at risk of immediate harm – for example, in a family where there has been significant previous child abuse, or where a mother has abused drugs or alcohol during pregnancy. If this is established, the child will be made the subject of an **inter-agency child protection plan**. The child's early years setting or school should be involved in the preparation of the plan.

The role of the school or early years setting to safeguard the child, and promote his or her welfare, should be clearly identified. Examples of this role might include:

- carefully monitoring the child's heath or well-being in the setting on a daily basis

- making referrals to specialist agencies – for example, educational psychology
- offering support and services to the parents – for example, a parenting class run at the setting
- monitoring the child's progress against the planned outcomes in the agreed plan.

Reflective practice

One of your key children is subject to an inter-agency child protection plan, under the category of neglect. During the day, you notice that the child looks rather grubby. Other children are avoiding him because he smells.

Discuss how you would talk to the parent at the end of the day and what information you would pass on to the child's social worker.

The rights of children and their families

Children are entitled to basic human rights such as food, health care, a safe home and protection from abuse. However, children are a special case because they cannot always stand up for themselves. They need a *special* set of rights that take account of their vulnerability, and ensure that adults take responsibility for their protection and development.

The rights embodied by the **UN Convention on the Rights of the Child** that particularly relate to early years care and education are as follows:

- Children have the right to be with their family or with those who will care best for them.
- Children have the right to enough food and clean water for their needs.
- Children have the right to an adequate standard of living.
- Children have the right to health care.
- Children have the right to play.
- Children have the right to be kept safe and not hurt or neglected.
- Disabled children have the right to special care and training.
- Children have the right to free education.

The causes and effects of discrimination in a multi-ethnic society

What is discrimination?

Discrimination occurs when someone is treated less favourably, usually because of a negative view of some of their characteristics. This negative – or pejorative – view is based on stereotypical assumptions that do not have a factual basis.

Types of discrimination

The most obvious types of discrimination occur as a result of the stereotypes described in Unit 1: racism, sexism, ageism and disablism. Children may also discriminate against other children on account of their differences. This often takes the form of **name-calling** and **teasing**, and may be directed at children who are either fatter or thinner than others in the group, or who wear different clothes.

Sometimes discrimination is **institutionalised**. This means that the particular institution is not organised to meet the needs of all the people within it; in other words, the structures are not in place to prevent discrimination taking place. Examples include:

- racism within the police force; many more black youths are still stopped by the police than are white youths
- children with impairments or learning difficulties are not provided with the equipment or resources to enable them to take a full part in the school or nursery planning
- adults who use wheelchairs may not be allowed access to cinemas or theatres, because of lack of suitable adaptations to comply with fire regulations
- the needs of children from minority religious or cultural groups are not recognised within the nursery or school.

Direct discrimination occurs when someone is treated less favourably on specific racial or other grounds than other people are, or would be, treated in similar circumstances. For example, if an Asian woman is turned down for a job as a shop assistant and told there are no vacancies, then a white woman with equivalent qualifications is offered the job a short while later, the Asian woman has been **directly** discriminated against.

Indirect discrimination occurs when a condition or requirement is applied equally to people of all racial or other groups, but far fewer people of a particular group are able to comply with it. Such indirect discrimination is against the law when it cannot be justified other than on racial or other grounds. For example, if an employer requires job applicants to have a qualification in a particular subject, but will only consider people whose degree is from a British university, this condition could amount to indirect discrimination.

The effects of discrimination on children's development

The early childhood setting – nursery, playgroup or nursery school – is often the first experience beyond their immediate family and friendship group that the child joins. When they join any wider setting, children need to:

- feel valued for themselves – as individuals
- feel a part of things, and a sense of belonging
- feel accepted by others
- develop a sense of self-worth (i.e. to feel that they matter to other people).

Discrimination of any kind prevents them from developing a feeling of self-worth or **self-esteem**. The effects of being discriminated against can last the whole of a child's life. In particular, they may:

- **be unable to fulfil their potential**, because they are made to feel that their efforts are not valued or recognised by others
- **find it hard to form relationships** with others because of lack of self-worth or self-esteem
- be so affected by the **stereotypes or labels** applied to them that they start to believe in them and so behave in accordance with others' expectations; this then becomes a **self-fulfilling prophecy** – for example, if a child is repeatedly told that he is clumsy, he may act in a clumsy way even when quite capable of acting otherwise
- feel shame about their own cultural background

- **feel that they are in some way to blame** for their unfair treatment and so withdraw into themselves
- **lack confidence in trying new activities** if their attempts are always ridiculed or put down
- **be aggressive towards others**; distress or anger can prevent children from playing cooperatively with other children.

Disability and discrimination

Children who are disabled (and their families) may be discriminated against in particular ways.

- They may face difficulty gaining access to shops. Most large stores have easy entrance arrangements, but smaller shops prevent access by wheelchair (and often by large pushchairs and prams, too).
- Children who look different often face more discrimination because the disability is seen first rather than the child; for example, they may be stared at and hear remarks about themselves when out with their families. Disabled children have even been barred from cafés and restaurants because of their differences.
- Children who look just like any other child may have a 'hidden' disability, such as autism, attention deficit hyperactivity disorder (ADHD) or deafness. Their behaviour may attract disapproval when out in public and the family will feel under attack.
- They may have financial difficulties. There are always extra financial costs involved in bringing up a disabled child in the family – for example, mobility costs, the costs of giving full-time care, and perhaps extra laundry costs. Parents may have to rely on state benefits to enable them to give their child the care they need.
- Parents who are caring for a disabled child may not have the time or energy to give equivalent attention to any other child in the family. This could restrict the other child's development.
- Parents often have to struggle 'against the odds' to obtain the best treatment and resources for their child. Many parents find it difficult to have to ask for help all the time; others find the process very tiring. (For example, the process of **statementing** can take many months or even years – see Unit 9.)

Strategies to promote and meet the needs of individual children and their families

Your role in challenging discrimination

The first step in being able to challenge discrimination is to identify when it is taking place. The most obvious and common form of indirect discrimination is when **labels** are applied to children. You may believe in private, for example, that Mark is a 'spoilt' child who gets away with the sort of behaviour that you personally think is unacceptable. It would be unnatural not to have an opinion on such matters. However, you should not initiate or join in any discussion that results in Mark being labelled as a 'difficult' or 'spoilt' child. Equally, you will find some children more likeable than others; again this is quite natural. What is important is that you are fair in your treatment of all the children in your care. You should treat them all equally and with respect.

Remember the poem on page 10 of Unit 1, 'Children learn what they live', and try to develop **positive attitudes** towards all the children you meet, so that they cannot feel the effects of discrimination. It is only natural to like some children better than others, but our behaviour should always reflect the principle that all children are entitled to the same love and respect.

How to encourage diversity and inclusive practice

Every child needs to be included and to have full access to the curriculum, regardless of their ethnic background, culture, language, gender or economic background. Some practical ways of valuing and encouraging diversity are listed below.

- **Provide positive images**: books and displays should use positive images of children with disabilities and from different cultures. Children also need positive images of gender roles (e.g. men caring for small children and women mending the car).

- **Arrange activities to encourage children with additional needs to participate fully with other children**: this might mean providing ramps for wheelchair users, or working with parents to find comfortable ways for a child to sit (e.g. a corner with two walls for support, a chair with a seat belt, or a wheelchair with a large tray across the arms).
- **Learn a sign language**, such as Makaton or Signalong, to help communicate with a child who has a hearing impairment or a learning difficulty.

Planning activities which promote equality of opportunity

Every child needs to feel accepted, and to feel that they belong in the setting. Try to find out as much as possible about different cultures, religions and special needs. Activities should be planned which enable children to:

- feel valued as individuals
- explore a wide range of everyday experiences from different cultures and backgrounds
- express their feelings.

Make sure that the books, posters and other resources include positive images of minority ethnic groups and children with impairments, and that gender roles are non-stereotyped and reflect the diversity of family life. Specific activities may include the following:

- Play with malleable materials such as play dough, sand or clay; drawing, painting and craft activities help children to express their feelings and are non-sexist activities; include examples from different cultures (e.g. papier mâché, origami, weaving).
- Provision of toys that offer a range of play opportunities rather than those that are aimed particularly at one sex or the other (e.g. provide a wide variety of dressing-up clothes that can be used by girls and boys). Include dress from different cultures and make sure that superhero outfits are available for either sex (e.g. Superwoman as well as Superman, Wonderwoman and Batman).

- Extension of the home corner to provide a wide range of play situations (e.g. a home corner plus an office or shop, or a boat).
- Using books and telling stories in different languages: invite someone whose first language is not English to come and read a popular story book – such as 'Goldilocks and the Three Bears' – in their language to the whole group; then repeat the session using the English text, again to the whole group.
- Playing music from a variety of cultures (e.g. sitar music, pan pipes, bagpipes), and encouraging children to listen or to dance to the sounds.
- Planning a display and interest table around one of the major festivals from different cultures (e.g. Diwali, Hanukkah, Easter, Chinese New Year).
- Using posters that show everyday things from different countries (e.g. musical instruments, fruit and vegetables, transport and wildlife).
- Organising the home corner to include a variety of equipment commonly found in homes in different cultures (e.g. tandoor, wok, chopsticks).
- Providing dolls and other playthings that accurately reflect a variety of skin tones and features.
- Arranging cookery activities using recipes from other cultures and in different languages; contact the relevant organisations to find out how to promote cooking skills for children with special needs.

See also Unit 9 for discussion of promoting individual children's needs and how you can support children with additional needs.

In practice

Exploring assumptions and stereotypes

The following adjectives are often used to describe children:

bossy	noisy	shy
energetic	competitive	helpful
aggressive	lively	gentle
warm	moody	quiet
kind	babyish	emotional
strong	lazy	sissy
clinging	cheeky	

Use the headings **girls, boys** and **either boys or girls** to create three columns. Then put the adjectives from the list into the appropriate column, according to whether you think they describe girls, boys or either girls or boys. Compare your lists with those of a friend.

- How similar were your choices? Discuss the similarities and the differences.
- Discuss reasons why some adjectives are so closely related to gender.
- Do your lists really apply to all the children you work with or know?

Assessment practice

1. How can you develop and maintain relationships with families?

2. What do you understand by diversity and inclusive practice?

3. Why is it important to record and report information in a professional manner?

4. What is the role of a key person in an early years setting?

5. How can you help to provide a diverse and inclusive environment?

8 Play activity for children from birth to 16 years: Unit 8

This Unit will teach you about how to provide play activities for children. This will include understanding about the main stages of play and the diverse play needs of individuals. You will learn how to support play opportunities and the key issues for you to consider as an adult. See more on play in Unit 4.

> ### Learning outcomes
>
> During this unit you will learn about:
>
> 1. How to meet the diverse play needs of children.
> 2. How to support a range of play opportunities for children.
> 3. The role of the adult in providing play activity for children.

The diverse play needs of children

The stages of play

The stages of play in young children are described fully in Unit 4.

In later childhood and early adolescence, children's play becomes more organised and structured as their enthusiasm for logical thinking shows itself through **games with rules** and in **team sports**.

Winning becomes important as they begin to understand that winning means following the rules. This is the age when team sports become important. However, even when teenagers are just 'hanging out' together, they are learning – sharing information and knowledge, and gaining a better understanding of social relationships.

As children enter their teenage years, they rarely refer to what they do outside school hours as playing; however, older children do need to play, just as much as do the under-fives. Many children from about 11 years and older have little opportunity for play. When school time is over, their leisure time is often taken up with household chores, sports activities, reading, using the computer or watching television or DVDs. Research has shown that older children also need time to **play**. They need free time – when nothing is planned or scheduled, nothing demanded, and during which they are discouraged from watching television or using the computer.

Play-based learning activities provide many different ways for children to learn a variety of different skills and concepts; they also enable children to feel competent about their ability to learn.

The interests of children from birth to age 16 years

Babies (from birth to 18 months) are totally dependent on caring adults to provide them with new play experiences; they show an interest in:

- watching movement and listening to rhythmic sounds
- holding rattles, chiming balls and musical toys
- exploring textures – for example, on an activity mat
- playing with stacking beakers and bricks
- exploring objects with their hands and their mouth
- active play with a caring adult
- making noises by banging toys
- playing with empty cardboard boxes
- looking at picture books.

Figure 8.1 Babies enjoy looking at picture books

Children aged 18 months to three years have an increasing desire for independence; they show interest in:

- playing with things that screw and unscrew
- paints and crayons
- sand and water play
- playing with balls – rolling, kicking and throwing.

Towards the end of this period, they show interest in:

- toys to ride and climb on
- matching and sorting games
- simple jigsaw puzzles
- puppet play and action rhymes
- musical games
- jumping, running and physical games
- role-play.

Children aged three to five play with other children; they show an interest in:

- playing outdoors
- active pretend play with other children
- jigsaw puzzles and making models
- simple craft activities and playing with dough
- playing on the floor with bricks, trains, dolls and boxes, alone and with others
- acting out puppet shows
- imaginative play.

Children aged five to eight are learning self-control and enjoy showing what they can do; they show an interest in:

- team games and games with rules

- complicated games on the floor with small-world objects
- more elaborate pretend play with others
- playing cooperatively with other children
- fantasy play
- activities that involve precise movements – such as hopscotch or skipping games.

Children aged eight to 12 usually have at least one special friend, but also like to belong to a group; they show interest in:

- being physically active outdoors
- cooperative and competitive games
- reading fictional stories, magazines and 'how to' project books
- games with rules – traditional board games such as draughts and chess, word games, card games and quiz-type games – as well as the more complex fantasy games
- craft activities and making things from construction kits
- collecting favourite things, producing topics and projects.

Adolescents (12 to 16 years) are becoming increasingly independent from their parents; they show an interest in:

- developing their own ideas and values – often becoming concerned about social issues such as global warming and poverty
- being with their friends; at first they socialise in mixed-gender groups – this gives way to one-to-one friendships and romances
- music, sports, computing and computer games
- role models – particularly media personalities – pop stars, sports stars and film stars.

The importance of consulting with children about their play environments

Children have the right to be consulted and involved in decision-making about the type of play provision they have. Involving children in making decisions is important because it helps them to develop:

- **independence**, which increases their feeling of confidence in their own abilities

- a sense of being in control of their own environment
- **trust** – knowing that adults trust their judgement and opinions
- **self-help skills** – for example, knowing that the adult will be patient in letting the child dress himself, even if it takes a long time and several attempts.

Teenagers would probably not refer to their social or leisure activities as 'play', but surveys of the views of children show that they want:

- opportunities to be physically active – indoors and outdoors
- the chance to meet with their friends
- the chance to be somewhere quiet
- choice and variety.

Children have also identified the following barriers to their play:

- fears for their safety, especially from bullying
- traffic
- dirty and/or rundown play areas and parks
- lack of choice
- play provision that is too far away.

How to recognise the individual play needs of children

What are play needs?

Play needs are individual to each child and are directly related to the age, stage of development and interests of the child.

 Progress check

Play needs

Play needs include opportunities to:
- play in safe places
- use a variety of objects and materials
- learn about the physical environment
- develop empathy (being able to imagine what someone else feels or thinks)
- take control of their own learning – at their own pace

- develop relationships with others – both other children and adults
- explore their own feelings – and learn how to control them.

Adults often make assumptions about the play needs of children, but these are not always an accurate reflection of what children both want (play preferences) and need (play needs).

Observing children during their play and **discussing their play preferences** with them will help to ensure that each child's play needs are met.

How to support a range of play opportunities for children

Play settings and resources

Children play in a great variety of settings, including their homes, nurseries, schools and playgroups. **Playworkers** work with school-aged children in *out-of-school* settings. Different playwork settings are run in different ways, but all aim to give the children choices about how they spend their leisure time. Playworkers work in a range of settings, both statutory and voluntary, which aim to provide for children's play, such as those in the examples listed below.

- **Breakfast clubs (8–9 am)**: parents bring children to the club; children can have breakfast; staff take children to school; some activities may be provided.
- **After-school clubs (3–6 pm)**: these cater for four- to 14-year-olds; parents book children in; clubs collect children from school; parents collect children from club; most clubs organise a refreshment break during the session.
- **Playbus**: open access; the bus goes to clubs, groups, play areas or other appropriate places; the children may come and go at will; activities can be organised; in some cases, the bus staff may organise something that is open only to members of a group or club.

- **Play centre/youth groups**: can cater for a variety of age ranges (e.g. 8–14 years, 11–14 years, 13–18 years, up to 25 years); venues vary from purpose-built buildings to village halls, church rooms and schools; opening times vary from one day to every day of the week.
- **Adventure playgrounds**: open access; children can come and go at will; children do not need to be booked in and out of the playground; the staff supervise outdoor activities and equipment; outdoor play equipment is often designed and built by the children; some activities may be available indoors, often led by the children.
- **Holiday play schemes**: usually for four- to 14-year-olds, but some may be open to older children; play schemes can be run by a variety of organisations – for example, the Church, voluntary organisations and uniformed groups; the times of opening and the number of days per week vary between schemes.

Playworkers may also work in a number of more *specialised* settings in which providing for play has been recognised as an important way of supporting children. For example:

- hospitals
- refuges
- family services.

Not all settings fit with these descriptions. For example, some after-school clubs may be open access; playbuses may run activities in a variety of settings, including open-access play in public parks or after-school clubs in village halls; some adventure playgrounds run sessions like after-school clubs.

Some disabled children using play settings need additional support; others who need extra help at school might not need it in a supervised play setting.

Playworkers are responsible for enabling or facilitating **play opportunities**. They should do everything possible to ensure that children have choice and control of their own play. How much enabling a playworker might do depends on the needs, personality, age and ability of the child or children – or even just the mood of the children on a particular day. Playworkers:

- offer a **range of activities**, including creative activities, sporty games, drama, den building, cooking
- provide children with a **safe place to play**, socialise, try out new things or just spend quiet time; safety in a play setting does not mean that children are not able to take risks; playing safely means that the playworker has thought about protecting the children from harm – for example, providing 'crash' mats for a made-up climbing game or helping the children work out their own safety rules.

Play rangers

Play rangers are adults who are trained in 'supporting children's outdoor play in public parks, housing estates, village greens and other open spaces'. The concept was set up in 2001 and there are now play ranger schemes in many parts of the UK – usually funded by local authorities. All sessions are **open access** and led by what the children want to do; they can drift in and away as they wish. Play rangers:

- provide simple raw materials, such as ropes for a swing, tools or dressing-up clothes, which can be transformed by children's imagination, and help to get things started
- usually work with children aged from five to 13; but in practice, three-year-olds turn up with older siblings, and older teenagers return to the play areas with younger children
- encourage families and the wider community to join in
- are not limited by bad weather – activities are provided under a temporary cover.

Resources for play

We all need to practise skills to become competent, but life would be boring and repetitive if we always had to do things in the same way. Children need to be given plenty of opportunities to practise their newly developing skills, and to express their thoughts, feelings and ideas in different contexts. This means that there should always be a wide range of resources from which children can choose. These include the following:

- **The outdoor environment** (e.g. gardening, parks and wildlife): to promote physical development and their understanding of the natural world.
- **Natural materials** (e.g. sand, water, flour): to promote exploration and investigation.
- **Recycled materials** (e.g. cardboard, plastic, clean clothing): for constructing models, dressing-up activities.
- **Commercially produced items** (e.g. Lego construction kits, wooden blocks and climbing equipment): to promote exploratory play.
- **Space for play**: for children to use their imagination in games that require few props (e.g. making a den from a table and a cloth).

Good use of resources

A painting or drawing activity that will allow them to develop their fine manipulative skills can be varied by using:

- different quality paper (e.g. sugar, cartridge, 'newsprint')
- paper of different colours
- different sizes of paper
- different media (e.g. pastels, wax crayons, colouring crayons, chalk)
- paint (e.g. ready-mixed, powder, thick, thin, fluorescent, pearlised)
- different techniques (e.g. finger, bubble, printing, marble-rolling, string).

While using such a variety the children are also learning about textures, which are appropriate materials to express an idea, colours and developing concepts about materials – how runny paint 'behaves', how chalk smudges, and so on. Other types of activity – construction, water, sand, small world, role-play and similar activities – can easily be varied to broaden children's experience.

Facilitating inclusive play

Boys often seem to dominate outside play and the use of equipment. As children become more aware of their gender, and of other people's expectations of their behaviour, they might reject activities they once liked and choose instead more 'gender-appropriate' activities. For example, girls might choose skipping games, while boys may prefer a game of football.

In order to challenge these stereotypes and to ensure equal opportunities are offered to every child, follow the guidelines presented here.

For more information on inclusive play, see Unit 4.

In practice

Facilitating inclusive practice

- **Avoid having expectations** of children's physical abilities based on stereotypes. *Example*: avoid saying things like, 'You're a big strong boy, Tom, please carry that chair inside for me.'
- Ensure that the provision of play does not reinforce stereotypes. *Example*: Allow only the girls to use the wheeled toys and bikes for one session.
- **Be a good role model**. You should be fully involved in children's physical play, rather than passively supervising. Show children that you are enjoying the session.
- **Be observant**. Take note of the child who seems reluctant to try new equipment, and offer gentle encouragement.
- Be aware of the use of gender-specific terminology. *Example*: use 'firefighter' instead of 'fireman'.
- **Be sensitive to requests for privacy** when changing for school PE lessons.
- **Respect dress codes** based on religious beliefs, ensuring safety guidelines are still followed.
- **Children with special needs** may need different equipment – according to the special need they have – or they may need it to be adapted: for example, by fitting Velcro straps to bike pedals or providing soft foam-filled blocks, soft balls, bean-bags and plastic bats. These can often be obtained from a charity or from a toy library.

How to use music, movement, rhythm and games to promote play

Musical activities

Although different cultures have their own traditions, music is a 'universal' language and is, therefore, accessible to everyone. Our bodies have a natural rhythm – the heartbeat and pulse – and even those with hearing impairments can be aware of rhythms and vibrations caused by sound.

Nursery, finger and action rhymes are often the first songs that children participate in, and each family will use its own favourites. Work settings usually introduce an even wider repertoire to children. These rhymes help to develop children's sense of rhythm as well as increasing their vocabulary and, perhaps, encouraging their number skills (counting up and down) or naming of body parts, and so on.

See Unit 10 for the benefits of providing singing opportunities in early years settings.

There is a range of musical activities that are appropriate.

Listening to music – live or taped

Try to introduce a wide range, including music from different cultures – oriental, folk tunes, pan pipes from South America, unaccompanied vocal music from other continents, as well as military band music and western styles. The extracts should not be too long and you can encourage active listening by asking them to focus on one aspect – the tempo (speed), the tune or the rhythm.

Singing

This can be well-known rhymes or games that involve the children in imitating a short tune sung by an adult (or – with older, confident children – a child). Regular singing games develop children's listening skills and ability to discriminate sound – particularly helping them to 'pitch' a note more accurately.

Playing instruments

This involves many skills – physical, listening, social and intellectual. The best and most available instruments are our own bodies. Body percussion involves hitting, flicking, tapping, thumping, etc. different parts of the body to produce a wide range of sounds – try chests, fingernails, teeth, cheeks with mouths open ... in fact, anything – not forgetting the human voice! Children learn to control their movements to create loud and soft sounds, fast and slow rhythms.

Any bought instruments available should be of good quality and produce pleasing sounds – cheap ones are not sufficiently durable and often create a poor sound. Although tuned percussion instruments (i.e. xylophone, glockenspiel, metallophone) are likely to be found in schools, individual, child-friendly instruments are better for younger children who may not be ready to share. A good range could include untuned percussion – tulip blocks, cabasa, guiro (or scraper), maracas, tambour (hand-held drum), tambourine (like a tambour, but with metal discs around the side), castanets (on a hand-held stick), claves (or rhythm sticks), click-clacks, bongo drums – as well as Indian bells, triangle and beater, individual chime bars and beaters, cow bells and hand-held bells. A group of instruments can be placed in a 'sound' corner for children to experiment with on their own or in pairs – perhaps all 'wooden' instruments on one occasion or 'ones that are struck with a beater' another time.

Playing musical instruments in a group

Large group sessions can be difficult to organise, but some **simple rules** can make them enjoyable for all and worthwhile.

- **Sitting in a circle** and reinforcing the names of instruments as they are given out helps to keep things under control. Even three-year-olds can understand that they must leave their instrument on the floor in front of them until asked to pick it up, although this is not easy in the first instance.
- **Having a go**: it is usually a good idea to allow children to 'have a go' with their instruments before doing a more focused activity. The whole point of the games is for children to experience music-making so there must be plenty of playing and experimenting, and not too much sitting around waiting!
- **Taking turns to listen** to each child make as many different sounds on her instrument in as many ways as she can is a good way of building her confidence and understanding that there is no right or wrong way.
- **Offer choices**: children can then choose the sounds they like best. Similarly, work can focus on dynamics – loud and soft – and children can be

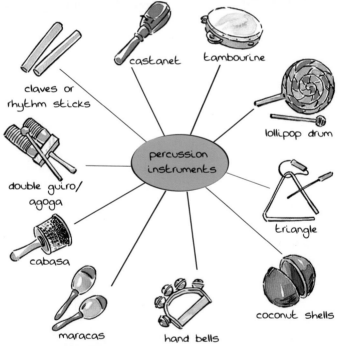

Figure 8.2 Percussion instruments

asked to play as loudly as they can and as quietly as they can. Which instruments were difficult to do this with? Why?

- **Taking turns to play**: another activity involves each child having an instrument – this time make sure there are some that resonate (i.e. go on

sounding after they have been played or struck) as well as the wooden percussion instruments. Going around the group, one child plays her instrument and the next child cannot play until the sound has died away. Discuss which instruments had 'long' sounds and which 'short' ones.

Moving to music

This allows children to respond creatively to different sounds and rhythms. A wide variety should be available, as for listening. Circle singing games such as 'The farmer's in his den', 'Ring-a-ring o' roses' and 'Here we go round the mulberry bush' all encourage children to move in time with the pulse or beat.

Composing music

Choosing sounds and putting them together in patterns around silence to create their own tunes and rhythms can develop listening and intellectual skills. (There are many useful books available with suggestions for games and activities.)

Using homemade instruments

These add variety and interest. The most successful are shakers made from 'found materials' using different containers – tins, plastic pots, boxes (these must be clean and have close-fitting lids) – and choosing contents that will produce interesting sounds. These could be rice grains, lentils, chickpeas, black-eyed beans, runner bean seeds, dried pasta, stones or sand.

Under supervision children can experiment and choose the contents, the amount and the container. If they are to be used continually it is a good idea to glue the lids on to avoid the danger of children putting small items in their mouths. They can also be decorated or covered in patterned sticky-backed plastic.

The opportunities for drama and imaginative play in a variety of settings

In imaginative play, children use their own real-life experiences and rearrange them. It provides opportunities for children to express emotions, such as jealousy, frustration or anger, in a safe and unthreatening way. Imaginative play links with:

- creative play
- role-play
- dramatic play
- domestic play

- fantasy play
- play with dolls and small-world objects.

Role-play (or pretend play)

Children act out roles, usually pretending to be parents or characters from television programmes or books. They benefit from having access to a home area, with scaled-down cooker, table and chairs, and so on.

Small-world play

Small-scale models of people, animals, cars, doll's houses and fake food are useful in imaginative play; children are familiar with these objects and playing with them helps them to relax and also to extend their language skills.

Dressing-up activities

Playing with dressing-up clothes stimulates imaginative play, and pretending to be an adult (parent, superhero, king or queen) allows children to feel in control and empathise with others.

Play with puppets and dolls

Puppets and dolls (or teddies) can often help a withdrawn or shy child to voice their hidden feelings – by using the puppet's voice. This type of play may also help children to vent their powerful emotions (e.g. jealousy of a new baby) by shouting at, say, a teddy.

Ways to support children to express their creativity

EYFS 2012

The requirements of the EYFS state:

'Children's creativity must be extended by the provision of support for their curiosity, exploration and play. They must be provided with opportunities to explore and share their thoughts, ideas and feelings, for example, through a variety of art, music, movement, dance, imaginative and role-play activities, mathematics, and design and technology.'

Creative development is strongly linked to play and involves children:

- taking risks and making connections
- exploring their own ideas and expressing them through movement
- making and transforming things using media and materials such as crayons, paints, scissors, words, sounds, movement, props and make-believe
- making choices and decisions about their own learning
- responding to what they see, hear and experience through their senses.

Creative play is about experimenting with materials and music. It is not about producing things to go on display or to be taken home. See Figure 8.3 for activities to promote creative play.

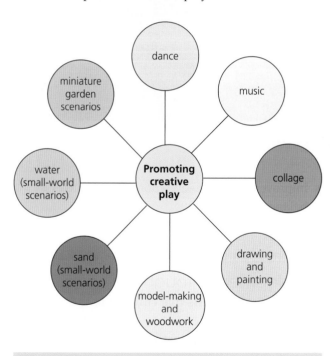

Figure 8.3 Promoting creative play

Providing a variety of resources for creative play

Adults need to choose play materials carefully and to create:

- play opportunities
- time to play
- space for play indoors and outdoors

- places for dens, physical play, manipulative play and creative play
- **play props** and clothes for dressing up and role-play
- an adapted play environment for children with disabilities.

Adults who provide **open-ended** materials create more play possibilities for children. You should provide:

- recycled junk materials (string, boxes, wood)
- natural materials (clay, woodwork, sand, water, twigs, leaves, feathers)
- traditional areas (home area, wooden blocks, work shop area with scissors, glue etc)

Key term

Play prop – Using objects in dramatic play or role-play; e.g. a cardboard box might represent a car or an oven; play dough might be made into cakes to go in the oven.

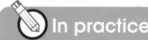 **In practice**

Providing variety in a drawing or painting activity

A painting or drawing activity that allows children to develop their creativity and their fine manipulative skills can be adapted to provide variety by using:
- different-quality paper – sugar, cartridge, 'newsprint', wall lining paper, etc.
- paper of different colours
- different sizes of paper
- different media – pastels, wax crayons, colouring crayons, chalk, etc.
- paint – ready-mixed, powder, thick, thin, fluorescent, pearlised, etc.
- different techniques – finger, bubble, printing, marble-rolling, string, etc.

While using such a variety the children are also learning about textures, colours and developing concepts about materials – how runny paint 'behaves', how chalk smudges etc. Other types of activity – construction, water, sand, small world, role-play, etc. – can easily be varied to broaden children's experience.

Figure 8.4 Playing with recycled materials allows children the choice of what to make

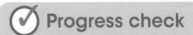

✓ Progress check

Materials for creative play

1. What is the meaning of 'open-ended' materials?
2. Why is it important to provide open-ended materials?
3. Give three examples of open-ended material provision and three examples of pre-structured material provision.

The role of the adult in supporting physical play opportunities

Outdoor physical play opportunities should, ideally, be provided every day. Children need physical play to:

- learn how to control their bodies
- develop their gross and fine motor skills

- improve their hand–eye coordination and body balance
- help them to use energy and prevent obesity.

Your role in promoting physical development through play activities

- Recognise the **skills** that children have developed.
- Provide plenty of **opportunities** for children to practise their skills.
- Make sure that children have the freedom to explore their environment **in safety**.
- Be there for children; offer them **reassurance**, encouragement and praise.
- Provide access to a **range of facilities and equipment**; this need not be expensive – a visit to the local park, a pre-school group (playgroup or one o'clock club) or an adventure playground will provide facilities not available in a small flat.

- Promote **outdoor play** whenever possible; even in cold or windy weather, children will enjoy running around outside as long as they are warmly wrapped up. (If you are supervising, make sure that you are warmly wrapped up too.)

Age/stage of development	Play activities	Benefits to child
3 years+ Walks with arms swinging Climbs upstairs with one foot on each step and downwards with two feet on each step	• Provide balls and bean-bags for throwing and catching • Simple running games	• Develops muscles and hand–eye coordination • Develops leg muscles
4 years+ Good sense of balance Catches, throws and kicks a ball Runs up and down stairs, one foot per step	• Climbing frames, rope swings, slides, suitable trees • Party games, e.g. musical statues • Running to music – fast or slow, loudly or quietly according to the music	• Develops confidence and control; leg muscles and spatial awareness • Promotes the idea of cooperation and learning rules of games • Develops a sense of rhythm and confidence
5 years+ Can run and dodge lightly on the toes Climbs, skips and hops forwards on each foot separately Shows good coordination and fine motor skills	• Climbing frames, rope swings etc. • Skipping ropes and hoops • Hopping and jumping • Action songs and games • Riding tricycles, bikes – with or without stabilisers • Swimming	• Develops confidence and control; leg muscles and spatial awareness • Stamina, sense of rhythm, coordination • Balance, coordination, develops leg muscles • Develops muscles, stamina, balance, hand–eye coordination, sense of speed • Overall muscle development, stamina and coordination
9 to 11 years Can ride a two-wheeled bicycle Learns to swim Can skip freely Shows body strength and good coordination	• Football, dancing, judo or gymnastics, bikes • Swimming • Team sports: five-a-side football, basketball	• Promotes social skills, independence, coordination • Overall muscle development, stamina and coordination • Teamwork, agility coordination, control, stamina
12 to 16 years Skilled at running, climbing, balancing, hopping and skipping Can do complex construction activities	• Team sports: five-a-side football, basketball • Construction kits • Adventure playgrounds and sports/leisure centres	• Social skills, teamwork, agility • Hand–eye coordination, control, fine motor skills • Overall muscle development, stamina and coordination

Table 8.1 Physical play: suggested activities and their benefits

In practice

Adapting activities for physical play

- Avoid running races where children may feel discouraged if they always come last. Try *imaginative* running (e.g. where the children pretend to be jet planes zooming down the runway).
- For children who have difficulty with throwing and catching, try using a small soft pillow, standing quite close at first and gradually stepping back as they gain control.
- Always supervise climbing play carefully. For children who seem nervous when climbing, stand close by to encourage and help if they falter.
- Make an obstacle course using planks, barrels, ladders and boxes, and rearrange them frequently. Children can climb up, over and under.
- Make a 'hopping trail' using cut-out contact footprints that show hopping steps on one foot; then hopping on the other foot, tiptoeing and jumping.

In practice

Observing children during physical activity

Select one child to observe during a period of physical activity (e.g. a gym or dance class, outdoor play with climbing equipment, or ball games). Devise a checklist (see Unit 2 for guidelines on making observations) to record the child's use of:

- gross motor skills (e.g. running, squatting, climbing)
- fine motor skills (e.g. throwing and catching a ball, picking up equipment and carrying objects).

Write a conclusion to show how the particular session of physical activity benefited the individual child; note if there were ways that the session could be extended to improve the development of these skills.

How to encourage children to explore and investigate through play

Exploratory play encourages children to use their senses to discover the properties of different materials in interesting and enjoyable ways.

Activities to promote exploratory play include:

- water play
- sand play
- clay and play dough
- drawing and painting
- cooking (see below)
- making music.

For more information on these categories of play, see Unit 4.

Learning through cooking activities

Almost all children have some experience of cooking or, at the very least, food preparation, in their own homes. This experience can range from watching tins being opened and the contents heated, seeing fruit being peeled and cut, or bread being put in a toaster and then spread, to a full-scale three-course meal (or more) being cooked. All cultures have their own food traditions, and cooking activities with young children provide an ideal opportunity to introduce and celebrate their diversity and richness.

Mealtimes are, for most of us, social occasions that involve sharing, turn-taking and an understanding of acceptable behaviour: 'table manners'! Apart from allowing children to develop these social skills, cooking activities are valuable in promoting **scientific understanding** in terms of materials and their properties and processes of change – both physical and chemical.

- **Physical changes** are those that can be reversed (e.g. water, when frozen, becomes ice but, when allowed to thaw, returns to its original state – water).
- **Chemical changes** are those that have brought about a change in the substance that cannot be reversed (e.g. a piece of bread once toasted will not return to its original state when left to cool, or cheese that has been heated and become melted will not return to its original form or texture even if it retains its essential flavour).

Most importantly, children are learning these fascinating facts in the context of an everyday activity.

Safety and hygiene are paramount considerations when planning and implementing such activities. Some people have food allergies that must be taken into account when planning what foodstuffs will be used. Less obvious may be skin conditions (e.g. eczema), which may be painful particularly if in contact with fruit juices or, sometimes, soaps and washing-up liquids. Some thought at the planning stage should enable you to check with parents and take the necessary steps (e.g. thin disposable gloves) to involve all the children.

As you make these preparations for the activity you can use them to develop children's understanding and awareness of hygiene. Whenever possible you should provide a set of equipment, appropriately sized, for each child and ensure that the finished product is given to the child who made it.

Strangely enough, cooking activities do not always need to involve using a cooker or even a microwave oven! Figure 8.5 highlights a wide range of processes that offer opportunities to use food with children. For some you need only the food and basic utensils (e.g. for spreading, decorating biscuits, preparing fruit salad); for others the use of a kettle or access to hot water may be sufficient. Use of a refrigerator will be needed for others.

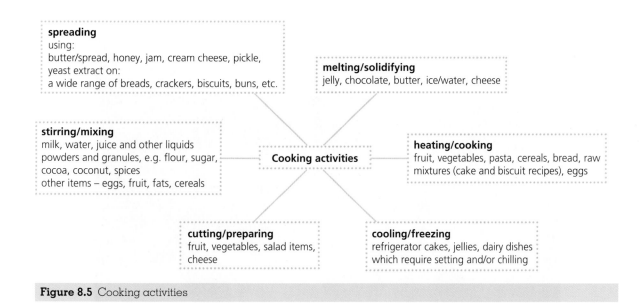

spreading
using:
butter/spread, honey, jam, cream cheese, pickle, yeast extract on:
a wide range of breads, crackers, biscuits, buns, etc.

melting/solidifying
jelly, chocolate, butter, ice/water, cheese

stirring/mixing
milk, water, juice and other liquids
powders and granules, e.g. flour, sugar, cocoa, coconut, spices
other items – eggs, fruit, fats, cereals

Cooking activities

heating/cooking
fruit, vegetables, pasta, cereals, bread, raw mixtures (cake and biscuit recipes), eggs

cutting/preparing
fruit, vegetables, salad items, cheese

cooling/freezing
refrigerator cakes, jellies, dairy dishes which require setting and/or chilling

Figure 8.5 Cooking activities

In practice

Cooking with children

- Always prepare surfaces with antibacterial spray and clean cloths.
- Always ensure children have washed their hands and scrubbed their fingernails.
- Always provide protective clothing and, if necessary, roll up long sleeves.
- Always tie back long hair.
- Always check equipment for damage.
- Always follow the safety procedures and policies of the work setting.
- Always ensure adequate supervision.
- Always remind children not to cough over food or put their fingers or utensils in their mouths when handling food.
- Always check the use-by dates of food items and store them correctly.
- Always check for 'E' numbers and artificial ingredients in bought food items.

Exploring scientific concepts through cooking activities

Changes in appearance

Through cooking activities children will be able to observe changes in appearance – colour, shape and texture – during all the processes. It is helpful to encourage children to look closely at the ingredients *before* they are cut, sliced, combined and/or cooked (or whatever process is being used) and, perhaps, to guess (or predict) what they think will happen. Children can extend their vocabulary to include not only words that describe the look and taste of food but also those instructions that are commonplace in recipes such as 'beating', 'creaming', 'sieving', 'grating'.

Raising awareness of healthy eating

These activities are also valuable in raising children's awareness of healthy and nutritious foods, educating them about diet and choice. By discussing the need for an ingredient to sweeten food, children can be introduced to the variety available and be made aware of healthy options – for example, using honey instead of sugar.

- Children learn through **active involvement** so any cooking activity must be chosen carefully to ensure that they can participate: there is very limited value in them watching an adult carry out the instructions and occasionally letting them have a stir!
- Other learning outcomes include: development of **physical skills** through using the equipment – pouring, beating, whisking, stirring, etc.

Figure 8.6 Cooking activities can support different areas of learning

- **aspects of counting, sorting, measuring** – size and quantity – sharing, fractions, ordinal number (i.e. first, second), sequencing and memory through following and recalling the recipe instructions
- **independence skills** through preparation, controlling their own food and equipment, tidying up
- **expressing their ideas**, opinions, likes and dislikes
- understanding **how to present food** attractively through arrangement and decoration.

In practice

Cooking activities

Remember, when choosing a cooking activity for children:
- that parental wishes must always be respected
- to check that all children can eat the food to be cooked
- to check that there are no problems regarding allergies or religious dietary restrictions
- to follow the basic food safety and hygiene guidelines in Unit 3.

Adapting cooking activities for children with particular needs

All children should have the opportunity to enjoy cooking and food preparation. The most important aspect of helping children with particular needs is to have knowledge and understanding of the difficulties facing each child. You may have to adapt some recipes, provide special gadgets or offer an extra pair of hands to enable children with particular needs to join in. The best people to ask are the child's parents or primary carer. Ideas for adapting cooking activities fall into the following categories.

- **Problems with mobility or coordination**: work with parents to find comfortable ways for a child to sit (e.g. a corner with two walls for support, a chair with a seat belt, or a wheelchair with a large tray across the arms). Children might need adult help with stirring, whisking and pouring. Provide

a non-stick mat placed under the mixing bowl and utensils with easy-to-grip handles.
- **Visual impairment**: children might need to have their hands guided to handle objects. They may need to sit where there is good light and have the use of magnifying glasses.
- **Hearing impairment**: remember to use touch, gesture and facial expression to help these children to participate. Use pictures to illustrate the steps of a recipe during cooking activities.
- **Learning disability**: allow more time to complete a task. It often helps to break each task down into more stages. Other children might need pictures of food to help them make choices. Encourage them to 'have a go', and praise their efforts.
- **Special dietary needs**: always find out about each child's special dietary needs (e.g. vegetarian, vegan, diabetic diet, diet for coeliac disease, lactose intolerance, obesity).
- **Food allergies**: the most common – and dangerous – of these is peanut allergy. Always check with parents before giving peanut butter to a child for the first time. Some children are more likely than others to develop an allergy to food additives, especially colourings, flavour enhancers and preservatives. Children with food-related problems such as asthma, eczema and skin rashes are often advised to avoid additives. For more information on food additives, visit www.nutrition.org.

How to create play environments indoors and outdoors that stimulate play opportunities

The provision of indoor and outdoor play environments is described in Unit 4.

Health and safety requirements for play settings

There is no specific legislation on **play safety** in the UK, and undertaking a 'suitable and sufficient' risk assessment is the primary legal requirement.

The general health and safety requirements relevant to most settings where children play are described in Unit 3. In addition, the following legislation may apply to certain play settings:

- The Day Care and Childminding (National Standards) (England) Regulations 2003.
- The Child Minding and Day Care (Wales) Regulations 2002.
- The Regulation of Care (Scotland) Act 2001.

The policies and procedures of a range of settings

See Unit 3 for detailed information on policies and procedures. All play settings must have policies with clear procedures to show how to implement them. These vary from setting to setting, but generally include the following areas:

- health and safety, including safety on outings, safety when escorting children to and from the setting, risk assessment, etc.
- child protection
- fire alarms and emergency procedures
- dealing with accidents and injuries
- health and hygiene.

 Progress check

Policies and procedures

Find out about your setting's policies and procedures for:
- health and safety
- child protection and bullying.

The importance of children's rights and making choices in play

Playing is integral to children's enjoyment of their lives, their health and their development. Children – disabled and non-disabled – whatever their age, culture, ethnicity or social and economic background, need and want to play, indoors and out, in whatever way they can. Through playing, children are creating their own culture, developing their abilities, exploring their creativity and learning about themselves, other people and the world around them. The right to play is enshrined in the UN Convention Rights of the child:

'Article 31 (Leisure, play and culture): Children have the right to relax and play, and to join in a wide range of cultural, artistic and other recreational activities.'

Play will have low status unless practitioners can help parents and colleagues to see how richly it helps children to develop and learn. Tina Bruce identified 12 features of play (see below). If seven or more of the 12 features are present, then it is probably a rich play scenario. If only a few of the features are present, it does not necessarily mean the child is not doing something worthwhile, but it may not be play.

The 12 features of play

1. Children use real, first-hand experiences in their play, such as going to the shops or preparing food.

2. Children have a sense of control when they play and they begin to make up rules – for example, the dog must be fed and his plate must be here, on the floor, because I say so. Children feel powerful when they play.

3. Children find, use and make play props when they play. This is creative, as they use things in flexible and new ways. It is imaginative, as they rearrange their experiences to suit the play, themselves and the characters.

4. Children choose to play. No one can make a child play.

5. When children play, they sometimes rehearse the future – for example, in their role-play, when they pretend to be adults.

6. Children might pretend when they play – for example, that they are the goodies chasing the baddies. They organise their thinking, transforming it as they do so.

7. Children might choose to play alone, needing some personal space and time to reflect and try out an idea they have – for example, with their small-world garage.

8. They might play with other children, in parallel, associatively or cooperatively.

9. When children play they have a personal play agenda. They might want to put pretend jam on all the pretend cakes, or bath the dog. They will find a way to carry this out. Adults are welcome to play with children, providing that everyone respects each other's personal play agenda.

10. Children involved in rich play become deeply involved and are difficult to distract. Children wallow in their play.

11. Children show use their latest learning when they play. They might have just mastered riding a bicycle, so in their play they keep riding the bike to post a letter, to go to the shops, to take their child to school – anything as long as they are on their bike!

12. Play brings together the learning children do. It organises the learning, so that it becomes connected and an integrated whole.

(from Bruce (1996) *Helping Children to Play* (London: Hodder Education))

Self-directed play

Self-directed play takes place when children are in charge. It is sometimes called free play or unstructured play. Children are able to follow their interests and inclinations freely without the constraints that adults – and computers – place upon their world.

Self-directed play requires **minimal adult intervention**. For example, a child might be shown how to use a glue stick and paper and be minimally supervised while they explore those materials on their own and create a picture or model. The adult only intervenes if the child does something potentially dangerous – for example, putting the glue in their eye – and otherwise refrains from limiting the child's creativity.

How to encourage children to direct their own play

Children of school age are expected to be given responsibility, and choice in play, according to their age. The play environment must support this by providing:

- a stimulating play environment, which also promotes their physical safety and emotional well-being
- a wide range of opportunities for play, including an element of challenge and reasonable risk-taking
- minimal adult supervision – so that the child feels in control
- opportunities to choose whether or not they want to be involved in certain play activities
- access to a wide range of materials and the freedom to choose how they use the resources, which will allow them to direct – or determine – their own play
- group activities that are not too large so that children feel pressured and unable to enjoy the activity.

 Progress check

Self-directed play

Self-directed play is:
- freely chosen: children choose *what* they do
- personally directed: children choose *how* they do it
- intrinsically motivated: children choose *why* they do it
- goal-less: they do it for no external goal or reward.

The role of the adult in providing play activity for children

Having respect for children and valuing their play preferences

Giving attention to children's play activities can range from being a passive observer through to being fully involved in their play. Our own experience of playing as children and our ideas about play are certain to have an influence on the way we think about how children play. Children quickly pick up on the way adults react when they are playing. For example, if you hover over a child who is using the climbing frame for the first time, the child will probably be less adventurous and turn to you for reassurance. Or, if you stereotype children's play by always encouraging boys to play as superheroes and girls to play with the pram and dolls, the children may alter their course of play to fit in with your ideas.

One of the most important skills to develop is being able to know when to get involved and when to allow children to carry on playing. The principle behind this is having respect for children and valuing their play preferences. Although you may be involved in planning the play environment, you are not planning the way children play in it. Children need to be able to initiate their own ideas and to be spontaneous.

Your role in supporting children in providing play opportunities and activities

Supervising children's play

Children need to be supervised carefully. Careful supervision does not mean standing over children all the time. Much of the supervision you do can be at arm's length. However, it is important for adults never to sit with their back to the group, either indoors or outdoors. Without supervision, children might become involved in unacceptable or inappropriate behaviour. If children rush about and become overexcited, you could join their play and help them to develop a storyline; they may have lost their play ideas in the excitement.

How to support children according to their age, needs and abilities

Showing you are interested

When interacting with children during play and leisure activities, practitioners should show that they are interested in what the children are saying and experiencing. This shows that their ideas and feelings are important to you – and that you value them. You can show your interest by:

- listening carefully to what they say
- maintaining eye contact
- sitting at their level

- nodding and smiling to encourage them to express their feelings
- praising them for achievements – and just as importantly – for their efforts
- responding to their questions and observations.

Respecting their need for privacy and to make choices

Even very young children show that they appreciate and need times when they can be alone – often choosing to sit quietly in the book corner when others are playing elsewhere. They also need to be able to talk with their friends and act out different roles without an adult presence. Older children often show a greater need for privacy.

Practitioners should always respect their need for privacy. The only times when it is appropriate to invade their privacy are when you believe the child to be at some sort of risk; then, your responsibility to protect them takes priority over their right to privacy. Encouraging children to make choices for themselves about how they play and spend their leisure time is also important. Practitioners should not try to impose their own ideas when children are involved in their activities.

Giving praise and encouragement

Praise is an expression of approval of a person's achievements or characteristics. Encouragement is when someone talks or behaves in a way that gives you confidence to do something. Both praise and encouragement are very important as they help children to:

- develop positive self-esteem
- become more confident in their own abilities
- keep trying and so develop their skills in building resilience.

 **In practice**

How to praise and encourage children
- Give praise and positive feedback for all achievements, however small.
- Be prompt in giving praise and encouragement: praise and encouragement work much better when delivered immediately after the effort or achievement.

In practice (cont.)

- Encourage children to make choices and to take risks and face challenges; sometimes they need to learn by their mistakes.
- Encourage children to discover and develop their talents: discovering something that they are good at will boost their confidence and self-esteem.
- Avoid making comparisons with another child.
- Always remember the child is an individual.
- Encourage them to feel included in decision-making and respond to their questions in a considerate way.
- Make sure the way you praise is appropriate to the age of the child: an older child might feel embarrassed by an effusive show of verbal praise and may prefer a high-five.
- Be specific about why you are praising them: Avoid general praise, such as: 'You've done well today.' Instead say: 'Well done, Jack, for helping to clear away all the blocks.'

Assessment practice

Planning for play and learning

1. Look at the following list of activities.

sand play	dressing up	outdoor game
board game	poetry	making music
painting	clay	role-play
home play	ring (or circle) game	songs
story telling	modelling	dough
natural materials play	water play	drama activity/ mime
cooking	listening game	finger rhymes
drawing	adventure playground	table-top game with rules

2. Choose **one** of the following age ranges:
- one to two years
- two to four years
- four to seven years
- eight to 11 years
- 12 to 16 years.

3. Select **three** of the listed activities that you have identified as particularly appropriate for that age range.

4. For **each** of the **three** activities describe:

• what equipment and resources you would provide	• the health and safety aspects you would need to consider
• how you would set up the activity and the immediate environment	• what the children will actually be doing and what experiences you want them to have
• what language you would want to encourage or introduce; for example, new vocabulary – names of objects and/ or descriptive terms, such as hot/cold, wet/ dry, etc.)	• how your activity will support and stimulate the play
• how the activity meets the individual needs of the children	• how you will provide for different cultural backgrounds
• how you will provide for children who have particular needs.	

Working with colleagues in the promotion of play

It is very important that you establish and maintain good working relationships with colleagues, so that a positive play environment is provided for children. Colleagues can support each other by giving each other feedback about planned activities. Being able to give and receive positive feedback encourages an environment of trust and cooperation, and will also help you to reflect on your own practice.

A positive play environment has the following features:

- a caring environment that promotes respect and cooperation
- promotes child development through play
- works in partnership with parents for the benefit of the children
- provides a wide range of play opportunities appropriate to the individual play needs of each child.

(For more information on working with colleagues, see Unit 7.)

Reflecting on your own practice

Being able to reflect on your practice in planning and providing opportunities for play will help you to understand which things have worked well – and which have not worked so well. This will help you to think of ways to improve your practice. There are various ways to reflect on your practice. These include:

- observing the children's responses during play – their enjoyment and skill development
- reviewing what worked well and what did not work so well – in terms of equipment provided, numbers of children involved and an assessment of how involved children were in their play
- asking children for feedback
- asking colleagues for feedback
- recording your reflections in a Reflective Diary.

Identifying your strengths and weaknesses and how to improve your practice

Practitioners need to reflect on their own contributions to good practice. This involves identifying their strengths and weaknesses. For example, here are three examples of practitioners identifying their own strengths and weaknesses and using them to improve their practice:

Reflective practice

Three case studies

1. Robbie recognises that he is particularly effective when supporting children to plan their own leisure opportunities. He finds it easy to build a rapport and to support their ideas. Identifying this strength will boost his confidence and enable him to model good practice within the team.
2. Leanne acknowledges a weakness when supporting young children during creative play. She admits to feeling frustrated, having prepared pretty paper flowers and scraps of lace for making Mother's Day cards, when two of the children completely covered their decorated cards with crayon scribble. Identifying this weakness will help Leanne to cope with the feelings of frustration when not in control of a planned activity. She will look again at what she had read about one of the benefits of creative play being 'an end in itself' and discuss the issue with colleagues to decide how best to improve her practice in this area.
3. Jodie identified a strength when carrying out a cooking activity at the after-school club. She found that she got a real buzz out of working in a small team supporting the primary school children in making pizzas with lots of different toppings. Jodie received positive feedback from the adult team and from the children. This boosted her confidence and she plans to write some basic guidelines about the activity for newcomers to use.

How to end a play session

You must be able to end each play session in a way that is appropriate to the children, their level of involvement and the requirements of your play setting. You can do this in the following ways.

- **Giving advance warning**: remember to warn the children five to ten minutes in advance that the play session is about to end – so that they have a chance to finish what they are doing.
- **Asking for feedback**: give children the chance to give feedback on the play opportunities and environments, and note this feedback for future sessions; this can be done informally, by chatting to them about their experiences, or – with older children – using a questionnaire or suggestion box.

- **Ensuring child safety**: following your setting's procedures for ensuring the safety of the children on departure – for example, young children must be collected by a known adult.
- **Tidying up the play environment**: follow your setting's procedures for tidying up the play environment and dealing with resources.
- **Completing all required records**: such as attendance logs, notification slips, and so on.

Activity

Research into playwork

Find out about the career of a playworker.

> **1** What is playwork?

> **2** What qualities do you need to become a playworker?

> **3** Where would you expect to find employment with a qualification in playwork?

Tidy-up time

The role of the adult is important at tidy-up time. This can be enjoyable if adults think of tidying up as part of the child's learning through play. Children love to sweep with dustpans and brooms with shortened handles, which can be made safe for the children to use. They enjoy wiping tables. If boxes have labels, pictures and words, they take pride in putting things away in the right box. If children have choices about taking things off shelves to use play materials, they know where to put them back when they have finished using them. Children will willingly help to water plants.

It is important to encourage both boys and girls to join in with tidying up. Knowing a child's interests helps adults to find something the child will enjoy tidying away. Children are eager to help put away large equipment in an outside shed. They will work as a team if encouraged.

 Useful resources

Play England
Promotes free play opportunities for all children, and works to ensure that the importance of play for children's development is recognised. Find out about the national play organisations relevant to where you work: Play Scotland, Play Wales and the International Play Association: www.playengland.org.uk.

9 Supporting children with additional needs: Unit 9

During this Unit you will learn how to support children with additional needs and their families. This will include knowledge of legal requirements and sources of support for children. You will consider the needs of the child in the setting and some of the possible barriers to participation. You will also think about your role as an adult and how you can adapt activities to assist participation.

> ## Learning outcomes
>
> *During this unit you will learn about:*
>
> 1. *How to support children with additional needs and their families.*
> 2. *How to support children with additional needs within the setting.*
> 3. *The role of the adult in enabling children with additional needs to participate in activities and experiences.*

Supporting children with additional needs and their families

Children with additional needs have needs that are 'in addition' to the general needs of children. Some children have a very obvious and well-researched **disability**, such as Down's syndrome or cerebral palsy; others may have a specific learning difficulty such as dyslexia or giftedness. What defines them as children with additional needs is the fact that they need *additional help* in some area of development, care or education compared with other children.

It is important to remember that children are more alike than they are different. *Every* child needs to:

- feel welcome
- feel safe, both physically and emotionally
- have friends and to feel as if they belong
- be encouraged to live up to their potential
- be celebrated for his or her uniqueness.

In other words, **children** are always **children first**; and the additional need is secondary.

Children with additional needs are often referred to as children with **special educational needs (SEN)**, and the current legislation in England and Wales reflects this; however, in Scotland, recent legislation emphasises children's need for additional support – to meet their additional needs.

The range of additional needs is enormous, from severe to relatively minor, from temporary or short-lived to permanent. Children with additional needs may be grouped into the following categories:

- **Physical disability**: needs related to problems with mobility or coordination, such as cerebral palsy, spina bifida or muscular dystrophy.
- **Speech or communication difficulties**: needs related to communication problems such as delayed language, difficulties in **articulation** or stuttering.
- **Specific learning difficulties (SLD)**: needs related to problems usually confined to the areas of reading, writing and numeracy; **dyslexia** is a term often applied to difficulty in developing literacy skills.
- **Medical conditions**: needs related to medical conditions such as cystic fibrosis, diabetes, asthma, chronic lung disease or epilepsy.
- **Sensory impairment**: needs related to problems with sight or hearing.
- **Complex needs**: needs related to problems many of which result from a **genetic disorder** or from an accident or trauma.

- **Behavioural difficulties**: needs related to aggression, challenging behaviour, hyperactivity, attention deficit hyperactivity disorder (ADHD) or antisocial behaviour.
- **Life-threatening illness**: needs related to a serious or terminal illness, e.g. childhood cancer, HIV, AIDS and leukaemia.
- **Emotional and social difficulties**: needs related to conditions such as anxiety, fear, depression or autistic spectrum disorder (ASD).

Key terms

Articulation – A person's actual pronunciation of words.

Disability – Under the Equality Act 2010, a person has a disability if they have a physical or mental impairment, and if the impairment has a substantial and long-term adverse effect on their ability to perform normal day-to-day activities.

Genetic disorder – A disease or disorder that is inherited genetically.

It should also be noted that a child may also have only a *temporary* or short-term need, such as when a child's parent or sibling has died, they are a victim of bullying or abuse, or they have a temporary hearing loss after a common cold.

Legal requirements relating to children with additional needs

A child with additional needs may need extra or different help at school or home because of:

- physical difficulties or disability
- communication problems
- a visual or hearing impairment
- emotional, social and behavioural difficulties
- a serious medical condition
- *or*a combination of any of these.

The main **Acts** that have shaped the way in which children with additional needs are cared for and educated today are:

- The Education Act 1996 and the Children Act 2004.
- The Education (Additional Support for Learning) (Scotland) Act 2004.

- The Equality Act 2010.
- The Special Needs and Disability Act (SENDA) 2001.

Key term

Special Educational Needs (SEN) – Legally, a special educational need means that a child has a learning difficulty, a behavioural, emotional or social difficulty, or a disability. As a result, the child finds learning or accessing education more difficult than most children of the same age.

The Education Act 1996

The Education Act 1996 says that 'children have SEN if they have a learning difficulty which calls for special educational provision to be made for them'. Children have a learning difficulty if they:

- have a significantly greater difficulty in learning than the majority of children of the same age, or
- have a **disability** that prevents or hinders them from making use of educational facilities of a kind generally provided for children of the same age in schools within the area of the LEA
- are under compulsory school age and fall within the definitions above, or would do so if special educational provision were not made for them.

The Children Act 2004

This Act defines learning disability as 'a state of arrested or incomplete development of mind which induces significant impairment of intelligence and social functioning'.

The Education (Additional Support for Learning) (Scotland) Act 2004

This Act places duties on local authorities and other agencies to provide additional support where needed to enable any child or young person to benefit from education. Additional support needs can be short or long term. For instance, additional support may be required for a child or young person who for example:

- is being bullied
- has behavioural or learning difficulties

- is deaf or blind
- is particularly gifted
- is bereaved
- is not a regular attendee
- is looked after by a local authority.

The rights of children with additional support needs (ASN) and their parents have been strengthened through changes to the original 2004 Act introduced by the **Additional Support for Learning Act 2009.**

The support provided will be tailored to the individual child and may include those shown in Figure 9.1.

The Equality Act 2010

The Equality Act 2010 was introduced to strengthen and simplify equality legislation by reforming pre-existing discrimination legislation into a single new law, replacing all the previous anti-discrimination law, including the Disability Discrimination Acts (DDA) of 1995 and 2005. The Equality Act considers that a person has a disability if he or she has a physical or mental impairment, or a severe disfigurement that:

- is long term (has lasted for 12 months, is likely to last at least a further 12 months, or is lifelong)
- has substantial adverse effects on the child's ability to carry out normal day-to-day activities.

There are **two core duties** under the Equality Act that are relevant to all early years settings. They apply to disabled children and to adults (i.e. to staff, parents, volunteers or any other disabled adults who may be involved in or use the service). These are:

1 A duty not to treat a disabled child (or adult) 'less favourably' than someone else for a reason related to the disability.
2 A duty to avoid 'less favourable treatment' for a reason relating to a disability through making 'reasonable adjustments'.

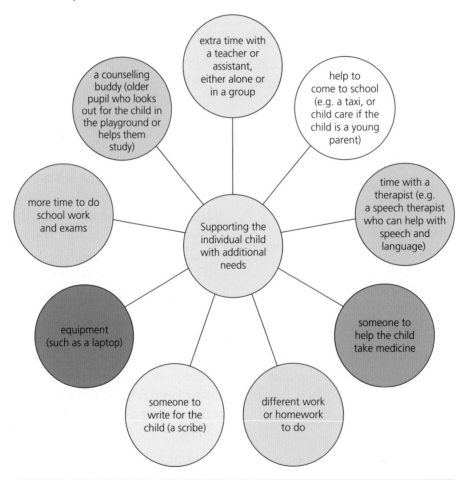

Figure 9.1 Supporting a child with additional needs

The Act also states that providers should *anticipate* both what an individual child or staff member might require at a particular time, and also the likely needs of disabled children and staff in the future in order to avoid less favourable treatment.

The Equality Act duties apply to all early years settings, whether or not they are in receipt of government funding. This includes:

- schools and pre-schools
- playgroups and crèches
- Children's Centres
- private, voluntary and independent settings
- individual childminders and networks of accredited childminders
- education and social services provision.

The Equality Act requires all providers of child care and education to have due regard to the need to:

- promote equality of opportunity between disabled people and other people
- eliminate discrimination that is unlawful under the Act
- eliminate the harassment of disabled people for reasons related to their disability
- promote positive attitudes towards disabled people
- encourage participation by disabled people in public life
- take steps to meet disabled people's needs, even if this requires more favourable treatment.

It is important to remember that these duties apply not only to disabled children, disabled staff and other disabled people such as parents or members of the public who may use a public service or its premises, but also to any other children or adults who use or are involved in a relevant service.

The Special Needs and Disability Act (SENDA) 2001

The Special Needs and Disability Act 2001 strengthened the right of children with disabilities to attend mainstream educational facilities. It was supported by the Code of Practice 2002 (see below).

Codes of practice and provision for children with special needs

The Special Educational Needs Code of Practice 2002 **has the following general principles**:

- A child with special needs should have his or her needs met.
- The special needs of children will be met in mainstream schools – wherever possible.
- The views of children should be sought and taken into account.
- Parents have a vital role to play in supporting their child's education – and must be seen as partners with LEAs and other agencies.
- Children with SEN should be offered full access to a broad, balanced and relevant education, including an appropriate curriculum for the Foundation Stage and the National Curriculum.
- All early years settings have a **SEN policy** and follow the integrated team approach of the Foundation Stage Profile.
- Early identification, early years action, early years action plus and for some children, statutory assessment.

The role of the Special Educational Needs Coordinator (SENCO)

According to the Code, every registered child care setting must have a SENCO – a member of staff who takes responsibility for special education needs. The SENCO is responsible for:

- making sure that all children with SEN are being helped appropriately, ensuring liaison with parents and other professionals
- talking to and advising any member of staff who is concerned about a child
- coordinating provision for children with special needs
- making sure all written records are completed and appropriate Individual Education Plans (see page 231) are in place
- ensuring relevant background information about individual children is collected, recorded and updated
- contacting the relevant Area SENCO at the earliest possible stage where there is a concern.

SEN policy

Every setting must have a SEN policy. This should include information about:

- how they identify and make provision for children with SEN
- the facilities they have, including those that increase access for pupils who are disabled, including access to the curriculum
- how resources are allocated to and among pupils with SEN
- how they enable pupils with SEN to engage in activities of the school, together with pupils who do not have additional needs
- how the governing body evaluates the success of the school's work with pupils with SEN
- their arrangements for dealing with complaints from parents.

The Statement of Special Educational Needs

The Statement of Special Educational Needs is a legal document produced by LEAs following multi-professional assessment and contributions from parents or carers. It specifies the precise nature of the child's assessed difficulties and educational needs, and the special or additional provision that would be made in order to meet that pupil's needs. Statements must then be reviewed at least annually.

An assessment must take account of the following five factors:

1 **Physical factors** – the child's particular illness or condition.
2 **Psychological and emotional factors** – the child's intellectual ability and levels of anxiety or depression will lead to different needs and priorities; for example, severe anxiety may adversely affect all daily activities, and its alleviation will therefore assume top priority.
3 **Sociocultural factors** – the child's needs will be influenced by being part of a family, the family's background and the relationships within the family. The individual's wider community and the social class to which they belong are also influential.
4 **Environmental factors** – a child living in a cold, damp house with an outside toilet will have different needs from someone who is more comfortably housed.
5 **Political and economic factors** – poverty or belonging to a disadvantaged group leads to less choice in day-to-day living.

 Progress check

SEN

- Know how to define SEN.
- Understand how an individual plan helps a child with special needs.
- Know how to define inclusion.

Key term

Assessment – Through observing children and by making notes when necessary, practitioners can make professional judgements about children's achievements and decide on the next steps in learning. They can also exchange information with parents about how children are progressing.

The Common Assessment Framework for children and young people (CAF)

The Common Assessment Framework is a key part of delivering frontline services that are integrated and focused around the needs of children and young people. It is a standardised approach used by practitioners to assess children's additional needs and to decide how these should be met.

The **CAF** is an assessment designed for universal services (health, education and early years services). A practitioner's decision to undertake a common assessment is dependent on whether:

- the child is not achieving one or more of the five priority outcomes, identified in the Early Years Foundation Stage (EYFS)
- there is uncertainty about the difficulty
- the support of another agency may be needed.

If observation and assessment lead to concerns about any area of a child or young person's development, senior practitioners should always discuss these concerns with the child's parents or carers first. The SENCO can help settings to plan activities and experiences that will support specific areas of development. The SENCO will also advise settings if it is necessary to seek extra information and advice from other professionals, such as an educational psychologist or a speech and language therapist.

Intervention

If a child has a diagnosed special need or disability (or if assessment reveals a special need), they are likely to be in need of some kind of intervention – to offer support for them and for their family.

The Early Support Programme

Early Support is an integral part of the delivery of the EYFS for babies and young children under five with disabilities or emerging SEN. It helps staff in early years settings to identify impairments early and to work in partnership with families and other services to provide the best possible care and support for young disabled children. An important part of the Early Support programme is the Family File, which the family holds. The Family File:

- is used by the professionals and the family together, to plan appropriate support to be provided for the child
- informs the family about the different professionals they may meet and what their role is
- explains how the different health, education and social services can provide support
- allows parents and carers to share information about their child with the professionals they meet, without having to say the same things to every new person
- provides information about sources of financial support and child care.

The benefits of early recognition and intervention

Sometimes parents are unaware that their child's development is delayed compared with other children of the same age, especially in the case of their first or oldest child. On other occasions, parents may have felt that 'something is not quite right', but have either been anxious about sharing their worries, or have talked to other professionals but not been fully understood. Sometimes a child can appear to be developing well during a check-up, but have difficulties in less structured environments or in the company of other children.

Early identification means that the child can be helped while still very young. In many cases, prompt intervention and support early on can prevent or minimise later difficulties.

Case Study   The importance of early recognition

When Matthew, Emma and their three-and-a-half-year-old daughter, Chloe, went on holiday to Portugal with another family, they found themselves in a nightmare situation. During the holiday, Chloe had not only pushed another child into the deep end of a swimming pool, where he had to be rescued by lifeguards, but she had also shoved an entire restaurant table into the harbour. For Matthew and Emma, it was the last straw. They had been concerned for some time that Chloe's development was slow, her hearing variable and her speech poor. But whenever they raised their anxieties with health professionals, they were told not to worry. Chloe had failed her first hearing test but had passed a subsequent one and a speech test at 18 months.

After the disastrous holiday, Matthew and Emma were so desperate that they consulted a child psychologist, who recommended ignoring Chloe

Case Study — The importance of early recognition (cont.)

for two hours every time she 'misbehaved'. After a few weeks, Chloe was transformed into a calm, compliant child. Now Emma believes it was the cruellest thing she has ever done and feels guilty about the whole episode.

What Matthew and Emma now know is that Chloe is deaf. In fact, she was born deaf. But even after numerous tests, Chloe's deafness was not diagnosed until she was nearly four years old. Chloe had somehow taught herself to lip-read. Matthew and Emma began to do their own hearing tests on Chloe; when they hid from her while speaking, they realised that she failed to respond – it was obvious she could not hear them. Chloe was just about to

start school at four when she was diagnosed with a moderate to severe hearing loss after a thorough hospital hearing check. She was fitted with hearing aids. Matthew remembers the moment well: 'She smiled the most enormous smile of her whole life,' he says. Now six years old, Chloe is still struggling to catch up with her 'normal hearing' peers. Matthew and Emma just wish they had known what to look for in those early years.

(Chloe's is a true story. Since she was born, the otoacoustic emissions test (OET) – a hearing screen that may have identified her hearing impairment – has been routinely offered to all babies in the UK within a few days of birth.)

The range of local and national support available for children and their families

Statutory support for children with additional needs and their families

Most families in an area use statutory services (i.e. the services provided by their local authority for *all* families and children, including health, education and social services). See Unit 1 for the range of provision for children and their families.

Local authorities provide some services directly – for example, benefits, schools and short break, or respite, schemes funded by social services.

Voluntary and independent support for children with additional needs and their families

In the independent sector, some services are provided by **charities** or commercial organisations with a particular interest in special needs or particular disabilities. Sometimes these services are funded by local authorities.

Example: Children with **ASD** might attend a nursery run by a local voluntary organisation with particular experience of supporting children with ASD, but with their local education authority or social services department paying for them to attend.

Problems occur when children are not recognised as having additional needs until their development begins to look different from that of other children. This is especially true for children with ASD or ADHD. Diagnosis of a disorder or disability is not always straightforward, and is often ambiguous.

Extra help or support in the pre-school years is provided at different levels, depending on how severe a child's need for extra help is, and on the approach taken by each individual local authority.

How to access available information to support children and their families

Parent partnership services

The Parent Partnership Scheme (PPS) is a statutory service that offers the following support:

- information, advice and support for parents of children with SEN

- putting parents in touch with other local organisations
- making sure that parents' views are heard and understood – and that these views inform local policy and practice.

Some parent partnerships are based in the voluntary sector, although the majority of them remain based in their LEA or Children's Trust. All parent partnerships, wherever they are based, work separately and independently from the LEA; this means that they are able to provide impartial advice and support to parents.

For more information, visit the NPPN (National Parent Partnership Network) website at www.parentpartnership.org.uk.

Every Disabled Child Matters (EDCM)

Every Disabled Child Matters is a campaign to make sure disabled children and their families get the same rights as everyone else. Learners are advised to check government policy for accurate updates to terminology with regard to the Every Child Matters 2002 Agenda.

The aims of the campaign are for disabled children and their families to:

- have the same rights as everyone else so that they are fully included in society
- get the services and support they need to live their lives in the way they want
- stop living in poverty
- receive education that meets their needs
- have their say about services for disabled children.

Supporting children with additional needs within the setting

The importance of inclusion

Inclusion is a term used within education to describe the process of ensuring **equality of learning opportunities** for all children, whatever their disabilities or disadvantages. This means that

all children have the right to have their needs met in the best way for them. They are seen as being part of the community, even if they need additional help to live a full life within that community.

Inclusion refers to *everyone*, no matter the ASN of an individual, their gender or sexual preference, religion, race or cultural background.

In practice

Inclusive practice

Inclusive practice is important in child care and education settings because it:
- promotes equality of opportunity for all children
- encourages the development of more flexible attitudes, policies and everyday practices
- promotes community integration through understanding of and respect for others
- recognises and celebrates diversity.

The government's aim is for all schools to become **inclusive schools**. These are schools that welcome all pupils, and develop values that promote pupils' educational, social and cultural development.

Despite the moves towards inclusion, there are arguments for keeping a minority of children in special schools. Inclusion is about much more than the *type* of setting that children attend – it is about the *quality* of their experience and how they are welcomed, helped to learn and enabled to participate fully in the life of the school or setting.

Mainstream education

Children with ASN have the right to be educated within a mainstream school alongside other children. Education authorities should provide education in mainstream school *unless:*

- education in a special school would better suit the ability or aptitude of a child with ASN
- mainstream education would not allow the other children in the classroom to get the most from their learning
- mainstream education for a child with ASN would result in unusually high public costs.

Special schools

Many special schools are developing their inclusive practice. They are educating children directly, and they also share their expertise with mainstream schools; this promotes inclusion by making provision more flexible.

Key term

Inclusion – 'Inclusion is a process of identifying, understanding and breaking down barriers to participation and belonging.' (Early Childhood Forum)

How inclusion should work in a range of settings

Under the Children Act 1989, all local authorities have to keep a register of local disabled children. This is to help the local authority plan services more effectively. Registration is not compulsory and failure to register does not affect a child's right to services. The professionals listed in Table 9.1 are all involved in the care and education of children with special needs. Many of them work in the community or in **special schools**; however, with the government's commitment to inclusive education, some are also involved in the education of children in mainstream settings.

Family doctors (GPs)

Family doctors are independent professionals who are under contract to the National Health Service, but who are not employed by it. They are the most available of the medical profession, and are also able to refer carers on to specialist doctors and paramedical services.

Physiotherapists

The majority of 'physios' are employed in hospitals, but some work in special schools or residential facilities. Physiotherapists assess children's motor development and skills, and provide activities and exercises that parents and carers can use to encourage better mobility and coordination.

Community nurses

Most community nurses work closely with family doctors and provide nursing care in the home. They also advise the parent or carer on specialist techniques (e.g. on how to lift, catheter care).

Health visitors

Health visitors are qualified nurses who have done further training, including midwifery experience. They work exclusively in the community, and can be approached either directly or via the family doctor. They work primarily with children up to the age of five years; this obviously includes all children with disabilities, and they carry out a wide range of developmental checks.

Paediatric occupational therapists

Paediatric occupational therapists (or OTs) specialise in working with children. They carry out assessments to see if children would benefit from using specialist equipment like adapted cups and cutlery, chairs or buggies, and provide advice on lifting and handling children safely. They also help children to improve daily living skills (e.g. eating and dressing).

They work in hospitals, schools and other residential care settings.

School nurses

School nurses may visit a number of mainstream schools in their health district to monitor child health and development – by checking weight, height, eyesight and hearing, and by giving advice on common problems such as head lice. They may also be employed in special schools to supervise the routine medical care of disabled children.

Speech therapists

Speech therapists may be employed in schools, in hospitals or in the community. They assess a child's speech, tongue and mouth movements, and the effects of these on eating and swallowing. They also provide exercises and activities both to develop all aspects of children's expressive and receptive communication skills and to encourage language development.

Communication support worker

A communication support worker works alongside teachers to provide sign language for young deaf children in nursery or school.

Play specialists

Play specialists are employed in hospitals and are often qualified child care practitioners who have additional training. They may prepare a child for hospitalisation and provide play opportunities for children confined to bed or in a hospital playroom.

Play therapists

Play therapists also work in hospitals and have undertaken specialist training. They use play to enable children with special needs to feel more secure emotionally in potentially threatening situations.

Clinical psychologists

Clinical psychologists usually work in hospitals. They assess children's emotional, social and intellectual development and advise on appropriate activities to promote development.

Dieticians

Most dieticians work in hospitals and can advise on a range of special diets (e.g. for diabetics or those with cystic fibrosis or coeliac disease).

Social workers

Most social workers now work in specialised teams dealing with a specific client group (e.g. a Disability and Learning Difficulties Team). They are employed by social services departments (called 'social work departments' in Scotland) and initially their role is to assess the needs of the child. They may refer the family to other departments, such as the Department of Social Security (DSS), the National Health Service (NHS) or voluntary organisations. A social worker may also act as an advocate on behalf of disabled children, ensuring that they receive all the benefits and services to which they are entitled.

Technical officers

Technical officers usually work with people with specific disorders (e.g. audio technicians or audiologists monitor the level of hearing in children as a developmental check, and sign language interpreters translate speech into sign language for deaf and hearing-impaired people).

Nursery officers

Nursery officers are trained child care practitioners who work in day nurseries and family centres. Such staff are involved in shift work, and they care for children under five years when it is not possible for those children to remain at home.

Family aids

Family aids (or home care assistants) used to be called 'home helps'; they provide practical support for families in their own homes (e.g. shopping, cooking, looking after children).

The SENCO

The special educational needs coordinator liaises both with colleagues in special schools and with the parents of children with special needs. They are responsible for coordinating provision for children with special educational needs, for keeping the school's SEN register and for working with external agencies (e.g. educational psychology services, social service departments and voluntary organisations).

Educational psychologists

Educational psychologists are involved in the educational assessment of children with special needs, and in preparing the Statement of Special Educational Needs. They act as advisers to professionals working directly with children with a range of special needs, particularly those with emotional and behavioural difficulties.

Portage worker	Orthoptist
Portage is an educational programme for children who have difficulty in learning basic skills due to either physical or behavioural problems. Home Portage Advisers are specially trained in understanding child development and come from a variety of professions, ranging from nurses or other health professionals to schoolteachers.	An orthoptist works with people who have visual problems and abnormal eye movements.
Special needs teachers	**Educational welfare officers**
Special needs teachers are qualified teachers with additional training and experience in teaching children with special needs. They are supported by: • **special needs support teachers** or **specialist teachers** who are often **peripatetic** (they visit disabled children in different mainstream schools) and who may specialise in a particular disorder (e.g. vision or hearing impairment) • **special needs support assistants** who may be qualified child care practitioners, and who often work with individual 'statemented' children under the direction of the specialist teacher.	As in mainstream education, educational welfare officers will be involved with children whose school attendance is irregular; they may also arrange school transport for disabled children.

Table 9.1 Professionals involved in the care and education of children with additional needs

The advantages and disadvantages of inclusion for the child

Each child will have individual needs, so the advantages and disadvantages of inclusion will vary according to these individual circumstances. Many parents of children with special needs believe that their child will benefit more from being in a 'special school'. Many teachers feel that trying to educate children with additional needs in a mainstream setting is demanding too much of the education system, and that the children *without* additional needs may find that *their* needs are not fully met.

The advantages of inclusion for the child
• The child gets the opportunity to be part of the bigger community – and not to feel marginalised.
• The child has peers on whom to model behaviour.
• The other children learn not to be scared of people who are different.

The disadvantages of inclusion for the child
• The child may disrupt the class and become resented both by other pupils and some staff.

• The child will not receive therapy as part of their school day – as they might in a special school.
• Teachers may not be experienced in teaching children with additional needs.
• The child may become isolated and feel different.
• There is often a risk of exclusion for a behaviourally challenged child.
• Bullying may be a problem.

Establishing and maintaining partnerships with parents and families

Working in partnerships with families is particularly important when a child has ASN. Each parent should be made to feel welcome and valued as an expert on their child, and that they play a vital role in helping practitioners to enable their child to participate and learn.

Parents and families:

• have a unique knowledge and expertise regarding their children, and local authorities need this to help them to provide the best education possible

- should be encouraged to participate in the decisions that affect their children and their education
- should be provided with the information they need to be informed about changes to legislation and practice in education
- should be given a named contact person for more detailed information; this person will provide them with details of local and national organisations that can offer more help, if required.

Parents should also be able to choose the extent to which they are involved in their child's setting. Not all parents have the time or the confidence to become involved in activities within the setting.

Providing support for children and families

Where factors that impact on a child's ability to learn and develop are just starting to become apparent, partnership working involving *all the adults* in a child's life becomes very important. The earlier a need for additional help is identified, the more likely it is that early intervention can prevent certain aspects of a child's development or behaviour developing into a persistent difficulty.

Information and advice

Parents find that getting a diagnosis for their child is important. Being given a name for their child's condition or special need enables them to discuss their child's development needs with health, social services and education professionals.

Shared experiences: parents often find that the most helpful sources of information and advice are others with shared experiences. There are many organisations that exist to provide support and answer questions. *Examples*: Contact A Family, the Down Syndrome Association, Mencap and the Royal Society for the Blind, but there are hundreds more – most with their own website and helpline.

Service provision: getting information about what they and their children are entitled to, as early

as possible, is very important. This applies to the **benefits** they are entitled to as well as the services.

Communicating with parents

The principles of effective communication are discussed in Unit 5. One of the main purposes of communicating with parents is to provide and to share information about the child and about the setting – both about the care and education setting and the home. Practitioners need to build up a partnership with parents, and to do this they need to promote a feeling of trust.

Providing flexible support

Parents want support that is flexible enough to respond to their particular families' needs, and that is both available in an emergency and can also be planned in advance.

Children want support that enables them to do the kinds of things their peers do; this can vary from going swimming with their siblings to spending time away from home with their friends.

The most popular services are generally those developed by parents themselves, or by local disability organisations. See also pages 224/5 for information about the PPS.

The impact on families

Each family will respond in their own way when they find out that their child has a disability or a special need. Common reactions of parents to having a child with disabilities include the following.

- **A sense of tragedy**: parents who give birth to a child with a disability experience complex emotions. They may grieve for the loss of a 'normal' child, but they have not actually been bereaved – they still have a child with a unique personality and identity of their own. Relatives and friends can be embarrassed if they do not know how to react to the event, and their awkward response can leave parents feeling very isolated at a time that is normally spent celebrating.

- **A fear of making mistakes**: sometimes there is an over-reliance on professional help. If the disability seems like the most important aspect of the child's personality, parents may believe that only a medical expert can advise on the care of their child. The reality is that the parent almost always knows what is required for their child. A great deal of what the child needs is not related to their disability in any case.
- **Being overprotective**: a desire to cocoon the child can be counterproductive. The child needs to be equipped for life and can learn only by making mistakes. In addition, siblings may resent the disabled child who is seen as spoilt or never punished.
- **Exercising control**: parents may take freedom of choice away from the child, so disempowering them. Parents and carers often dictate where and with whom the child plays, thus depriving them of an opportunity for valuable social learning.

There are other factors that will have an impact on family life; these include:

- financial worries, especially when parents have to juggle work commitments with child care
- feeling guilty that other children in the family are missing out on family fun because of their child's special needs
- parents feeling tired and stressed because of the extra attention required by their child, especially during bouts of illness.

 Progress check

Support for the family

What sort of difficulties might be experienced by the family of a child with an additional need or disability?

How can staff in early years settings help the family?

The role of the adult in enabling children with additional needs to participate in activities and experiences

How to recognise and plan for individual needs and learning opportunities

Practitioners should plan to meet the needs of:

- both boys and girls
- children with SEN
- children who are more able
- children with disabilities
- children with complex health needs
- children from all social, family, cultural and religious backgrounds
- looked-after children
- children of all ethnic groups, including Traveller communities
- refugees and asylum seekers
- children from diverse linguistic backgrounds.

... in other words, *every child in their care*! This may seem a daunting task, but if you get used to focusing on each child as an individual, with their own needs and personalities, then it does not seem so difficult!

 Progress check

Supporting children with special needs

Practitioners need to:
- be aware that all children have different experiences, interests, skills and knowledge which affect their ability to develop and learn
- provide a safe and supportive learning environment, free from harassment, in which the contribution of all children and families is valued
- challenge all stereotypes and expressions of discrimination or prejudice
- value the fact that families are all different – that children may live with one or both parents, with other relatives or carers, with same-sex parents or in an extended family.

Planning for individual needs

Practitioners should work with parents to identify **learning needs** and respond quickly to any area of particular difficulty. In nurseries and schools, teachers and other staff **observe** and note children's ways of learning, and monitor their progress. They do this in many different ways, as shown in Figure 9.2.

Individual Education Plan (IEP)

Every child with SEN should have an IEP. The IEP's purpose is to detail the ways in which an individual child will be helped – for example:

● what special help is being given
● who will provide the help
● how often the child will receive the help
● targets for the child
● how and when the child's progress will be checked
● what help parents can give their child at home.

The child's teacher is responsible for the planning and should discuss the IEP with the parents or carers and with their child, whenever possible. IEPs are usually linked to the main areas of language, literacy, mathematics and behaviour and social skills. Sometimes the school or early education setting will not write an IEP but will record how they are meeting the child's needs in a different way, perhaps as part of the whole class lesson plans. They will record the child's progress in the same way as they do for all the other children.

In addition, practitioners should:

● assess how accessible the setting is for children who use wheelchairs or walking frames or who are learning English as an additional language, and take appropriate action to include a wider range of children
● work together with professionals from other agencies, such as local and community health services, to provide the best learning opportunities for individual children.

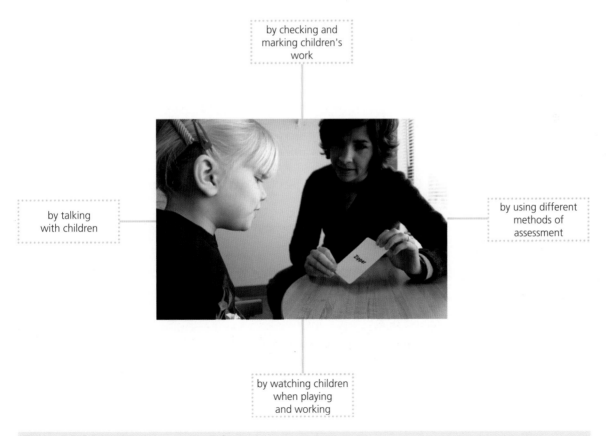

by checking and marking children's work

by talking with children

by using different methods of assessment

by watching children when playing and working

Figure 9.2 Adults identify learning needs…

Multi-agency approach

In order to provide inclusive care and education, settings and individual practitioners need to know when to call in help from outside and whom to approach when more specialist expertise and help is needed. **Specialist help** may include any of those professionals listed in Table 9.1 on pages 226–228.

The importance of avoiding labelling and stereotyping

As we have seen in Units 1 and 7, stereotyping often leads to **discrimination**. It also matters a great deal how we 'label' people who are different from us. Many years ago, people who were obviously *different* – that is, they were perhaps unable to walk or talk or they seemed to be a bit 'simple-minded' – were believed to be in some way evil; some were even burnt to death as witches. Today we are much more aware of individual differences and have much more knowledge about diverse needs and abilities. It is still very important that we do not apply labels to anyone.

Disabled children are often stereotyped and labelled. This *always* has a negative effect on the child and his or her family. Table 9.2 shows you which terms are appropriate to use and which should be avoided.

Avoid	Use instead
The handicapped	Disabled people
The disabled	Disabled people *or* people with an impairment
The deaf	Deaf people/hard of hearing people (depending on which group) *or* hearing-impaired
The blind	Blind people *or* partially sighted people (depending on which group), or visually impaired
Using the collective noun ('the ...') implies that all disabled people have the same needs and issues, and reinforces their supposed separateness from the rest of society.	
Deaf and dumb *or* deaf mute	A person who is deaf without speech *or* deaf sign language (or British Sign Language) user (BSL is a recognised language, and for many deaf people it will be their first language)
Able-bodied, healthy, normal	Non-disabled
Handicapped, cripple, invalid	Disabled *or* disabled people/person, *or* if appropriate, a person with a mobility impairment
Victim of *or* suffering from	Has (an impairment), a person with, *and* avoid using medical labels that define people by their disability
Wheelchair bound *or* confined to a wheelchair	Wheelchair user *or* a person who uses a wheelchair
An epileptic	A person with epilepsy
A spastic	A person with cerebral palsy
Mentally ill, insane, crazy, psycho, schizo, etc.	A person with mental health problems

Avoid	Use instead
Mental handicap, retarded	A person with learning disabilities/learning difficulties
Dwarf *or* midget	Restricted growth *or* short stature
Fits, spells, attacks	Seizures

Table 9.2 Children with additional needs: terms to use and terms to avoid

The importance of realistic expectations of children's development

Having positive, realistic expectations for children's achievements and behaviour is something both parents and practitioners should strive for. When expectations for children are set at the right level – not too high and not too low – then children can expect to have high self-esteem and also fulfil their potential.

A good understanding of child development is vital to your work with children. You need to be aware that every child varies as to when they pass through the normative stages of development described in Unit 2.

You – and the child's parents – need to have realistic expectations for each child, based on both the child's stage of development and his or her temperament and any additional needs.

You also need to take account of special or additional needs, where development may be very different from the norm.

It is very important to promote the strengths of the children as well as assisting with their difficulties. You can achieve this by choosing some of the activities that you know the child is good at. For example, Child A may have difficulties tying her shoelaces, but may be very skilled at cutting out shapes; therefore, do some cutting-out sessions and always offer plenty of praise and encouragement, both for *achievement* and for the *effort* the child has made.

In practice

Having realistic expectations

Temper tantrums in children usually occur from between one and three years of age, and are a normal developmental stage that reflects a child's inner struggle to establish his own sense of self. Temper tantrums are often called 'the terrible twos' and may involve crying, screaming, head-banging, breath-holding, breaking objects and/or jumping up and down. However, if you were to see a colleague behaving in this way, you would be very alarmed! Your realistic expectations fit with the boisterous two-year-old but not with an adult in their 20s.

How to use specific methods of communication

Many children with SEN have difficulties with language and communication. Most will benefit from learning a 'sign language', such as Makaton, PECS (Picture Exchange Communication System), Signalong or BSL/Signed English.

Makaton

The Makaton vocabulary is a list of over 400 items with corresponding signs and symbols, with an additional resource vocabulary for the UK National Curriculum. The signs are based on BSL, but are used to support spoken English. The Makaton Project publishes a book of illustrations of the Makaton vocabulary. Most signs rely on movement, as well as position so you cannot really learn the signs from the illustrations. Also in many signs *facial expression* is important. If a child at a school or nursery is learning Makaton, the parents should be invited to learn too. The Makaton Project will support schools and parents in this, as they know that everyone involved with the child must use the same signs.

Signalong

Signalong is a sign-supporting system, which is also based on BSL; it is designed to help children and adults with communication difficulties – mostly associated with learning disabilities – that is user-friendly for easy access. The Signalong Group has researched and published the widest range of signs in Britain.

PECS

PECS begins with teaching children to exchange a picture of an object that they want with a teacher, who immediately gives it to them. For example, if they want a drink, they will give a picture of 'drink' to an adult, who directly hands them a drink. Verbal prompts are not used; this encourages spontaneity and avoids children being dependent on the prompts. The system goes on to teach recognition of symbols and how to construct simple 'sentences'. Ideas for teaching language structures, such as asking and answering questions, are also incorporated. It has been reported that both pre-school and older children have begun to develop speech when using PECS. The system is often used as a communication aid for children and adults who have an **ASD**.

The barriers to participation for children and families

There are certain potential barriers to participation – or access to provision – for children with additional needs and their families. These include the following.

1 **Physical barriers**: this does not refer only to the more obvious physical barriers, such as not having any ramps nor sufficiently wide doors for wheelchair access; it also refers to such facilities as toilet and washing facilities, appropriate signage for people with visual impairments, etc.

2 **Attitudes of staff**: settings may exclude children from participation in group activities because of their special needs; this exclusion can sometimes be justified on health and safety grounds, but usually could be remedied with some planning and communication with the child's family.

3 **Poverty**: the cost of high-quality early years care is simply not affordable for those families living in poverty. Children are more likely to be living in poverty in:
   - *families with one or more disabled persons*
   - *lone-parent households*
   - *inner-city areas.*

The following activities show how early years settings can present barriers to equality of access for children and their families.

Case Study — Excluded from an outing

The nursery manager at a private nursery explains to a child's parents that their son, Thomas, will not be able to join the rest of his group on a visit to a local children's theatre production of 'The Gruffalo's Child'. Thomas has Down's syndrome and learning difficulties. The nursery staff had met to discuss the problem and had concluded that there was no point in Thomas going as he would not appreciate the show and would probably disrupt the other children. Thomas's mother is very unhappy with their decision and has accused the nursery of discriminating against Thomas on account of his disability.

Discuss the following questions in a group.
1. Do you think the nursery staff were justified in their decision?
2. Do you believe the nursery has discriminated against Thomas?
3. What could the nursery staff have done in order to enable Thomas to join the others?

In practice

A hearing problem

Carla, a baby of 15 months, has just been diagnosed with a severe hearing impairment. When she has her nappy changed, Mary, the baby room supervisor, notices that Laura, one of the early years practitioners, changes her nappy in silence, although she always smiles, chats and plays with the other babies during nappy-changing routines. When Mary asked her why she does not do the same with Carla, Laura replied that she did not see the point because Carla cannot hear anything.

1. Why is Mary concerned about Laura's child care practice?
2. Discuss ways in which practitioners could promote Carla's development and meet her holistic needs.

How to review activities and experiences to ensure an inclusive approach

Even when a setting has experience in providing inclusive care and education, it is still important that activities and experiences within the setting are regularly reviewed and evaluated. In order to ensure an inclusive approach, you should:

- review the setting's policies, procedures and codes of practice on equality of opportunity

- review activities and trips away from the setting to determine whether the practice is inclusive and that there was no discrimination against disabled children (or adults)
- obtain feedback from the children: find out their views by listening to them as well as observing them; ask open-ended questions, such as 'What did you like about the activity? Which bits did you find easy and which difficult?' in order to gain valuable feedback
- encourage children to participate: show them that you value their ideas and be ready to adapt your practice to suit their individual needs and preferences
- be reflective in your practice – this means that you are constantly learning from experience, and learning how to improve your practice.

Reflective practice

Supporting children with additional needs

1. How well does your setting provide for the additional needs of children?
2. Is there effective communication between the child's parents or carers and the setting?
3. Do the play experiences and activities avoid stereotyping and ensure that each child has an equal opportunity to take part in activities?

Types of adaptations to equipment and the environment	
Minor adaptations to the home such as grab rails and temporary ramps. **Bathing, feeding and walking equipment.**	**Major adaptations** including door widening for wheelchair access, lowering worktops, bathroom alterations and purpose-built extensions.
Providing ramps for wheelchair users.	**Providing thick pencils and brushes** for children with poor fine motor skills.
Adapting standard equipment: for example, by having a tray on the table so that objects stay on the table, and a child with a visual impairment does not 'lose' objects that fall off.	**Helping children to manage eating and drinking:** there is a wide range of specialist aids for eating and drinking, such as angled spoons and suction plates.
Using specialist environments: for example, ball pools, warm water pools or light and sound stimulation or sensory rooms.	**Promoting children's autonomy and independence** through the use of specialist aids and equipment: for example, hearing aids, non-slip table mats and special 'standing' chairs.

Table 9.3 Adaptations that may be required

Specialist aids and equipment

Many children with learning difficulties will have **personal priority needs** that are central to their learning and quality of life. Some children may need the provision of a specific **therapy** or may require paramedical care – for example, supervising medication. Others need to have existing equipment or activities modified or adapted to suit their particular needs.

Helping children without using special equipment

You can often meet children's additional needs without needing specialist aids and equipment. For example, by:

- positioning children so that they learn effectively – for example, by making sure the light falls on the adult's face, so that a child wearing a hearing aid is able to lip-read and a child with a visual impairment can use any residual eyesight to see facial expressions
- providing the opportunity to learn sign languages – for example, Makaton or Signalong
- developing children's self-esteem (e.g. by encouraging and praising effort as well as achievement)
- allowing children's behaviour and alternative ways of communicating to be acknowledged and understood
- providing appropriate therapies – for example, speech and language, occupational or physiotherapy (support from health services is generally set out as non-educational provision in a child's **statement**); however, speech and language therapy may be regarded as either educational or non-educational provision)
- planning the use of music, art, drama or movement therapy – these therapies may play a complementary role in the curriculum for individual children and will need to be planned as part of the whole curriculum
- helping children to maintain good posture, appropriate muscle tone and ease of movement, and promoting skills in independent mobility
- promoting relaxation and support to help children manage stress and anxiety; some settings use a sensory room, but a quiet, comfortable area will benefit all children.

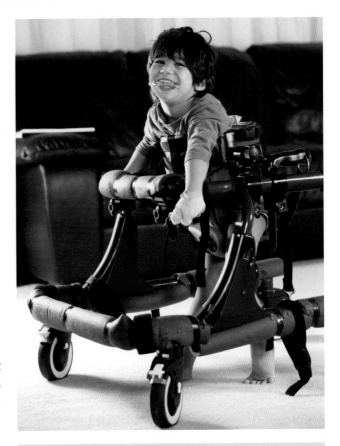

Figure 9.3 Using a walking frame or rollator

The safe use of specialist aids and equipment

Using specialist aids and equipment safely is important – both for the children's health and your own safety. Some equipment should not be moved without taking certain precautions.

- All equipment and furniture must be installed correctly and maintained adequately.
- Children and adults must know how to use the equipment correctly and follow the manufacturer's instructions.
- Help other non-disabled children to understand the importance of specialist equipment for disabled children.
- Encourage non-disabled children to treat specialist aids with respect: for example, a child who uses a hearing aid or who wears glasses needs to know that their valuable aids will be kept safely for them when not being used.

In practice

Providing for Selma's needs

When Selma, a partially sighted baby, joined the nursery, her key person, Josh, discussed her needs with her parents and contacted the RNIB for information about ways of supporting her development. Josh decided to plan a set of activities that could be used by Selma – and by sighted babies too – based on his research, which found that for profoundly blind and partially sighted babies it is important to do the following:

1. Offer as wide a range of *tactile experiences* as possible right from the beginning: Josh started collecting tactile objects, such as:
   - a foil survival blanket to scrunch and reflect
   - a flat silky cushion containing polystyrene beads
   - panscourer, lemon reamer, pasta strainer, dishwashing brush.
2. Encourage movement: helping babies to become aware of whole body movements and to learn to tolerate different positions, such as being placed on their stomach. Josh:
   - provided some brightly lit and sound-producing toys to provide the motivation to roll and reach
   - rearranged the nursery furniture to provide a logical sequence to support the baby when moving and to help 'mental mapping' of her environment.
3. Encourage exploration of sound, rhythm and timing. Josh provided:
   - tactile nursery rhyme prompt cards: He made these using A4 cards and stuck on different fabrics to link touch to a particular song. For example, a piece of fur fabric stuck on card to make a link with 'Round and round the garden like a teddy bear', or a single shiny silver star stuck onto dark blue card to make a link with 'Twinkle, twinkle little star'.
   - a handbell, rolling chime ball, musical xylophone and a drum.
4. Josh used some of the tactile objects in a treasure basket that could be enjoyed by all the babies in the setting.

Assessment practice

Identifying children with additional needs in your setting

Select a child or young person in your setting who has an SEN or disability. Find out all you can about:
- the type of disability or special need
- the type of support that needs to be provided
- where to go for further information.

Useful websites and resources

Contact A Family – helps families who care for children with any disability or special need: www.cafamily.org.uk
Council for Disabled Children: www.ncb.org.uk
Cystic Fibrosis Trust: www.cftrust.org.uk
Down's Syndrome Association: www.downssyndrome.org.uk
MENCAP: www.mencap.org.uk
National Deaf Children's Society: www.ndcs.org.uk
National Parent Partnership Network: www.parentpartnership.org.uk
National Society for Epilepsy: www.epilepsysociety.org.uk
Royal National Institute of Blind People: www.rnib.org.uk
SCOPE – for children with cerebral palsy: www.scope.org.uk
SENSE – supports and campaigns for children and adults who are deafblind: www.sense.org.uk

10 Introduction to children's learning: Unit 10

This Unit provides an introduction to frameworks for learning and the different ways in which children learn. You will study some of the key issues that affect children's learning and find out how the adult can create opportunities for learning that meet individual needs.

Learning outcomes

During this unit you will learn about:

1. The different frameworks for learning for children from birth to 16 years.

2. The principles of how children learn.

3. The role of the adult in supporting children's learning from birth to 16 years.

The different frameworks for learning for children from birth to 16 years

Each country of the UK has a government department that deals with education curriculum requirements. These are:

- **England** – Department for Education
- **Wales** – Education, Lifelong Learning and Skills Department within the Welsh Government
- **Scotland** – Education and Lifelong Learning Department within the Scottish Parliament
- **Northern Ireland** – Department of Education for Northern Ireland (DENI).

The curriculum frameworks in UK countries

The Early Years Foundation Stage (EYFS) in England

The EYFS was revised in 2012 and sets the standards that all early years providers must meet to ensure that children learn and develop well and are kept healthy and safe. It promotes teaching and learning to ensure children's 'school readiness' and gives children the broad range of knowledge and skills that provide the right foundation for good future progress through school and life.

The **EYFS** seeks to provide:

- **quality and consistency** in all early years settings, so that every child makes good progress and no child gets left behind
- **a secure foundation** through learning and development opportunities which are planned around the needs and interests of each individual child and are assessed and reviewed regularly
- **partnership working** between practitioners and with parents and/or carers
- **equality of opportunity** and anti-discriminatory practice, ensuring that every child is included and supported.

The learning and development requirements in the EYFS

The learning and development requirements cover:

- the areas of learning and development which must shape activities and experiences (**educational programmes**) for children in all early years settings;

- the **early learning goals** that providers must help children work towards (the knowledge, skills and understanding children should have at the end of the academic year in which they turn five); and
- **assessment arrangements for measuring progress** (and requirements for reporting to parents and/or carers).

The seven areas of learning and development

There are **seven areas of learning and development** that must shape educational programmes in early years settings. All areas of learning and development are important and inter-connected. Three areas are particularly crucial for igniting children's curiosity and enthusiasm for learning, and for building their capacity to learn, form relationships and thrive. These three areas, *the prime areas*, are:

1 communication and language
2 physical development, and
3 personal, social and emotional development.

Providers must also support children in four *specific areas*, through which the three prime areas are strengthened and applied. The *specific areas* are:

1 literacy
2 mathematics
3 understanding the world, and
4 expressive arts and design.

Assessment in the EYFS

1 **Ongoing assessment** (also known as formative assessment): This involves practitioners observing children to understand their level of achievement, interests and learning styles and then shaping learning experiences for each child reflecting those observations. Practitioners should address any learning and development needs in partnership with parents and/or carers, and any relevant professionals.
2 **Progress check at age two**: When a child is aged between two and three, practitioners must review their progress, and provide parents and/or carers with a *short written summary* of their child's development in the prime areas. This progress check must identify the child's strengths, and any areas where the child's progress is less than expected. If there are significant emerging concerns, or an identified special educational need or disability, practitioners should develop a targeted plan to support the child's future learning and development involving other professionals (for example, the provider's SENCO) as appropriate.

Assessment at the end of the EYFS – the Early Years Foundation Stage Profile (EYFSP)

In the final term of the year in which the child reaches age five, the EYFS Profile must be completed for each child. The Profile provides parents and carers, practitioners and teachers with a well-rounded picture of a child's knowledge, understanding and abilities, their progress against expected levels, and their readiness for Year 1. The Profile must reflect:

- ongoing observation
- all relevant records held by the setting
- discussions with parents and carers, and any other adults whom the teacher, parent or carer judges can offer a useful contribution.

Each child's level of development must be assessed against the early learning goals. Practitioners must indicate whether children are meeting expected levels of development, or if they are exceeding expected levels, or not yet reaching expected levels ('emerging'). This is the EYFS Profile.

The National Curriculum in England

The National Curriculum sets out the statutory requirements for the knowledge and skills that every child is expected to learn in schools. The National Curriculum framework enables teachers to provide all school-aged children with challenging learning experiences, taught in ways that are both balanced and manageable. It sets out the standards used to measure the progress and performance of pupils in each subject, to help teachers plan and implement learning activities that meet the individual learning needs of pupils.

The National Curriculum applies to children of compulsory school age (five to 16 years) in schools in England. It sets out what pupils should study, what they should be taught and the standards that they should achieve, and is divided into four Key Stages:

- Key Stage 1: children aged between five and seven (Year groups: 1 and 2)
- Key Stage 2: children aged between seven and 11 (Year groups: 3, 4, 5 and 6)
- Key Stage 3: children aged between 11 and 14 (Year groups: 7, 8 and 9)
- Key Stage 4: children aged between 14 and 16 (Year groups: 10 and 11).

In Key Stage 1 of the National Curriculum, the compulsory subjects consist of: English, Mathematics, Science, Information and Communication Technology, Design and Technology, History, Geography, Art and Design, Music, Physical Education. In addition there is a non-statutory framework for Personal, Social and Health Education (PSHE) and Citizenship. Primary schools must also provide religious education and sex education, although parents may withdraw their children from these lessons if they wish to do so.

The early years framework in Scotland

The key documents are Birth to Three: Supporting Relationships, Responsive Care and Respect and the newly developing generic framework for the curriculum, known as the '3–18 framework', 'Excellence for All'.

Birth to Three

The document is based on principles summarised as:

- the best interests of children
- the central importance of relationships
- the need for all children to feel included
- an understanding of the ways in which children learn.

Curriculum for Excellence: three to 18 years

The purpose of the curriculum framework is captured in four capacities. It aims for every child to be:

1 a successful learner
2 a confident individual
3 a responsible citizen
4 an effective contributor.

Areas of experience and outcomes are:

- expressive arts
- health and well-being
- languages
- mathematics
- religious and moral education
- sciences
- social studies
- technologies.

Skills for learning, life and work are linked to literacy, numeracy, health and well-being.

Assessment

Assessment is required to support the purposes of learning. This is sometimes described as 'assessment is for learning'.

The early years and early primary level

The early years and early primary level (three to eight years) emphasises active learning, real-life and imaginary situations, and the importance of parents' and children's interests and experiences from home as the starting point from which to extend learning.

The curriculum framework in Wales

The Foundation Phase (three to seven years)

The basic message of the Foundation Phase in Wales is that it offers children a sound foundation for their future learning through a developmentally appropriate curriculum. It brings more consistency and continuity in a child's learning:

'Emphasis has been placed on developing children's knowledge, skills and understanding through experiential learning – learning by doing and by solving real-life problems both inside and outdoors.'

Key elements in the curriculum framework are:

- learning by doing
- the importance of first-hand experience (experiential learning)

- learning though play
- active involvement in learning (not exercises in books)
- time to develop speaking and listening
- time to develop confident readers and writers
- practical mathematical experiences through everyday problem-solving experiences
- emphasis on understanding how things work and finding different ways to solve problems.

In addition, the curriculum places more focus on:

- skills and understanding
- the whole child – personal, social, emotional, physical and intellectual well-being
- positive attitudes to learning (enjoying it and wanting to continue the learning)
- giving children high self-esteem and confidence so that they experiment, investigate, learn new things and make new relationships
- encouraging children's development as individuals through creative, expressive and observational skills, and recognising that different children have different ways of responding to experiences
- learning about conservation and sustainability through outdoor, first-hand experiences involving real-life problems.

The areas of learning

There are seven areas of learning in the Foundation Phase:

1 personal and social development, well-being and cultural diversity
2 language, literacy and communication skills
3 mathematical development
4 Welsh language development
5 knowledge and understanding of the world
6 physical development
7 creative development.

Assessment: the Foundation Phase outcomes

At the end of the Foundation Phase when children are seven years old, there is a statutory teacher assessment of each child. Teachers are required to make rounded judgements of children, based on their knowledge of the way in which a child performs across a range of contexts. Strengths and

weaknesses are identified. The child's progress is checked against adjacent outcomes to see which makes the best fit to the child's performance: the best possible match is made. This takes place in the following areas of learning:

- personal and social development, well-being and cultural diversity
- language, literacy and communication skills (in English or Welsh)
- mathematical development.

The curriculum framework in Northern Ireland

The 12 years of compulsory education in Northern Ireland are divided into five Key Stages of which Foundation and Key Stages 1 and 2 are primary education, and Key Stages 3 and 4 are post-primary education. The Foundation Stage in primary schools is for children in Year 1 (four- to five-year-olds) and Year 2 (five- to six-year-olds). They begin the curriculum which goes through to Stage 4 in the secondary school.

The Foundation Stage (Northern Ireland)

The **Foundation Stage** aims to provide a programme for children that will:

- promote children's personal development
- promote positive attitudes and dispositions to learning
- promote children's thinking skills and personal capabilities
- encourage creativity and imagination
- enable children to develop physical confidence and competence
- develop children's curiosity and interest in the world around them
- enable children to communicate in a variety of ways
- motivate children to develop literacy and numeracy skills in meaningful contexts.

The seven areas of learning in the Foundation Stage (Northern Ireland)

The statutory curriculum in the Foundation Stage is set out under the following areas of learning:

1 religious education
2 language and literacy

3 mathematics and numeracy

4 the arts

5 the world around us

6 personal development and mutual understanding

7 physical development and movement.

All schools in Northern Ireland are required to include religious education (RE) as part of the curriculum for all pupils from Foundation Stage to Key Stage 4. RE is taught in accordance with the core syllabus drafted by the four main Christian Churches in Northern Ireland and specified by the Department of Education.

There is **assessment** for learning, and reporting to parents through a meeting and an annual report.

The Northern Ireland Curriculum (Key Stages 1 to 4)

The areas of study are:

- language and literacy
- mathematics and numeracy
- modern languages
- the arts
- environment and society
- science and technology
- learning for life and work
- physical education
- religious education.

Cross-curricular areas (which continue through the education stages) are:

- communication
- using mathematics
- using ICT.

Thinking skills are developed to enable the child to:

- think critically and creatively
- develop personal and interpersonal skills and dispositions
- function effectively in a changing world.

Personal capabilities aim to encourage:

- lifelong learning
- contributing effectively to society.

Children are assessed at the end of each Key Stage.

Key term

Statutory framework – This means that a document is required by law to be followed and carried out in practice. It is not a matter of choice; it is a legal requirement.

The principles and approaches of competing frameworks for learning

The principles set out in Table 10.1 have a long tradition and have influenced the early childhood curriculum frameworks of countries around the world.

The overarching principles of the EYFS

(The principles underpinning the Foundation Phase in Wales are similar to those for the EYFS in England.)

1 Every child is a **unique child**, who begins learning at birth and can become resilient, capable, confident and self-assured.

2 Children learn to be strong and independent through **positive relationships** with their parents and carers and with others, including their key person at their early years setting.

3 **A positive environment** – in which children's experiences are planned to reflect their needs, and help build their confidence, and in which there is a strong partnership between early years practitioners, parents and other professionals – is crucial if children are to fulfil their potential, and learn and develop well.

4 **Children develop and learn in different ways and at different rates.** All areas of learning and development are important and are interconnected.

Evidence shows that the right foundations of early learning (from pregnancy until age five) make significant differences to outcomes for children and to future life chances. Physical and mental health and the establishment of positive attitudes to learning that will continue throughout the EYFS into the school years and beyond are all affected by what happens at the beginning of children's lives.

Principles influencing early childhood curriculum frameworks in the UK

1. The best way to prepare children for their adult life is to give them a good childhood that meets their needs and builds on their interests.	6. There are times when children are especially able to learn particular things.
2. Children are whole people, who have feelings, ideas, relationships involving a sense of self and others, a sense of awe and wonder, and who need to be emotionally, physically and morally healthy.	7. What children can do (rather than what children cannot do) is the starting point for a child's learning.
3. Children do not learn in neat and tidy compartments. Everything new that they learn links with everything they have already learned.	8. There are many different kinds of symbolic behaviour. These show the inner thoughts, feelings and ideas of the child, through the way they draw, paint, make things, dance, sing, talk/sign, enjoy making stories, mark-make or pretend play. The Italian educator Malaguzzi called this the 'hundred languages' of children.
4. Children learn best when they are respected and helped to be autonomous, active learners.	9. Relationships with other people are central to a child's emotional and social well-being, and for opening up their possibilities for an intellectual life and sense of fulfilment.
5. Self-discipline is emphasised as the only kind of discipline worth having. Children need their efforts to be valued in their own right.	10. A good education is about the child, the context in which development and learning takes place, and the knowledge and understanding that evolves as part of the child's learning journey.

Table 10.1 Principles influencing early childhood curriculum frameworks in the UK

Each principle is further broken down into four commitments. These describe how the principles are put into practice (see Table 10.2).

The principles underpinning A Curriculum for Excellence 3–18 (Scotland)

The Scottish curriculum framework is based on the following principles:

- challenge and enjoyment
- breadth
- progression
- depth
- personalisation and choice
- coherence
- relevance.

1 **Challenge and enjoyment**: young people should find their learning challenging, engaging and motivating. The curriculum should encourage high aspirations and ambitions for all. At all stages, learners of all aptitudes and abilities should experience an appropriate level of challenge, to enable each individual to achieve his or her potential. They should be active in their learning and have opportunities to develop and demonstrate their creativity. There should be support to enable young people to sustain their effort.

2 **Breadth**: all young people should have opportunities for a broad, suitably weighted range of experiences. The curriculum should be organised so that they will learn and develop through a variety of contexts within both the classroom and other aspects of school life.

3 **Progression**: young people should experience continuous progression in their learning from three to 18 within a single curriculum framework. Each stage should build upon earlier knowledge and achievements. Young people should be able to progress at a rate that meets their needs and aptitudes, and keep options open so that routes are not closed off too early.

Theme and principle	Commitments
A unique child Every child is a competent learner from birth who can be resilient, capable, confident and self-assured.	1. **Child Development**: Babies and children develop in individual ways and at varying rates. Every area of development – physical, cognitive, linguistic, spiritual, social and emotional – is equally important. 2. **Inclusive Practice**: The diversity of individuals and communities is valued and respected. No child or family is discriminated against. 3. **Keeping Safe**: Young children are vulnerable. They develop resilience when their physical and psychological well-being is protected by adults. 4. **Health and Well-being**: Children's health is an integral part of their emotional, mental, social, environmental and spiritual well-being, and is supported by attention to these aspects.
Positive relationships Children learn to be strong and independent from a base of loving and secure relationships with parents and/or a key person.	1. **Respecting Each Other**: Every interaction is based on caring professional relationships and respectful acknowledgement of the feelings of children and their families. 2. **Parents as Partners**: Parents are children's first and most enduring educators. When parents and practitioners work together in early years settings, the results have a positive impact on children's development and learning. 3. **Supporting Learning**: Warm, trusting relationships with knowledgeable adults will support children's learning more effectively than any amount of resources. 4. **Key Person**: A key person has special responsibilities for working with a small number of children, giving them the reassurance to feel safe and cared for, and building relationships with their parents.
Enabling environments The environment plays a key role in supporting and extending children's development and learning.	1. **Observation, Assessment and Planning**: Babies and young children are individuals first, each with a unique profile of abilities. Schedules and routines should flow with the child's needs. All planning starts with observing children in order to understand and consider their current interests, development and learning. 2. **Supporting Every Child**: The environment supports every child's learning through planned experiences and activities that are challenging but achievable. 3. **The Learning Environment**: A rich and varied environment supports children's learning and development. It gives them the confidence to explore and learn in secure and safe, yet challenging, indoor and outdoor spaces. 4. **The Wider Context**: Working in partnership with other settings, other professionals and with individuals and groups in the community supports children's development and progress towards the outcomes of *Every Child Matters*: being healthy, staying safe, enjoying and achieving, making a positive contribution and economic well-being.
Learning and development Children develop and learn in different ways and at different rates, and all areas of learning and development are equally important and interconnected.	1. **Play and Exploration**: Children's play reflects their wide-ranging and varied interests and preoccupations. In their play children learn at their highest level. Play with peers is important for children's development. 2. **Active Learning**: Children learn best through physical and mental challenges. Active learning involves other people, objects, ideas and events that engage and involve children for sustained periods. 3. **Creativity and Critical Thinking**: When children have opportunities to play with ideas in different situations and with a variety of resources, they discover connections and come to new and better understandings and ways of doing things. Adult support in this process enhances their ability to think critically and ask questions. 4. **Areas of learning and development**: The EYFS is made up of seven areas of learning and development. All areas of learning and development are connected to one another and are equally important. All areas of learning and development are underpinned by the Principles of the EYFS.

Table 10.2 The EYFS: themes and principles

4 **Depth**: there should be opportunities for young people to develop their full capacity for different types of thinking and learning. As they progress, they should develop and apply increasing intellectual rigour, drawing different strands of learning together, and exploring and achieving more advanced levels of understanding.

5 **Personalisation and choice**: the curriculum should respond to individual needs, and support particular aptitudes and talents. It should give each young person increasing opportunities for exercising responsible personal choice as they move through their school career. Once they have achieved suitable levels of attainment across a wide range of areas of learning, the choice should become as open as possible. There should be safeguards to ensure that choices are soundly based and lead to successful outcomes.

6 **Coherence**: taken as a whole, children's learning activities should combine to form a coherent experience. There should be clear links between the different aspects of young people's learning, including opportunities for extended activities that draw different strands of learning together.

7 **Relevance**: young people should understand the purposes of their activities. They should see the value of what they are learning and its relevance to their lives, present and future.

The principles underpinning the Foundation Stage (Northern Ireland)

Young children learn best when they:

- have opportunities to be actively involved in practical, open-ended and challenging learning experiences that encourage creativity
- have opportunities to initiate experiences that capitalise on their individual interests and curiosities
- are actively involved in planning, reviewing and reflecting what they have done
- are enabled to express themselves by creating images, sounds, movements, structures and invented stories
- are involved in play that is challenging, takes account of their developmental stage and needs and builds on their own interests and experiences

- work in stimulating environments and have access to a range of resources
- develop secure relationships with peers and adults
- have choice and exercise autonomy and independence in their learning, and are encouraged to take risks.

Alternatives to mainstream education

All children attending early years settings and schools must follow the appropriate curriculum for their age group and their location. A minority of children attend settings that offer an alternative approach and curriculum. Such schools and nurseries are usually – but not always – in the private sector, but are included within the relevant statutory inspection framework (e.g. Ofsted in England). These settings include those described below.

Montessori nurseries and schools

Maria Montessori (1870–1931) became the first female doctor in Italy and worked with children with learning difficulties. Montessori:

- used her observations of children to create new techniques of education that emphasised the unique development of each child
- created an environment in which the child is free to develop their own skills and abilities; **Practical Life** exercises develop gross and fine motor skills, concentration and responsibility in independently chosen activities
- designed a set of learning – or **didactic** – materials that encourage children to use their hands – developing a strong grasp of abstract concepts through concrete or 'hands-on' experience
- believed that mixed age groups provide children with the opportunity to help and to be helped by other children, and to take part as both the youngest and oldest member
- thought that the highest moment in a child's learning was what she called the polarisation of the attention – the child is completely silent and absorbed in what they are doing.

Montessori teachers are specially trained to observe, to respond to the needs of each child and to **direct** the whole group. They do not teach in the traditional sense, but rather guide each child forward.

Steiner (Waldorf) nurseries and schools

Rudolf Steiner (1861–1925) believed (as did Froebel – see below) in the importance of the **community** and that children need a carefully planned environment in order to develop in a rounded way. Steiner schools are called **Waldorf** schools, and follow the principles outlined below.

- Children do not learn to read or write formally until they are around seven years old.
- The design of the environment emphasises warm colours, soft materials and rounded corners – and is without plastic toys.
- Outdoors the equipment is minimal, but logs and trunks are plentiful to encourage children's use of their own imagination.
- The use of televisions and computers with younger pupils is strongly discouraged.
- Pupils usually retain the same classmates throughout school and have the same class teacher from the age of six to fourteen.
- Festivals and seasons are given special attention so that pupils appreciate the rhythms of nature.

There are now about 40 Waldorf/Steiner schools in Great Britain and Ireland, which together make up the Steiner-Waldorf Schools Fellowship.

High/Scope

High/Scope is an educational programme originally designed for children in the USA in the 1960s. The High/Scope Approach is based on the following principles.

- **Active learning**: this involves the child having choice of a range of materials and activities. They are free to manipulate those materials, and encouraged to use their own language and have adult support.
- **Plan–Do–Review process**: children are encouraged to use a **Plan–Do–Review** process to give them the opportunity to use their initiative, to generate their own learning experiences and to reflect on those experiences.

- The environment includes **four base areas**: a book, a home, a construction and an art area. Other areas are added depending on the children's interests (e.g. computer, woodwork, gardening, office or shop). Materials are labelled and stored so that children can find, use and return the materials they need. Children's work is carefully displayed.

The High/Scope Curriculum has been developed through **extensive observations of young children** learning, and supports the EYFS in creating confident learners.

Figure 10.1 Children should be free to express themselves in many different forms

The Reggio Emilia approach

Loris Malaguzzi (1920–94) founded the Reggio Emilia approach at a city in northern Italy called Reggio Emilia. Malaguzzi is often credited with inspiring the philosophical underpinning to the movement; however, the approach is also based on the ideas of both Piaget and Vygotsky. The main features of the approach are:

- the belief that children are capable of long-term, sustained learning when the topic is of interest to them

- teachers listen to and observe the children closely, ask questions and explore the children's ideas; they then provide experiences that stimulate children's thinking and learning
- the school environment is designed so that every part has its own purpose and identity, and spaces encourage communication through interaction; the *piazza* (communal areas) and *atelier* (art studios) are considered the core of the schools
- children are assisted in their discovery of ideas by both teachers and the *atelierista* (all pre-schools in Reggio have an artist based at the school)
- the 'hundred languages of children' – children should be free to express themselves in many different forms (e.g. painting, drawing, singing, puppetry, acting, dancing)
- parents provide ideas and skills that make them active partners in the children's learning through the interests of children.

The topics for study are derived from the talk of children, through community or family events, as well as the known interests of children (puddles, shadows, dinosaurs); they are then pursued in depth through projects. The role of the educators is not to answer questions for pupils or inform them if they are correct or not, but instead to help children discover the answer for themselves and question further.

Home education

Elective home education is where parents or guardians decide to provide education for their children at home instead of sending them to school; they are entitled to do this under Section 7 of the Education Act 1996. Where parents opt for elective home education, the LEA needs to satisfy itself that the education being provided is 'efficient' and 'suitable'.

Forest Schools

The philosophy of Forest Schools, which started in Denmark in 1950, is to encourage and inspire individuals of any age through positive outdoor experiences. Forest Schools have demonstrated success with children of all ages who visit the same local woodlands on a regular basis, and through play have the opportunity to learn about the natural environment, how to handle risks and most importantly how to use their own initiative to solve problems and cooperate with others. Forest School programmes run throughout the year, for about 36 weeks, going to the woods in all weathers (except for high winds).

Forest Schools aim to develop:

- a greater understanding of their own natural and man-made environments
- a wide range of physical skills
- social communication skills
- independence.

Your role in supporting different approaches to learning in a range of settings

You have a vital role to play in supporting children's learning. When planning for children's learning you should consider both the needs and achievements of the child, and the range of learning experiences that will help children to progress in different aspects of their learning and development.

Planning learning experiences

In order to plan learning experiences that will meet each individual child's needs, it is important to find out as much as possible about the child and to build on this by:

- regularly observing children
- working together with parents and families
- taking account of special educational needs
- promoting equal opportunities
- collaborating with other agencies, when necessary, and
- supporting transitions.

The principles of how children learn

The stages and sequence of cognitive development

The normative stages and sequence of cognitive development are summarised in the charts in Unit 2.

As is emphasised throughout this book, each child is unique. Just as children vary in the rate at which they grow and develop *physically*, so their cognitive development occurs at different rates and in different ways, with some children needing more attention at different stages than others.

Theories relating to cognitive development

Jean Piaget (1896–1990)

Jean Piaget, a Swiss psychologist, identified particular stages of cognitive development that continue to influence how we work with children. His stage theory stated that:

- children move through a series of stages, which are loosely related to age ranges
- children progress through the stages in a particular **sequence** (or order)
- no stage can be missed out or 'jumped over'
- basic concepts are formed early and are refined as children gain first-hand experiences
- very young children are 'egocentric' (i.e. they see things from their own viewpoint and have difficulty in putting themselves in another's place).

Sensorimotor stage (birth to approximately 2 years)	
Main feature: the child begins to interact with the environment, using sensory and motor skills	
0–6 months	Babies explore objects around them using their **senses** – squeezing, sucking, shaking, etc. They enjoy bright colours and can recognise familiar objects. They begin to differentiate familiar sounds, tastes and smells. They use their voices to produce a range of sounds. Their developing physical skills mean they can coordinate movements to help them explore their environment.
6–12 months	During this period babies learn that objects exist even when they cannot be seen – this is know as developing '**object permanence**'. They may repeat actions to watch cause and effect. They watch and imitate adults, and at this stage develop memory of events they have experienced. This helps them to understand familiar routines.
1–2 years	Increasing physical skills and mobility help children to play with a wider range of objects. They can understand the names of objects and can follow simple instructions. They continue to experiment by repeating actions and movements, and are developing early concepts linked to them. They begin **symbolic play** – using toys or objects to represent things in real life (e.g. a doll becomes a baby, a box becomes a car or television). They will also 'talk' to themselves and be aware of other children playing, although they will not necessarily play 'with' others.
Pre-operational stage (2 to 6–7 years)	
Main feature: the child begins to represent the world symbolically	
2–3 years	Manipulative skills develop and children are more able to control their movements to use tools and implements (e.g. hold a crayon and move it up and down, connect construction materials). They have some understanding of their own daily routine and are developing memory skills, which help their understanding of basic concepts. They can often match two (sometimes three) colours – usually yellow and red – and begin to name them. Children are still egocentric – that is, they are unable to see or understand things from another person's viewpoint. They are becoming able communicators. Play may involve 'looking on' at others and, sometimes, joining in, although they may still play alone or in parallel.
3–4 years	Pincer grasp is developed and helps them to use paintbrushes, pencils, beads (large) and other play materials with increasing control. They are developing independence in everyday tasks (e.g. toileting, hand washing, dressing). Play with a wide range of materials helps to develop

Pre-operational stage (2 to 6–7 years) (cont.)

	their understanding of concepts (e.g. colour, weight, size, number – they may say the number sequence up to ten but with varying degrees of accuracy). They are becoming fluent speakers and beginning to use written symbols to represent an object or word ('pretend' writing). They can also recognise environmental print (e.g. road names, shop signs). Play may now involve cooperation with others, and they learn through trial and error and opportunities to solve relevant problems.
4–5 years	Physical skills help children to do up buttons, zips and other fastenings. They are becoming more independent in managing their own routines but still need adult help. They are developing concepts of time (day and night, sequence of their day), number (know number sequence to ten and may count reliably up to ten), colour (can name some accurately and sort objects by colour), size (can identify big and small when given two appropriate objects and begin to order by size), shape (can identify and name basic 2D shapes and some 3D shapes). They can remember and talk about their own experiences and are beginning to recognise letter shapes and associated sounds. Play is often cooperative and can involve taking on identified roles.
5–7+ years	Increasing independence through developing physical skills and ability to choose and make decisions. During this period they are usually able to conserve (see next stage). They are increasingly able to express their ideas and creativity in a variety of ways – through words (spoken and written), movement, music, pictures, models and other craft work. Their drawings include greater detail. Concepts are becoming more refined (e.g. time – understanding of seasons, months of the year, days of the week, hours in the day). They are able to play more complex games, and sustain interest and cooperation for longer periods of time. They are beginning to develop own research skills – knowing where to find information they are interested in.

Concrete operational stage (6–7 years to 11–12 years)

Main feature: the child learns such rules as conservation

7–12 years	Children are now less egocentric; they can increasingly see things from another's point of view – they decentre and are able to concentrate on more than one thing at a time. They understand the concept of reversibility – that both physical actions and mental operations can be reversed (e.g. a ball of play dough can be made into a cylinder shape and then be reformed into a ball shape). They master conservation at about the age of 8 years: quantity, length or number of items is not related to the *arrangement* or *appearance* of the object or items. They also master seriation: the ability to arrange objects in an order according to size, shape or any other characteristic.

Formal operational stage (11–12 years to adulthood)

Main feature: the adolescent can transcend the concrete (the 'here and now') and think about the future

12 years – adulthood	Adolescents now begin to understand abstract concepts such as fairness, justice and peace. They use deductive logic; this means that they create rules that help them to test things out – to have a hypothesis and to solve problems.

Table 10.3 Piaget's stages of cognitive development

Schemas and cognitive development

Piaget uses the term **schema** to describe the skills and concepts that children acquire through the following processes.

- **Assimilation**: the child takes in information from their experiences and constructs a theory or schema.

- **Accommodation**: the child has learned from new experiences and has to adjust (or accommodate) the original schema to fit with the new information.
- **Adaptation**: the child now knows more about certain aspects of the world and can act upon this knowledge.

Piaget used the term **equilibrium** to describe the stage at which the child has successfully incorporated new understanding into an existing schema. He believed that the experience of **disequilibrium** was a crucial motivation to learning.

 Progress check

Examples of assimilation and accommodation

1. A child believes that 'all furry four-legged animals are dogs'. One day he sees a breed of dog that he has never seen before and says, 'That's a dog.' The child recognises the similarities and makes the assumption. This is **assimilation**. Then the child sees a squirrel and the child says, 'That's a dog.' But his parents tell him it is not a dog, it is a squirrel. The child alters his perception. This is **accommodation**.
2. A child learns that her father is called daddy, so she calls other males (e.g. the postman) daddy. This is **assimilation**. She is quickly told that the other man is not daddy, he is Harry, the postman. Again, the schema for daddy is modified. This is **accommodation**.

Lev Vygotsky (1896–1934)

Vygotsky believed it was very important for cognitive development that someone who knows more than the child is available to help them to learn something that would be too difficult for them to learn on their own. He believed that 'what a child can do in cooperation today he can do alone tomorrow'.

The main features of Vygotsky's theory of child development are as follows:

1 **The zone of proximal development (ZPD)**: (proximal means 'next') also sometimes called the zone of *potential* development, the ZPD is defined as the difference between problem-solving the child is capable of performing *independently*, and problem-solving he or she is capable of performing with *guidance* or collaboration. Every child has a ZPD, which is achievable only with help and encouragement from another person; this could be guidance from an adult, or collaboration with more competent peers. This 'expert intervention' can only enable learning if it is far enough ahead of the child's present level to be a challenge, but not so far ahead that it is beyond comprehension.

2 **The importance of play**: play provides foundations for children's developing skills, which are essential to social, personal and professional activities. Children benefit from play as it allows them to do things *beyond* what they can do in 'real' life – such as pretend to drive a car. Play is another way through which children can reach their ZPD.

3 **Reconstruction**: children experience the same situations over and over again as they grow, but each time they can deal with them at a higher level and reconstruct them.

4 **The importance of social interactions**: knowledge is not individually constructed, but co-constructed between two people. Remembering, problem-solving, planning and abstract thinking have a social origin. What starts as a social function becomes *internalised*, so that it occurs within the child.

Jerome Bruner (1915–)

Bruner's work was influenced by both Piaget and Vygotsky. He claimed that children's learning moves through three stages: enactive, iconic and symbolic, in that order. Unlike Piaget's stages, Bruner did not state that these stages were necessarily age-dependent or inflexible. Bruner's theory has the following features.

- **Enactive stage**: we learn by enacting – or *doing* – things. This applies to adults as well: many adults can perform a variety of physical tasks (e.g. operating a lawn mower or learning to drive a car) that they would find difficult to describe in **iconic** (picture) or **symbolic** (word) form. Children need to have real, first-hand, direct experiences; this helps their thought processes to develop.
- **Iconic stage**: we learn by using visual images. This may explain why, when we are learning a new subject, it is often helpful to have diagrams or illustrations to accompany verbal information.

Children need to be reminded of their prior experiences; books and interest tables with objects laid out on them are useful aids to this recall of prior experiences.

- **Symbolic stage**: we learn by making what we know into symbolic codes – languages, music, mathematics, drawing, painting, dance and play are all useful codes, which Bruner calls **symbolic thinking**.

Scaffolding

Bruner believed in the importance of 'scaffolding' in helping children to learn. Adults can help develop children's thinking by being like a piece of scaffolding on a building. At first, the building has a great deal of scaffolding (i.e. adult support of the child's learning), but gradually, as the children extend their competence and control of the situation, the scaffolding is progressively removed until it is no longer needed.

Scaffolding can be described as anything a teacher can provide in a learning environment that might help a student to learn. This includes anything that allows the student to grow in independence as a learner, such as:

- clues or hints
- reminders
- encouragement
- breaking a problem down into smaller steps
- providing an example.

The same scaffolding may be provided to all children, or teachers may offer customised scaffolding to individual learners.

The features of scaffolding

- Recruitment: the adult's first task is to engage the interest of the child and to encourage them to tackle the requirements of the task.
- Reduction of degrees of freedom: the adult has to simplify the task by reducing the number of actions required to reach a solution. The child needs to be able to see whether or not they have achieved a fit with the task requirements.
- Direction maintenance: the adult needs to maintain the child's motivation. At first, the child will be looking to the adult for encouragement;

eventually, problem-solving should become interesting in its own right.

- Marking critical features: the adult highlights features of the task that are relevant; this provides information about any inconsistencies between what the child has constructed and what they would perceive as a correct construction.
- Demonstration: modelling solutions to the task involves completion of a task or explanation of a solution already partly constructed by the child. The aim is that the child will imitate this back in an improved form.

Parents routinely act as teachers – or enablers – in the ways outlined above, through rituals and games, which are a part of normal adult–child interactions.

In practice

Scaffolding an activity

Daniel and his father were out shopping. Daniel stopped walking and was obviously struggling to do up the zip on his jacket, but was becoming increasingly frustrated. His father stood behind him and – using his own hands to guide Daniel's – helped him to insert the end of the zip into the metal fitting. When Daniel had managed to slot it in, he was easily able to pull the zip up by himself and was delighted.

In class, think about the following scenarios and discuss how you could scaffold the child's learning:
1. about the difference between weight and mass
2. how to ride a two-wheeled bike
3. how to tie shoelaces.

Friedrich Froebel (1782–1852)

Froebel founded the first kindergarten in 1840 and his ideas have been very important in shaping the way early years services are integrated. He placed a great deal of emphasis on ideas, feeling and relationships. Froebel's theory has the following features.

- Children have inborn knowledge and skills and are innately **creative** beings.
- The curriculum consists of a set of special shaped wooden blocks – known as **Gifts** – and a set of

craft projects known as **Occupations** (songs, movements and dancing, and crafts – such as modelling and drawing).

- There is a focus on mathematical and language skills, and on the adult–child relationship.

The critical (or sensitive) periods for learning

The human brain has a huge capacity to change; it is often referred to as being 'plastic', which means that it grows and develops all the time. *Critical* or *sensitive periods* are windows of opportunity in time, where a child is most receptive to learn with the least amount of effort.

There certainly seem to be critical periods – or sensitive times – when the brain develops in specific ways. For example:

- when in the womb, there is a critical time for brain development during the first three months of pregnancy
- during a baby's first few months, the hearing and sight pathways in the brain are particularly sensitive to stimulation.

Recent research in the field of neuroscience shows that – although there are certain 'sensitive' times when children are particularly receptive to learning – they are rarely so critical that a child cannot 'catch up' in their learning. For example, a child who has missed a lot of schooling through being in hospital for a series of operations will usually catch up when given the opportunity. He or she may find it more difficult once the sensitive period has passed, but will learn when certain skills are introduced with patience and sufficient time.

Studies of children who have been severely deprived, abused or neglected show that it is particularly difficult for them to catch up once the sensitive periods have been passed. The case study presented below shows how a young child was deprived of emotional, cognitive and social stimulation. There are many other sad cases of so-called 'feral' – or wild – children whose development has been severely delayed. The most famous documented case is that of Genie in the USA; another is that of Isabel Quaresma (see case study box below).

Case Study — Confined to a hen coop

Isabel was born in 1970 in Tabua, Portugal, to a mother with learning difficulties. Isabel was the only one of three children not fathered by a family member. When she was found in January 1980 at the age of nine, she had spent the previous eight years shut in a hen coop. Isabel's growth was seriously stunted, she was not toilet trained, and of course she could not talk. She held her arms in the position of hens' wings, and the palms of her hands were covered in hard, scaly patches – or calluses. She had been fed on scraps – the same food as the hens received.

Eventually she was taken to an institution for children with learning difficulties. Some 18 years later, Isabel had not grown much and had made little progress generally. She could understand simple orders, but if asked to fetch two items, would only understand one request and return with one item. Her mental age was estimated at about two years. Physically, she had learned to walk, but she was unable to talk.

The effective types of environments that encourage learning

The things that matter most when creating a rich learning environment are:

- your relationship and communication with children, their families and the team of staff (i.e. people)
- how you support the children in using core experiences and open-ended, continuous material provision, equipment and resources, indoors and outdoors.

Children need:

- people who give them interesting and engaging experiences
- carefully thought-through and organised materials indoors and outdoors
- to be greeted and made to feel welcome with their parent/carer as they arrive

- to be connected with their key person when they part from their parent/carer
- to feel physically, socially and emotionally safe, so that their intellectual lives open up as they relax and enjoy learning.

It is very difficult for children when adults flit about and do not stay in one place for long enough for children to engage with them in focused ways.

 Progress check

Providing an effective environment to encourage learning

The role of the adult in supporting children's development and learning through developmentally appropriate materials provision, equipment and resources is central. The environment (people and provision) needs to support all children, including those with special educational needs, disabilities, boys and girls, children from diverse backgrounds and different cultures, or with English as an additional language.

Clutter confuses children. There should be nothing in a learning environment, indoors or outdoors, that has not been carefully thought through and well organised. Children need to know what they are allowed to do, and what they are not allowed to do, and the environment needs to signal to children how it should be used and kept. When children feel insecure, they test boundaries to find out if there are any and what they are.

The space indoors and outdoors should be flexible, so that it can be set up and transformed for different uses in a variety of ways. Attention should be given to light, because the way that it shines into a building changes the atmosphere. If the sun is shining onto a child's face during story time, it will be difficult for the child to become engaged.

The temperature is important. Being too hot or too cold makes it difficult to learn. Outdoors, children need suitable clothing, for all weathers (and so do the adults!), and indoors, the rooms should have good air circulation, so that heads are clear and the spread of infection is reduced.

The role of active learning and the importance of play in a variety of settings

What is active learning?

Active learning is learning that engages and challenges children's thinking using real-life and imaginary situations. It takes full advantage of the opportunities for learning presented by:

- spontaneous play
- planned, purposeful play
- investigating and exploring
- events and life experiences
- focused learning and teaching.

These opportunities for learning are supported when necessary through sensitive intervention to support or extend learning. All areas of the curriculum can be enriched and developed through play.

The importance of play in active learning

As we have seen in Unit 4, well-planned play is important for the following reasons. Play:

- helps children to think and make sense of the world around them
- develops and extends their linguistic skills
- enables them to be creative
- helps them to investigate and explore different materials, and
- provides them with opportunities to experiment and predict outcomes.

Children need opportunities to follow their own interests and ideas through free play. Children's learning is most effective when it arises from **first-hand experiences** (whether spontaneous or structured) and when they are given time to play without interruptions and to a satisfactory conclusion.

Play underlies a great deal of young children's active learning. In order to promote active learning through play, practitioners need to provide:

- a carefully planned and organised environment – with varied resources

- challenging and interesting play opportunities appropriate to children's needs, interests and abilities
- opportunities for creative play – intervening only when necessary to avoid repressing language or imagination
- enough time for children to develop their play
- opportunities for social interaction – promoting cooperation, turn-taking and sharing
- links between play activities and real-life situations (e.g. shop play linked with real shopping trips)
- opportunities to observe children's activities in order to plan for the future and to enable regular assessment.

The factors that can affect the child's ability to learn

Recently there have been many advances in the way we understand the brain and its functions – and particularly in our understanding of how children learn. It used to be accepted that the structure of our brains are fixed from birth, as a result of the genes we inherit from our parents. Neuroscientists now believe that while the *basic* brain structure is determined by our heredity, this serves only as a framework. Cognitive development is influenced by many factors; these include:

- **genetic factors** (e.g. sensory impairments, Down's syndrome)
- **physical factors** – general health, quality of nutrition, opportunities for physical activity, the development of physical skills (e.g. fine motor skills for hand–eye coordination)
- **environmental factors** – effects of poverty, provision for play and active learning
- **emotional factors** – self-esteem and confidence, effects of trauma (such as bereavement, abuse, a new baby in the family)
- **social factors** – role models, amount of opportunities to socialise, stability of relationship with adults
- **cultural factors** – different cultural experiences and expectations.

One factor may affect another. For example, physical factors such as a hearing impairment may affect a child socially and emotionally, which in turn may lead to lack of confidence and motivation. If children lack stimulation in their environment – in any area of development – they will miss out on important learning experiences that help in the formation of concepts.

The skills children need to learn effectively

The frameworks for learning for children from birth to 16 in the UK are designed to promote these skills, and to assess each child's skills throughout their schooling.

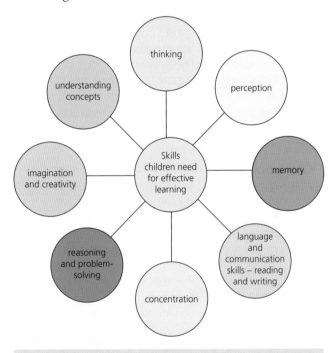

Figure 10.2 Skills for learning

How to encourage concentration and attention in children

An important part of the learning process is being able to concentrate and to keep one's attention focused on one activity at a time, without being distracted by other things. We all use our attention and concentration skills every day, often without really noticing them. These skills help us to:

- select and focus on what is important (e.g. what the teacher is saying)
- ignore irrelevant things that we do not need to pay attention to (e.g. what you can hear going on outside)
- maintain our effort or attention over time (e.g. concentrate for the necessary amount of time).

Sometimes we need to pay attention to more than one thing at a time; this may require certain skills – for example, copying work from the board while the teacher is explaining the information being given.

There are two types of concentration required in different situations:

- **active concentration** – construction, creative activities, imaginative play, sand and water play, problem-solving in maths and science, and literacy activities.
- **passive concentration** – watching television or videos, listening to stories, sitting in assembly, and so on.

Some children can concentrate passively for fairly long periods, while others are better able to concentrate actively when building a model or taking part in imaginative play.

Difficulties with attention and concentration

All children have times when they find it difficult to concentrate. This could be because they:

- are too tired or unwell
- are unable to focus in a busy environment (e.g. with other children talking to them or around them)
- are easily distracted by things going on around them
- are easily distracted by thoughts or feelings that are unrelated to the task at hand (daydreaming)
- are easily overwhelmed by large amounts of information
- are emotionally distressed
- have attention deficit hyperactivity disorder (ADHD).

In practice

How to encourage concentration and attention in children

There are many ways in which you can help children to concentrate. These include the following.

- **Minimise distractions**: children need a quiet area for activities that require more concentration; carpets and rugs can be used to keep noise levels down.
- **Respond to individual needs**: some children react badly when they feel rushed in their learning – others become bored and may disrupt others if given too much time for one activity.
- **Time activities appropriately**: avoid situations where the students are passive listeners for long periods of time; keep activities brief, or structure them into short blocks; provide a clear beginning and end.
- **Provide children with hands-on activities**: for example, experiments, orienteering activities, projects.
- **Use children's names and make eye contact**: when giving instructions, get the child's attention by calling their name and making eye contact.
- **Use memory games** and encourage participation in classroom discussions and other collaborative activities.
- **Use songs and rhymes**: these will improve memory and concentration.
- **Use praise and positive feedback**: children benefit from having targets to improve their concentration, and incentives or rewards when they reach them.

The role of the adult in supporting children's learning

How to support the development of skills for children to become effective learners

Research shows that children develop and learn through their play and the first-hand experiences they are offered by adults who are interested in what they do, and who support and extend their learning. Children benefit from the relationships and companionship they find with other children. But none of this can happen if the conditions are not favourable. The role of the adult is crucial in creating, maintaining and planning the general environment.

Children need to learn to be capable and independent in order to learn new skills. The child who is self-reliant will be more active, independent and competent: he or she will have the confidence necessary to cope with situations on his/her own and to become an effective learner.

How to promote self-reliance

All children should be allowed and encouraged to do the things that they can do from an early age – and be praised and rewarded for their efforts.

- **Allow children to do things for themselves.** Even very young children begin to show an interest in doing things for themselves. Encourage independence by letting children do things for themselves as soon as they express a desire to do so.
- **Focus on the effort made by the child** and avoid being critical of the 'end product'. Always praise children for doing things on their own. As children grow and mature, they will naturally want to do more and more for themselves.
- **Encourage children to help with new and challenging tasks.** This helps to promote self-confidence. Remember to choose tasks that children can accomplish.
- **Encourage children to make decisions.** Children learn to make good choices by being given choices. At first, choices should be kept simple, like allowing children to choose what to wear out of two outfits. As children get older, encourage them to make more and more complex decisions.
- **Be a good role model for responsibility and independence.** Children learn by watching adults. Let children see you making decisions without wavering, and also taking care of responsibilities in an appropriate manner.
- **Help and encourage children to solve their own problems.** Problem-solving is a skill that must be learned. Encourage children to come up with their own solutions to their problems. The ability to problem-solve is a skill that will be useful throughout children's lives. It will also help in the development of confidence and independence.
- **Encourage children to take risks.** Taking risks involves facing potential failure. Many parents – and other adults – try to shield children from the disappointment of failure. However, children need to take risks in order to grow. Children must experience failure in order to learn how to cope with it.
- **Be there to provide support, when needed.** Even the most independent-minded children need adult support on certain occasions. Make an effort to be available to the children in your care and to provide support when needed. Children who are secure in their relationships will have the confidence needed to explore the world.
- **Praise children.** Children should receive praise when they display responsible and independent behaviour. Adults who praise such behaviour are letting children know that they notice and appreciate their efforts.
- **Give children responsibilities.** One of the best ways for children to learn how to behave responsibly is to be given responsibilities. Make sure that the tasks assigned to the children match their capabilities. Take the time to show them how to do their assigned tasks properly. However, how well children perform a task is not as important as what they are learning about responsibility.

From birth, babies and children need to be encouraged to 'have a go' even if their early efforts are not always successful. You have an important role in helping to develop self-reliance at all stages of children's development (see Table 10.4).

How to provide an environment that supports and encourages children's learning

Learning requires the active, constructive involvement of the learner. Learning in groups at school requires children to:

- pay attention and concentrate
- observe

- memorise
- understand
- set goals
- assume responsibility for their own learning.

All children will flourish in a good learning atmosphere – or ethos – in which adults support and extend the development and learning of all the children. Every child needs full access to the curriculum in order to learn effectively. This applies to all children – regardless of their ethnic background, culture, gender, language, special educational (or additional) needs, or economic background.

The different learning opportunities in everyday situations and daily routines in a variety of settings

Each everyday situation and daily routine will provide plenty of learning opportunities. Practitioners have an important part to play in recognising when opportunities for learning occur and in providing the right conditions for learning.

Babies

- Encourage babies to cooperate when getting them dressed and undressed (e.g. by pushing their arms through sleeves and pulling off their socks)
- Provide finger foods from about eight months and tolerate mess when babies are feeding themselves
- Set out a variety of toys to encourage them to make choices

Children aged 2–4 years

- Provide a range of activities – both indoors and outdoors
- Encourage children to help tidy away toys
- Allow children to have a free choice in their play
- Encourage children in self-care skills – washing hands, brushing hair and getting dressed; be patient and provide them with adequate time
- Build choice into routines such as meal and snack times
- Encourage children to enjoy simple cooking activities

Children aged 5–8 years

- Provide activities that promote problem-solving skills, such as investigating volume and capacity in sand or water play
- Allow children to take responsibility for set tasks (e.g. wiping the tables, caring for plants)
- Encourage them to learn specific skills – such as using scissors and threading large needles
- Allow children the opportunity to make choices, and encourage them to assess risks when supervised

Children 8–12 years

- Allow children to choose – for example, the choice of playing sports, musical instruments, a dance class, or nothing at all
- Encourage them to set goals and work towards achieving them
- Provide opportunities for them to plan and organise their own activities
- Allow children to make mistakes and to learn from them
- Encourage them to ask for support – but avoid taking over completely

Young people 13–16 years

- Allow them to take some control over their own learning, deciding what to learn and how
- Assist them in creating learning goals that are consistent with their interests and future aspirations
- Provide opportunities for them to demonstrate their skills and achievements (e.g. organising fundraising events or a display board)

Table 10.4 Promoting self-reliance skills throughout childhood

In practice

Your role in providing the right conditions for learning

- Ensure that children feel known and valued as individuals, safe and cared for.
- Respect each child's rate of development, so that children are not rushed but are supported in ways that are right for each child.
- Take into account the children's previous experiences, current interests and developmental needs.
- Identify learning opportunities that arise spontaneously through play, indoors or outside.
- Ensure that children have uninterrupted time in which to explore their environment independently, setting their own challenges and making their own discoveries.
- Provide access to a wide range of materials, and opportunities for children to manipulate these materials.
- Encourage the use of language and provide access to a rich vocabulary.
- Manage children's time so that they have the opportunity to become deeply involved in their activities.
- Plan activities to allow children to follow their ideas through, including returning later to continue their explorations or creative expressions.

Case Study

Using everyday events for learning

At lunchtime, a group of sitting babies and toddlers were encouraged to choose their pudding. A plate of freshly prepared fruit was placed on the table. A tiny portion was given to the babies to try out. Several showed they wanted more through their movements. The key person passed the plate to the babies, who were allowed to take more for themselves. This encouraged:

- learning that one portion of fruit is the same as the next
- physical coordination
- a feeling of control over what happens
- decision-making.

The different types of activities that meet the diverse needs of children

Planning activities to meet children's needs

See Unit 4, pages 176–177 for the different aspects you will need to consider when planning activities to meet children's needs.

Adult-directed activities

These are planned, prepared and, often, initiated by adults. For example, a water activity might be planned that focuses particularly on 'force' or 'pressure'. The adult may have selected the equipment that lends itself to using water under pressure – squeezy bottles, thin plastic tubing, a water pump – and allowed children to use it in their own way, or played alongside the children, talking about what was happening and questioning them so that they express their ideas.

Progress check

Encouraging children's active participation

- Even when an activity is adult-directed, it should always involve active participation by the children.
- Activities that have an 'end product' (e.g. a model or a special occasion card) must allow for children's experimentation and creativity so that each one is different and original.
- There is absolutely no value in directing every aspect of a task. You should not aim to have all the children's work looking the same or 'perfect' (i.e. your idea of what the finished article should look like).
- Ownership is very important: children need to feel that their work is their own.
- What children learn from doing the activity – practical skills, understanding of materials, textures, sounds, and so on – is far more important than the finished article.
- Young children should also be able to choose whether or not to make a card or a model.

Observing and monitoring progress

Planning activities an experiences to suit the individual interests and needs of an individual child

Talking with children about the experience/activity they are involved in, and extending their vocabulary

Providing appropriate activities and experiences

Ensuring a wide range of materials and resources is available

Supervising to ensure safety

Showing genuine interest in the children's activity/experience and sometimes joining in with sensitivity to the child's interests

Being a good role model

Intervening when appropriate with sensitivity

Encouraging children to participate and experiment

Figure 10.3 How adults can support children's learning

Child-initiated activities

These occur when children make their own decisions, without suggestion or guidance from adults, about the way in which they use the equipment and resources provided for them. For example, although an adult may have chosen which construction materials to set out (e.g. wooden blocks) two children may decide to work together to build a castle for 'small-world' figures or 'play people'. This, then, is a child-initiated activity.

Structured activities

These should be carefully planned to develop a particular aspect of understanding or skill. They are structured in that there are resources, carefully chosen, and usually a sequence of tasks, or steps, that may lead to a desired learning outcome or objective. An adult usually leads, supervises and monitors children's responses.

 In practice

A simple sorting activity

Aim: To find out if children can identify and sort all the blue objects from a selection of objects of different colours.

- Ask the children individually to find something blue and put it in the sorting 'ring' with other blue things – this ensures that all children participate, and enables the adult to find out if the child has understood the task and can carry it out.
- For this task the child has to know what 'blue' means and be able to distinguish objects of that colour from others.
- Some children may not realise that there are different shades of blue that are still 'blue'.
- Adults working with children on an activity such as this need to talk to them. Asking questions and enjoying a chat together helps adults check each child's understanding.

Spontaneous activities

These can be stimulated by natural events – a hailstorm, snow, a rainbow, puddles – or by an experience a child has had and wants to share with you (e.g. the arrival of a new baby, a new pet, a birthday). The excitement generated by such occurrences makes the learning opportunities too good to let pass without capitalising on them. Planned activities can be postponed to another time in order to make the most of spontaneity. Other spontaneous activities arise when children make their own decisions about how they use the play equipment – perhaps arranging chairs to pretend they are travelling on a bus.

The benefits of singing

Singing can meet all five outcomes of *Every Child Matters* and can also create a greater sense of community and increasing social cohesion within the school.

Music lessons in school can help foster individuality, improve social skills and help create more positive attitudes in general. In studies, these effects have been particularly marked in low-ability, disaffected pupils.

Singing can be used to prepare to start or finish routine activities such as settling down to take the register or signifying the end of the school day.

Music can be used to reinforce mathematical development through the use of finger and counting games, and exploration of musical instruments and sound-makers through sequencing and patterning.

Studies have shown that school music lessons can benefit reading and language skills. Very young children have been shown to increase the amount, quality and understanding of speech developed through singing activities.

There are also many physical advantages to singing, such as increased blood flow and lung capacity. Combined with movement or dance, it can be used to help combat obesity and increase general physical fitness.

Sing Up is a not-for-profit organisation providing the complete singing solution for schools, with access to the unique Song Bank, tailored resources, training and personalised support. Sing Up transforms school life, improves learning and builds stronger communities: www.singup.org.

 **In practice**

Planning a singing activity

- Think about songs from your childhood, and discuss what makes them memorable.
- How many mnemonics do you know? (A mnemonic is a short rhyme, phrase or other mental technique for making information easier to memorise – e.g. the colours of the rainbow or the number of days in each month.)
- In groups, plan a simple singing activity for a group of children aged three to five years. Include visual props and musical backing where appropriate.

The adult role during an activity

The most obvious role is that of ensuring safety by supervising effectively. Regardless of age and setting there are always some activities that *must* be supervised. These include:

- cooking
- tasting
- activities involving living things
- those involving equipment that could be dangerous if wrongly used
- physical – particularly those involving climbing frames and/or gymnastic equipment.

Another role is to encourage children to try new things and to express their ideas. This involves the adult showing genuine interest in the children's activities and talking with them about the activities they are involved in. It is important that children experiment themselves, explore the materials and use them in creative ways rather than follow an adult's directions. Asking 'open' questions (see the section on effective communication in Unit 5) encourages children to put their thoughts into words, and the adult can extend their vocabulary by offering the new words in context and at the right time.

The important thing to remember is that children learn best by finding answers for themselves with encouragement and support. The adult role is *not* to take control of the activity away from the children and 'do the difficult bits' for them.

Choosing when to intervene in children's activities

There will be certain instances when you *must* intervene – see Progress check below – but you will need to use your discretion in other instances. The following scenarios may lead you to intervening in children's activities:

- **children become frustrated** – offer support to help them through the difficult stage and move them on to the next step, e.g. if they are having trouble joining two pieces of Lego, assist them by calming them and then, perhaps, holding one piece firmly while they fit the other. **Do not** take both pieces and do it for them.
- **play is becoming rough or too boisterous** – sometimes just a look or a word will be enough to remind them of acceptable behaviour.
- **children are losing interest** – talk to them about the activity, ask questions that might prompt them to try something new or creative **or** suggest they move to another activity.
- **some children appear to be excluded from an activity** – this may result from strong personalities 'taking over'. Just talking to the group and asking what each is doing may be enough to solve the problem.
- **children are experiencing difficulties** – this may result in them losing concentration and not managing to persevere with what they are trying to do. A little encouragement and praise for their efforts can give them the confidence to try again.
- **children deserve praise** – for effort, acceptable behaviour, achievement.
- **you notice the children are experimenting and you see an opportunity to develop their understanding**, e.g. rolling toy cars down a slope and talking about which one is fastest. Questioning – 'Why do you think the blue one reached the carpet first?' encourages them to express their ideas – they may be on the wrong track 'because it's blue' or they

might think of a reason that could be tested 'because it has more wheels than the red one' or 'because its wheels are bigger'.

Progress check

When you must intervene

You *must* intervene when:
- children are likely to harm themselves
- children could hurt others
- there is a risk of damage to property or equipment
- children are behaving unacceptably (e.g. showing discrimination by name-calling, physical aggression or spitefulness).

The principles of effective communication when supporting children's learning

Unit 5 discusses the principles of effective communication with children. In brief, when communicating with children you should:

- show respect for other people's beliefs and views
- establish boundaries by managing children's expectations
- show interest in the individual child, their needs and preferences
- use appropriate body language
- practise active listening
- convey warmth
- convey understanding
- convey sincerity
- seek feedback, paraphrasing and reflection.

The importance of consulting the child when supporting children's learning

It is important to recognise that children have a right to participate in the key decisions that affect their lives. Article 12 of the United Nations Convention on the Rights of the Child states that children should have the opportunity to express their views on matters that concern them, and to have those views taken into account when decisions are made. It is generally agreed that participation by children and young people results in real benefits for themselves and for the organisations that consult them. These benefits include:

- skills development – communication, negotiation and teamwork
- educational experience
- promoting a sense of responsibility for oneself and others
- providing an enjoyable and social environment
- raising self-esteem.

Recent research into consultation with pupils found that children's learning experiences could be enhanced if tasks were more closely aligned with the social worlds in which they lived – both inside and outside the classroom. They said they found it helpful when teachers used materials, objects and images that they were already familiar with.

Motivation to learn

Being able to make decisions about their activities is a very important aspect in children's active learning because it ensures that learning is matched to what they *want* to do and achieve. It also enables children to be in control and independent.

Reflective practice

Allowing children to be in control of their own play

Harry is sitting in the nursery playing with a train. Phoebe is Harry's key person and is sitting next to him. Harry makes a 'Brrm' noise and says, 'Train,' as he pushes the train along the floor. Phoebe smiles and nods and says, 'That's right, it's a train, a blue train.' Harry stops pushing the blue train and picks up a red car. He says, 'Car,' and shows Phoebe, who says, 'Yes, that's right. It's a car, a red car.' By simply commenting, rather than asking questions, Phoebe is allowing Harry to be in control of his own play and he is not under any pressure to communicate.

Think about the ways in which you have allowed children to be in control of their own play, and why this is important.

11 Supporting children and families: Unit 11

During this Unit you will learn about the range of support available for children and families and how to build positive relationships. You will consider your role as an adult in managing potentially sensitive situations, and take into account your responsibilities.

> ## Learning outcomes
>
> During this unit you will learn about:
>
> 1. The range of support available for children and families.
>
> 2. How to build positive relationships with children and their families.
>
> 3. The role of the adult when supporting children and their families in a social care setting.

The range of support available for children and families

Vulnerable children and families

Children and families living in poverty

In the UK in 2011, *Save the Children* estimated that 1.6 million children were living in **severe poverty.** Overall, one in three children in the UK today are living in poverty. Poverty causes a poor quality of life. It brings stress and sometimes also despair. These can affect social relationships and health.

Low educational achievement is strongly connected with poverty and disadvantage. For example, a young child in a well-off home will hear every day more than three times the number of words heard by a child with parents who are less well-off.

- Children living in poverty start school less ready to learn, less able to understand the importance of learning and less able to benefit from the teaching they receive in school.
- In many homes, there is nowhere quiet to study as the only warm room houses the television; there is no table on which to work, no books, very few toys and certainly no computers.
- Almost a quarter of children cannot afford to go on school trips.
- Children in urban settings (located in the inner city rather than in the suburbs) are more likely to experience poverty, a lack of facilities for play, fewer swimming pools and parks, and poor school buildings. Because of the difficult conditions in many urban areas, teachers, doctors and other professionals do not always stay in their jobs for long and children experience a lack of continuity in their care.

Poverty of aspiration

Apart from poverty in wealth or income, children and their families also have a poverty of aspiration. This means that they have low self-esteem, often believing there is little point in making the effort to improve their education.

Housing

The welfare state made cheap, rentable council housing a priority. During the market forces approach of the 1980s, people were encouraged to buy their council houses, and local authorities have not been permitted to build more. This has meant that:

- government funding has supported **housing associations** (these are voluntary organisations) to develop alternatives to council housing (funding for these has, however, been reduced over recent years)
- there is less cheap **rented property** available
- nearly two-thirds of people have **mortgages** and are buying their own homes; this has led to

increased homelessness through evictions when people cannot keep up mortgage payments

- some families rent in the **private sector** but may also be evicted if they cannot keep up with payments
- some families live with relatives in **overcrowded** circumstances
- some families have to move into **temporary housing**; constant moves mean a lack of stability for children
- some families are unsuitably placed in **bed and breakfast accommodation**, with inadequate space for basic cooking and washing facilities.

Different problems exist in rural and urban areas respectively. In the UK, fewer children live in the country, but the children of low-paid casual farm workers often grow up in poverty. They are also often lonely and isolated.

Gypsies and Travellers

There are several different groups of Gypsies and Travellers living in the UK, including Romany Gypsies, Irish Travellers, New Travellers, and Circus and Fairground families. Some cultural values and traditions are shared, including a nomadic lifestyle or heritage.

Travellers face many difficulties in the UK. These include the following:

- drastically reduced stopping places for Travellers
- inconsistent health care, because it is difficult for Travellers to register with GPs
- patchy education provision, because most local authorities do not take account of the needs of Travellers when planning services.

Early childhood practitioners need to implement the **equal opportunities policy** and **code of practice** devised in their work setting. They can incorporate aspects of the Traveller's way of life when setting up the home area. For example, they can make a caravan. This helps children to focus on the positive aspects of the travelling life.

Traveller Education Services provide support for all groups of Travellers – for example, Gypsies and Romanies, including English, Welsh and Scottish Romanies, and Irish and Scottish Travellers; some Traveller Education Services work with European Romanies seeking asylum.

Supporting vulnerable children and families through a multi-agency approach

Sure Start is an extensive government programme launched in the late 1990s as a cornerstone of the government's drive to eradicate child poverty in 20 years, and to halve it within a decade. The first Sure Start local programmes were established in 1999, with the aim of improving the health and well-being of families and children from before birth to four years, so that they can flourish at home and when they begin school. They started in the most disadvantaged areas in the UK. Sure Start local programmes are delivered by local partnerships and work with parents-to-be, parents and children, to promote the physical, intellectual and social development of babies and young children. All Sure Start local programmes are now called Sure Start Children's Centres.

Sure Start Children's Centres have the following four key objectives:

1 **Improving social and emotional development** – by supporting early bonding between parents and their children, helping families to function and enabling early identification and support of children with emotional and behavioural difficulties.
2 **Improving health** – by supporting parents in caring for their children to promote healthy development before and after birth.
3 **Improving children's ability to learn** – by providing high-quality environments and child care that promote early learning and provide stimulating and enjoyable play, improve language skills and ensure early identification of children with special needs.
4 **Strengthening families and communities** – by involving families in building the community's capacity to sustain the programme and create pathways out of social exclusion.

The emphasis is on prevention in order to reduce social exclusion later on, and to improve the chances of younger children through early access to education, health services, family support and advice on nurturing. These projects include support for:

- special educational needs
- outreach services and home visiting
- families and parents
- good-quality play, learning and child care
- primary and community health care
- advice about child health and development
- advice about parent health.

Children's Centres

The majority of Children's Centres have been developed from Sure Start local programmes, neighbourhood nurseries and Early Excellence Centres. Children's Centres are places where children under five years old and their families can receive seamless, holistic, integrated services and information, and where they can access help from multidisciplinary teams of professionals. Children's Centres serve children and their families from the antenatal period until children start in Reception or Year 1 at primary school. They also offer a base within the community, linking to other providers of day care, such as childminder networks and out-of-school clubs.

Each centre offers the following services to families with babies and pre-school children:

- good-quality early learning integrated with full day care provision (a minimum of ten hours a day, five days a week, 48 weeks a year)
- family support services
- a base for a childminder network
- child and family health services, including antenatal services
- support for children and parents with special needs
- links with Jobcentre Plus, local training providers and further and higher education institutions.

Children's Centres may also offer other services, including:

- training for parents – for example, parenting classes, basic skills, English as an additional language

- benefits advice and information
- toy libraries.

Family centres

The main function of a family centre is to support families to stay together whenever possible and help family life to be a positive and happy experience for parents and their children. Most family centres work with families who have been referred by social workers, health visitors and professionals from schools, probation officers and mental health visitors. Referrals are made to meet a variety of needs, including:

- family support – where there are relationship difficulties between family members
- where there is a risk of family breakdown
- when a child is believed to be at risk from significant harm
- where families are experiencing problems in managing their children's behaviour
- where a family has experienced loss
- where children and/or parents have experienced – or are experiencing – some form of abuse in their lives.

Services provided may include:

- Individual child work – work on keeping safe, disclosure, self-esteem and life story work
- Individual adult work – positive parenting, self-awareness and self-esteem, anger management, life story and parent and child play sessions
- Counselling for both adults and children to help them come to terms with their particular worries or concerns
- Supervised contact as part of ongoing work
- Positive parenting group
- Family support group
- School holiday clubs (for children aged five to 12)
- Outreach sessions within family homes.

Residential children's homes

Children's homes exist to ensure that the needs of children are met when they cannot live with their own family. They offer a safe place for children to develop and grow, as well as providing food, shelter, and space for play and leisure in a caring environment. Generally, when children need to live away from their families, they will stay with foster carers. It is only when foster care is either not possible or not desirable that residential care is chosen.

Children have to live away from their own families for all sorts of reasons. These include:

- their parents are unwell
- they have problems with their family and need to spend some time away from home (e.g. behaviour problems or educational difficulties)
- they may have a disability and need a break from living with their families
- they are in the care of local authority subject to a Court Order or Voluntary Agreement.

All children who come to live in a children's home must have a **Care Plan**. Their Care Plan states:

- why a child is living in a home
- what is supposed to happen while they are living there
- what is supposed to happen at the end of their stay.

Most children *will* go home, but a few go to live with other families and some go to live in other homes. Older children who are not planning to return home are given help to prepare them for living on their own; this is called the 16+ Careleavers Service (formerly Aftercare). Children go to their own school if they have a school place, or social workers help to get them back into school.

It is considered very important that children stay in touch with their family and friends. It is only when they might be hurt, or a Court Order says that contact is not allowed, that some children will not be able to have visits from their family or will not be able to visit them.

Foster care

Foster care is also social care; it is arranged through local social services departments or through **independent** fostering agencies. There are different types of foster care depending on the needs of both the child and their family. These include short-term care for just a few days or weeks, or longer term placements, as well as care for disabled children or children with behavioural problems.

The main categories of foster care are as follows.

- **Emergency**: when children need somewhere safe to stay for a few nights.
- **Short-term**: when carers look after children for a few weeks or months, while plans are made for the child's future.
- **Short breaks**: when disabled children, children with special needs or children with behavioural difficulties regularly stay for a short time with a family, so that their parents or usual foster carers can have a break.
- **Remand**: when children are remanded by a court to the care of a specially trained foster carer.
- **Long-term**: not all children who need to permanently live away from their birth family want to be adopted, so instead they go into long-term foster care until they are adults.
- **'Family and friends'** or **'kinship'**: a child who is the responsibility of the local authority goes to live with someone they already know, which usually means family members such as grandparents, aunts and uncles or their brother or sister.
- **Specialist therapeutic**: for children with very complex needs and/or challenging behaviour.
- Anyone can apply to be a foster carer, so long as they have the qualities needed to look after children who cannot live with their parents. There is no maximum age limit for being a foster carer.

The national and local support available for children and families

If a family has too little income to keep themselves, the Social Security Act 1986 provides a safety net and social security payments are made. Contributory benefits are available to those who have paid National Insurance during periods of employment. Non-contributory benefits are either:

- **available as of right** (Child Benefit is payable to all mothers, and Income Support is available to families provided there is no other source of income)

- **means tested** – your income is calculated and, if it is higher than a certain level, no benefit will be paid; because the forms are complicated to fill in and people feel anxious about the process, these benefits are often not claimed. Examples of this type of benefit include help with rent for elderly people, or family tax credit for families where a parent is working full-time but the income falls below a certain level.

The Department for Work and Pensions is responsible for a range of benefits and services for families (its website address is: www.dwp.gov.uk).

The range of statutory, private and voluntary organisations that support children and families

We have already seen how Children's Centres and Family Centres support children and families. Communities throughout the UK provide a range of services that are available to help children and families who are in need of support.

Support for children and families from statutory organisations

Social services: Children and Families section

Social workers who work in the Children and Families section within a local authority are professionals – usually trained to degree level – who form relationships with children and families who are facing challenges. By supporting and working with them, the social worker finds and develops long-lasting solutions.

Social workers help children and families in the following ways. They:

- provide support and advice to keep families together
- assess children when they may be in need

- investigate situations where children may be suffering abuse or neglect and take action that will protect them
- look after children who cannot live with their families
- ensure that children and families have access to the most appropriate services available, by putting people in touch with other helping agencies
- provide access to services for children with disabilities and their families
- manage adoption and foster care processes, and provide access to support for private foster carers
- provide support for children who have problems at school or are facing difficulties brought on by illness in the family
- provide a service to the courts.

The health visitor service

The health visitor service is an integral part of the NHS Community Health Service. The service works with mothers, their families, and community groups to promote the health and well-being of children between the antenatal period and the age of five. Health visitors are registered nurses with specialist qualifications in community health, which includes child health, health promotion and education.

Health visitor teams work in a range of locations in the community including people's homes, health centres, schools and Children's Centres. The health visiting team is multidisciplinary, and often includes the following professionals:

- specialist health visitors
- community nursery nurses
- community staff nurses
- health visitor assistants
- immunisation nurses.

The role of the health visitor service

The health visitor team works closely with GPs, schools, Children's Centres, and other health and social care professionals in the acute and community settings. They provide advice and support in a number of areas including:

- new birth visits, including advice on feeding, weaning and dental health
- physical and developmental checks

- general parenting support
- advice on family health and minor illnesses
- specific support on subjects such as post-natal depression
- deliver immunisation and national screening programmes
- support children and families during the transition to school.

Most health visiting services also run a targeted support service for children and families who require extra support. This service assesses each child and family and introduces them into appropriate services, such as speech and language therapy.

Support for children and families from private, independent and voluntary organisations

Some private and voluntary organisations provide support for children and families in Children's Centres, neighbourhood nurseries and extended schools. These programmes are founded on partnerships between local authorities, schools and providers. Others provide support within their own privately managed settings: nurseries, crèches, day nurseries and playgroups.

Childminding

Childminders are often the child care of choice for working parents. Childminders can:

- provide consistent one-to-one care, tailored to the individual needs of a child
- form a stable ongoing relationship with the child, continuing from infancy through to when they need care around schooling
- provide care for siblings together
- be very flexible over the hours of care provided, and can pick up or deliver children to and from other forms of care
- provide care in a home that can include involvement in activities such as cooking, shopping, gardening and family mealtimes.

A **registered childminder** works in his or her own home, and is registered and inspected by Ofsted, demonstrating the quality and standards of their care. Ofsted ensures that every registered childminder meets the national standards, such as:

- ensuring that they are suitable to be with children
- checking that they provide a safe, stimulating and caring environment, giving children opportunities for learning and play
- making sure they work in partnership with parents and carers.

In addition, in order to become registered, a childminder must undertake police and health checks, have a regular inspection of their home, and take an introductory childminding course and first aid training. Registered childminders can look after only a certain number of children at any one time, which allows them to focus more on each child.

The National Childbirth Trust (NCT)

The NCT is the UK's largest charity for parents. NCT's services include:

- providing accurate, impartial information to parents so that they can decide what is best for their family
- introducing parents to a network of local parents to gain practical and emotional support
- offering information and support in pregnancy, birth and early parenthood
- campaigning to improve maternity care and ensure better services and facilities for new parents.

Family Action

Family Action is a charity – founded in 1869 – that works with children and families by providing practical, emotional and financial support through over 100 services based in communities across England. Family Action offers the following services:

- **Building Bridges** services: supporting children and parents where the parent has an enduring mental health problem.
- **Perinatal Project**: supporting mothers at risk of depression during their pregnancy and up to one year after the birth of their child.
- **Valuing Families** services: where parents have learning difficulties.

- **Newpin** services: intensive support to mothers and fathers of children under five whose mental health is impacting on their ability to provide safe parenting.
- **Wellfamily** services: holistic support to families linked to GP practices.

Family Action also provides family support services to Children's Centres in 15 local authorities.

Action for Children

Action for Children is a voluntary organisation – or charity – that has been working with the UK's most vulnerable and neglected children since 1869. Until 2008, Action for Children was called The National Children's Home, or NCH. Services offered by Action for Children include the following:

- **Fostering**: a range of placement types – specialising in helping children who have encountered severe disruption or emotional trauma
- **Adoption**: finding caring adoptive families for children of all ethnic backgrounds and ages, disabled children, sibling groups and older children
- Family-based **short breaks**
- **Residential care**: range of residential short breaks and residential permanent homes for those unable to live with their families and who need a supportive home.

Support through multi-agency services

Through the Change for Children programme there has been an increase in the range of multi-agency services available to children and families, from integrated working within Children's Centres and extended schools through to multi-agency teams and panels supporting groups of local schools.

There are many other local support groups, including **Gingerbread**, which works on behalf of lone parents, and **Contact A Family**, which provides independent information, advice and support to parents of children with disabilities or special needs.

The range of challenges experienced by children and their families

Every family undergoes periods of strain or difficulty from time to time. For some it is short term, while for others it is prolonged and may give rise to tensions and problems that affect children's daily lives. When working with children and their families, you need to be understanding of the needs of individuals as well as the whole family unit in order to support them effectively.

Many families experiencing any of the challenges listed in Figure 11.1 will cope well with the difficulties, finding support among relatives and friends and other organisations. Indeed, some of the factors (particularly those marked with an asterisk: *) can have very definite positive aspects to them.

Case Study — A young family

Samantha is 19 and lives in a first-floor flat in a large inner-city area. She has one child, Jamie, who is two years old. Jamie's father, Kevin, lived with Samantha until Jamie was two years old but has now returned to his mother's home because he felt he could not cope with all the arguments over money and child care. Kevin's mother dislikes Samantha and feels that she 'trapped' her son by becoming pregnant. Samantha is very close to her own parents, who live around the corner. Her mother has a full-time job but helps out by baby-sitting. Samantha has the opportunity to return to study to take GCSEs. Kevin has offered to look after Jamie for one day a week and will take him to the college nursery the following morning. Samantha is excited by the prospect of this new opportunity but anxious about Kevin caring for Jamie overnight because of his mother's feelings.

1. Identify some of the difficulties that each person may have.
2. How can the staff at the nursery support Jamie and all the family members involved in his care?

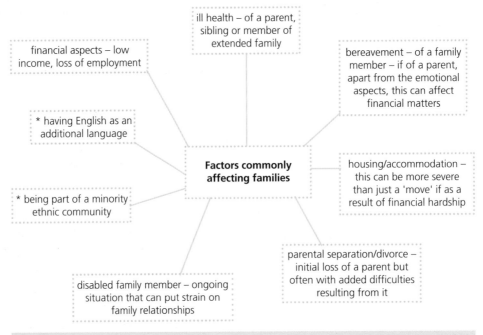

ill health – of a parent, sibling or member of extended family

financial aspects – low income, loss of employment

bereavement – of a family member – if of a parent, apart from the emotional aspects, this can affect financial matters

* having English as an additional language

Factors commonly affecting families

housing/accommodation – this can be more severe than just a 'move' if as a result of financial hardship

* being part of a minority ethnic community

parental separation/divorce – initial loss of a parent but often with added difficulties resulting from it

disabled family member – ongoing situation that can put strain on family relationships

Figure 11.1 Challenges experienced by children and their families

Activity

Challenges experienced by children and their families

1 In pairs, choose one factor from those detailed in Figure 11.1 and create an imagined situation for a family with a young child in a work setting. Try to use children of different ages for each factor. Then identify:
   • the different ways in which staff might know about the situation
   • what extra provision might be needed for the child
   • how staff might approach the parent(s) to talk about how the child is behaving or progressing
   • what other support would be available to them from state or voluntary organisations.

2 Present the results of your discussions and research to the rest of your group.

How to build positive relationships with children and their families

Positive relationships are relationships that help and support children by improving their ability to participate in and benefit from the setting. Working with parents is an essential aspect of work with children. Parents are the first and primary educators of their children. You can strengthen and build on this responsibility so that parents experience an increase in enjoyment of their children and an understanding of child development. Remember that it takes time and regular communication to build good relationships with parents that are founded on mutual trust and respect.

How to interact with and respond to children and their families

Starting the relationship: making parents welcome in the setting

Parents start off in an unequal relationship with child care staff. Some parents may feel very anxious, as they are not familiar with the building, the staff or the rules and relationships within the setting. Other factors may increase their uncertainty and feelings of helplessness. For example:

- they may speak a different language from that spoken in the setting
- they may be under emotional pressure about leaving their child
- they may have other worries (e.g. about getting to work, financial problems).

You need to be able to see things from a parent's point of view and to do everything possible to make them welcome in the setting.

Progress check

Making parents and carers welcome in the setting

Some useful ideas include the following:

- **Names accurately recorded**: first of all, make sure that you have the parents' names accurately recorded. Find out how they want to be addressed – do not assume that their surnames will necessarily be the same as that of the child.
- **Greeting**: make a point of greeting parents and smiling at them.
- **Name badges**: these are useful so that parents know to whom they are talking and who their children are talking about.
- **Photos**: a board with staff names and regularly updated photos could be put in the reception area and in newsletters.
- **Key person**: parents need to know which staff member will be working most closely with their child. Most nursery settings have an identified key person, who will be responsible for keeping notes and records of progress for a small number of children; the key person will be the main point of contact for the families of those children.

In many nursery settings the children are cared for in groups according to age and/or stage of development, and there may be one supervisor for each group. The manager or supervisor of a nursery, or the head teacher in an infant school, would still retain overall responsibility.

How to allow children to express themselves to enable a supportive framework

Adults need to give babies and young children respect as people in their own right, competent to express their views. Children need to feel confident that they can express their needs and wishes, and that you will listen carefully and respond to them. **Active listening** means responding to what children are saying; it means recognising that children know and can tell us things without necessarily being able to put them into words. They express themselves through body language, expression, actions and behaviour as well as their voice.

When you listen and 'tune in' to children and respond to them, you can help them to become aware of how they are feeling. This will include noticing changes in a child's behaviour and emotional well-being, and developing a trusting relationship so that the child can tell you if things are upsetting him or her. If a child is allowed to express sadness and anger, as well as happiness and enjoyment, he or she may feel more confident that it is all right to have a range of emotions. The child will be more likely to tell other people how he or she is feeling.

Allowing children to express themselves is important for the following reasons:

- **Professional responsibility**: It is your responsibility to develop the skills of active listening (described on page 151) and of taking children's concerns seriously.
- **Empowerment**: When children understand that you will listen to them and treat their concerns in a professional way, they will become empowered – and so feel more confident about expressing themselves. A key person system enables the practitioner to get to know the child and their family to recognise and be responsive to their individual needs.
- **Children's rights**: All children have a right to express and have their views taken into account on all matters that affect them. This is a basic human right under the UN Convention on the Rights of the Child (1989).
- **Child protection**: All children have a right to grow up in an environment that ensures that they are protected. Taking a child's concerns seriously is important. Often, when a child has been bullied or abused in some way, he or she will try to communicate what has happened. The child needs

to know that you are there to listen and, most importantly, that you will believe what he or she tells you.

- **Choices and decision-making**: The Children's Plan (first published by the Department for Children, Schools and Families in 2007) states that services for children 'need to be shaped by and responsive to children, young people and families'. Children who are encouraged to consider choices and to make decisions will learn to feel more confident, and by taking on this responsibility their self-esteem will also improve.
- **Developing life skills**: Children need to be motivated in order to develop important life skills, such as self-care and socialisation. Encouraging children to express their feelings will increase their motivation to become independent and to interact with others.

The importance of valuing the role of families in building relationships with children and families

The importance of understanding the wide variety of parenting and family approaches is discussed in Unit 7, pages 188–189.

The value of involving families in the setting

There are many reasons why it is valuable to involve parents, carers or family members in the work setting. See this Unit, page 277 for more information about involving families.

Settling-in policies

Many parents and carers find the settling-in period for their child very difficult to cope with – particularly if it is their first child. Most work settings will have a settling-in policy to make the transition from home to day care, nursery or school, or from one care setting to another, as smooth as possible. Unit 2, pages 79–81 deals with these in considering the children and their needs; here we need to think about them from the viewpoint of the child's family.

Helping a distressed or concerned parent to separate from their equally unhappy child is one of the main issues in nursery settings. This particular age group (under four years) finds it particularly hard to separate. This is not helped by a system of often irregular attendance, which makes continuity of settling difficult. Some children sail through this process – however, many do not.

 Progress check

Good practice for settling-in procedures

- **Training**: training should be provided to enable staff to gain skills in interacting with and settling babies and children for whom they are not the key person.
- **Arrival and greeting**: a child's key person should greet parents each time their child attends and leaves the setting. The key person should always ensure that time is allowed for two-way communication to take place with each parent on these occasions.
- **Key person**: parents need to meet and get to know the adults who will be caring for their child. They need to know that their anxieties will be taken seriously and that they can trust staff to support them.
- **Policies, procedures and routines**: parents should be given full information about how the nursery or other setting operates when they apply for a place, both verbally and in booklet form. The policies and procedures should be openly available and parents should be able to discuss them with staff if they have any concerns.
- **Child's preferences**: parents should be given the opportunity to explain their child's likes and dislikes, routines, and so on, so that the work setting may take them into account. Ideally, there will be a home visit made by the setting's staff prior to the child attending. Encourage parents to provide the child's favourite teddy or comfort object.
- **Parental preferences**: it is important to find out, in the event of the child becoming upset, whether the parents would prefer to be called immediately or would be happy for staff to persist for a bit longer with trying to settle her. Find out how and when parents can be contacted if there is a problem with settling in.

Progress check (Cont.)

- **Communicating with parents**: the needs of parents whose first language is not English should ideally be met through translation services, interpreters and staff language skills. The local Early Years Development and Childcare Partnership (EYDCP) can offer useful advice.
- **Supporting parents**: staff should also be skilled in identifying ways in which all parents, including those with disabilities or learning difficulties, can be supported in their contribution to their child's learning and development.
- **Keeping parents informed**: parents need to be reassured that they will be told about their child's day and progress, with the opportunity to check that she or he has settled. This is particularly important in the early stages of settling in.

Respecting the values and beliefs of others

The training you have received will have emphasised the richness and variety of child-rearing practices inthe UK. It is an important part of your professional role that you respect the wishes and views of parentsand other carers, even when you may disagree with them. You should also recognise that parents are usually the people who know their children best. In all your dealings with parents and other adults, you must show that you respect their cultural values and religious beliefs.

How to communicate with children and their families

Ongoing communication with parents is essential if children's needs are to be met. For many parents there can be regular and informal communication when children are brought to, or collected from, the work setting. However, it is unusual for both parents to perform this task and, therefore, it is often the same parent who has contact. The methods below can usually work for both parents and practitioners. Finding ways to communicate with parents can sometimes be difficult, especially when staff may not feel confident themselves.

- **Regular contact with the same person:** always meet and greet parents when they arrive. At the start, it is very important that parents meet the same person – preferably their child's teacher or key person – on a daily basis.
- **A meeting place for parents:** ideally, there should be a room that parents can use to have a drink and a chat together.

How to share information when requested, in line with procedures

Exchanging routine written information

Information that applies in the longer term should, ideally, be given in writing – for example, information concerning food allergies or medical conditions, such as asthma or eczema. As well as telling staff, notices may need also to be attached to a child's own equipment or lunchbox, or displayed in particular areas (e.g. food preparation, nappy-changing). In a school setting, the class teacher should ensure that any other adults involved in the child's care receive information as appropriate.

Copies of all letters received and sent, and a record of all communication should be kept for future reference.

Verbal information

Routine information can be – and often is – exchanged verbally. This usually happens at the start and end of the session, when parents and their child's key person chat informally.

- **Talking with parents**: always let parents know about their child's positive behaviour, and take the opportunity to praise the child in front of their parents. Then, if you need to share a concern with them, they will already understand that you are interested in their child's welfare and are not being judgemental. (Many adults associate being called in to see the person in charge with their own experiences of a 'telling off'.)
- **Recording information and passing on messages**: you will need to record some information the parent has talked to you about – especially if you are likely to forget it! You should

Written information	How and when it is used
Formal letter	<ul><li>Welcome letter prior to admission to the setting</li><li>To give information about parents' evenings or meetings</li><li>To alert parents to the presence of an infectious disease within the setting</li><li>To advise parents about any changes of policy or staff changes</li></ul>
Email	<ul><li>To give information about an event</li><li>To respond to a request from parent or colleague</li></ul>
Newsletters	To give information about future events – fundraising fairs, open forums and visiting speakers etc.
Noticeboards	To give general information about the setting, local events for parents, support group contact numbers, health and safety information, daily menus, etc.
Activity slips	To inform parents about what their child has been doing
Admission form	All parents fill in an admission form when registering their child. This is confidential information and must be kept in a safe place where only staff have access to it
Home books	To record information from both staff and parents. Home books travel between the setting and the home and record details of the child's progress, any medication given, how well they have eaten and slept, etc.
Accident slips	To record information when a child has been ill or is injured when at the setting
Suggestions box	Some settings have a suggestion box where parents can contribute their own ideas for improving the service
Policy and procedure documents	These official documents should be openly available, and parents should be able to discuss them with staff if they have any concerns

Table 11.1 Exchanging routine written information

always write down a verbal message that affects the child's welfare, so that it can be passed on to other members of staff – for example, if someone else is collecting the child, if a favourite comfort object has been left at home, or if the child has experienced a restless night. The person delivering the message also needs confirmation that it will be acted upon. Where there are shift systems in operation, a strict procedure for passing on messages needs to be established.

- **Telephone calls**: information received or delivered by telephone should be noted in a diary so that action can be taken.

Barriers to communication: how you can help

- **Time constraints**: there may be several children arriving at the same time, which puts pressure on staff at a busy time. Parents may be in a rush to get away when bringing their children. It is important that you do not interpret this as a lack of interest. Greet them with a friendly nod and pass on any information as briefly as possible.
- **Not seeing parents regularly**: when someone other than the parents brings and fetches the child, staff will need to find other ways to maintain regular communication.
- **Body language and non-verbal communication**: be aware of how parents may be feeling at a particular time, even when they do not mention anything specific; for example, if a parent does not make eye contact, it may be that they are depressed.
- **Written communication**: unless sent in the post, there is a chance that some letters and other written notes may not reach the parent. Also, some parents might have difficulty reading and writing, and may not want to seek help. The noticeboard can also be used to display a general letter sent to all parents.

- **Making messages clear**: remember that we understand messages not only from what is said but also from *how* it is said – our tone of voice, gestures and facial expressions can change the meaning of a message. The person on the receiving end of a written message has no such clues. It is important to give careful consideration to the wording of any letter and try to make sure that it cannot be misinterpreted.

- **When English is not the parent's first language**: you can help by signing or – where possible – by involving bilingual staff or translators. Notice boards can display signs in picture form – for example, showing the activities their child will be doing during the session. Having written information in a number of different languages is also helpful.

 In practice

Communicating with parents

1. The parents of three-year-old Thomas have been anxious about their son's appetite since he was ill with a virus. The staff at the day nursery have been observing Thomas, keeping written records and taking photographs, at snack and mealtimes over a period of a week. They have made sure the food is attractively presented, includes some of Thomas's favourite items and offered in small portions. They have noticed a great improvement and want to share their findings with his parents and discuss how he is at home.

2. Charlotte, who is five, has recently become withdrawn, both from adults and other children. For the past week or so she has needed encouragement to complete work tasks that are within her capability, and when she has had free-choice activity she has tended to sit alone in the home corner with a soft toy. This represents a change in Charlotte's behaviour and the teacher wants to discuss her concerns with Charlotte's parents.

- In each case, what method would you use to contact the parents?

- Explain what you would say/write and what you would arrange in order to deal with each situation.

Case Study   A conflict between school and home

An infant school clearly states in its prospectus that there is a uniform and gives reasons why it wishes pupils to wear it. Ryan, who is four years old, has just started in the Reception class and his parents believe that:

- uniforms prevent children from being seen as individuals, and

- wearing uniforms is inappropriate for very young children.

Ryan's teacher believes that Ryan has noticed that he is the only child in the class not in a school sweatshirt, and he keeps asking when he will be given his own sweatshirt.

In your group, think about and discuss the following questions.

1. What reasons might the school have for wanting its pupils to wear a uniform?
2. What should the teacher's first step be?
3. How can the situation be resolved to everyone's satisfaction?
4. What are your views about uniforms, generally, and why?
5. List the advantages and disadvantages of having a school uniform.

The importance of treating adults with courtesy and respect

Adults and children you work with may be from different cultures and their values and beliefs may be very different from yours. Parents and practitioners should work together in an atmosphere of mutual respect within which children can have security and confidence. Children will need to receive respect and courtesy from us in order that they can extend these skills to others.

Progress check

How to treat adults with courtesy and respect

- Acknowledge and respect the views of others at all times.
- Be friendly and approachable – using positive body language – and a smile!
- Speak clearly and maintain eye contact.
- Take time to remember names and preferred forms of address.
- Be a good role model by showing courtesy – e.g. always saying 'please' and 'thank-you'.
- Encourage parents to share their knowledge and views of their child's development.
- Ensure that the displays and resources reflect children's home and community experience.
- Ensure that the family or child's particular interests and experiences, such as the birth of a sibling, are used in planning work with the child.

Reflective practice

Interacting with others

Think about the way you interact with people in your setting:
- Have you made an effort to show respect and courtesy?
- Do you act as a positive role model, showing children how you value and respect differences?
- How could you improve the way you interact with others – to demonstrate your promotion of equality and diversity?

Planning activities and experiences to meet the needs of individuals and their families

Most social care settings have a busy programme of activities and experiences that aim to meet the needs of children and their families. The ways in which these are planned and organised will depend on the needs of the families involved with the setting.

Parent-and-baby and parent-and-toddler group (or Stay and Play group)

These groups are often offered from a Children's Centre and are an effective way of introducing parents and children to being in a group setting in an informal way. Parents might bring their toddler to the group once a week.

There will be drinks and healthy snacks for parents and children, together with activities appropriate for toddlers. Adults can talk, exchanging ideas and feelings. Babies can also be brought to the group. The group may have a regular programme of visits from a range of professionals – for example, a speech and language therapist and a clinical psychologist. Planning for the group may draw on best practice in early years education, offering high-quality treasure baskets for babies, a range of play and first-hand experiences, and outdoor play.

Workshops

Parents appreciate workshops run by the setting. These usually take place in the evening; parents come to experience some of the things their children do and staff explain what the children get out of the activities – for example, parents may be surprised to find out about the mathematics that their children are learning when involved in a cooking activity.

Toy libraries

Toy libraries are run by skilled staff and may be based in schools, community centres, public libraries, hospitals, Children's Centres, or health centres. Some also offer a mobile service, even delivering to homes. These can be very beneficial to families, especially those on a low income. Instead of needing to spend a great deal of money on an expensive toy, families can see if the interest in a particular toy is short-lived.

Children can get a broader play experience through regular borrowing, and can enjoy a range of high-quality toys and materials. A good toy library can show how open-ended equipment – for example, a Duplo® set with bricks, animals and people – provides long-lasting and rich play opportunities.

On the other hand, many 'educational toys' that are advertised on TV and in catalogues – for example, an electronic toy that speaks the names of letters when you push the buttons – will not usually hold a child's interest for more than a few hours at best. Toy libraries can have a particular role in supporting families with a disabled child, by offering specialist play equipment.

Leisure libraries were pioneered in the UK in 1988, evolving from toy libraries for **children with special needs**. They are often run by groups of parents and by the users themselves, with the support of social services. They provide facilities, advice, equipment to borrow and a social meeting place for adults with learning difficulties and their families.

Book packs and activity packs

The BookStart programme, which began in Birmingham in 1992, initially aimed to provide a pack of free books to every family with a baby. The programme has now expanded to provide a free pack to every baby, toddler and three- to four-year-old child, with bilingual packs, packs for children who are deaf, and packs for children who are blind or visually impaired.

In addition, some Children's Centres have developed packs to help parents to provide opportunities for early language and literacy, and maths and science experiences in the family home, at no or low cost. They encourage parents to enjoy books and educational activities with their children. Children can begin to learn mathematics and science in a very natural way. Eastwood Nursery School and Children's Centre in London has developed an exciting set of mathematical packs for families to borrow. Southway Nursery School and Children's Centre in Bedford has developed multicultural recipe packs for its resource centre.

Progress check

Encouraging partnership with families

- Do parents feel welcome in the setting? Can you think of ways to make your setting more welcoming to parents?
- Do all parents have the opportunity to contribute to the setting?
- Are parents asked for feedback on any concerns they have about the setting – for example, the outdoor play area?
- Do parents know whom to contact if they wish to seek further advice?
- Are there fun activities – such as fun days, picnics and local visits – to take part in for families to get to know each other outside the setting?

Assessment practice

Planning an outing to the local park

You have been asked to help to organise a visit to the local park, involving as many parents and carers as possible.

Draw up an outline plan, including the following:
- what to take
- how to get there – consider risk assessment
- staff members to be included
- fathers and mothers to be involved
- resources for activities and games
- food and drink
- safety measures: contact numbers, any special needs, etc.

Discuss how you will share relevant information with parents and staff, and how you can prepare for the outing.

Activity

Designing a newsletter

Design a newsletter for parents of a Reception class child. It should include information about the topic being studied for the forthcoming half-term, suggest what items the children might like to bring in, what parents could do to support the topic or get involved in school. Include some reminders about days when children need their PE kit and any school fundraising events coming up.

The role of the adult when supporting children and their families in a social care setting

The importance of working in a team and providing feedback to colleagues

To meet the needs of all the children, the staff members must work effectively together as a team. The roles and responsibilities of individual team members will depend on the organisation of the work setting. In your role as a learner you will be supporting the work of others. You will usually work under the direction (or sometimes supervision) of a manager or teacher, depending on the setting.

There may also be professionals from other disciplines (medicine, social services, dentistry, etc.) who are involved with the families and children you work with. A special school or nursery that cares for children with physical disabilities will have a **multidisciplinary team**; this may include teachers, early years practitioners and assistants, trained special care assistants, physiotherapists, paediatricians and, possibly, social workers.

Effective teamwork is vital in such settings to ensure that:

- everyone knows their individual roles and responsibilities
- parents and primary carers know which team member can deal with any specific concerns.

The importance of working in a team and providing feedback to colleagues is covered in Unit 1.

The importance of maintaining confidentiality

In order to establish a relationship of mutual trust and respect, you must ensure that you practise confidentiality at all times. Information about the children in your care is confidential and should be kept in a safe place where only staff members may have access to it. The supervisor or manager must check that all staff members are aware of medical conditions or cultural issues that affect the day-to-day care of a child. It is also important to ensure that these details are updated regularly. Most settings have a Confidentiality Policy.

In most instances you will be working under the supervision of others and it is likely that parents will pass confidential information directly to a staff member. However, there may be occasions on which you are given information and asked to pass it on, or that you may hear or be told confidential information in the course of the daily routine. This issue is dealt with in the section on confidentiality in Unit 5, and as long as you follow the guidelines, procedures and practices that apply to the work setting, you will not go far wrong.

Remember that there are lines of management in place in most work settings and you should follow them if you need to check your understanding or to ask advice. Try to be aware of the ways in which staff members relate to, and communicate with, parents, and try to identify which methods seem to be most effective.

Your role in supporting the individual needs of the child

What interests a child at any particular time is the starting point for deciding how best to support his or her learning and development. Practitioners need to provide relevant learning and development opportunities and set realistic and challenging expectations that meet the individual needs of children. Meeting individual needs must be based on *observing* the child in action and finding out about their needs and preferences.

Children feel secure when they take part in activities that interest them, for example role-play or stories. You can help children to build on prior learning by pitching the play or story at a level that is demanding but still within the child's reach. Your role is to provide an *inclusive* environment that promotes the needs of every child. In order to achieve this, you should develop an awareness and understanding of:

- the requirements of equal opportunities that cover race, gender and disability
- the code of practice on the identification and assessment of special educational needs

In order to meet children's diverse needs, and help all children make the best possible progress, practitioners should:

- plan opportunities that build on and extend children's knowledge, experiences, interests and skills and develop their self-esteem and confidence in their ability to learn
- use a wide range of teaching strategies, based on children's learning needs
- provide a wide range of opportunities to motivate, support and develop children and help them to be involved, concentrate and learn effectively
- provide a safe and supportive learning environment, free from harassment, in which the contribution of all children is valued and where racial, religious, disability and gender stereotypes are challenged.

Unit 4 provides information on providing well-planned play to meet the developmental needs of young children.

In practice

Supporting the individual needs of the child

The early years setting should:
- take account of each child's individual needs and provide for them appropriately
- be stimulating – it should offer a wide range of activities which encourage experimentation and problem-solving
- provide opportunities for all types of play
- provide support for children who may be experiencing strong feelings – for example, when settling in to a new setting or when they are angry or jealous (see Unit 3)
- encourage children who use them to bring in their comfort objects – for example, a favourite teddy or a piece of blanket
- encourage the development of self-reliance and independence
- ensure that children who have special needs and disabilities are provided with appropriate equipment and support.

In practice

Meeting individual needs

1. Choose a child in your setting who requires additional help with some aspect of communication, language and literacy.
2. Make an assessment of the child's needs.
3. Plan a programme or activity that will help to meet those needs.
4. Implement the activity.
5. Evaluate the activity.

The role of the key person

A key person is a designated member of staff who is responsible for the care of one or more children within the setting. Their responsibilities might include:

- planning the child's day
- monitoring and recording the child's development
- liaising with the child's parents
- welcoming and settling in the child and returning the child to the parent at the end of a session.

The key person system helps children to cope with separation and change; it also enables the key person and the child to form an attachment. Parents who have to work full-time may not be able to spend time settling their children in to the nursery, and the key person needs to adapt their practice to fit in with parents' needs.

Your personal role and responsibilities in a social care setting

Your specific role and responsibilities will be governed by the area in which you work. You should always act in a professional manner and be prepared to ask for guidance when new to the job. (Unit 5 covers the professional skills required when working with children and their families.) Generally, when working in a social care setting, you will need to have a thorough understanding of child development and behaviour. You will also need to know how to promote and maintain:

- a family-centred (not only a child-centred) approach

- multi-agency working – including agencies such as housing, leisure and the benefits agency
- health and safety
- confidence and self-esteem
- diversity and understanding of heritage
- appropriate family contacts.

If you work in a residential children's home, you will be required to undertake a special induction programme within six weeks of starting work. This applies to *all* children's home staff, including any agency, temporary, volunteer and student staff). The induction programme teaches you how to follow procedures relating to:

- emergencies
- health and safety
- child protection (prevention of abuse, recognition of abuse – including its recognition in non-verbal children – dealing with disclosures or suspicions of abuse) and notification of incidents.

How to deal with sensitive situations in a positive way

Practices in child-rearing vary around the world, and many cultures have strong traditions as to the role of each parent and in relation to discipline. Whatever the children's backgrounds, the parents are their earliest educators. While some parents will have looked at many different care and education settings before deciding which suits them and their child best, others will have had little choice. It is likely that they will have read the prospectus or brochure, which explains the aims and ethos of the work setting, but that does not necessarily mean that they share *all* those views and attitudes.

Managing sensitive situations

It is not the job of staff in a work setting to tell parents how to raise their children. They can, however, offer suggestions and support, when appropriate, in the best interests of the child. To be able to do this effectively a good, trusting relationship between parents and staff needs to be established. Parents need to feel able to express anxieties and difficulties in confidence and without feeling their parenting skills are being judged.

Assessment practice

Your role in relation to children and their parents

1. (a) For each of the following settings, and working in pairs, make a list of the main concerns parents might have about their baby or child starting and settling into the setting:
   - day care setting
   - nursery class
   - school setting.

   (b) Compare your list with that of another pair, and discuss any similarities and/or differences.

2. Working in small groups, choose *one* of the settings and write a list of the ways in which the setting would welcome a baby or child and parents, and how the settling-in period can be eased. (Note: try to use your own practical experiences in placement to help you – for example, what information do parents provide about their child? Is there a key person system?)

3. The amount of parental involvement varies from setting to setting and depends on the age of the children concerned. Thinking about your answers to questions 1 and 2, and using the same setting you chose for question 2, explain how a parent will be involved in the settling-in process.

4. Complete a chart, as in the example below, to show the role of the practitioner during the settling-in process in relation to the child and to the parent(s).

Role in relation to child	Role in relation to parent
Learn child's name quickly	Greet by name
Always welcome child by name	Make time to discuss any concerns
Be ready to give assurances and attention, etc.	Be ready to give assurances and attention,etc

5. A strong partnership between parents and carers helps a child to develop and to make good progress. Most settings provide parents with information about various policies (for example, discipline or behaviour), explain why they have certain procedures and how they will care for, and educate, the children. As a member of staff (in the setting chosen in question 2), you have been asked by some parents what they should be doing to ensure their child's care and education progresses well, and how they can support you and your work. **Create a leaflet** to give to parents, identifying their role. It must suggest what they can do to support different areas of your work (for example, feeding or mealtimes, behaviour, politeness, getting enough sleep), and explain how it helps the child, the parents and you!

Answers

Below are the answers to the First Aid quiz on page 93, Unit 3.

1 b
2 b
3 a
4 c
5 b
6 b
7 c
8 b
9 c
10 a

Index